1990

University of St. Francis

W9-ACQ-378

3 0301 00090644 2

Cambridge Studies in French

NATURALIST FICTION

NATURALIST FICTION
THE ENTROPIC VISION

DAVID BAGULEY

Professor of French, University of Western Ontario

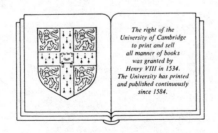

CAMBRIDGE UNIVERSITY PRESS

CAMBRIDGE

NEW YORK   PORT CHESTER

MELBOURNE   SYDNEY

LIBRARY
College of St. Francis
JOLIET, ILLINOIS

Published by the Press Syndicate of the University of Cambridge
The Pitt Building, Trumpington Street, Cambridge CB2 1RP
40 West 20th Street, New York, NY 10011, USA
10 Stamford Road, Oakleigh, Melbourne 3166, Australia

© Cambridge University Press 1990

First published 1990

Printed in Great Britain at the University Press, Cambridge

British Library cataloguing in publicaton data
Baguley, David
Naturalist fiction: the entropic vision. − (Cambridge
studies in French)
1. Fiction in French, 1848−1900. Naturalism. Critical
studies
I. Title
843′.8′0912

Library of Congress cataloguing in publication data
Baguley, David.
Naturalist fiction: the entropic vision / David Baguley.
p.   cm. − (Cambridge studies in French)
Bibliography.
Includes index.
ISBN 0-521-37380-8
1. French fiction − 19th century − History and criticism.
2. Naturalism in literature. I. Title. II. Series.
PQ653.B34   1990
843′.70912 − dc20   89-32593CIP

ISBN 0 521 37380 8

WS

843.7
B144

For Natasha and Alexander

135,815

CONTENTS

ACKNOWLEDGMENTS

I am deeply indebted to numerous colleagues and friends who have provided me with many useful suggestions and much practical help essential to the completion of this book. I should also like to thank the editorial and production staff of Cambridge University Press for their invaluable assistance. In certain parts I have reworked studies that have previously been published, either in English or in French, in the journals *Canadian Review of Comparative Literature*, *L'Esprit créateur*, *French Forum*, *Romance Studies*, *University of Toronto Quarterly*, and in the collection *Le Naturalisme en question* (ed. Yves Chevrel). I wish to express my thanks to the editors in question for permission to take up this material again. I am most grateful also for generous grants from the Faculty of Arts of the University of Western Ontario and from the Social Sciences and Humanities Research Council of Canada that have made possible the research which, over a number of years, has gone into this study.

INTRODUCTION

A brief preamble on the genesis of this book will perhaps not seem out of place in a study of a type of literature much concerned with origins and frequently intent upon defining its originality in relation to other literary models. The book was conceived, some considerable time ago, as an introductory study to the French naturalist movement for (mainly) English-speaking readers. Had that project come to fruition, it would undoubtedly have followed a most predictable plan. There would have been the requisite initial chapter on usages of the term 'naturalism' in philosophy, in art criticism and in literary aesthetics, followed, no doubt, by a study of positivist and scientific thought in mid-nineteenth-century France, then by a summary of the main ideas of Hippolyte Taine, all of which supposedly provided an impetus to the movement. There would have been sections on the literary precursors of the naturalist writers, 'realists' like Balzac, Duranty, the Goncourt brothers, on Zola's early works and aesthetic principles, on the formation of the so-called 'Médan group' (officially Paul Alexis, Henry Céard, Léon Hennique, Joris-Karl Huysmans and Guy de Maupassant) with mention of the celebratory dinner offered by the five above (plus Octave Mirbeau) to their elders, Flaubert, Edmond de Goncourt and Zola (plus the publisher Charpentier), at the restaurant Trapp on 16 April 1877, an occasion usually considered to have been the founding event of the naturalist school in France. Special prominence would have been given, in the anecdotal history of the movement, to the publication, exactly three years later, of the collection of stories by the same five plus Zola, *Les Soirées de Médan*, a work usually held to have been a kind of manifesto of the group. But the main body of the book would almost certainly have consisted of a series of monographs on the principal naturalist writers (including Alphonse Daudet), with due but modest recognition afforded the minor figures, and an attempt to gauge the degree of adherence of all and sundry to the tenets of the school. Each writer's idiosyncrasies would have been cheerfully explained away by reference to Zola's

1

famous formula to describe a work of art, 'a corner of nature seen through a temperament', as long as hefty 'slices of life', 'studies of nature', 'human documents' prevailed in his works, for the master himself never failed to emphasise the individuality of his fellow writers. Then, towards the end of the book, there would have been the inevitable chapter on the inevitable decline of the movement in the late eighties and early nineties with the onset of the idealist reaction, the religious renewal, the Russian evangelical novel, symbolist poetry, psychological novels, and with the decline of the prestige which science was supposed to have enjoyed in the heyday of the movement. Special significance would have been given to the infamous 'Manifeste des Cinq' in *Le Figaro* of 18 August 1887, with which five upstart young writers, Paul Bonnetain, Lucien Descaves, Gustave Guiches, Paul Margueritte and J.-H. Rosny – a kind of anti-Médan group – posing as Zola disciples, attacked the master and his latest novel, *La Terre*, thereby signalling, so it is usually claimed, a repudiation of naturalism and its leader by the new generation of writers. By the time the journalist Jules Huret published in 1891 the opinions of sixty-four men (and women) of letters in his *Enquête sur l'évolution littéraire* – a final chapter of the book would have shown – there was general agreement, even among the naturalists themselves, that the movement was over, though the famous telegram from Zola's ever faithful disciple, Paul Alexis: 'Naturalisme pas mort. Lettre suit' – his finest literary achievement according to a sardonic Catulle Mendès[1] – would have provided the pretext for a concluding section on the lasting impact of the naturalist movement in France and abroad.

Certain traces of this happily aborted project still remain within the present book, particularly in chapters 1 and 2, which deal in part with the history of the naturalist movement in France (and with the apparent lack thereof in Britain) and with naturalist aesthetics.[2] But this material will be presented as much for the problems and uncertainties that it illustrates as for its informational value. For mainly methodological reasons the kind of serene exposition outlined above is no longer possible. Traditional studies of naturalism have been excessively anecdotal and biographical to the detriment of an understanding of the literature that they often purport to explain. Furthermore, they have almost invariably been limited to a single national tradition such that recent surveys of research have emphatically deplored the lack of studies from a more international perspective.[3] The main focus of this book, nevertheless, as the subject dictates, is French naturalist literature, with particular reference to fiction. I am not, therefore, attempting a comparative study. But the generic approach that I wish to adopt does require frequent reference to texts from other national traditions, particularly, with the English-speaking reader in mind, to works written in English.

A further reason for abandoning the traditional approach, of which my scheme above provides a kind of parodic reduction, is that the decentred method that is regularly employed by such surveys tends to perpetuate or to gloss over certain paradoxes, contradictions and ambiguities, for they are often content to trace loose associations among writers rather than to make rigorous studies of relationships among their texts. How do we explain, for example, the problematic association between realism and naturalism, 'a great, perhaps the greatest, bug-bear of this topic' according to two recent interpreters of the movement?[4] How do we reconcile the apparent disparity between the doctrines and the practices of certain naturalist writers? Is it enough merely to assert that they failed to put their theories into practice – and so much the better for their works![5] How do we account for the fact that most naturalist writers, certainly in France, were refined aesthetes, yet seem to have relished writing on the most sordid themes? Is the nature of naturalist literature so disparate – to raise another vexed question – that it inherently defies attempts to define a specifically naturalist poetics?[6]

In his landmark study *Le Naturalisme* (1982), a work which alone represents the final and decisive reason why to go back over the well-trodden paths of the familiar survey would be impossible, Yves Chevrel raises a number of these key questions. In this book Chevrel breaks completely with the approach of his predecessors in the field, refraining from applying any a priori definitions and seeking factors of coherence, not in the often contradictory declarations of the naturalist writers themselves nor in the circumstances of their varied careers, but in the common themes and practices of their texts. Furthermore, as a comparatist, he adopts a resolutely international perspective, dealing, for example, with the question of periodisation within the broad context of Western literature as a whole. But Chevrel's book is particularly useful for the eclecticism of its approach, for the variety of critical resources that are brought to bear on the elusive topic, notably those of comparative literary history, literary poetics, narratology, thematics, stylistics, reception theory and sociological criticism. It is a work which opens up the whole field of naturalist studies to fresh perspectives and from which all subsequent studies will, to some degree, be derivative.

This present study is more limited in its methodological scope than

Chevrel's book, but my attempt to deal with naturalist literature as
a distinct literary genre and to define its primary characteristics is
prompted by a shared conviction that 'il s'agit d'abord de rassembler
un corpus de textes qui, dans les années 1870–1900, ont été perçus
comme possédant des traits communs et de les éclairer les uns par
rapport aux autres en utilisant l'œuvre et l'action de Zola comme
repère, mais non comme critère unique'.[7] A similar point is made by
Haskell M. Block in an earlier study: 'If naturalism represents not
only an attitude but also a literary tradition and style, it should be
possible to discover common devices and techniques in particular
naturalistic novels, as well as common underlying assumptions and
processes of composition.'[8] But Block's own corpus of texts, though
taken from different national traditions, is far too restricted, consisting only of three works, *L'Assommoir*, *Buddenbrooks* and *An
American Tragedy*. In fact, as well as the methodological considerations that I have so far indicated, it was precisely a growing awareness
of recurrence on reading a much larger number of naturalist texts that
led to the approach that I have adopted. One would expect, of course,
to be totally subjected to the mimetic effect on reading a broad sample
of naturalist works, based, as they are usually claimed to be, on a
thoroughly documented or observed reality. One would expect, on
encountering the hundreds of characters that there are in these works,
in an immense variety of situations, to be impressed by their
multifariousness. Instead, the reader becomes increasingly aware of
their fundamental repetitiveness and conventionality. Very soon, the
tell-tale signals become clear: the heroine's hopes – to be dashed by
a series of deceptions; the calm bourgeois interior – to be disrupted
by some secret vice; the hard-working plebeian – to be brought down
by a propensity for drink; the respectable and virtuous maiden – to
be ruined by some inherited, hysterical weakness. The registry of
scandals and disasters becomes all too predictable. No doubt the
contemporary occasional reader was surprised, often outraged,
sometimes titillated by these texts. But the modern critic reading a
number of them soon comes to feel at times like some industrious
social anthropologist engaged upon the study of the dens of vice of
some vast metropolis, whose senses (and sense of shock) are dulled
by the familiarity but who hopes nevertheless to gain insights from
the continued frequentation. Already in 1880, with typical prophetic
intuition, Henry Céard saw danger in the growing conventionality
of naturalist subjects: 'Défions-nous des mastroquets, faisons
attention aux bordels: tâchons que dans le naturalisme il n'y ait pas
de sujet classique.'[9] Likewise, at roughly the same time, Flaubert,

a reluctant inspiration to the movement, warned Huysmans, the young author of *Les Sœurs Vatard*, on the question of style: 'Prenez-garde; nous allons retomber, comme au temps de la tragédie classique, dans l'aristocratie des sujets et dans la préciosité des mots. On trouvera que les expressions canailles font bon effet dans le style, tout comme autrefois on vous enjolivait avec des termes choisis. La rhétorique est retournée, mais c'est toujours de la rhétorique.'[10]

This is not to accuse naturalist literature of being given to tedious repetitiveness. The simple explanation lies in the fact that, like all literature, naturalist literature is generic, having definable relations (whether derivative or transgressive) and sharing common character-istics with one or more general literary classes. Even the most startlingly original texts, or those which seek to deny such affiliations, are subject to the same law and are part of a larger system. As Laurent Jenny argues, literary works always enter into a relationship of realisa-tion, transformation or transgression with regard to archetypal models: 'Hors système, l'œuvre est donc impensable.'[11] From the same premise derives the main purpose of this book: an attempt to describe and define the 'literariness' of naturalist fiction in the essential aspects of what might be called its 'genericness', an aim which is clear-ly in defiance of the traditional tendency to interpret naturalist texts as almost outside the scope of literature, as a set of documents, records, *procès verbaux* of their age. In more straightforward terms, the purpose will thus be, in the words of E. D. Hirsch Jr, 'to describe the common elements in a narrow group of texts which have direct historical relationships'.[12] This generic approach, I would hasten to emphasise, does not involve the mere categorising, classifying and, no doubt, disparaging of naturalist literature in relation to some fixed, monolithic, hierarchical, essentialist typology inherited from the past. By consciously attempting to avoid writing biographical or social history, I shall be more disposed to write what might be called – to borrow Brunetière's notions, ironically so in a study of the literature he abhorred – an 'internal literary history', seeking to trace a 'filiation of texts' and to define the generic links between them. An appropriate balance will be sought between the abstract scheme and the historical fact, between the model and the text, in the hope of avoiding certain of the excesses of traditional studies of naturalism, which tend either to reduce the literature to the pure historicity of the literary movement and to the biography of its participants, or to assimilate the literature too abstractly to the principles of naturalist aesthetics, thereby losing sight of the reality of the texts themselves. As Gérard Genette has emphatically argued, a genre cannot be defined exclusively in transhistorical or historical terms: 'à quelque niveau de généralité que l'on se place, le fait générique mêle inextricablement, entre autres, le fait de nature et le fait de culture'.[13]

Inevitably, therefore, if the historical development of our genre is to be studied as much as its more abstract characteristics, as modern theoreticians would require,[14] at least in the French context where this can more easily be achieved, we must be sensitive to its mutability and to the main phases of its development: roughly, a period of inception, in which certain models are established, a period of crisis, in which rival types conflict, then a decadent stage, in which the conventions are used and abused. There are indeed those who would argue, like Jean-Marie Schaeffer, that the mobility of a genre is such that each text modifies it: 'Pour tout texte en gestation le modèle générique est un "matériel" parmi d'autres sur lequel il "travaille".'[15] Thus the generic nature of texts is to a considerable degree explainable as a series of imitations, borrowings, modifications, derivations, adaptations, parodies, working from text to text and from model to text. Clearly, in such a scheme, the exemplary texts deserve special attention for the authority with which they establish the parameters of the genre. Accordingly, chapter 3 of this study will seek to identify and analyse the influential, prototypical naturalist texts which seem to sum up the essential properties of the genre, inspiring transtextual reworkings, establishing a continuity, forming models. Clearly also, in such a study, minor works and writers have their place and must be given a certain prominence, which their reputation may not seem to justify. But, minor works frequently better display and exploit the favoured conventions of a genre than do the more generically complex, acknowledged masterpieces.

Just as there are complex texts which derive from a variety of genres, there are hybrid genres which draw characteristics from a variety of literary types, even from types of discourse that are not necessarily literary. Zola made the extravagant claim that naturalist literature embraces *all* genres (for reasons that we shall explore in chapter 2). He could more reasonably have made a case for stating that its boundaries do in fact overlap with many a neighbouring territory. Thus, in asserting the specific nature of naturalist fiction as a 'genre' and in seeking to define its primary characteristics, I am not by any means claiming that this specificity is exclusive. On the contrary, I shall attempt to demonstrate that the typical naturalist text is the meeting place of several types of discourse whose combination alone determines the distinctive character of naturalist fiction. Once these elements have been defined, it will be possible to go on (in chapters 4 and 5) to demonstrate the existence of certain recurrent combinations, certain fundamental types of naturalist texts, species within the genre – to use a problematic and discredited analogy – as well as certain recurrent character types and even certain recurrent localities favoured by naturalist fiction, with their characteristic functions.

All this conventionality is, of course, disguised by the mimetic, realistic practices of naturalist literature and is not acknowledged by naturalist aesthetics, which tends to perpetuate the realist myth of the direct representation of an inexhaustibly rich, complex, observable reality of situations, people and sites to be depicted like some vast Balzacian enterprise. Realist literature – and naturalist literature in so far as it shares this common, fundamental design – can be situated in what Paul Hernadi calls 'the area of fading distinctions, between the highly polarized universe of the imagination and its undifferentiated "center" – the actual world'.[16] Yet, more patently directed towards the representation of this so-called 'actual world' (than to featuring the fundamental literary structures), it (unnaturally) seeks to conceal literary distinctions, to disguise its 'literariness', hide its 'genericness'. A major purpose of this book is to counter that process and restore to naturalist literature its generic identity.

In a similar way, this book also seeks to counter the tendency to interpret naturalist literature as a *passive* depiction of reality, usually the sordid, ill-chosen aspects of reality. Just as, in the field of linguistics, the discipline of pragmatics puts into question the priority given to the descriptive and representational functions of language, an attempt will be made here to draw attention to the more active, performative, operative functions of naturalist literature. Hence a chapter on the ironic, satirical and parodic dimensions of naturalist fiction (chapter 6), followed by a chapter which looks to define the kind of effects that the naturalist text produces in the reader and the strategies by which these effects are brought about. Even naturalist description, the subject of chapter 8, can be shown to partake, in some degree, of this intentionality.

But the principal factor of unity in naturalist fiction, I shall be arguing, is thematic. The final chapter will therefore attempt to define essential thematic constants in the corpus of texts used for this study. Thematic criticism is hardly a fashionable venture these days. But, it seems to me, it is an essential part of the generic study of literature and of naturalist literature in particular, for it is in its 'thematic content' that naturalist fiction asserts most specifically its literary characteristics. In Gérard Genette's terms, two of the essential dimensions of literature (along with the *formal*), are the *generic* and the *modal*. 'La différence de statut entre genres et modes', he writes, 'est essentiellement là: les genres sont des catégories proprement littéraires, les modes sont des catégories qui relèvent de la linguistique, ou plus exactement de ce que l'on appelle aujourd'hui la *pragmatique*.'[17] Now naturalist fiction shares its modal determinants with the broader categories of realist fiction and representational fiction. But, it is in its thematics, informed by a common view of man's newly perceived relationship to nature in the scientific age, that can be discerned its essential, specific generic features.

Theorists frequently comment on the awful methodological pitfall that attends generic studies, the vicious circle of auto-justification in which the analyst may so easily founder. Heather Dubrow describes the danger in the following way: 'Underlying all of these morphological considerations is the central problem that definitions of genres, like those of biological species, tend to be circular: one establishes such a definition on the basis of a few examples, and yet the choice of those examples from the multitude of possible ones implies a prior decision about the characteristics of the genre.'[18] However, in the face of such a dilemma, to avoid being paralysed into inertia, the critic must find some mean approach between the deductive and the inductive methods, between the models and the texts, between the general scheme and the particular cases in point. In fact, this book is made up of a series of such mediations: between a historical and a non-historical approach, between theory and textual analysis, between national and international perspectives, between detailed studies and sweeping generalities, between selectiveness and inclusiveness.[19] But it is in the nature of genre criticism to seek such mediation, as a number of theorists have pointed out. Claudio Guillén, for instance, argues that the concept of genre itself 'occupies a central position in the study of literary history, very probably, because it has succeeded so well and for so long in bridging the gap between critical theory and the practice of literary criticism'.[20] Tzvetan Todorov frequently makes the same point: 'Les genres sont précisément ces relais par lesquels l'œuvre se met en rapport avec l'univers de la littérature.' The same critic even goes so far as to claim: 'Le genre est le lieu de rencontre de la poétique générale et de l'histoire littéraire événementielle; il est à ce titre un objet privilégié, ce qui pourrait bien lui valoir l'honneur de devenir le personnage principal des études littéraires.'[21]

Clearly the danger with such an approach is of being caught

between the Scylla of the too-general and the Charybdis of the too-specific, or, more humbly, of falling between a whole series of stools. This may even be the case with the decision to use both English and French in this study, a solution likely to displease polyglots and unilinguals alike.[22] But in this, as, no doubt, in a host of other matters, the well-intentioned author can only crave his reader's indulgence.

1
HISTORIES

Just as narratologists have recently made much of the fundamental distinction between the events that are supposed to have occurred in a story and the narrative that relates them (*histoire* and *récit* in Genette's terminology), historiographers have long since distinguished between, on the one hand, history as the happenings of the past and, on the other hand, accounts that have been or could be produced to relate those happenings. Hegel referred respectively to *res gestae* and *historia rerum gestarum*, while other Germans later – and more economically – differentiated between *Geschichte* and *Historie*. Italians, after Croce, contrasted *storia* and *storiografia*, while a French translator of Heidegger, Henry Corbin, was even more economical in distinguishing between *Histoire* and *histoires*.[1] In the actual practice of history writing, so it seems, this fundamental distinction is more complex and far from absolute. As Walter L. Reed points out: 'The referential gap between history-as-account and history-as-events [rather] has become the mechanism for a history interminable, as newly identified events have demanded newly constructed accounts and old accounts (like Hegel's *Philosophy of History*) have themselves acquired the status of events that need accounting for.'[2] In the field of *literary* history there is the same complication, in kind if not in degree, with the added problem that literature itself is largely composed of accounts, stories, *histoires*.

If we bear in mind, therefore, the difference between 'History' and 'histories', it is clear that the former is unique, being the happenings themselves, and has no inherent, natural pattern, but remains open, at least in theory, to an incalculable number of accounts, of 'histories' in the second sense of the term.[3] Inevitably, therefore, there would seem to be, in any historical field, a totally impossible situation: an infinite number of different histories seeking to account for an infinitely complex History. However, an important corrective to this apparent multifariousness is, of course, the simple fact that historical accounts, like literary texts, even realist novels, are derivative of one another. Histories borrow their plots from previous histories. In other words, whereas, as we know, History never repeats itself, histories certainly do.

In a chapter dealing with the problem of the historical approach to naturalist literature, it is clearly as important to take into account the nature of, and the motivations behind, previous histories, with their characteristic ordering principles, as it is to attempt a further, necessarily incomplete and inadequate account of some aspect of naturalism's complex History. Let us proceed, therefore, directly to what is probably the main source: Zola's own 'accounts'. Unlike his contemporary naturalists, the Goncourt brothers, Zola never wrote any straight historical works, but as one would expect of a man of Taine's and Michelet's era and of an admirer of their works besides, he was imbued with the historical spirit and, as we shall see, eager to situate, explain and justify naturalist literature from a historical perspective. In fact, his critical works are replete with brief lessons in literary history. He would no doubt have preferred Taine himself to have accomplished the task, but he was never reluctant to attempt it himself.

In an early review of a book on Roman history, an *Histoire de Jules César* (1865), the novelist discusses in general terms the problem of writing history. He characterises two types of historian: (1) those who neglect details, 's'attachent à l'ensemble', 'embrassent d'un coup d'œil l'horizon d'une époque' (X, 158),[4] imposing a system and, in doing so, Zola argues, depriving history of its vitality; (2) those who belong to the opposite school, thriving on detail and attempting to render the figures, events, spirit and customs of an age in all the vivid colours of reality: 'Elle est analyse, et non pas synthèse' (X, 159). Now being, as he puts it, 'fou de réalité', Zola clearly prefers the analytical method, the realist approach, and he condemns the providential, synthetic type of history of the author of the text under review. But his objections are not only methodological, for he is still writing under the Second Empire as an opponent of the régime and the anonymous author in question is none other than Louis Napoleon himself. It is hardly surprising, therefore, that, pretending to write himself without 'le moindre sous-entendu', he ironically condemns the author's partiality: 'Il est presque juge et partie à la fois, et bien que personne ne se permette de soupçonner un instant sa bonne foi d'historien, il se trouve dans la position fausse d'un homme qui fait par moments sa propre apologie' (X, 162).

Now exactly the same objections could be raised against Zola himself when he later came to give his version, more imperial than empirical, of the history of naturalist literature. In a study of Sainte-Beuve, for example, which he wrote for the Russian review *Vestnik Evropy*, we see that he completely reverses his position. He imagines a model history of French literature (significantly) written by Taine, which would be 'un édifice complet avec ses fondations, ses premières assises, ses étages successifs; et le tout sera déduit logiquement, démonté et remonté d'après certaines lois' (XII, 449). In his own little literary histories he adopts a thoroughly synthetic and schematic approach. His collections of articles dating from the period 1875 to 1880 – *Le Roman expérimental* (1880), *Les Romanciers naturalistes* (1881), *Nos Auteurs dramatiques* (1881), *Documents littéraires* (1881) and *Le Naturalisme au théâtre* (1881) – abound in such sketches.[5] But the best example appears in the more varied collection of articles that Zola wrote for *Le Figaro* in 1880–1 and published under the title *Une Campagne* (1882). 'Le Naturalisme' (*Le Figaro*, 17 January 1881) is his attempt to put the record straight once and for all on this troubled question that has caused so much fuss in the press and brought so much vituperation on his head. The novelist's explanation and defence of naturalism consists almost entirely of a historical survey tracing a prestigious lineage of naturalist writers. The outline is remarkably simple. 'Sans remonter au déluge', he begins with the eighteenth century, matching off the pantheist Rousseau, father of the Romantics, against the positivist Diderot, 'le véritable aïeul des naturalistes' (XIV, 507). The Romantic line runs on through Chateaubriand, Victor Hugo and what Zola contemptuously calls 'la queue romantique'. In Diderot's line, which, he claims, is now dominant, there is Stendhal, the link with the eighteenth century – 'La chaîne est ininterrompue' – followed by Balzac, another 'père du naturalisme', Flaubert, Edmond and Jules de Goncourt, then finally 'nous, les cadets, qui sommes encore trop dans la bataille pour être classés et jugés froidement' (XIV, 509). Since the demise of the Classical formula, a battle has raged between the two. The battle lines are still drawn, but the outcome is inevitable: 'Mon credo est que le naturalisme, j'entends le retour à la nature, l'esprit scientifique porté dans toutes nos connaissances, est l'agent même du dix-neuvième siècle' (XIV, 511).

This highly schematic interpretation of two centuries of French literary history is remarkable in several respects. Firstly, for its combative view of literary history, which, reflecting as it does the rigours of literary life in France, also, and mainly, serves to lend a heroic stamp to Zola's own efforts and to those of his associates. The naturalist legions are winning the day, he asserts, and, despite his frequent disclaimers – 'Je ne suis pas un chef d'école, et je raie gaiement cela de mes papiers' (XIV, 510) – Zola himself implicitly emerges as the new Imperator of this naturalist hegemony. Indeed, his scheme is extraordinarily authoritarian, exclusively national (at this stage at least), though claiming universal validity, and thoroughly utopian. In *Le Naturalisme au théâtre*, for example, he writes: 'La force du naturalisme est justement d'avoir des racines profondes dans notre littérature nationale, qui est faite de beaucoup de bon sens.' Then, unabashedly, the novelist adds: 'Il vient des entrailles mêmes de l'humanité' (XI, 284). The naturalists of Zola's (almost equally fictitious) masterplan recall the all-conquering Froments of his final series of novels, *Les Quatre Evangiles*.

Zola's grand design is also noteworthy as an example of the not uncommon practice among literary polemicists of fabricating a tradition and of claiming to descend from prestigious ancestors. Zola's recuperation of the Classics is a very selective business, as well as being a relatively arbitrary fabrication, vested with absolute prestige and authority, sweepingly dispatching all literary works and writers to one of two rudimentary categories. Undoubtedly, had they been alive to do so, both Stendhal and Balzac would have protested as vigorously as did Flaubert at being included in Zola's great tradition. Where precisely were those battalions of naturalists that he wrote about before 1880? On what basis did he expect his contemporaries to believe that by 1879 'le romantisme ... s'est effondré devant le naturalisme, revenu plus fort et maître tout-puissant, menant le siècle dont il est le souffle même' (X, 1236)? It is quite extraordinary that Zola could be making such extravagant claims at a time when the accomplishments of the writers associated with him and with his ideas were so limited, when only a handful of naturalist novels had been written – and mostly by Zola himself! Clearly, for polemical purposes, the novelist is fabricating a largely mythical heritage in the guise of literary history. Better than any claims to innovation, the purposeful continuity of the tradition that he has created is the most powerful vindication of the type of literature that he favours and is seeking to promote.

What is even more significant, for our purposes, in Zola's scheme is the fact that it appears to have provided the model for a number of standard historical studies of naturalism, even though their authors were presumably prompted far less, if at all, by such polemical imperatives. The most obvious example is Charles Beuchat's massive two-volume *Histoire du naturalisme français* (1949), the product of twenty-five years of research and a mine of information (in volume II) on the minor writers of the naturalist period. The author casts his net over an extraordinarily wide sea, making half of French literature naturalist in kind and making no attempt to distinguish between realism and naturalism. Naturalism is for him a movement of reaction against Romanticism, the conventional, the grandiloquent, the cult of form, in the name of 'simple reality'. It is 'an eternal need of man', expressing his sense of reality and of present circumstances. Homer is the first naturalist, Rabelais 'le véritable père du naturalisme' and Diderot the movement's first theoretician. But, like Zola, Beuchat begins his history proper in the eighteenth century, with Diderot and Rétif de la Bretonne, yet another 'père et initiateur du naturalisme' (p. 33). As the biographies and the plot summaries pile up, the military and heroic metaphors, reminiscent of Zola's campaigns, spring forth. By the end of volume I, 'grâce à des génies de la force d'un Balzac, d'un Stendhal ou d'un Flaubert, le naturalisme poursuit joyeusement sa marche triomphale. Il a doublé le cap des tempêtes. Tel un vaisseau de haute mer, il vogue vers le large' (p. 287). By the end of volume II, subtitled *Le Naturalisme triomphant*, the author's evangelical spirit knows no bounds in his paean to the heroic age of the Goncourt brothers and of the true hero himself, a pugnacious Zola, 'qu'enivrait le bruit de la mitraille', taking head-on assailants from the enemy camp: 'Le diable d'homme rendait coup pour coup, blessure pour blessure. Il tint bon, jusqu'à l'arrivée de renforts. Alors, la victoire récompensa ces braves et la renommée répandit au loin les noms de Maupassant, de Huysmans, de Céard, d'Hennique et d'Alexis. Le naturalisme triomphait sur toute la ligne' (p. 433).

Most other literary historians, as one would expect, are more restrained in their views, but there are frequently more than a few vestiges of the same overall vision and spirit. For example, in a standard study which predates Beuchat's book and which, typically, consists of a series of (mainly) biographical studies of the major naturalists within the framework of the now familiar overview of the movement, Pierre Martino writes: 'C'est pourtant vers 1890, à une date où, après une courte bataille d'une dizaine d'années, le petit groupe naturaliste était devenu une grande armée victorieuse ...'[6] Even in such an authoritative study as Gustave Lanson's *Histoire de la littérature française*, in which there is not the slightest trace of bias in favour of Zola and the naturalist movement and in which there is certainly no hint of a heroic conception of the naturalist struggle, the author, nonetheless, places the whole of the literature of the period 1850–90 under the naturalist banner and declares: 'L'essor du naturalisme est le grand fait littéraire qui domine la seconde moitié

du XIXe siècle.'[7] Yet, extraordinarily, this movement which supposedly dominated a whole age is not embodied in a single writer.
Even Zola, the leading figure of this 'mouvement de réaction contre
le romantisme', is paradoxically 'avant tout un romantique'.[8] 'Pour
Lanson', as Jacques Dubois neatly puts it, 'le naturalisme est un de
ces cercles dont le centre est partout et la circonférence nulle part.'[9]
Thus, whereas Zola and the critics intent upon establishing the
credentials and viability of the naturalist movement muster up an
almost infinitely extendible series of portraits of literary figures
stretching back into the past, in Lanson's gallery there are only empty
frames. Nevertheless, there is still the supposition of continuity and
unity. Such studies impose and seek to uphold a clear pattern of
development which, inevitably, is undermined by more detailed and
more narrowly focused analyses of individual writers and texts. An
evident feature of historical studies of the naturalist movement in
France is the blatant disparity between the disarming orderliness of
the patterns of development established by the general studies, and
the contradictions, dissensions and uncertainties that the detailed
studies expose. 'La véritable histoire du naturalisme', writes Jacques
Dubois, 'se noue peut-être dans un ensemble de discordances.'[10]

Literary history, it can be argued, is essentially the awareness of
relationships and consists of establishing transitions. The objection
that much literary history gives rise to is, of course, that the coherence,
the unity, indeed the very truth, that literary historians establish derive
from their modelling and are not inherent features of History itself.[11] Yet, as one might legitimately object, the alternative approach
being proposed in this book is in itself a concatenation of data. Just
as we can be aware, along with modern historians, that the writing
of history is to a considerable degree a *literary* undertaking, we must
also acknowledge that the study of a literary genre is itself a literary
genre. Nevertheless, the claim would be that the immense advantage
of this approach over the type of historical studies which we have just
reviewed is that we are dealing with a homogeneous set of data, a series
of texts, which, for all their complexity, belong to the same order of
reality. Literary histories, on the contrary, tend to subsume disparate
elements: biographical details, texts, manifestos, social, political and
historical events, etc. Hence their need to rely upon external principles
of ordering into epochs, schools, movements. Hence, too, the fact
that they frequently consist of a series of biographies strung together,
as Roland Barthes noted some time ago: 'L'histoire n'est ici que
succession d'hommes seuls; bref, ce n'est pas une histoire, c'est une
chronique ... Toute histoire littéraire nous renvoie ainsi à une séquence

de critiques closes.'[12] Or, as we have seen in the cases of Zola and Lanson, the principle of unification may be provided by an antithetical formula like Romanticism versus Naturalism, a type of differentiation which, as Françoise Gaillard writes in the wake of Barthes, 'masque, sous l'hypertrophie d'une tendance unifiante, les contradictions existant au sein même de ces "écoles" ou "mouvements" ... De cette occultation du véritable lieu de conflits ne peut naître qu'une histoire apparente ou, mieux, qu'une apparence d'histoire.'[13]

We should look more closely, therefore, if only briefly, at certain of what are usually recognised as the most significant 'historical' events and developments in the French naturalist calendar, with a view to approximating in part the History of the movement in all its complexity rather than to add to, deny or confirm the histories that exist already. Three prominent incidents, the Trapp dinner, the publication of *Les Soirées de Médan* and the 'Manifeste des Cinq', landmark events which contain the potentiality of a convenient historical pattern – an inauguration, a manifesto and a collective attack from a new generation of writers; or, in short, a birth, a flourish and a decline – will be the central points of focus. It is not unusual for the publication of *Les Soirées de Médan* to be heralded as naturalism's founding event. 'Evénement repère dans l'histoire littéraire du XIXᵉ siècle', writes Alain Pagès, '*Les Soirées de Médan* apparaissent comme un exemple particulièrement riche permettant de réfléchir au problème de l'origine.'[14] However, unless we believe, as the same critic playfully suggests, that 'l'origine est aussi une fin',[15] we might easily be led to conclude in the light of what follows that, if that particular event was the beginning, the whole movement was still-born or at least expired before it received its ritual sanction.

Be that as it may, what is usually acknowledged as the baptismal event of the naturalist movement in France is the Trapp dinner, which took place on 16 April 1877. But why, we may ask, is this particular occasion any less arbitrary than any other as an initial point of reference? There is, of course, in France, a long tradition of literary alliances being sealed in a café or restaurant, in locations like the café Procope in Saint-Germain which served the function of literary meeting place for generations and was frequented by Rousseau and Voltaire. According to Paul Bourget, his own friendship with Zola dated from a dinner held there in 1875, one of a whole series called 'le Bœuf nature'.[16] Other 'Bœuf nature' dinners were still taking place three years later at another restaurant, chez Brébant, where, since 1870, the famous 'dîners Magny' had been held and where, appropriately, the more professional Société des Gens de Lettres would later gather. Zola saw naturalist significance in the name, as he explains in 1877: 'Il contient toute une profession de foi, il est le drapeau du *naturalisme*, la revendication du vrai dans les arts et dans les lettres.'[17] Then there were the 'Flaubert dinners', or the 'dîners des auteurs sifflés' as they were also called – each participant having had a play or two hissed and booed – which were held quite frequently after April 1874 and brought together Flaubert, Daudet, Edmond de Goncourt, Zola and Turgenev. According to Léon Deffoux: 'Le dîner Flaubert apparaît comme la réunion la plus significative des débuts du naturalisme.'[18] There were other regular gatherings too, at which some or other of the (future) naturalists met: Sunday afternoons at Flaubert's, when he was in Paris; Friday receptions held by Madame Charpentier, the publisher's wife. There were Zola's own Thursday gatherings – a longstanding tradition going back to the early days (1863–4) when more painters than authors came – which, at the time of the publication of *L'Assommoir*, attracted the young writers, Huysmans, Céard, Hennique, Alexis, Maupassant and Mirbeau.

Why then, the question remains, single out the 'dîner Trapp' when there were apparently so many literary meals taking place? An extract from an unpublished diary by Henry Céard provides a succinct account of the occasion and some interesting indications of its significance:

Un jour l'envie venait à Zola de voir l'endroit de nos réunions: il acceptait un dîner, et le dîner était si mauvais qu'un peu honteux, nous nous proposions de lui en offrir un autre plus correct, ailleurs dans un endroit où il pourrait manger. Maupassant alors proposait d'y amener Flaubert; Flaubert amené on songeait à Goncourt; et l'on écartait Daudet sans discussion. Il n'était pas considéré comme un maître. Puis c'était Charpentier qu'on invitait, avec l'arrière-pensée que cette politesse le déciderait à publier les romans à venir. On s'attablait chez Trapp, auprès de la gare St Lazare, et ce dîner intime, par une indiscrétion d'Alexis, était annoncé et commenté aigrement par *La République des Lettres*. La maison même d'Hugo s'en occupait, prenait même un peu d'ombrage, les familiers s'inquiétaient de ce qu'ils considéraient comme l'affirmation d'une école nouvelle hostile au romantisme, et Daudet, humilié de son exclusion, en présence de Mme Charpentier, les larmes aux yeux, disait avec amertume: 'C'est le salon de Zola qui a fait cela.'[19]

Even allowing for distortions and mythical accretions – not to mention the absurd implication that the naturalist movement owed its foundation to a gastronomical fiasco – the dinner, we clearly see, had, so to speak, all the trappings of a founding event: the merging of two groups of participants, certain inclusions, certain exclusions, a rival party and, already, certain potential tensions. The 'arrière-pensée' of inviting Charpentier is indicative also of the young writers' real motives.

But the occasion was most significant as what we would call nowadays a 'media event'. The newspapers had a field day commenting satirically on the dinner. *La République des Lettres* even published a (fantasy) naturalist menu:

> Potage 'purée Bovary'.
>
> Truite saumonée à la 'fille Elisa'.
>
> Poularde truffée à la 'Saint-Antoine'.
>
> Artichauts au 'Cœur simple'.
>
> Parfait 'naturaliste'.
>
> Vin de 'Coupeau'.
>
> Liqueur de l''Assommoir'.[20]

This kind of persiflage in the press indicates the seriousness with which the event was really taken, but it does also lend a certain aura of credibility to the myth of the founding of a new literary school. It certainly reflects the tone of the dinner itself, as we can tell from Edmond de Goncourt's brief account in his *Journal*: 'Ce soir ... la jeunesse des lettres réaliste, naturaliste, nous a sacrés, Flaubert, Zola et moi, sacrés officiellement les trois maîtres de l'heure présente, dans un dîner des plus cordiaux et des plus gais. Voici l'armée nouvelle en train de se former' (16 April 1877). But was the new literary school, movement or 'army' really formed that evening? We can confidently assume that nothing approaching a common naturalist agenda would have been discussed at this or at any other similar event. On such occasions conversation seems to have turned to far racier matters than naturalist aesthetics and, as several entries in the Goncourt *Journal* show, the mere presence of Flaubert, with his undisguised scorn for Zola's, or for anybody's, pet theories was a guarantee that no possible doctrinal consensus could ever have been achieved. In fact, at an earlier gathering, no more than two months before the Trapp dinner, again according to Goncourt's account, Zola had been forced into the following much-quoted apostasy:

Flaubert attaque, – toutefois avec des coups de chapeau donnés à son génie, – attaque les préfaces, les doctrines, les professions de foi naturalistes, enfin toute cette blague un peu Mangin, avec laquelle Zola aide le succès de ses livres. Zola répond à peu près ceci: 'Vous, vous avez eu une petite fortune, qui vous a permis de vous affranchir de beaucoup de choses. Moi qui ai gagné ma vie absolument avec ma plume, qui ai été obligé de passer par toutes sortes d'écritures honteuses, par le journalisme, j'en ai conservé, comment vous dirai-je cela? un peu de *banquisme* ... Oui, c'est vrai que je me moque comme vous de ce mot *Naturalisme*; et cependant, je le répéterai sans cesse, parce qu'il faut un baptême aux choses, pour que le public les croie neuves ...' (19 February 1877)

Thus, even if, here again, we make due allowance for some natural overstatement of the case by Zola, clearly on the defensive in the face of Flaubert's formidable onslaught, we see once more that strategy, opportunism, *réclame*, mystification are primary motive forces behind the movement. A shared sense of purpose and common aesthetic principles are obviously of secondary importance.

Along with the long tradition of literary junketing in France, there is the equally long tradition of contention in the literary arena, where it is not enough for writers to write, for they must engage in polemical battles over manifestos, slogans, critical reviews and so on, in order to make their mark. Groups like the one we are describing are a natural form of defence ... and attack. Paul Alexis was particularly adept at exploiting the press for advertising purposes, often to the annoyance of the more scrupulous members of the group.[21] The Trapp dinner, as it turned out, was one such venture. In a similar, but more restrained fashion, Zola wrote articles in support of his younger associates to draw them into the limelight and he found openings for them in the press both in France and abroad. As Goncourt sourly put it in his *Journal*: 'Zola a une *gens* de jeunes *fidèles*, dont le *malin* écrivain entretient et nourrit du reste l'admiration, l'enthousiasme, la flamme par l'octroi de correspondances à l'étranger, le faufilement bien payé dans les journaux où il règne en maître, enfin par des services tout matériels' (28 May 1879). But such mutual services were a part of the cut and thrust of the literary order. Zola had a practical sense of the advantages of a group effort, as his correspondence shows, where he is constantly urging the younger writers to add 'des œuvres de combat' to their modest achievements. 'Nous devons d'ici à quelques années', he writes, 'écraser le public sous notre fécondité.'[22] It was probably more than anything else this kind of effective complicity that brought the group together and held it together in the (late) 1870s. Of the three 'maîtres', the triumvirate of Flaubert, Edmond de Goncourt and Zola, each of whom, in his own way, as we shall see, influenced the younger writers and the course of the movement, it was Zola who had the clout and, for the very reasons that he gave in his dispute with Flaubert (quoted above), drew them by his sense of enterprise into the orbit of his rising star.

'Les groupements', Léon Hennique later observed to an interviewer, 'viennent de la cameraderie plutôt qu'ils ne sont la conséquence des mêmes idées ... Les naturalistes, nous nous groupâmes autour de Zola, parce que nous étions outrés des attaques dont son œuvre littéraire était l'objet, sinon, nous ne nous connaissions ni les uns ni les autres.'[23] This alliance of younger writers with Zola was in fact both much looser and more extensive than has often been supposed. Curiously it was in all probability through the Parnassian journal, *La République des Lettres*, that the first encounters took place, among Hennique, Huysmans, Maupassant and Alexis.[24] Curiously too, these far from conventional writers were mostly in government service, like Maupassant, who met Zola when he was with the Ministère de la Marine at Flaubert's Sunday gatherings. Céard worked for the War Ministry and was introduced to Huysmans, another civil servant, in the Ministry of the Interior by a colleague, Ludovic de Francmesnil. Like Zola's old friend, Marius Roux, and Octave Mirbeau also, Gabriel Thyébaut, yet another *fonctionnaire*, who later formed close ties with Zola, was as much a part of the company as the contributors to *Les Soirées de Médan*. According to C. A. Burns, Céard, Huysmans, Thyébaut, Francmesnil and François Coppée held regular meetings to share in their enthusiasm for the works of Balzac, the Goncourt brothers and Flaubert, and only discovered Zola's novels in the early months of 1876.[25] Alexis was the only one of the later 'Médan group' to have already formed by this time a close association with Zola. Thus it was that in April 1876 Céard paid a respectful visit to Zola one Sunday (and, so the story goes, was taken for a wine merchant) to express the group's admiration for the novelist's works. Shortly afterwards he brought Huysmans along. These meetings were, no doubt, of considerably more consequence than the Trapp dinner, for Céard and Huysmans would appear to have been key figures in the network of associations established thereafter. The group's 'adoption' of Zola, their vigorous defence of *L'Assommoir* and their respect for his novels in general, irrespective of the determination of the press to perpetuate the myth of the existence of a new literary school, were important factors in contributing to a certain unity of purpose and agreement among these writers.

If, however, we look at the same relations from the point of view of a number of detailed, well-researched studies of individual naturalist writers, the sense of unity virtually disintegrates. According to B. H. Bakker, for example: 'L'"école" naturaliste se réduit en somme à un maître et à un disciple, à Zola et à Alexis; et il n'y a que ce dernier qui souscrive strictement à la pure théorie naturaliste.'[26] As for Huysmans − the most successful of the younger naturalist writers before 1880, vigorous defender of Zola and his text in 'Emile Zola et *L'Assommoir*' (1877), author of two naturalist novels, *Marthe, histoire d'une fille* (1876) and *Les Sœurs Vatard* (1879), the latter of which was dedicated to Zola by 'son fervent admirateur et dévoué ami' − he kept a discreet silence on Zola's theories and by 1879, so it seems, was having serious doubts about his association. Hennique, for his part, also charged to the defence of *L'Assommoir* in a controversial lecture at the Salle des Capucines (on 23 January 1877), but, in O. R. Morgan's estimation, his links with Zola and his literary campaign were no more than 'the flirtation of a *bourgeois révolté*, an aspirant to literary success, with the newest and most original theories of his day'.[27] In his massive study of Maupassant, André Vial makes a similar point on all the members of the group: 'Tous les cinq rendent un juste hommage à leur aîné [Zola], mais à l'écrivain et non au doctrinaire, le jour où, pour faire leur trouée, ils s'associent à une gloire jeune et bon teint.'[28] The other 'aînés', like Flaubert, we recall, did not hide their disdain for Zola's formulas. Edmond de Goncourt was privately undermining Zola's influence by all accounts and, in the preface to *Les Frères Zemganno* (1879), made a public and barely veiled attack on the author of *L'Assommoir* with derogatory references to what he called *canaille littéraire*. But it was Maupassant who, privately at least, was the most scornful of Zola's theories, even though publicly he also defended the novelist with apparent conviction. 'Selon que Maupassant s'adresse à Zola ou à Flaubert,' Vial notes,

au public ou aux intimes, selon que le document date de la période des ambitions poétiques ou de celle qui s'ouvre avec le succès de *Boule de Suif*, selon même que l'on s'éloigne davantage de cette inauguration triomphale vers le temps des ventes toujours mieux assurées, la sincérité le cède à l'esprit d'intrigue, ou, lorsqu'elle s'affirme, s'accommode volontiers de quelque fanfaronnade ou de surenchère courtisane, avant de trouver sa vraie mesure, − dans le silence et l'oubli; c'est au début de 1882, que Maupassant écrit pour la dernière fois le mot 'naturaliste': il n'a publié encore, sous son unique signature, qu'un seul recueil de nouvelles, *La Maison Tellier*.[29]

Paradoxically it was the very issue of a unified aesthetic that caused the most dissension among the group and it was the critics' determination to lump them together as a school that caused resentment.

Paradoxically also, though it is perhaps a general law of the group dynamics of literary movements that professional success as much as failure brings about disruptions,[30] the more successful members of the group, Huysmans and Maupassant, inevitably drew away as soon as they had made their mark.

In a sense it was Flaubert rather than Zola who was the real mentor of the group, the focal point, the dominating spirit, the major inspiration, in these early years. He was not only the author of works that inspired them, but was a kind of measure of their artistic integrity, a writer of conscience, of utter conscientiousness, of impeccable standards. In his letters to Flaubert, we see Zola almost panic-stricken in case he may have offended the 'maître de Croisset'. 'Je vous ai écrit, il y a plus de quinze jours,' he writes on 7 October 1877, 'et vous ne m'avez pas répondu, vous si exact. Etes-vous fâché?' Then five days later, in great relief at having received replies: 'J'avais eu une folle idée que je dois vous confesser, pour me punir: je croyais de vous avoir fâché par quelques feuilletons où j'ai soutenu des idées que je ne sais pas être les vôtres.'[31] Zola was clearly fully aware of Flaubert's fulminations against his ideas and against those who seemed likely to espouse them.[32] As Henri Mitterand puts it, Flaubert was the 'figure tutélaire' who dominated this 'naturalist period', from 1877 to 1880, ironically the very period of Zola's most intense theorising, much to the older writer's dismay.[33] It is therefore surprising, but far from unreasonable, to suggest that Flaubert's death on May 8 of that crucial year (1880) struck a fatal blow to the Médan group and marked the end of an era.

Against this background of tensions and dissensions the publication of the (now) famous collection of six short stories, *Les Soirées de Médan* (1880), by the so-called 'groupe de Médan' needs to be set. Here again our literary histories have not always proved reliable in attributing considerable significance to this single event. Maupassant set the tone. In a famous account of the origin of the collection, he spins a yarn about balmy summer evenings at Zola's country house in Médan, where, in a Boccaccian manner, the six naturalists had taken a turn in telling a tale and Zola had suggested that they publish the stories together.[34] This account, as has been pointed out numerous times, is pure fantasy, for the book was almost certainly planned in Paris and not at Médan in the winter of 1879, as a result – so Léon Hennique informs us in a much more credible version – of a discussion at dinner of the Franco-Prussian war, the common theme of the six texts.[35] Now the whole episode, so it appears, was a rather makeshift matter to which the five attached little importance and Zola even less, for he was at the time racing against the clock to finish writing *Nana*.[36] 'En somme', writes Alain Pagès in an article on this overblown event, 'une histoire médiocre, marquée par le hasard, le désintérêt, la rapidité.'[37] Potentially then, yet another naturalist non-event, but one which clearly gave rise in fact to considerable mystification. The publication of *Les Soirées de Médan* and the critical reaction to it, as Alain Pagès has shown, created what he calls the 'myth of Médan', the illusion of a group of writers solidly united behind 'le maître de Médan'. To a considerable degree, the myth was fostered by Zola and his friends, but it was confirmed and perpetuated by the press. Thus, Pagès concludes, '*Les Soirées de Médan* restent importantes pour nous, non pour le contenu de quelques nouvelles rassemblées dans un recueil, mais pour le mythe qui s'attache à elles. Dans ce mythe, se projettent des rêves, des désirs, le rêve d'un groupe uni, le rêve d'un écrivain maître de l'avenir.'[38]

But, for all the fantasy that it inspired, *Les Soirées de Médan* should not be too readily dismissed. The brief preface to the collection, which either Zola or Céard composed and which is dated (Médan, of course, rather than Paris) 1 March 1880, is in itself an interesting pointer in view of its double design:

Les nouvelles qui suivent ont été publiées, les unes en France, les autres à l'étranger. Elles nous ont paru procéder d'une idée unique, avoir une même philosophie: nous les réunissons.

Nous nous attendons à toutes les attaques, à la mauvaise foi et à l'ignorance dont la critique courante nous a déjà donné tant de preuves. Notre seul souci a été d'affirmer publiquement nos véritables amitiés et, en même temps, nos tendances littéraires.

On the one hand, we see a provocative defiance of the critics, a challenge to the dominant literary institutions and tastes of the time, another skirmish in the struggles that are part of this history of the naturalist movement in France that we are here retracing (and, to some degree, 'deconstructing') in a necessarily summary and incomplete manner. But, on the other hand, the preface contains a confident assertion of the common character of the literature that the group was writing (or hoping to write) and indeed *Les Soirées de Médan* is a significant work precisely because it represents a collective effort with a shared sense of *literary* purpose, instead of being a theoretical statement, a programme or a manifesto, for, as I shall attempt to show later (in chapter 6), this rather disparate group of texts, collected opportunely together, does reveal a unified design. This preface sends us thus in two directions: the one which we shall follow in the main body of this book, attempting to define those common literary tendencies in naturalist texts. The other brings us back, still somewhat reluctantly but only temporarily and quite briefly, to the tangled threads of the History/histories of the movement.

If, as we can confidently state, the naturalist group, in so far as it had ever functioned in this way, was after 1880 no longer a coherent active force, then perhaps the greatest irony of the whole situation is the fact that its virtual disintegration coincided exactly with the beginning of a period of great productivity of naturalist texts in France and abroad. As we can see from the tables in Yves Chevrel's book *Le Naturalisme* listing the most significant naturalist publications, the years 1879–80 are marked as the period of what he calls the first 'ground-swell', arising after a surprisingly considerable hiatus following the years 1864–9 when the very first texts had appeared.[39] Thereafter, Zola himself dictated the pace, withdrawing for most of the year to Médan, producing in regular succession, after *Nana* (1880), a remarkable series of texts: *Pot-Bouille* (1882), *Au Bonheur des Dames* (1883), *La Joie de vivre* (1884), *Germinal* (1885), *L'Œuvre* (1886) and *La Terre* (1887). 'Je me tiens à l'écart', he wrote in April 1884; then, in March of the following year, to Octave Mirbeau: 'Mais pourquoi dites-vous que je conduis le naturalisme? Je ne conduis rien du tout. Voici bientôt quatre ans que je n'ai écrit une ligne dans un journal, je travaille dans mon coin, en laissant rouler le monde où il lui plaît.'[40]

Now, ironically again, it was precisely this almost serene detachment from literary politics in his own country, sustained by his confidence in his fame and influence abroad,[41] that became one of the principal grievances brought against Zola by the signatories of the 'Manifeste des Cinq' – a fact which usually goes unnoticed.[42] We know that in November 1886 he had refrained from commenting publicly on J.-H. Rosny's novel, *Nell Horn*, much to the author's indignation; it was probably Rosny who wrote the manifesto. Zola also failed to give sufficient encouragement and support, at least in Paul Bonnetain's estimation, when, in 1884, the latter had faced a lawsuit for immorality at the time of the publication of his novel on onanism, *Charlot s'amuse* (1883);[43] it was probably Bonnetain who had the original idea to write the manifesto.[44] Zola was therefore not a king to be toppled, but a general who had fallen asleep on the battlefield and was accused of neglecting the literary struggle for his own selfish purposes. 'La surprise fut pénible', so the accusation runs, 'de voir Zola déserter, émigrer à Médan, consacrant les efforts – légers à cette époque – qu'eût demandés un organe de lutte et d'affermissement, à des satisfactions d'un ordre infiniment moins esthétique.' Thus we could quite easily, and perhaps just as convincingly, attribute to this episode a significance that would be almost the very opposite to the one that it has acquired for most literary historians. Instead of being a repudiation of their leader by a group of naturalist writers, and therefore the evident sign of the disintegration of the movement, it appears as a gesture of frustration and resentment by a group of would-be or pseudo-disciples directed against a figure of towering authority both at home and abroad. As Zola was quick to point out, he barely knew his detractors and had only ever met one of them (Bonnetain). And all the time, as Guy Robert has shown, the output of naturalist texts in the years 1886–7 in France was 'massif et puissant'.[45]

But the 'Manifeste des Cinq' is also significant for our purposes because it contains the outline of yet another historical reading of the naturalist movement in France, one which runs counter to the optimistic versions that we have seen, and one which is even more polemical and reductive in its distortions than they, a kind of 'Decline and Fall of Emile Zola' from the heights of *L'Assommoir* to the putrid depths of *La Terre*. The signatories recall the heady days of yore when the Master was so courageous and strong, the days of his 'rout of the Romantics'. But now he has lapsed into clichés and obscenity; 'le charme du Maître', they claim, has come to 's'embourber dans l'ordure'. Though the five pretend that their long repudiation of Zola is made in the name of 'ambitions saines et viriles', in the name of their 'cult', their 'deep love', their 'supreme respect' for Art, it is a scurrilous document, a vile *ad hominem* attack, literally a series of low blows, for they attribute Zola's decline, on the one hand, to what they variously call a 'malady of the lower organs', his 'manies de moine solitaire', a 'maladie rénale', the 'irrémédiable dépravation morbide d'un chaste', and, on the other hand, to what they term 'une boulimie de vente', a crass desire for commercial success. The terms of the assault are, of course, themselves mock naturalist, dwelling upon morbid physiology as Zola was often accused of doing and as we also see in their ludicrous prescription for Zola's literary malady: 'Peut-être Charcot, Moreau (de Tours) et ces médecins de la Salpêtrière qui nous firent voir les coprolaliques pourraient-ils déterminer les symptômes de son mal ...'

But this sally by the five would-be rebels turned out to be more of an Aunt Sally than a serious threat to Zola's reputation, for the offensive proved to be far too offensive to be convincing. Edmond de Goncourt and Alphonse Daudet, both much more closely associated

135/815

College of St. Francis Library
Joliet, Illinois

with the five than Zola – four of them frequented the former's Grenier and Descaves was a great friend of the latter – and both suspected of being behind the attack, were caused more embarrassment than pleasure or amusement by an incident that they may have unwittingly inspired by their caustic private criticisms of Zola. Even though the 'Manifeste' provoked a great stir in the press, it soon became evident that the missile had backfired, for the excesses of the attack, the relative obscurity of its perpetrators and, in particular, the apparent hypocrisy of the author of *Charlot s'amuse* meant that the protest was not taken seriously. *Chroniqueurs* relished trivialising the incident, hoisting the five, as it were, on their own petard. In *Le Voltaire* of 26 August, for example, there appeared a pseudo 'Manifeste des Cinq' in which it was recounted that the authors of *Les Soirées de Médan*, along with a doctor, had accompanied Zola to a 'maison Tellier' in Saint-Germain where the author of *La Terre* had acquitted himself rather well of certain of the charges contained in the original 'Manifeste'.[46] It was, of course, the month of August, the 'silly season' for the journalists. But other commentators were more serious in denouncing the upstarts. 'Vous avez fait là, mes garçons,' Henry Bauer wrote in *Le Réveil*, 'une vilaine besogne qui se retournera contre vous-mêmes, vous avez oublié que le peu que vous êtes, vous le lui devez: vous n'existez que par lui ... Apprenez, mes petits, que toute la littérature contemporaine a pris son essor dans ses *Rougon-Macquart*.'[47]

Clearly this at times burlesque incident is far from having the historical significance with which it is often graced and, in a number of ways, it may be interpreted very differently. In a rigorous, sociological study of literary groups in the latter half of the nineteenth century, for example, Christophe Charle sees in it the very opposite of a manifesto:

Dans une certaine mesure, ce manifeste est un succès puisqu'il fait parler des auteurs, mais il repose sur de telles ambiguïtés et de telles contradictions, et surtout sur une conjoncture tellement fragile, qui dépasse largement les auteurs (concurrence entre journaux, entre chapelles, réaction anti-naturaliste, etc.), que ce n'est qu'un feu de paille. Surtout, c'est un antimanifeste qui critique la première génération mais ne propose rien qu'un retour à un réalisme adouci, c'est-à-dire insipide.[48]

Indeed, set against the realities of the literary institutions of the time and against the almost desperate need of young writers to impose themselves on a shrinking literary market dominated by the novel and by the financial success of an ever limited number of writers like Zola, the gesture was a decided failure, for it had the opposite effect to the one intended, reaffirming the pre-eminence of the author of the *Rougon-Macquart* and leading to a dispersion of this new group.[49] 'Ainsi le scandale du *Manifeste*', writes Christophe Charle, 'prend place à une plus large échelle dans le processus de dissociation du courant réaliste et naturaliste, sous l'effet de la concurrence entre individualités.'[50] Paradoxically then, it would seem, Zola's five *detractors* of 1887 were motivated by the same ambitions that ten years earlier had led five other young writers to *defend* him. But times had changed and so had the strategy.

We have seen, therefore, in this chapter so far that the forming and disbanding of alliances, polemical exchanges, celebratory gatherings, manifestos and so on, are all part of the complex web of the History of the naturalist movement in France. Within certain limits any of these events – and others, no doubt, that have fallen into complete oblivion – could be given special significance and be said to illustrate general trends. On the basis of the same evidence, furthermore, we could even go so far as to claim that there was or was not a Médan group. In view of such indeterminacy, we must also regard with scepticism attempts to establish firm and precise dates to demarcate the period of the naturalist movement. Traditionally, historical dates or the biographical dates of major literary figures provide the markers. Literary history, as Gérard Delfau points out, tends to favour 'les "grandes dates" et les "grands auteurs", à redoubler l'histoire politique en lui empruntant les éléments de sa propre périodisation. De là ces "écoles" qui s'installent et tombent en même temps que les régimes politiques.'[51] The most common division for late nineteenth-century France, as we have seen above, is: 1850–70, le Réalisme; 1871–1900, le Naturalisme, with the fall of the Second Empire and the Commune providing a convenient split. But such divisions, in the light of the sort of historical evidence that we have rapidly reviewed, are clearly arbitrary in the extreme. So too are attempts to attribute writers to literary categories, leading to such unavailing questions as 'Maupassant fut-il en définitive totalement naturaliste?'[52] or to speculation as to whether or not Daudet was a naturalist writer. It is not that we should dismiss such questions because of the writers' own disclaimers. If we merely did so, we might readily conclude that, like some rare tropical bird, the species of naturalist writer was in danger of extinction even before it could be identified. The point is that a naturalist writer can only be defined as one whose works betray to some significant degree the features identifiable as characteristic of the naturalist 'genre', and we cannot expect the whole of the writer's works, not even Zola's, nor even a single one of his texts, to conform entirely to the canons of a particular genre. Likewise, the naturalist movement itself cannot be equated with the circumstantial associations of a group of writers, brought together by certain common interests, and the literary polemics in which they were engaged. It can only reside in the recurrence of certain common characteristics in a significant number of works. Thus, in France, long after the members of the 'Médan group' had gone their separate ways and long after the 'Manifeste des Cinq' had lost its topicality (and supposedly decisive effect), naturalist texts were being written and published.

Outside France, Furst and Skrine observe, even though the 'adherents to Naturalism tended to congregate in groups, to publish manifestos and to proclaim their artistic theories', there was 'no single, unified movement with a clear-cut outline, as has sometimes been suggested'.[53] Groupings, they argue, occurred and dispersed quite rapidly (as we have seen to be the case in France); naturalist movements arose at different times in different countries;[54] and the movement took on a different character in each country according to native traditions and conditions. One suspects also that this lack of unity is due to the same kinds of indeterminacies and contradictions that we have seen exemplified in the French situation – though only a thorough-going, comprehensive, international history of the movement could properly demonstrate the fact. To pick on just a couple of inconsistencies to illustrate the point, we note firstly that, according to the section on Germany in Furst and Skrine's study, Hauptmann's play *Vor Sonnenaufgang*, which appeared in 1889, is said to be the first major work of naturalism in the country, yet, by 1891, according to Hermann Bahr, the movement was declared to be over.[55] Similarly in Belgium, we learn from Gustave Vanwelkenhuyzen's study, a courageous group of young writers, Jeune Belgique, emerged towards the end of 1881 sympathetic to Zola and naturalism, yet, after the publication of *Pot-Bouille* (in 1882), only a few months later, the same young writers turned against the author of *Les Rougon-Macquart*. Nevertheless, as the same critic interestingly observes, 'de nouvelles œuvres à caractère naturaliste continuent à paraître: à coté des *Kermesses* de G. Eekhoud et des *Béotiens* de Nizet, signalons *L'Hystérique* de Camille Lemonnier qui suscite l'indignation du public puritain par la hardiesse de sa conception et le réalisme de ses peintures'.[56] Clearly, in these cases too, a period of polemics, manifestos, groupings and theorising, which is often taken to be the essence of the naturalist movement itself, does not coincide with the far more extensive and far less easily definable period of the production of naturalist texts.

The situation of naturalism in Victorian Britain shows an interesting contrast with the French pattern, for all those usual indications of the existence of a literary movement (groups, manifestos, polemics, theoretical writings) seem to have been virtually non-existent, such that one might be legitimately led to wonder, on the basis of the usual evidence, if indeed there was any English naturalist literature at all. If we remain faithful to the stereotypes, of course, we could not imagine a less appropriate terrain for the spread of naturalist literature than the land of Mrs Grundy and Mr Pecksniff, with its respectability and its prudery, with its queen so difficult to amuse, with its modestly draped furniture, a land in which 'French' and 'immoral' were almost synonymous and in which, according to Trollope, 'it behooves the English novelist to be pure'.[57] Yet, at the same time, we could not imagine a more suitable arena than the country dominated by the Victorian ethic for a trial of the strategies of unmasking and demystification of the naturalist aesthetic, for we know that the Kingdom was less united than many believed. 'It is a curious paradox of Victorianism', Clarence Decker writes, 'that the great Victorians were strenuously anti-Victorian.'[58] The incursion of naturalism onto English soil was not without its paradoxes and peculiarities — and not merely because the best representative of English naturalism, to remain with the stereotypes, was George Moore, an Irishman!

Comparative literary history, no less than the other branches of history upon which we have touched, is a matter of point of view. From a broad, panoramic perspective, we would have to agree that the reception of naturalism in Britain followed the general pattern of development traced by F. W. J. Hemmings for the reception of Zola's works abroad, with its 'variations in pace and stress' from country to country: first, a campaign of detraction on the part of the traditionalists, followed by the launching of translations, then a phase of violent argument between the old guard and a group of younger critics and writers favouring certain of Zola's innovations, and, finally, the production of works in more or less conscious imitation of his masterpieces.[59] As far as 'pace' and 'stress' are concerned, Britain was among the slowest and most recalcitrant in her response, for, as the same critic observes: 'Hostility to Zola's novels was nowhere more marked than in the Anglo-Saxon countries.'[60] From a closer perspective, however, the reception and development of naturalism takes on particular national features. Closer still, as we

have already had occasion to observe in the case of France, we see
that contradictions and uncertainties appear, for in Victorian Britain,
as we know, more often than not appearances were deceptive.

There are, for example, significant disparities among historians
of English literature on the importance of naturalism in their field.
There are volumes of literary history that do not contain a single
mention of the phenomenon. There was, for example, no entry for
'Naturalism' in the *Oxford Companion to English Literature* until
the 5th edition, where it is presented as 'primarily a French movement'
and where there is curiously no mention at all of any English naturalist
text or writer.[61] In the *New Pelican Guide to English Literature*,
English naturalism is summarised in a single sentence,[62] whereas in
Raymond Williams's important book, *The English Novel. From
Dickens to Lawrence* (1970), it does not rate a single mention.
According to Walter Allen, in his authoritative study, *The English
Novel*, 'while there is plenty of realism in English fiction' between
the mid-eighties and 1914, 'there is little true Natur^{X}lism'.[63] Clearly
there is neither a place for naturalism nor even, for some, a trace of
naturalism in the Great, or any other, Tradition.

When critics take the trouble to ask why the movement did not
take root in English soil, they offer a variety of explanations. Often,
like William Frierson, they merely point to the Anglo-Saxon temperament uncongenial to 'undiluted naturalism' or, like Edward McInnes,
to 'the English mind, traditionally disinclined to all extremes'.[64] The
explanation of Furst and Skrine is somewhat mystifying, for, whereas
a 'powerful current of Realism' in France 'encouraged the rise of
Naturalism', they argue that in England the realist tradition seems
'perversely' – [O perfide Albion!] – to have 'militated against it'.[65]
Many, no doubt, would have agreed with the solution proposed by
the great contemporary critic, George Saintsbury, writing on the
same problem, when he argues that the 'habits and public opinion
of the nation', its 'healthy beefiness and beeriness', have preserved
it from the 'curious scholasticism of dull uncleanliness' of French
novelists![66] Yet other historians of English literature present quite a
different version of the History of naturalism across the Channel.
According to Enid Starkie, for example: 'Everything that was most
vital and original in English fiction, during the last quarter of the
nineteenth century, came from France.'[67] Clarence R. Decker makes
a similar claim: 'It is clear that practically all of the important English
writers of the late nineteenth century were, in one way or another,
influenced by foreign Naturalism.'[68]

There are also considerable differences of opinion on the question of deciding which texts do in fact form part of a naturalist corpus. William Frierson's list would be extensive indeed, for, as well as bringing under the naturalist banner a whole host of minor novelists and short story writers, he claims that 'the great figures of 1900–1917 were all in one way or another subject to strong naturalistic influence – Gissing, George Moore, Henry James, Arnold Bennett, Galsworthy, Wells, Maugham, Joyce'.[69] Most other critics, however, are far more selective and tend to agree, if not on their choice, at least on the fact that their choice is limited. F. W. J. Hemmings, for example, refers to only one novel, George Moore's *A Mummer's Wife*, as showing 'unmistakable signs of having been affected by French naturalism', whereas other works that one might be tempted to include, like Kipling's 'Badalia Herodsfoot', Arthur Morrison's *Tales of Mean Streets* and *A Child of the Jago*, Somerset Maugham's *Liza of Lambeth* and George Gissing's *The Nether World*, 'follow on the tradition of the "social novel" deriving from Dickens as much as Zola'.[70] According to Walter Allen, Moore remains 'almost the only English Naturalist in the French sense',[71] but Yves Chevrel includes in his charts not only Moore's *Esther Waters* but also Gissing's *Workers in the Dawn* (and, curiously, G. B. Shaw's *The Quintessence of Ibsenism*).[72] Furst and Skrine give a longer list, which consists essentially of 'a few scattered works, mainly in the 1890s, by Gissing, George Moore, Morrison, Whiteing'.[73] The only common factor in these lists seems to be a text or two by George Moore. But, in a recent study, Lilian Furst has emphasised the elements of exaggeration, of posturing and of 'blarney' in George Moore's naturalist professions of faith, and reduces the association of the so-called 'English Zola' with the movement to a mere flirtation, resolutely situating *Esther Waters* in the tradition of the English novel.[74] What precisely, then, is this English naturalism? It seems to be both all and nothing, and to be as elusive as the Scarlet Pimpernel!

In the face of such a lack of consensus and of such uncertainty, we may wish to stick to certain historical facts. But even there we find no lack of anomalies and singularities. If we look, for example, at the chequered history of the introduction of translations of French naturalist texts into Britain, we inevitably come across some peculiar occurrences. A few statistics show how very late, selective and sudden this was. Before 1900 there appeared translations of forty-five works by Zola, thirty-five by Daudet, twelve by Maupassant, five by the Goncourt brothers, two by Huysmans (*En route* and *La Cathédrale* however!), but nothing by the other members of the Médan group. Daudet was being translated by 1877, but the first British translation of a Zola text did not appear until 1883; the first Goncourt text in 1886; and the first Maupassant translation in 1887. Only in 1886 was *Madame Bovary* translated and *L'Education sentimentale* had to wait until 1898! But when the translations did come, they came with a vengeance, for, between 1884 and 1889, there was an invasion of novels from France rendered into English. During that period Henry Vizetelly published, along with other naturalist works, seventeen novels by Zola and, according to the publisher's son, Ernest, a million copies were in circulation at one time.[75] It is more than likely that, rather than the content of the translated and *expurgated* texts, as is usually supposed, it was the suddenness of Vizetelly's commercial success and the explosiveness of the phenomenon that led to the famous proceedings against the publisher.

On 8 May 1888, in the House of Commons, a certain Mr Smith from Flintshire led a debate on the topic of 'pernicious literature' and cited in particular Vizetelly's Zola translations, expressing, according to Hansard, the considered view that they 'were only fit for swine, and their constant perusal must turn the mind into something akin to a sty'.[76] Curiously, the leader of the attack on behalf of the National Vigilance Association, W. T. Stead, had himself been prosecuted in 1885 for publishing a pamphlet on the brothels of London. Curiously too, one of the prosecutors at the first of the two Vizetelly trials (31 October 1888) was the future Lord Asquith, Britain's first 'Liberal' Prime Minister, while at the second trial (30 May 1889) Sir Edward Clarke played the same role, six years before *defending* Oscar Wilde in a more famous series of suits. There is also the curious fact that it was as much the result of the incompetence of his own lawyers as the soundness of the prosecution's case against him that led to Vizetelly's three-month prison term. As Robert Buchanan, one of the very few writers to defend Vizetelly publicly, observed, his crime was to have 'published in the English language what nearly every educated person reads in French'.[77] Yet the true irony of the situation is that the offending translations had already been expurgated; then, between the first and second trials, they underwent a second purging; then, when the publication of translations started up again after 1892, with publishers circumspectly profiting from the gap left by the ruin of Vizetelly's business, most of the same translations were refined for a third time and re-issued. Yet, all this time and despite all this effort, the original French texts continued to circulate freely!

Vizetelly's enterprise was clearly a vital factor in the introduction, diffusion and development of naturalist literature in Britain. But it was also a no less significant defiance of not just the prevailing moral order, but also the established order of the literary institutions of the country and, in particular, of the system of book distribution at the time. It was the age of the 'three-decker' and of the circulating libraries, notably Mudie's Select Library, which exercised a near total monopoly over the distribution of novels and even controlled what was being published. Probably at Zola's suggestion, George Moore launched a fierce campaign against the system, which led him, in 1885, to have published by Vizetelly a threepenny pamphlet entitled *Literature at Nurse, or Circulating Morals*. In this work he bitterly complains that in Britain the writer is subject to the censorship of the tradesman and that artistic aspirations are being crushed 'beneath the wheels of these implacable Juggernauts' (p. 4). He attempts to expose the hypocrisy of Mudie's venture with a few revealing quotations of a suggestive kind taken from books handled by the firm, before launching, in a far more unrestrained and scornful manner, reminiscent of the author of *Mes Haines*, into a litany of his hates:

I hate you [Mr Mudie] because you dare question the sacred right of the artist to obey the impulses of his temperament; I hate you because you are the great purveyor of the worthless, the false and the commonplace; I hate you because you are a fetter about the ankles of those who would press forward towards the light of truth; I hate you because you feel not the spirit of scientific enquiry that is bearing our age along; I hate you because you pander to the intellectual sloth of to-day; I hate you because you would mould all ideas to fit the narrow limits in which your own turn; I hate you because you impede the free development of our literature. (pp. 16–17)

An earlier attack by Moore on the same topic had appeared in the *Pall Mall Gazette* (10 December 1884) under the title 'A New Censorship of Literature'. Soon after, Moore reported back to Zola on his campaign and, with more than a trace of flattery, declared: 'Selon vos conseils, j'ai attaqué notre système de librairie ... *Cent* articles, de longs articles (dans les différents journaux de l'Angleterre) ont été écrits sur la question de la librairie ... Le système est fini. Alors c'est à Médan qu'on arrange les choses littéraires du monde!' In his reply, Zola returned the compliment, with a little French 'blarney' of his own:

Vous voilà devenu le champion de la vérité en Angleterre. C'est un beau rôle que vous tiendrez vaillamment. Et c'est aussi excellent, ce que vous me racontez sur votre prompte victoire, au sujet de vos librairies circulantes; car je suis persuadé que ce mode de publication avait un effet considérable sur la douce niaiserie où était tombé le roman anglais. Maintenant que les auteurs sont libres de s'adresser au grand public sans passer par les familles, vous allez voir les œuvres prendre des audaces d'analyse. – C'est à vous que l'Angleterre devra son roman viril de demain.[78]

Moore's burial of the circulating libraries was somewhat premature, despite his claims.[79] But this exchange of correspondence does show, for all the bombast, that Moore was 'Zola's ricochet', as he once called himself, not only as the author of one, two or more naturalist novels, but also as a writer who took seriously the task, inspired by Zola's own campaigns in that direction in France, of creating for the new literature of naturalism new market conditions to reach a new public. In his pamphlet Moore takes up again an oft-repeated theme, the problem of the nature, tastes and expectancies of this new reading public for the novel, and argues against the assumption that novels should be written for young unmarried women, deploring the situation of English literature, as he puts it, 'sacrificed on the altar of Hymen'. 'Let us renounce the effort', he exhorts, 'to reconcile those two irreconcilable things – art and young girls' (p. 21). And, once again echoing one of Zola's favourite arguments, he declares that in any case it is the romantic tale with its false ideals that corrupts; the truth, as the naturalists believed, has its own morality.

We see, then, that less than a generation after the introduction of a national system of primary schools through the reforms of Gladstone's first ministry (by the 1870 Education Act), Moore, in his way, was trying to alter the literary institutions of his country to reach a potentially new source of readership, as Zola was doing in France not only through his own campaigns but also through the mammoth and unprecedented sales of his novels.[80] Nevertheless, in official circles in Britain, particularly at the time of the Vizetelly trials, it was still the question of the morality of the novel that was uppermost in the minds of responsible men. The venerable Gladstone himself was worried by the threat to the country, as he saw it, of the appearance of the works of this 'school of foul novelists', seeing, no doubt, as it were, a French plot in every naturalist novel, in works which he held to be a 'dissolvent' of 'all that binds a people into a progressive nation'.[81] The Grand Old Man of English politics was far from being the only one to sound the alarm. Critics, journalists, men of the cloth, members of the general public joined in the denunciations. Like Miss Emily Crawford, they saw the works of Zola and the French naturalists as a source of 'purulent contagion'. The lady in question attributed Zola's taste for the lubricious to his Italian blood, but there was no such excuse for his disciples. 'The underlings of the naturalist school', she wrote, 'are like dogs battening upon carrion offal.'[82] As for one of the indignant readers of *The Sentinel*, he had only to scan two pages of a Zola novel on display in a bookshop window to arrive at the considered opinion that 'the matter was of such a leprous nature that it would be impossible for any young man who had not learned the Divine secret of self-control to have read it without committing some form of outward sin within twenty-four hours'.[83] 'Leprous', Enid Starkie states, 'was the favourite term of abuse used against any literature coming from France.'[84] Yet curiously — or perhaps quite logically so in view of the Wonderland logic that seems to prevail in this field — once the naturalist conventions had been accepted (at least by some), Zola was treated as a moralist for the same reasons that he had been denounced as immoral. For example, Miss Vernon Lee wrote in *The Contemporary Review* that 'it is salutary to be horrified and sickened when the horror and the sickening make one look around, pause, and reflect'.[85] Clearly, for the English critics of naturalism, morality was in the eyes of the beholder.

More generally, therefore, however bewildering the contradictions and anomalies attendant upon the History of the reception of naturalism in Britain might be, a number of factors emerge that are directly relevant to a study of the naturalist genre in its aesthetic intentions, its pragmatic effects and its textual manifestations. It seems, firstly, to be evident from these examples that the naturalist fiction, whether English or foreign in origin, in which the traditional morality of the text was superseded by some other principal motivating factor, scientific, sociological, or biological, clashed not only with the moral expectations of the English public, but also with the literary expectations of writers, critics and readers accustomed to the realist novels of the English tradition or the romances supplied by the circulating libraries. It is clear also that, as far as French imports were concerned, there was a kind of threshold of tolerance beyond which these texts were considered to be a violation not only of literary proprieties, but also of the purity of virgin girls and youths into whose hands they might fall. Furthermore, there was, as we have seen to be the case with translations and as we shall later see to be the case with adaptations, a tendency to react to the foreign naturalist invasion by modifying, adapting and purging these works to render them consonant with national norms. They were admitted in their integral state only under strictly controlled conditions, as were the faithful translations of six of Zola's novels done by a group of distinguished men of letters for The Lutetian Society and issued privately in 1894–5 at too high a price for the general public.[86] But texts were also translated in different ways, adapted, modified, parodied, transformed. Come what may, naturalist tableaux were forced into English frames, creating a naturalism with its own national design. Such textual transformations, as I hope to demonstrate later in this book, are much more revealing than the moral denunciations of writers, critics and public figures, for they go to the essence of the literature itself.

Once again, therefore, we are directed away from the uncertainties and contradictions of the historical approach towards a study of the texts themselves and their generic features. Even the heated debates in England tended eventually in the same direction, once the cries of moral indignation had somewhat abated. The more serious discussions of the new literature were more specifically literary and often turned on certain guiding dichotomies like 'romance–novel', 'romantic–naturalist', 'realism–idealism'. Clearly, naturalist fiction was either welcomed or, usually, rejected to the extent that it ran counter to the conventional Victorian novel, to that 'loose baggy monster', as Henry James termed it, or, as Thomas Seccombe characterised it, to 'the legacy of the mid-Victorian novel – moral thesis, plot, underplot, set characters, descriptive machinery, landscape colouring, copious phraseology, Herculean proportions, and the rest of the cumbrous and grandiose paraphernalia of *Chuzzlewit*, *Pendennis*, and *Middlemarch*'.[87] If we consider the almost complete lack of theorising on naturalism in England and the readiness of English writers to deny any affiliation with the movement, it becomes all the more important for us to define the naturalist text in relation to the type of literature to which it was opposed, for it is quite probable that the naturalist novel in England, as George Moore wished it to do, was instrumental in breaking the stranglehold that the realistico-didactic novel held over the Victorian literary scene.

None of the English writers to whose works I shall refer publicly declared at all, or for long, an allegiance to naturalist tenets. By 1887 George Moore was openly stating that he had forsaken the methods of naturalism. But no matter how short-lived or sincere his discipleship – Moore was prone to passing bouts of enthusiasm – his texts were recognised as innovative. Arnold Bennett, for example, calls his *A Modern Lover* 'the first realistic novel' in England, inspired by the 'grave and scientific fiction' of France.[88] As for Bennett himself, there are some harsh public statements on Zola and the naturalists in his critical works. He wonders, for instance, if the technical accomplishments of Maupassant and Flaubert can 'atone in the slightest degree for the defects of their mind', for they are both, in his view, 'second-rate artists'. Zola, he argues, 'carried the novel no farther than Balzac', 'did nothing new', was a kind of industrious craftsman who had but 'hours of genius'.[89] Yet it is well-known that Bennett was steeped in the works of the French realists and naturalists, borrowing from them freely. One of his earliest (unpublished) works was an imitation of *L'Assommoir* and a number of his novels, like *A Man from the North*, were written, as he put it, 'under the sweet influences of the de Goncourts, Turgenev, Flaubert, and de Maupassant'.[90] Bennett also, like Moore, though his originality is less evident, acquired the reputation of having rejected certain fundamental novelistic conventions. According to John Wain, for whom Bennett is 'the only English writer to have captured anything of the spirit of Balzac, Flaubert, and Zola', he broke with 'the tradition of English fiction that runs down from Fielding through Dickens and Thackeray and expresses itself in kindliness, sentimentality, profusion of incident, and love of oddities'.[91] Bennett, in turn – to complete the round – emphasised Thomas Hardy's great originality.[92] Now Hardy, too, is a case of a writer who openly distanced himself from Zola and the naturalists, criticising the disparity between the theory and the practice of the author of the *Rougon-Macquart* and claiming that, in any case, he was himself 'read in Zola very little'. Yet his notebooks reveal a familiarity with a number of Zola's novels and have inspired in their editor the suspicion that the English writer's appreciation of his French counterpart was more pronounced than he liked to admit.[93] And, if any other kind of evidence were needed to justify considering these works as part of our corpus of naturalist texts, there is the fact that they were greeted in England with the same kind of opprobrium and indignation that was usually reserved for the French naturalist novel, a sure sign that they were challenging the conventions that the Victorian reading public assumed it should find in the novels that it read.

Histories of naturalism in Britain always tend to be studies of the reception of foreign texts, of expressions of moral outrage, of the reluctance of English writers to commit themselves to naturalist aesthetics, then of the suggestion or two, the example or two, that show that perhaps there *was* interest and influence and that perhaps, in a few isolated cases, native dispositions were indeed fashioned by foreign naturalist modes. But, in following much the same path, I have attempted to show that the external evidence remains problematic, bringing us back once again to the view that the naturalist 'movement', on whichever side of whichever channel or sea it might be, is best studied internally, at the level of the interrelatedness of texts and of their relatedness to texts of other national traditions. On this whole general problem, Françoise Gaillard most pertinently writes:

Ainsi donc s'il peut y avoir une histoire littéraire qui soit une série spécifique, dont l'interdépendance avec d'autres séries sera postulée, ce ne peut être qu'au niveau des formes du discours, non prises en elles-mêmes dans l'achronie, mais envisagées dans leur actualisation en genres concrets, par leur singularité, genres dont l'apparition ou la prééminence historiquement analysées donneront lieu à une ébauche de périodisation.[94]

There is, then, a need to define naturalist literature as a genre, irrespective of the public pronouncements of authors and without necessarily heeding traditional categorisations, both of which may have owed as much to strategic considerations, to only marginally relevant moral preoccupations or to a process of ideological appropriation, as to any attempt to explain the literature. A generic approach would be a much surer guide both to an understanding of the nature of the body of naturalist literature with which we are concerned, and to the possible elaboration of a synthetic view. We are, therefore, naturally directed towards a type of approach of which the Russian Formalists are usually considered to have established the theoretical basis, one that involves studying genres, on the one hand, synchronically in their systematic relation to other contemporary types of discourse and, on the other hand, diachronically as a function of the evolving process of literary systems or combinations in their phases of inception, canonisation, discredit and renewal.[95] But, if we are to consider our 'genre' in this way, as a system, we cannot expect to be able to trace its development in neat systematic phases. This would be merely to attempt to replace one set of historical schemata with another. The task will be rather like tracing – to use a Zolaesque analogy – family resemblances in their diverse ramifications in individuals who retain the distinctive traits of the family line despite their intermingling with other strains.[96] The main focus will be on the issue of texts contemporary with, usually written in the same language as, and, in many cases, akin to the novels of the famous fictional family of the *Rougon-Macquart*, for in the dynasty of texts by Zola and his associates the generic similarities are most evident and concentrated. But we shall not, by any means, overlook different members scattered abroad, in particular those across the Channel. We are concerned, then, with a complex set of features and inherited codes that relate works to one another and form a tradition, but a tradition that is constantly subject to the conscious modifications and the accidents of reproduction that broaden the scope of the genre and bring about, eventually, its assimilation into other strains. Like Zola's family, indeed like most others, it has its divisions – and it has more than its fair share of black sheep and scandals.

2

THEORIES: REALISM,
NATURALISM, GENRE

'Writers and readers of certain historical periods', states Alastair
Fowler, 'have ignored genre. But while doing so, they have unconsciously engaged in generic transactions all the same. In fact,
ignoring genre has often meant passively accepting the conventions
prescribed by custom and fashion.' As examples of this process Fowler
cites the accommodating attitude of medieval readers to allegory and
our own tendency to 'generalize, without much thought, naturalistic
presuppositions and criteria'.[1] We obviously could not charge the
age of Darwin and Brunetière with an indifference to generic problems, but, as far as the naturalist writers of the period are concerned,
their particular aesthetic principles, in so far as they were clearly
formulated at all, were decidedly unaccommodating to an awareness
of the generic features of their literary works. Indeed, as we can clearly
see today, their theories are precisely characterised by the assumption
of 'naturalistic' presuppositions which, then as now, lead to an
underestimation of the relevance of generic criteria to an appreciation
of the literariness of their texts. There is then, unquestionably, a
problem of genre in relation to naturalist aesthetics, which it is the
main purpose of this chapter to explore, along with a brief survey
of the theories concerned.

The problem is due in part to the fact that there was no coherent,
unified body of theory among the naturalists. Not only did the French
naturalists, to take them again as our primary object of study, tend,
surprisingly so, to be largely indifferent to theoretical questions, but
also many of their programmatic statements were in fact directed
against the views of Zola, who was supposedly their chief theoretician.
There was from the start, for instance, considerable reluctance on their
part to accept the word 'naturalism'. Edmond de Goncourt preferred
'naturisme'. Huysmans came to favour 'intimisme'. Maupassant, at
least in his preface to *Pierre et Jean*, wrote about 'Réalistes' and suggested that they be called 'Illusionnistes'. As for the ill-fated young
naturalist Louis Desprez, in what was the first general study to be

published on the movement, he writes: 'Il y a un terme appliqué depuis longtemps à la peinture de Manet et de M. Bastien-Lepage qui caractérise certainement mieux la manière des Goncourt, de M. Daudet, de M. Zola, et même de Flaubert et de Balzac. C'est le terme d'impressionnisme.'[2] Flaubert, we know, scoffed at all such labels – and at most of the contents – and would have continued doing so, no doubt, if he had lived past 1880. It was, however, largely through Zola's insistence and persistence that the term 'naturalisme' came to achieve widespread acceptance, even though, of course, in other countries rival terms prevailed, like 'verismo' in Italy. Elsewhere, as in England, 'naturalism' tended to refer to the nasty French version of realism that was invading the native tradition. Yet Zola, characteristically, denied inventing the word even more vigorously than he denied inventing the thing:

Mon Dieu! oui, je n'ai rien inventé, pas même le mot naturalisme, qui se trouve dans Montaigne, avec le sens que nous lui donnons aujourd'hui. On l'emploie en Russie depuis trente ans, on le trouve dans vingt critiques en France, et particulièrement chez M. Taine. Je le répète un beau jour, à satiété il est vrai, et voilà tous les plaisantins de la presse qui le trouvent drôle et qui éclatent de rire. Aimables farceurs! (XIV, 510)

Previous usages of the terms 'naturalisme' and 'naturaliste' have been traced back to various sources and ages, notably (to be a little more precise) to: the natural sciences since the seventeenth century, art criticism from the same period but more particularly from mid-nineteenth-century France, philosophy from at least the time of the *Encyclopédie*, Russian literary criticism since 1846, Victor Hugo's works and even, as Zola insisted, (more or less) in those of Montaigne, but especially in Hippolyte Taine's writings. There the scientific, philosophical, artistic and literary usages converged and directly inspired Zola, who had been using the words since 1866 – that is well before the preface to the second edition of *Thérèse Raquin*, where, it is often claimed, he employed them for the first time.[3] Doubtless the rich and varied pedigree of the terms has led in part to the difficulties that critics encounter in attempting to define what they are supposed to denote. Charles Child Walcutt, for example, believes that current theories of naturalism 'disagree so fundamentally that they give diametrically contrary statements about the matter'.[4] According to another critic, Oscar Cargill, attempts to distinguish between 'realistic' and 'naturalistic' literature are 'probably an exercise in utter futility, like tilting at windmills', whereas for Joyce Hamilton Rochat the problem stems from the fact that 'naturalism is not a single form that can be grasped and examined at leisure, but a constantly changing, sometimes shapeless shape'.[5] Indeed, as our standby critics Furst and Skrine even go so far as to claim, 'as a term "Naturalism" is not readily comprehensible'.[6]

The problem with definitions of literary naturalism is, however, a more fundamental one than that of terminological fluctuations or vagaries, or even of a lack of agreement among the various theorists who have ventured to propose such definitions, for there is, in fact, a certain consistency in their diversity and in their insufficiency. The problem is, I would suggest, that these definitions invariably remain firmly rooted in one of the three allied but alien disciplines from which, as we have seen, literary naturalism is said to have derived: philosophy, science and art. They therefore tend to fall short of providing a specifically literary explanation. Thus the philosophical definitions offer too vague and general an interpretation to provide an adequate statement on the nature of the literary phenomena for which they seek to account. The scientific tendency is the most reductive of all three, making of naturalism an abstract method and giving rise, as in the famous case of Zola's theory of the 'experimental novel', to certain fundamental dilemmas when it comes to expounding the analogy. The artistic explanations are almost as restrictive, enclosing the literature within the limits of the aesthetics of realistic imitation or representation.

Nevertheless, each one of these tendencies deserves to be examined in some detail, not only to provide a framework for this review of naturalist theory, but also as an explanation of the misunderstandings that often arose among naturalist writers, their critics and their readers. But before doing so – and with particular regard to the latter point – we should be reminded of the fact that the naturalists' own definitions of their art were rarely dissociated from the polemical situation in which their views were shaped. Thus it frequently occurred, particularly in France, that in the heat of polemical exchanges raised by the appearance of naturalist texts, writers would invoke the philosophical, scientific or artistic *contexts* of their works as a defence against attacks on the *contents* of their literary texts. This situation, quite naturally, gave rise to cross-purpose polemics between writers and critics, the former professing that their literature resulted from a new method, the latter contending that it resulted in despicable characters and scenes. Zola would vaunt his new 'formula' in reply to critics' attacks on his 'putrid' or 'pernicious' literature. There is, then, a fourth type of definition, which belongs mainly to the anecdotal history of the movement and its reception, which is almost exclusively polemical (moralistic and conservative) and which reduces naturalist literature to its more scandalous subject matter. In its most spirited form, this tendency manifested itself in the endless stream of lampoons and caricatures in the popular press, of which Zola amongst all the naturalist writers took the brunt. From the time of the stage adaptation of *L'Assommoir* (January 1879), which first inspired them, and subsequently on any significant occasion, like the publication of *Nana, Pot-Bouille, La Terre* or *La Débâcle*, the caricaturists never tired of satirising the leader of the naturalist school, either by placing him in compromising postures with his own characters, like Nana in her underwear, or by engaging him in what they considered to be an appropriate occupation: as a cesspool cleaner or a rag-and-bone man. Chamber pots and pigs most frequently recur in these images; Zola is variously shown sitting on, in, emptying, or dipping his quill in the former, and usually riding the latter. In a striking variation on the theme in *Le Sans-Souci* (25 June 1881), the head of a huge pig is shown gazing into a trough at its reflection which has taken on the form of Zola's familiar face. The imagery of the trough was, alas, one of the constants of naturalist criticism! But, to give briefly a more serious example, we can simply refer to the definition of naturalism proposed by Charles Bigot in an article on 'L'esthétique naturaliste' published in the ultra-conservative *Revue des deux Mondes* in 1879, at the very time when Zola was elaborating his theory of the 'experimental novel'. 'Deux traits caractérisent proprement la littérature naturaliste', Bigot writes. 'D'un côté, elle s'attache surtout à la peinture du vice, à la laideur morale, à la maladie répugnante à voir du corps ou de l'âme; de l'autre, elle emprunte de préférence les sujets de ses peintures aux classes inférieures de la société.'[7]

This kind of dismissive view was shared by many critics and readers of the naturalist period and forms the basis of many subsequent and lasting prejudices. It also provided a context of contention in which the naturalists themselves were often led to (over)state their case by merely situating their literary texts within a broader philosophical framework. 'Le Naturalisme est l'évolution même de l'intelligence moderne', Zola goes so far as to claim in his reply to an attack by Gustave Rivet.[8] But the American novelist, James T. Farrell, writing at a time and place far removed from the controversies of Parisian literary circles, provides us with a better example of the broad, philosophical definition of naturalism. For the creator of Studs Lonigan, 'naturalism' and 'materialism' are synonymous. 'I would really prefer the word naturalism', he writes, 'and I would define it in a Deweyian sense. By naturalism, I mean that whatever happens in this world must ultimately be explainable in terms of events in this world.'[9] This kind of definition brings us back to the main tenets of *philosophical* naturalism: the view that the entire knowable universe consists of phenomena that are subject to, and thereby explainable in terms of, regularly recurrent natural causes, open to scientific investigation and forming a self-contained system of natural explanations. Implicitly contained in this view, it is true, are certain fundamental aspects of the naturalist writer's or artist's programme. Since the universe of matter is, in fact, the whole universe, which is 'self-existent, self-explanatory, self-operating, and self-directing', the role of the writer, like the scientist, will be to describe and represent what is seen, to still the imagination and to 'limit to a minimum the intrusion of the subjective, the feelings – often a synonym for falsehood and error in naturalism'.[10] In short, naturalism is materialistic in its ontology, mechanistic in its cosmology, empirical in its epistemology and relativistic in its ethics, and its main direction is towards reconciling, even to the point of assimilating, the natural world and human experience. Hence the tendency to distinguish two forms of naturalism: a Romantic version which 'places man in nature as its center, as the supreme, the reasoning climax of the concrete world', and an analytical, mechanistic version, which subjects man to nature's deterministic laws and with which the naturalist writers are usually linked.[11]

Such definitions more than adequately explain the intellectual climate in which naturalist literature was written. Sometimes, however, and somewhat defensively, one feels, this context is evoked to bolster the public image of a literature so frequently under attack and so often disdained. Literary naturalism gains in dignity, in continuity, by being equated with a broader philosophical framework, but, of course, it thereby loses its literary specificity, for a whole host of phenomena, literary or not, can be explained by reference to the same context. As D. A. Williams similarly and pointedly argues with respect to realism in general, there is a tendency to treat it 'as though it were *given* as a philosophical rather than a literary problem, to emphasize theory and intention rather than actual practice and, indeed, to subsume realism as an artistic mode used in different arts at different periods under the more or less scientific determinist philosophy broadly underlying the aesthetic theories of nineteenth-century Realist movements'.[12]

This is not to dismiss as irrelevant, by any means, the philosophical aspects of naturalism, for as well as providing this common ideological context for a variety of realistic movements and a bulwark against their critics, it also established new bases and justifications for certain of the literary practices of the naturalist writers. If, for example, it could be argued that the world in itself has no moral character, then naturalist writers are freed from the obligation to moralise. The supposition that 'naturalistic philosophy, unlike other philosophies, claims no special subject matter' and that its 'method is the natural method',[13] serves in addition to liberate them from the need to define the real substance of their work and to justify the liberties that they took with traditional expectations in the area of subject matter. This is true also of our second type of definition. If naturalism is fundamentally a method, then all subjects fall into its purview. Zola, as we know so well, was the writer most insistent in repeating that naturalism was not a school, not the work of a particular writer, nor a distinct genre, but the application of a method, or more precisely, as he came to define it, of the 'experimental method'.

'All too often', write Furst and Skrine, echoing Zola's own assertions down to the present day, the label 'Naturalist' is attached to a work 'merely because its subject is of a type associated with Naturalism, such as slum life or alcoholism or sexual depravity'. But – they go on to argue – it is essential to realise that 'true literary Naturalism is at least as much a question of method as of subject; only when the writer treats his subject with the objectivity of the analytical scientist, can we speak of Naturalism'.[14] Yet it is surely not in the least coincidental that the main bout of Zola's theorising about the naturalist 'method' occurred precisely during the period between the publication of *L'Assommoir* (1877) and *Nana* (1880), novels of slum life, alcoholism and sexual depravity, as, in part, an attempt to justify their apparent excesses. Instead, therefore, of the method bringing forth the works in the neutral permissiveness of scientific endeavour, as the theorists would have us believe, it was to a considerable degree, no doubt, the practices of the novelists themselves that prompted the need to elaborate a theoretical method.

Zola was not (quite) alone, as has often been supposed, in equating naturalist writing with scientific procedure. Alexis, as we might expect, followed his lead, declaring in 1884 in his typical, informal, journalistic manner: 'Le naturalisme ne consiste pas à nier les règles, à outrer plus ou moins la forme, à rechercher l'ordure pour l'ordure. Non! mille fois non! D'autres avant moi, et celui qui écrit ces lignes, nous nous sommes égosillés à répéter sur tous les tons, à démontrer de notre mieux, que le naturalisme n'est pas une rhétorique, mais une méthode.'[15] Other minor writers held a similar position, but, of the

French naturalists, it was Henry Céard who the most sagely articulated the belief in the scientific method applied to literature and who, as C. A. Burns has shown, the most faithfully continued to reflect on, and to defend, his views even in his latest works.[16] Ironically, for all that, it was Céard who lent Zola a copy of Claude Bernard's *Introduction à l'étude de la médecine expérimentale* and was thereby responsible in part for the dubious use to which the text was put. But it was Céard who, as we shall see, proved to be one of the first to point out to Zola how problematic his theory of the 'experimental novel' really was. Yet, even as late as 1918, Céard was theorising upon the analogous relationship between the novelist and the scientist, still expressing reservations about the notion of an experimental method in literature and about the equivalent tasks of the novelist and the chemist, but drawing a more appropriate parallel with the doctor's approach:

... il est de l'écrivain comme du médecin, lequel *n'invente pas la maladie*, mais par l'étude des phénomènes qu'elle présente, retrouve le point de départ de la lésion et fixe les stades cliniques de sa progression. Le roman m'apparaît ainsi comme une sorte de radiographie des âmes, nécessitant moins d'imagination que de science des rapports. L'art, ensuite, consiste à mettre en action dans les phrases, les intérieurs, les paysages, tous les mouvements décomposés des passions et de leurs secrets symptômes.

Vaille que vaille, voilà l'idée que j'ai toujours conçue du 'Naturalisme'.[17]

Charting the development of human disorders, studying the effects of the passions, showing the consequences of secret symptoms are, in fact, expressions that are much more descriptive of the actual practice of naturalist writers than are Zola's analogies with the work of the pure scientist, and the doctor is, as we shall later have occasion to observe, most decidedly a central figure in the naturalist scheme of things.

It is probably, thus, a law of naturalist aesthetics that the more intensely the moral reprobation was expressed to attack them from without, the more insistently did the naturalists claim the neutral ground of a scientific method or, as I shall indicate next, of mimetic representation. This insistence also precludes the role of the individual artist in the creative process, a position which Zola himself would only countenance at the time of the fiercest polemics. It is not only true, therefore, that 'the theories of Naturalism, if taken literally, amount in fact to a formidable anti-aesthetics in their deliberate exclusion of the creative power of the artist's individual imagination'.[18] They constitute also a formidable 'anti-poetics', in their emphasis on method and in their denial of the thematic, generic, specifically literary essence of naturalist literature. The very same can be said of our third, and by far the most commonly expressed strain of naturalist aesthetics: its mimetic postulates.

We are now directly confronted with what Yves Chevrel calls 'le problème réalisme–naturalisme' and what Furst and Skrine consider to be, as we have noted, 'perhaps the greatest bug-bear' of our topic.[19] So many attempts have been made to define 'realism' that it would, of course, be totally unrealistic to attempt even to summarise them. It would even be unfeasible to attempt to summarise the various arguments of theorists as to why the term is so elusive. Added to this is the complication, as we have also seen in the case of 'naturalism', of the writers' own free, and often indifferent, usage of the term. In his introduction to an important compilation of realist documents, George J. Becker writes: 'Though the words *realism* and *naturalism* are freely, even rashly, used, there is no general agreement as to what they mean. For many they have come to be merely convenient pejoratives, especially when qualified as *stark*, *raw*, *unimaginative*, *superficial*, *atheistic*, and more recently *socialist*.'[20] The same editor, in his preface, also points to another attendant problem, the fact that 'much of nineteenth-century writing about realism–naturalism was of an *ad hoc* nature, addressed to a book under review rather than to the broader implications of the work'[21] – or, we might add, to the theoretical implications of what was written. In view of all these difficulties, how then can we expect to define the relationship between realism and naturalism when, even assuming that we have by now acquired at least an adequate notion of the latter, the former is so problematic a concept? How can we choose amongst the manifold notions of realism in literary scholarship one, some or any of the following alternatives: a faithful representation of the real world, a study of contemporary mores, a mirror of reality, a rejection of romanticism and fantasy, a break with previous conventions, a set of mimetic textual strategies, the art of illusion, the art that dispels illusion, referential discourse, ironical discourse, mythical forms in a context of plausibility, a movement succeeding romanticism, a constant of Western literature since Homer, and so on.[22]

At the risk of grossly simplifying an obviously highly complex question, a useful, fundamental distinction might be made for our purposes between realism as (1) a *mode*, that is as a set of linguistic practices conducive to the plausible representation of reality, a fictional mode which, however dominant in much of the literature of the nineteenth century, remains transhistorical and transgeneric;

and as (2) a (historical) *genre*, rendered, of course, with the techniques of the realistic 'mode', with its specific content – roughly speaking, the deceptions of the sensitive ('problematic') individual in a given contemporary social milieu – and with its own periodisation – more roughly still, for the French context, from Balzac to Flaubert. Now, in the first sense of the term, it is important to emphasise that 'realism' is an essential and permanent feature of several narrative genres, indeed of all genres which require for their particular effects that the reader be engaged in the mimetic illusion. Thus, in this sense, the Gothic novel may depict its horrors *realistically*, for a basis of mimetic plausibility, a screen of realistic effects, the detailed depiction of a particular milieu, a convincing use of dialogue are indispensable to genres as varied as romance, the grotesque, satire, the detective novel, the thriller, science fiction or the fantastic tale. Naturalist literature is, therefore, only one of several such representational genres, though the degree to which it exploits the strategies of the realist *mode* (as well as some of the thematic features of the realist *genre*) is such that critics have tended to assimilate the genres of naturalism and realism or to interpret the former as an outlandish outgrowth of the latter. It would be much more accurate to say that naturalist literature fully exploits the mimetic procedures of the realist *mode* and has a close historical link with the realist *genre* in a number of thematic characteristics, but enjoys its own particular combination of themes and procedures.

The distinction between a realist mode and a realist genre, to press the point a little more for the purpose of clarification, is comparable to the contrast between two types, recently defined in an article by Jan Bruck denouncing the careless identification of the two terms 'mimesis' and 'realism'.[23] 'Mimesis' is a universal concept which can be traced back to the *Poetics* and which for Aristotle is a basic characteristic of all art and literature that *represent* without being a part of the reality context which they depict. 'The term "mimesis" denotes both these aspects: the unreality of aesthetic representations and their likeness to real objects and actions.' The aesthetics of 'realism', however, is a largely nineteenth-century phenomenon, with its new social consciousness, its demand for a new range of subject matter and for a contemporaneous reality (rather than a mythical or ideal context) depicted with objectivity.[24] The artifices of mimetic literature seem to make the discourse indistinguishable from the reality that it evokes. There is, then, a kind of mimetic pact, an understanding between readers and novelists that the former will take as true the events that the latter relate and, in so far as the medium allows them, imitate. When, in the nineteenth century (if not before and when not after), what is represented becomes the very world of the reader, the mimetic pact is completed by the realist pact or exchange, whereby the writer provides both the manner and the matter of the representation of the familiar world of the reader, who tacitly agrees to accept the conventional representation as being natural. As we shall later see, this process does not by any means account fully for the functioning of naturalist literature, which, though it shares many of its conventions, has its own particular designs.

The theoretical statements of the naturalist writers themselves do not lend themselves to such distinctions. They were much more preoccupied with establishing their mimetic credentials than with elaborating a specifically naturalist aesthetics, that is when they were not like Daudet or Edmond de Goncourt, largely indifferent to theoretical matters. As for the Médan group, Furst and Skrine remark, its members did not, with the obvious exception of Zola, make 'any substantial contribution to the theory of Naturalism'.[25] This is not completely true, as we have just noted, of Céard and Alexis, but certainly does apply to Maupassant, who, in the wake of his mentor Flaubert, was scornful of theorising about literary art. 'Le talent seul existe', he writes in his preface to Jules Guérin's *Fille de fille* (1883). 'Quant au genre de talent, qu'importe! J'arrive à ne plus comprendre la classification qu'on établit entre les Réalistes, les Idéalistes, les Romantiques, les Matérialistes ou les Naturalistes. Ces discussions oiseuses sont la consolation des pions.' But, as with Flaubert, there are in his correspondence, prefaces and occasional writings, elements of an aesthetics, but one which is significantly opposed to Zola's naturalism. Maupassant's belief in objectivity is more a Flaubertian strategy than a scientific or epistemological article of faith, for, in general, he was guided more by Herbert Spencer's relativism than by Taine's or Comte's positivism. He expresses his relativistic views (significantly) in his essay on Zola, boldly stating that 'la vérité absolue, la *vérité sèche*, n'existe pas, personne ne pouvant avoir la prétention d'être un miroir parfait ... Prétendre faire vrai, absolument vrai, n'est qu'une prétention irréalisable.'[26] Maupassant was as much interested in depicting subjectivist delusions as in attempting to render objective truths. His most famous theoretical statement, his essay 'Le Roman', better known as the preface to *Pierre et Jean* (1888), is Olympian in its attitudes and mainly consists of a series of similar arguments *against* the notion that truth can be rendered in fiction, as well as of recommendations on the art of the *vraisemblable*, a doctrine that is worlds apart from Zola's positivistic faith in objective representation and in the analytical mission of naturalist literature.[27] 'Faire vrai', Flaubert's disciple writes in a famous passage, 'consiste donc à donner l'illusion complète du vrai, suivant la logique ordinaire des faits, et non à les transcrire servilement dans le pêle-mêle de leur succession.' He concludes with the much-quoted assertion that 'les Réalistes de talent devraient s'appeler plutôt des Illusionnistes'.[28]

Even the enthusiastic study by Huysmans, 'Emile Zola et *l'Assommoir*', which Helen Trudgian describes as 'le grand manifeste du mouvement naturaliste, vigoureux et sincère',[29] resounding as it is with Zola's ideas, remains nevertheless a meagre contribution to naturalist theorising. It contains a vigorous tribute to Zola and his talent, followed by a flattering portrait of the novelist and his wife, a homage to Balzac's originality and influence, then the familiar denial of the charge that naturalism means sordid themes (and the now familiar assertion that it has no specific subject matter at all[30]), an attack on the sentimental, romantic, didactic, conventional novel forms, a defence of the intrinsic morality of realist fiction ('faire vrai, c'est faire moral') – all ideas to which Zola was even then giving currency. But there is, in the whole essay, only one sentence that truly approximates Zola's more specifically naturalist aesthetic, one that in fact looks directly back to the preface to *Thérèse Raquin* of ten years previously: 'Etant donné, comme sujets à étudier, un homme et une femme, nous voulons démontrer, si faire se peut, le mécanisme de leurs vertus et de leurs vices, disséquer l'amour, l'indifférence, ou la haine qui résulteront du frottement passager ou continu de ces deux êtres; nous sommes les montreurs, tristes ou gais, des bêtes!'[31] But the actual definition of naturalism that he gives is no more than a vague realistic ideal: 'le naturalisme, c'est l'étude des êtres créés, l'étude des conséquences résultant du contact ou du choc de ces êtres réunis entre eux; le naturalisme, c'est, suivant l'expression même de M. Zola, l'étude patiente de la réalité, l'ensemble obtenu par l'observation des détails.'[32] Then, fundamentally, when all this has been said, Huysmans, the aesthete, cannot hide the fact that what really enthuses him in Zola's work are the *natures mortes* in *Le Ventre de Paris*.

In general, the paucity of naturalist theorising about science in France is matched by other countries. There would seem to be much truth in the claims of Furst and Skrine that 'scientific determinism never caught on in England in spite of Spencer and some interest in Comte's Positivism' and that 'the English writers remained true to their tradition of a realism spiced with humour and keenly aware of human oddities with only an occasional passing glance at Naturalism',[33] though only, I would stress again, at the level of their theoretical statements. Much the same could be said, so it seems, of other national traditions. According to H. Markiewicz, for instance, 'verismo' became an extraordinarily elastic term: 'Ainsi les savants italiens parlent sans façon du "vérisme instinctif, anti-zoliste, entièrement non-scientifique de Verga".'[34] Moving north, we might observe that Strindberg, author of important naturalist dramas which can undoubtedly be associated with the movement thematically, is above all concerned in his theoretical writings with realistic illusion in the theatre and the two naturalisms that he defines, the 'greater' and the 'lesser', are two versions of the mimetic aesthetic: significant and trivial realism.[35] Furthermore, Markiewicz writes, surveying the large body of German theorising: 'le plus souvent, on oppose au naturalisme – le réalisme, qui exige le choix, l'anticipation et la modification des éléments de la réalité'.[36] Certainly, the most famous German example of a naturalist theory, by Arno Holz in *Die Kunst: Ihr Wesen und Ihre Gesetze* (1891), provides the perfect illustration of what I am attempting to show. 'Art has the tendency', he writes, 'to be nature again. It becomes nature in proportion to the conditions for imitation and the way they are handled.' Seeking, Zola-wise, a scientific law and a formula to oppose to Zola's own famous definition ('l'art est un coin de la nature vu à travers un tempérament'), he sets forth the following equation: $art = nature - x$, where x is the artist's temperament (or, as Furst and Skrine put it, 'any deficiency in the artist's imitative skill').[37] This is clearly a formula for absolute mimeticism and suggests to us a further rule: theoretical naturalism has the tendency to be theoretical realism again.

Obviously, one of the more significant consequences (at least for the purposes of this book) of the insistence of naturalist writers on the mimetic function of their art is for them to downplay the importance of its literary and generic essence. In fact, it could rather naïvely be argued that, in so far as their texts achieve the representational effect, merging in with the reality that they purport to depict, they become non-generic, dissociated from the recurrent forms, codes and conventions of literature itself. This is, as we now know after many modern exposures of the unreality and conventionality of realism, just another stage of the mimetic illusion, for realistic conventions are no more natural and no less generic than more manifestly literary conventions. There is no such thing as a 'real' or 'realistic' novel, as Philippe Sollers trenchantly writes, for, 'la notion de *réalité* étant

elle-même une convention et un conformisme, une sorte de contrat
tacite passé entre l'individu et son groupe social', the real 'n'est pas
manifesté ailleurs que dans un langage, et le langage d'une société,
ses mythes, est ce qu'elle décide d'être sa réalité'.[38] Yet a notion of
the fundamental incompatibility of the 'realism' of naturalism (in the
modal sense) and generic principles, and of the threat to the structure
of the latter by the former, was a common concern, if not of the
naturalist theorists themselves, then certainly of some of the critics of
naturalist texts. For them the traditional distinctions (and prejudices)
were still very much in place, usually in the form of the rudimentary
tripartite scheme of poetry (lyric), theatre (tragic and comic) and prose
(deriving from the epic) according to which they vainly sought to
situate the naturalist novel. Brunetière's collection of articles, *Le
Roman naturaliste*, constantly comes back to the problem of the
confusion of genres and of the breakdown of traditional distinctions.
In the chapter on the origins of the naturalist novel, he significantly
complains: 'De même qu'il y a des crises politiques ou financières,
il y a des crises littéraires ... Il n'y a plus de direction commune; les
principes chancellent; les bornes des genres se déplacent; le sens même
des mots s'altère; on perd jusqu'aux vrais noms des choses.'[39]

The naturalists themselves showed considerable hesitation over 'les
vrais noms des choses' and a significant reluctance to employ even
the term 'novel' for the most flexible of literary forms because of its
inherited generic associations. As Edmond de Goncourt writes in the
Journal: 'Décidément, ce mot *roman* ne nomme plus les livres que
nous faisons ... Non, il faudrait, pour dénommer le roman du XIXe
siècle, un vocable unique.'[40] 'Human documents', as the naturalists
frequently considered their works to be, were not to be read as
'novels', for the former are supposed to arise directly and naturally
from life, while the latter are the product of the writer's imagination
and are written according to conventional (i.e. generic) dictates.
Poetry, patently genre-bound by its very nature, obviously verbal and
the least representational of the three fundamental traditional modes,
was consigned in the naturalist scheme of values to an inferior status,
usually a peccadillo of the naturalist writer's Romantic youth or, as
Zola argued, a form thoroughly inappropriate to the temper of
modern times and the serious purposes of naturalist art. Contemporary poetry, he declared, was still too Romantic. The poet who
would bring 'la note naturaliste dans toute son intensité' (XII, 388)
was still to appear − and he never did![41]

As for the theatre, the French naturalists, 'auteurs sifflés' and their
disciples alike, did write extensively for the stage, adapted (or had

adapted) their stories and novels and energetically sought to make their mark. But, despite the great prestige attached to theatrical success in France and despite the fact that, outside France, writers like Strindberg and Hauptmann wrote significant naturalist dramas, the theatre was never to become a thoroughly appropriate medium for naturalist artists. Here too, we should observe, whether in France or abroad, their theorising was largely directed towards a more *realistic* drama, as in Zola's relentless campaigns against theatrical conventions. Pierre Martino is barely overstating the case when he bluntly asserts: 'La pièce naturaliste sera donc une sorte de calque du roman naturaliste.'[42] Similarly, Yves Chevrel, in a thorough-going study of the question, declares: 'Il semble que les écrivains français n'aient pas su voir avec netteté les impératifs précis d'une représentation et aient négligé, Zola tout le premier, la spécificité d'une œuvre dramatique; ils se sont montrés incapables de proposer une formule neuve, bien qu'ils aient vu les insuffisances du théâtre de boulevard qui règne à cette époque.'[43] But the problem of naturalist theatre does clearly bring into focus the question of the generic status of naturalist literature, which is of particular relevance to the aims of this book. As we have seen Brunetière disapprovingly argue, the naturalist age was a time of crisis when generic distinctions were seemingly no longer in effect. The dominance of the novel, a kind of omni-generic form, looked to be making such distinctions, whether rudimentary or fine, totally irrelevant. Thus, naturalist fiction was not only *non*-generic, in theory at least, in supposedly not being literature at all, but in being a faithful representation of life instead; it was also *multi*-generic in being at once narrative, dramatic and poetic, thereby rendering generic distinctions redundant. Yves Chevrel even suggests that naturalism perhaps involves 'la ruine d'une littérature constituée en genres'.[44]

We can therefore conclude that the naturalist theorising that I have surveyed had the effect of disguising the generic nature of the literature that it was supposedly promoting. But it was also, implicitly at least, an attack on generic conventions themselves. On the one hand, the theories of the naturalists were in one respect part of the necessary and natural process whereby writers of a new generation attack the formulas and conventions of the established literary insti-tutions as a defence against their detractors and as an attempt to create new expectations in their readers. But, on the other hand, instead of truly defining their own practices and describing the specific literary features of their texts, the naturalists tended to argue away the conventional nature of their own work by claiming it as part of a time-honoured philosophical tradition or by relating it to the currently prestigious scientific method or, most commonly, by invoking a mimetic aesthetic to promote the illusion of a literature aligned with reality and thereby liberated from the restraints of literary paradigms. Yet their works themselves exhibit the essential characteristics of a distinct literary genre, however deceptive their mimetic strategies and however varied their features, for they are, even to the same extent as much more obviously codified literary works, like fairy tales or detective novels, subject to, and the product of, the coercive dynamics characteristic of literary genres in their recurrent practices, themes, patterns and pragmatic effects.

Zola's theories are particularly significant for our purposes, not because they represent, as they are often held to do, an especially narrow brand of naturalist doctrines, the sectarian tenets of the Médan school, but, on the contrary, because the author of the *Rougon-Macquart* gave expression to *all* the aesthetic tendencies that have just been defined, in all their ambiguity and complexity. For this reason, we need to dwell a little on his views, even on the much maligned essay 'Le roman expérimental'.

We have already noted how it was Zola, above all, who sought to trace and establish links between naturalism and the whole positivist tradition in philosophy. The novelist's criticism and theoretical essays also contain frequent assertions of his fundamental belief in the mimetic purpose of literature, in a realist aesthetic, a belief that is obscured by the more strident scientism of his more familiar theories and is often ignored by their expositors. The naturalist novel is, Zola writes, 'un lambeau d'existence', the novelist 'un greffier, qui se défend de juger et de conclure' (X, 1240). As the theatre should also be, in his opinion, the true novel is wrought out of a constant struggle against conventions, those 'barrières entre la vérité absolue et nous': 'En somme, une œuvre n'est qu'une bataille livrée aux conventions, et l'œuvre est d'autant plus grande qu'elle sort plus victorieuse du combat' (XI, 332). The aim is to abolish all generic attachments, to still the imagination, to represent reality itself without mediation. As he writes in the most articulate expression of this view, in his article 'Le sens du réel' (1878): 'Tous les efforts de l'écrivain tendent à cacher l'imaginaire sous le réel ... Le sens du réel, c'est de sentir la nature et de la rendre telle qu'elle est' (X, 1285–6).

Yet, despite all this, Zola did, after all, achieve notoriety as a theoretician for his attempts to marry literature and the scientific method, principally in that extraordinary piece of discursive prose

'Le roman expérimental', an article published first in *Vestnik Evropy* in September 1879, then in *Le Voltaire* from 16–20 October the same year, then in the volume which bears the title of the essay in 1880. So much is controvertible not only in this essay but also in what has been written about it that it is necessary to limit our discussion to certain key points.

There is, to begin with, the basic claim that Zola makes on the first page of the article:

Je n'aurai à faire ici qu'un travail d'adaptation, car la méthode expérimentale a été établie avec une force et une clarté merveilleuse par Claude Bernard, dans son *Introduction à l'étude de la médecine expérimentale*. Ce livre, d'un savant dont l'autorité est décisive, va me servir de base solide. Je trouverai là toute la question traitée, et je me bornerai, comme arguments irréfutables, à donner les citations qui me seront nécessaires. Ce ne sera donc qu'une compilation de textes; car je compte, sur tous les points, me retrancher derrière Claude Bernard. Le plus souvent, il me suffira de remplacer le mot 'médecin' par le mot 'romancier', pour rendre ma pensée claire et lui apporter la rigueur d'une vérité scientifique. (X, 1175)

Now Zola certainly does *not* follow Claude Bernard 'sur tous les points' and the basis of the argument of his essay does *not* derive from the famous treatise. In fact it had been a part of Zola's theorising for at least ten years, since well before Céard lent him Bernard's book. It derives in the main from Taine's ideas. The key notion appears in the first page of the essay:

Je vais tâcher de prouver à mon tour que, si la méthode expérimentale conduit à la connaissance de la vie physique, elle doit conduire aussi à la vie passion- nelle et intellectuelle. Ce n'est là qu'une question de degrés dans la même voie, de la chimie à la physiologie, puis de la physiologie à l'anthropologie et à la sociologie. Le roman expérimental est au bout. (X, 1175)

The essential dynamic of Zola's essay could be characterised as a constant shift between two positions: on the one hand, a series of quotations and paraphrases recently culled from Claude Bernard's book on the experimental method and, on the other hand, this 'naturalist' thesis acquired much earlier from Taine. Already in 1866 (in *L'Evénement* of 25 July) the latter is very much in evidence as Zola writes of Taine: 'Il est le naturaliste du monde moral. Il croit qu'on peut arriver à classer les faits de la vie intellectuelle comme on classe les faits de la vie physique.' On this occasion too the novelist is moved to add: 'Je l'aime, cette méthode, parce qu'elle apporte la vérité' (X, 564–5).

At this early stage Zola's admiration was not limited to Taine's method alone. For the novelist, Taine was a kind of perfect *alter ego*, the 'compleat' naturalist, a man of his age, a man of energy, science and art, 'mathématicien' and 'poète' at the same time, the ideal critic. In his study 'M. H. Taine, artiste', Zola seeks, in the Tainean manner itself, to define his mentor's own 'facultés maîtresses'. With the reservation — ironically the same charge that would later be levelled against Zola himself — that the thinker applies his formulas too systematically, the young novelist proclaims his total allegiance: 'Je me reconnais comme l'humble disciple de M. Taine' (X, 563). However, over the years, Taine did not live up to Zola's expectations, as we see, for instance, in a later article called 'La formule critique appliquée au roman', published in *Le Voltaire* on 27 May 1879, shortly before the appearance (in October) of the essay on 'Le roman expérimental'. The novelist expresses his disappointment: 'C'est M. Taine qui est actuellement le chef de notre critique, et il est à regretter qu'il s'enferme dans l'histoire et la philosophie, au lieu de se mêler à notre vie militante' (X, 1295). He had earlier argued (in February 1877), in an article on contemporary criticism, that France had no great critic, nobody to act as an intermediary between the new generation of writers and the public, to fight for the new literature. Each age needs its critic, but Taine will not comply — 'le professeur repousse' — and, 'M. Taine mis à l'écart, il n'existe pas un seul critique de valeur' (XII, 468). Zola's own efforts are meant to fill the gap, take on the task, Taine's task, with Taine's ideas. Thus, even though his name is never invoked, the *deus absconditus* is very much present in Zola's essay, and Taine's writings, in particular his *Histoire de la littérature anglaise*, had as intense an impact on Zola as Claude Bernard's book and a far more lasting appeal, for he had read it fifteen years before and it clearly still represents an important subtext of 'Le roman expérimental'.

The general argument of Zola's essay is well-known enough for a brief passage or two to suffice to convey the main idea. After a long quotation from Claude Bernard's book on the experimental method, Zola adds:

Eh bien! en revenant au roman, nous voyons également que le romancier est fait d'un observateur et d'un expérimentateur. L'observateur chez lui donne les faits tels qu'il les a observés, pose le point de départ, établit le terrain solide sur lequel vont marcher les personnages et se développer les phénomènes. Puis l'expérimentateur paraît et institue l'expérience, je veux dire fait mouvoir les personnages dans une histoire particulière, pour y montrer que la succession des faits y sera telle que l'exige le déterminisme des phénomènes mis à l'étude. C'est presque toujours ici une expérience 'pour voir', comme l'appelle Claude Bernard. Le romancier part à la recherche d'une vérité. (X, 1178)

Balzac's *La Cousine Bette* is offered up as an example. Then the argument resumes:

En somme, toute l'opération consiste à prendre les faits dans la nature, puis à étudier le mécanisme des faits, en agissant sur eux par les modifications des circonstances et des milieux, sans jamais s'écarter des lois de la nature. Au bout, il y a la connaissance de l'homme, la connaissance scientifique, dans son action individuelle et sociale. (X, 1179)

For Zola's purposes, it should be emphasised, the originality of the theory of the experimental method is twofold. On the one hand, in relation to experimental science, it *advances* the method to the social sphere, as the novelist compounds Taine with Bernard, though he is careful to make it clear that he is not actually vying with the scientist (X, 1185). On the other hand, in relation to *realist* literature (in the modal sense of the term), the experimental novel is also an important *advance*. 'Un reproche bête qu'on nous fait', Zola argues, 'à nous autres écrivains naturalistes, c'est de vouloir être uniquement des photographes.' But with the application of the experimental method to the novel, he confidently asserts, 'toute querelle cesse. L'idée d'expérience entraîne avec elle l'idée de modification.' In this active direction of phenomena resides what he calls 'notre part d'invention, de génie dans l'œuvre' (X, 1180). We see, then, that the adaptation of Claude Bernard's system to the novel had not only the advantage of promoting the pretension of scientific truth in literature but also the advantage of allowing Zola to maintain, to further and to bolster his own deeply rooted, long-standing conviction about a work of art, as the product of a writer's 'temperament', as realism plus the artist's genius. In the double operation of 'observation' and 'expérience' Zola equates the writer's genius, subjectivity, temperament with the process of experimentation. We therefore arrive at the somewhat paradoxical view that Zola's theory was not merely an attempt to arrive at a more scientific type of realism, but also, on the contrary, a way of vindicating scientifically his deep-seated Romantic belief in individual genius.

When the essay was first published, it was not well received, though, contrary to a common belief or to what one might expect, it did not provoke a storm of protests.[45] It is true that certain of Zola's friends and enemies alike did denounce the untenability of the central notion of experimentation in a work of fiction. The most quoted objections are those raised by Henry Céard and Ferdinand

Brunetière, the former's discreetly and politely in a private letter,[46] the latter's publicly and derisively in his *Revue des deux Mondes* article.[47] In fact Céard later claimed, rather improbably, that he had lent Zola Claude Bernard's book for the very purpose of warning him against the dangers of applying the experimental method to literature.[48] For lack of evidence we do not know what the scientific community thought of Zola's advances into their field. Claude Bernard himself was spared, we must presume, any knowledge of the text that he had inspired by his death in 1878. However, one of his disciples, a certain Dr René Ferdas, was unimpressed enough by Zola's ideas to write a lively pamphlet protesting against the novelist's text. He claims that 'M. Zola n'a pas compris un traître mot du livre de Claude Bernard', makes the ironic suggestion that a Chair in the Experimental Novel be established at the Medical School in Paris and – what is perhaps most significant about his attack – uses the opportunity to remonstrate against the crudities of *L'Assommoir*, parodying Zola's own text by juxtaposing passages from Claude Bernard and quotations from Zola's novel.[49] Clearly, at least for Dr Ferdas, the seriousness of Zola the theoretician was no compensation for the excesses of Zola the novelist.

Subsequently, Zola critics have been hardly any kinder towards the novelist's theory of the experimental novel. According to F.W.J. Hemmings the concept is 'infantile' and its manner of presentation 'unbelievably naïve'. Angus Wilson calls *Le Roman expérimental* 'peculiarly silly'. Furst and Skrine quote further derogatory comments and conclude that to equate the arts with the sciences is 'patently absurd', as does Philip Walker in his recent biography of the novelist.[50] However, in opposition to the prevailing view, certain scholars have adopted a fresh approach to Zola's essay and have taken the work more seriously. Aimé Guedj, for example, explains – without explaining away – Zola's ideas by reference to the prevailing epistemological assumptions of his age and suggests that, considering the status of the biological model at the time and its widespread applications, there is in fact nothing unusual in Zola's ideas. Furthermore, he makes the telling point that *L'Introduction à l'étude de la médecine expérimentale*, 'par les ambiguïtés et les présuppositions idéologiques qu'elle comporte, *autorise* en effet certaines des conceptions les plus aventureuses du *Roman expérimental*'.[51]

There is, of course, no denying the defects of Zola's argumentation. At one point, to take an obvious example, he claims that the role of the experimental method is to 'pénétrer le pourquoi des choses', whereas three paragraphs earlier he agrees with Claude

Bernard that 'nous ignorerons toujours le *pourquoi* des choses; nous ne pouvons savoir que le *comment*' (X, 1188, 1185). At times he respects the limited goals of the method, elsewhere he extrapolates freely and makes extravagant claims.[52] There are dogmatic formulas and the style is at times painfully declamatory. But, if we allow for the fact that the references to the scientific method should be taken less literally than has often been the case, that is, more precisely, as a series of analogies, and if we recognise that what Zola is proposing, as he clearly states, is a departure from the *realist* practice of literature, his central argument is not without a certain validity. It turns on the difference between 'observation' and 'expérimentation', problematic terms for which we might usefully substitute the terms 'representational' and 'representative' practices. The object of the first process, the 'representational', realist enterprise, is the imitation of the unique, whereas the second process, the 'representative', introduces a higher degree of typicality and is closer to the illustration (if not the discovery) of generalisable, 'scientific' laws. Obviously, as Céard and Brunetière pointed out, a novelist cannot strictly speaking perform an experiment whose outcome is unknown, since the novelist is constantly in control of the conditions and the result. But, *like* the scientist, the naturalist novelist can illustrate and demonstrate in fiction a generalisable (though necessarily provisional) 'truth'. Thus naturalist fiction can be ascribed to two distinct tendencies: on the one hand, the representation of the *unique*, the representational tendency according to which the events (x) of realistic novel (N) occurred at time (y) in conditions (z); on the other hand, the representation of the *typical*, the representative tendency according to which novel (N) illustrates that in conditions (z) at time (y) events (x) occur. The distinction is naturally one of degree and is not absolute. The realist novel only *tends* towards the particular and moves away from the 'scientific', for there can be no science of the particular. Yet there is always a degree of typicality in the realist novel. How many Julien Sorels or Madame Bovarys, for example, were there supposed to have been at loose or in bondage in their age? The naturalist novel, of course, presents itself as a set of singular occurrences, but *tends* towards a more general understanding. Within the framework of this distinction, Zola's summary statement makes sense: 'En somme, on peut dire que l'observation "montre" et que l'expérience "instruit"' (X, 1178).

The naturalist novelist is bound then by 'le déterminisme des phénomènes' and remains within the 'laws of nature' which naturalist texts as a whole *represent*, that is fictionalise (realistically) and illustrate (naturalistically). Thus Zola's scheme emerges as an elaborate motivating system of fictional representation, one which is perfectly logical and understandable in the age of the powerful dominance of the biological *episteme* and one which is fundamentally no more objectionable than the realistic strategies that purport to represent reality itself. The scientifically verified laws of nature provide established, guiding sequences of consequentiality to motivate naturalist fiction, whose domain remains, as Zola emphatically argues, the world of the novelist, the world of the individual in society: 'Dès lors, dans nos romans, lorsque nous expérimentons sur une plaie grave qui empoisonne la société, nous procédons comme le médecin expérimentateur, nous tâchons de trouver le déterminisme simple initial, pour arriver ensuite au déterminisme complexe dont l'action a suivi' (X, 1189).

One final perspective on Zola's essay has recently been convincingly argued, the not unreasonable view that the excesses of 'Le roman expérimental' are to be explained as polemical and rhetorical strategies which, however effective they were at the time of publication, clearly appear to be ill-conceived when we consider them from a more distant perspective and with the advantage of retrospection. As Henri Mitterand writes: 'Le propos du *Roman expérimental* apparaît moins théorique que stratégique.'[53] This text needs therefore to be considered in the context of that continuous battle of prefaces, manifestos and journal articles to which we have referred and which was the reality of literary life (and survival) in Zola's time. We have already seen that privately he was far less doctrinaire. If we were to approach his essay from the familiar Russian Formalist standpoint with regard to literary evolution, his overstatements and emphatic formulas would appear perfectly normal as part of the process of challenge, conflict and renewal whereby new styles, new genres, new forms and devices have to be forcefully imposed to discredit the canonised forms and to reinvigorate the literary system with new elements. Ultimately it is really only in relation to this kind of view of literary development, and with an awareness of the demands of the polemical situation in which Zola was working, that the private disclaimers and the public statements can be reconciled.

Furthermore, the text itself bears the evident marks of the author's polemical intentions. Viewed in isolation, the theory does not stand up well to close scrutiny. But, viewed in its polemical situation, the essay is perfectly acceptable, in Henri Mitterand's words, as a 'texte vécu, un texte–acte, la performance d'un homme qui, en l'énonçant, se place délibérément en position d'affrontement face aux discours jusque-là dominants et occupant encore des places stratégiques essentielles sur le champ intellectuel (l'Académie, les grandes revues, l'Université)'.[54] We note, for instance, that Zola is still arguing on behalf of a collectivity, 'nous', the growing army of naturalists. The familiar defence against the detractors of *L'Assommoir* also appears: 'Certes, je suis un homme de paix, mais il me prend des besoins farouches d'étrangler les gens qui disent devant moi: "Ah! oui, le naturalisme, les mots crus!"' (X, 1224). Indeed, the essential structure of Zola's essay may be seen as an elaborate polemical device, consisting of a whole battery of more than fifty substantial quotations from Claude Bernard's book, from 'ce livre, d'un savant dont *l'autorité* est *décisive*' (X, 1175), as Zola significantly presents it. The quotation is, of course, generally recognised as a common rhetorical strategy, as a feature of authoritarian forms of discourse or of forms of discourse that seek to be authoritative. By subjecting his readers to this relentless process of quotation, to this array of resounding scientific statements, Zola clearly intended them to succumb under the very weight and mass of arguments mobilised for the occasion. But, in general, the status of the quotation necessarily remains ambivalent in any discursive context. The borrowings become to some degree a part of the main argument, but can never be totally integrated. They remain, by virtue of the patent signs of their otherness (the inverted commas, the different style), the discourse of another, belonging to an alien (con)text. This fact is evident to the reader of 'Le roman expérimental' who resists the bludgeoning effect of the quotations, but not necessarily to Zola's discredit. In this way we see that the author's 'compilation de textes' is in fact a manipulation of texts and, in the space between the substratum of Zola's own discourse and the citational superstratum derived directly from Claude Bernard, the novelist indirectly preserves the integrity of his own more flexible views.

Even in Zola's theoretical works, therefore, the relationship between naturalism and science remains problematic. In the fiction we are led even more to wonder if the human dramas are there to illustrate the scientific principles or if the science merely serves to motivate the human dramas. Do we give primacy to the science or to the fiction? Jean Borie points to this kind of indeterminacy as being generally prevalent in the 'medical' literature of the second half of the nineteenth century, 'qui n'arrive pas à décider ce qu'elle veut être: illustration d'un mécanisme scientifique ou représentation d'une tragédie'.[55] The evidence and arguments to support the former view are largely limited to the essay that we have just considered and to a few derivative statements. To support the opposing stance — as we are naturally inclined to do in a study which seeks to emphasise the literariness of naturalist fiction and which will therefore inevitably attach far more importance to its 'tragedies' than to its 'science' – various arguments may be invoked. Not only did the scientific method, as we earlier observed, provide a prestigious defence against the moralists' attacks, but it also justified the apparently dispassionate method of naturalist depiction, which, as we shall later observe, was a further justification for an essentially ironic mode of fictional presentation. As a strategy for the furtherance of a new generic model, the scientific analogy was ideally suited for the naturalists' purposes. It was, as Jean Borie notes, the most readily available objective type of discourse, impersonal, rational, dispassionate.[56] It also provided a more pragmatic model for naturalist literature beyond the search for truth or the representation of reality, for scientific progress is inherently dependent upon the process of a continual refutation of error. In fact, naturalist literature in general is far more concerned with the dissipation of human errors and illusions than it is with adding to the sum of scientific knowledge. Finally, this sceptical view of naturalism's scientific aims could be further supported by reference to Zola's often quoted statement in the preparatory files of his *Rougon-Macquart* series, which constitutes a kind of recantation *avant la lettre* of the doctrines espoused in *Le Roman expérimental*. Amongst a mass of notes culled from scientific sources we read the following self-instruction: 'Prendre avant tout une tendance philosophique, non pour l'étaler, mais pour donner une unité à mes livres. La meilleure serait peut-être le matérialisme, je veux dire la croyance en des forces sur lesquelles je n'aurai jamais le besoin de m'expliquer ... Je préfère être seulement romancier.'[57] Clearly *le vraisemblable* is a far more important consideration than *le vrai*, even, we can assume, in Zola's own works.

Nevertheless, we cannot entirely argue away the relevance of the scientific model to naturalist literature, lapse into extreme formalism and merely dismiss it as a motivating device. In Zola's age – the point bears repetition – there was nothing aberrant about this recourse to the scientific method. 'Fiction in the second half of the nineteenth century', writes Gillian Beer, 'was particularly seeking sources of authoritative organisation which could substitute for the god-like omnipotence and omniscience open to the theistic narrator.'[58] It was quite natural, for example, for Hardy to draw upon the current interest in heredity to add a seemingly plausible mode of explanation to the theme of the fallen woman already elaborated in the early drafts of *Tess of the d'Urbervilles*. In this case, most decidedly, the 'tragedy'

came first. Elsewhere, naturalist writers drew upon the rich source
of thematic material provided by 'science', usually medical science
and anthropology, for the dramatic potential of the dramas of
heredity, criminality, atavism, pathology. Sometimes the science
was crudely applied and the authenticity effect rebounds against
the work, as in the famous case of Antoine Macquart's spontaneous
combustion in Zola's *Le Docteur Pascal*. At times, also, the theorising
seems clumsily applied, almost arbitrary in its effects. But, however
suspicious we might be of the analogy between the novelistic practices
of the naturalist writer and the scientific method, however easily
we can point to the abuses in the uses made of scientific concepts
and information in naturalist literature, we must acknowledge
the profound impact that science had in general at all levels on
an art that was very much in tune with the spirit of its age. 'Zola's
assertion of analogies between fiction and experimental science',
writes Gillian Beer, 'his emphasis upon the double sense of "expérience" and "expérimental", is a procedure quite in accord with
current intellectual endeavour in the sciences which were preoccupied
with the demonstration of hidden relations and analogies.'[59]

Science, however, was not only a guarantee of authenticity,
but also a mark of originality, a source of generic renewal. In
flagrant contradiction, therefore, to his numerous attempts to
assert the existence of a long-standing naturalist tradition, Zola
can write in 1880: 'Notre roman est donc absolument original et
ne tient en rien au roman du passé; ou, du moins, depuis le commencement de ce siècle, l'ancienne formule a été tellement modifiée par
l'emploi des méthodes scientifiques, qu'il en résulte une formule
toute nouvelle, apportant avec elle un art et une morale' (XII,
503). Thus, conveniently, by invoking the innovativeness of scientific
literature, the novelist is divorcing it from past conventions, just
as equally conveniently in other circumstances, as we saw earlier,
he does the very opposite. The new novel of Zola's age, as the
novelist sometimes chose to regard it, was not only realistic, as
we already know, and therefore beyond the pale of literary conventions, but it was also totally new, as we see here, and therefore
free from the conventions of the inherited order. These new assertions
bring us face to face with an essential dilemma of our topic. How
can we interpret naturalist literature from a generic perspective
if, as its chief proponent implicitly claims, generic considerations
have no relevance to it? There is, apparently, a fundamental contradiction between naturalist aesthetics and our approach. We
should therefore, finally, examine a little more closely some of

the suppositions of Zola's theories from the more precise angle of his views on genre.

'Concepts of genre', writes Heather Dubrow, 'carry with them so many general implications about literature that they regularly reflect in microcosm the poetics of their author and of his age. If one knew nothing about a given writer save his pronouncements on genre, one could predict many of his other aesthetic principles, and predict them with great accuracy.'[60] In Zola's case there is a kind of converse relevance to these remarks, for we know much and much has been written about his aesthetic principles, whereas very little attention has been given directly to defining (or devining) his concepts of genre. This apparent indifference to the general theory of literary species is all the more surprising in relation to a writer who was Brunetière's contemporary and who was so imbued with the scientific, classificatory spirit. It cannot be entirely explained by a lack of interest in, or even by a profound scepticism about, the value of a generic approach to literature among critics since Zola's time, with their suspicions of essentialist thinking, of biological analogies, of rigid taxonomies. Other critics and poeticians, nonetheless, particularly in more recent times, have brought compelling arguments in defence of genre theories and genre criticism, affirming, for example, that they are strategically important in filling the gap between critical theory and the practice of literary criticism, that they are vital in the field of literary history to explain why some forms flourish while others perish, that they are indispensable for the understanding of texts, since, as E. D. Hirsch Jr observes, 'all understanding of verbal meaning is necessarily genre-bound'.[61] In Zola's case, however, critical disregard for generic considerations is no doubt also due to the novelist's own inclination to depreciate generic distinctions and categories, particularly with respect to his own works, for reasons which need to be explored.

It could be suggested, in general terms, that there are two extreme and complementary theoretical positions that dismiss generic factors in defining the nature of literary works. One view, as it were, tends to collapse genres into texts, whereas the other view collapses texts into genres. In the first instance each work is considered to be unique, a genre unto itself, outside the scope of generic categories. This *dispersive* tendency is usually identified with Benedetto Croce, who, in his *Estetica* (1902), argues that genre classifications are extraneous to aesthetic appreciation, for significant literary works are particular creations and, in any case, violate generic norms.[62] The other view simply presents each text as belonging to a single genre or seeks to fit all works into some rudimentary general scheme like the traditional triad of *lyric, epic* and *dramatic,* or the modal version of the same: *poetry, prose, drama.* This *reductive* tendency clearly cannot take into account the true generic complexity of texts, nor does it consider the varied responses of different readers and different ages to the manifold generic codes in a given text. We find ample evidence of both tendencies in Zola's (often implicitly stated) views on genre.

In some of his earlier theoretical works, however, the future author of the *Rougon-Macquart* series shows a lively interest in genre and some advanced views on the question. In a study of the novel submitted to the Congrès scientifique de France in 1866, he traces the development of the form from ancient times, links generic evolution with changes in societies and attacks the rigid systems of classification of the 'rhéteurs' of the past: 'les caractères des divers genres littéraires ne sont que les transformations de la pensée écrite soumise aux influences des civilisations' (X, 282). He even expresses the hope that one day he will write a book on this whole question, a book which he will call *Essai de rhétorique historique* (X, 282). Had he made good his promise, Zola might well have written an *Evolution des genres* long before his later arch-rival Brunetière. But such a literary irony was not to be, for Zola's views are concomitant with, and, to a considerable degree, irreconcilable with an overriding conviction that genres are embodied in 'grandes personnalités' (X, 313), that the whole of literary history proves the complete freedom of the great writer (X, 545), that 'une œuvre n'est que le produit d'une individualité' (X, 795). This Romantic exalting of the individual tempers Zola's Tainean convictions at this stage. In 1865, in a review of *Germinie Lacerteux,* which is not yet the canonical work that it will become, he pleads Croce-wise for a criticism that will respect the uniqueness of each work. Remarkably, in view of later pronouncements, he argues: 'Vouloir rapporter toutes les œuvres à une œuvre modèle, se demander si tel livre remplit telles et telles conditions, est le comble de la puérilité à mes yeux' (X, 62).

To some extent Zola will remain faithful to these premises in his later criticism, particularly when writing about certain great individual talents like Hugo or Daudet. But in the years when he was compelled to defend his own and other naturalist works and when he sought to impose his naturalist principles (from 1877 to 1882), his views became more dogmatic, more polemical, and there occurred an evident shift to the second, *reductive* attitude to genre that I have defined. Zola's general aesthetic concepts, his theory of the novel, and the necessities of his campaign for naturalism, as we shall see in turn, were even less conducive than his earlier views to a proper conception of the function of genre in literary texts. Though he does not openly state the negative case in the general theories that we have already surveyed, Zola does present naturalist literature as being totally undefinable in generic terms, as being in no way interpretable as a group of literary texts partaking of certain recurrent, conventionalised features of form, mode and theme. Naturalism, we recall, is a *method*, of universal application, one that is, therefore, too vast to be contained in a single school, system or genre. And, of course, it is totally 'ungeneric' in being, theoretically at least, a representation of reality itself. It is thus both abstract (a method) and concrete (reality, nature), both universal and historical, both general and specific. There is clearly no place in such a scheme for concepts of genre which mediate these oppositions. Furthermore, this occultation of genre extends to the text itself in its true literariness. As Zola observes in his article on 'Le naturalisme' (*Une Campagne*), where, in this regard at least, he unwittingly points to the severe limitations of his views, 'le naturalisme n'est qu'une méthode, ou moins encore, une évolution. *Les œuvres restent en dehors*' (XIV, 511).[63]

Inevitably the novel has a special place, not only in Zola's theory of naturalism, but also in his theory of genre. For the author of *Le Roman expérimental*, it is both a 'non-generic' and an 'omni-generic' form. Like Goncourt, he complains of the inappropriateness of the term 'roman', with its generic connotations, to denote naturalist works: 'Ce mot entraîne une idée de conte, d'affabulation, de fantaisie, qui jure singulièrement avec les procès-verbaux que nous dressons' (X, 1297). The work of the naturalist *novelist* is not to be categorised in literary terms, but, by contrast, it is noticeable that Zola's theatre reviews, collected together in the volume *Le Naturalisme au théâtre* (1881), are systematically arranged according to genre divisions and subdivisions (tragedy, drama, historical drama, comedy, pantomime, etc.) and, in his own plays, he is clearly more inclined openly to conform to the established conventions of dramatic forms.[64] But the naturalist 'novel' – to keep the unfortunate term – is free of conventions, emancipated from genre, boundless, unclassifiable. What is more, the novel 'n'a donc plus de cadre, il a envahi et dépossédé les autres genres' (X, 1240). Zola frequently states the conviction that the novel has 'absorbed' all other genres. The assertiveness with which he proclaims the hegemony of the (naturalist) novel, the reductiveness of his approach to genre and the combative-ness of his views remind us once again that his theories were prompted by the necessities of his own very generic struggle: 'Dans cette terrible lutte pour la vie qu'est la littérature, tout nouveau venu a le besoin de faire la place nette, d'égorger ses aînés, s'il veut pour lui tout le champ, tout l'empire' (XIV, 724).

In the cut and thrust of this battle of the books, Zola's generic categorisation is simple and schismatic. Here again he reduces all literature to two contending types: naturalist literature, which is allied with the scientific movement, identified with the future and characterised by a return to nature and reality; Romantic literature, which is idealistic, belonging to the past despite its anachronistic survival in the present and above all marked by rhetoric and convention. Balzac opposed to Hugo, realities to mere words! It is a struggle of form(ula)s: the one 'formule naturaliste', which guarantees truth, against the empty 'formules' of Romantic rhetoric (X, 1209–11). Zola's polemical articles would provide a remarkably pertinent illustration of the point of view, to invoke again the Russian Formalists, according to which literary evolution is a process prompted by the constant 'laying bare' and discrediting of the conventions and procedures of a previous generation when a 'formula' has lost its ascendancy and is due to be replaced. They would also illustrate the fact that such attacks are frequently made against conventions in the name of a conventionless representation of nature or the truth, when in reality what is proposed in their place is another set of conventions. 'En somme,' Zola writes, 'une œuvre n'est qu'une bataille livrée aux conventions, et l'œuvre est d'autant plus grande qu'elle sort plus victorieuse du combat' (XI, 332).

Genre, therefore, as Zola conceives it, is a kind of affliction of literature, a sum of moribund conventions from which naturalist works strive to extricate themselves. Most aesthetics are argued in the name of beauty or truth and naturally eschew the conventional. Zola's own faith in the power of mimetic literature, and in the capacity for scientific literature to attain the truth, further nourished and sustained his dismissive attitude towards generic conventions. But, above all, he provides the perfect example of a writer who, to impose his aesthetic principles, to assert the originality of his works, argues away their generic traits and imputes such features to the works of his adversaries.

In keeping with this polemical stance, there is also, in Zola's case, an equivalent attempt to establish norms and models to set against the conventions that he disdains. We have noted how, all the more effectively to affirm his own principles and practices, he created a lineage of prestigious predecessors stemming mainly from Balzac but extending beyond his own century. In his particular studies of their works, he may be seen directing readers to modify their preconceptions and to accept the new norms, seeking to establish a new generic contract, fully aware that naturalism can only flourish if a cohesive group of writers shares its literary practices and has models to which it can relate. Critics have often rightly commented upon the disparity between Zola's theories and his creative powers. But there is a close correlation between his theories and his practices as a professional writer. Thus, without acknowledging its generic status and maintaining the illusion of the 'non-generic' nature of the literature that he favours, Zola must fabricate a genre, impose norms, establish paradigms. This process, not by any means uncommon in the field of literature, is described by Jean-Marie Schaeffer as 'la procédure qui consiste à "produire" la notion d'un genre non à partir d'un réseau de ressemblances existant entre un ensemble de textes, mais en postulant un texte idéal dont les textes réels ne seraient que des dérivés plus ou moins conformes, de même que selon Platon les objets empiriques ne sont que des copies imparfaites des Idées éternelles'.[65] In Zola's criticism, an ideal text is similarly projected onto certain significant novels of the past, which are thereby made to conform to a prototype. Or, to describe the same process in the more recondite terminology of modern narratology, Zola's metatext generates an ideal hypotext from which naturalist hypertexts are supposed to derive.

There are some well-known examples of this strategy. Not unexpectedly Balzac provides the first, for, writes the author of *Les Rougon-Macquart*, 'l'auteur de *La Comédie humaine* a créé une formule' (X, 952). *La Cousine Bette* becomes the chosen text to exemplify the 'experimental novel', for, according to Zola, Balzac took as his subject in this work le baron Hulot, with his 'tempérament amoureux', and conducted an experiment, 'en soumettant Hulot à une série d'épreuves, en le faisant passer par certains milieux, pour montrer le fonctionnement du mécanisme de sa passion' (X, 1178). Whatever the merits of this interpretation, Zola clearly passes over the whole complexity of Balzac's novel: the web of psychological, social and moral issues, the socio-historical panorama, the melodrama, the myths, the intricate plot, the array of characters like Crevel, Valérie Marneffe, even Bette herself, as significant as Hulot, who, in any case, is as much a social and political figure as he is a 'tempérament amoureux'; all this is reduced to the simplistic scheme of the so-called experiment. Flaubert, too, is dragged (kicking and screaming) into the naturalist fold. After *Madame Bovary* had been presented earlier (in 1875) as 'le modèle définitif du genre' (XI, 97), *L'Education sentimentale* comes to fulfil the role. Flaubert, in Zola's assessment, is an epic and lyrical writer who has become a naturalist novelist, founding 'une poétique nouvelle' (XI, 99) and in a sense giving up genre: 'Un poète changé en naturaliste, Homère devenu Cuvier' (X, 917). On *L'Education sentimentale* Zola writes in 1879 a much-quoted passage: 'Voilà le modèle du roman naturaliste, cela est hors de doute pour moi. On n'ira pas plus loin dans la vérité vraie, je parle de cette vérité terre à terre, exacte, qui semble être la négation même de l'art du romancier' (XII, 608). A work, then, that is purged of all generic taint, untarnished by the stigma of genre! 'Tous nos romans', Zola adds, 'sont des poèmes à côté de celui-là.' Thus, evacuated from Flaubert's text, like Balzac's, is all its generic complexity.[66] Zola even performs a similar operation – to give a final example – on one of his own (future) texts, in a passage from *Le Roman expérimental* purporting to describe the genesis of a possible naturalist novel on the theatre, a work which would, as it were, write itself (*s'établir*) out of the documents that the novelist would have collected together. As he puts it, 'le romancier n'aura qu'à distribuer logiquement les faits' (X, 1286). But neither the genesis of *Nana*, the novel to which this passage indirectly refers, nor the text itself, one of Zola's most complex and elusive works, with its constantly shifting perspectives, bears much resemblance to what the critic describes. Yet, once again, we see that he has argued genre away, conceived of an ideal text with no genetic or generic links to other texts nor to the literary classes to which all texts necessarily belong.

There are several reasons why Zola should, in these various ways, systematically downplay and neutralise generic parameters. In the first place, realist literature always seeks to promote the illusion of what we might (most inelegantly) call 'ungenericness', presenting itself in the guise of a neutral mode directed more towards the undifferentiated forms of the real world than towards the codified structures of literature. There is also the tendency of naturalist literature, as I shall later show in the chapter on naturalist satire and parody, to be anti-heroic, 'anti-romanesque', to subvert generic distinctiveness as well as generic distinctions. Then there is the fact that, in the rivalry and struggle of literary schools, movements and formulas, the partisan critic will not fail to focus on the artificiality of the generic conventions of his opponents' work and emphasise the naturalness of the convention-free creations that he wishes to defend. Finally, the novel, Zola's chosen form, seems naturally ungeneric in itself, almost hostile to other genres. As Bakhtin observes, it 'parodies other genres (precisely in their role as genres); it exposes the conventionality of their forms and their language'.[67] Zola boldly, stubbornly, theorises all of these tendencies.

Yet, notwithstanding Zola's views, we, in our post-formalist, post-structuralist age, have come to recognise that even what is seemingly the most natural(istic) piece of literature remains a codified artifact. 'Là, néanmoins, où les écritures de la modernité entendent exhiber la conventionnalité de la littérature en tant que telle', writes Menachem Brinker, 'le réalisme se contente de dénoncer celle de la génération précédente.'[68] The naturalists, for their part, writing in the name of a realistic aesthetic, or attempting to elaborate a naturalist doctrine inspired by the methods and spirit of the biological sciences, were unaware of, or sought to disguise, the conventionality of the literature that they recommended and, in most cases, composed. Hence their particularly un-literary, un-generic view of their art. Henri Mitterand has noted, for example, 'l'étrange silence de la théorie naturaliste, qui se veut une théorie du roman, sur deux composantes essentielles du genre: la fiction et la narration – le fantasme et le récit'.[69] It doubtless requires a certain distancing to become fully conscious of generic conventions, an especially difficult process in relation to a type of literature held to be other than literature, to be science or life itself, to belong, at least in aspiration, to a different order of reality from literary norms, and one which, in any case, is of such a complex, hybrid nature that it defies simple classifications. In any case too, as Gérard Genette points out, of the different types of transtextual links that a literary work maintains, the generic are usually the most implicit, hence the most elusive, representing what he calls 'une relation tout à fait muette', a relationship that it is the generic critic's business to explore.[70] Finally, the point must be made (even though it will threaten to undermine in the eyes of some the very project of this book) that, however much the theoretician seeks to establish the generic limits of texts, the texts themselves will invariably transcend them. Indeed, as Zola put it, '*les œuvres restent en dehors*'. Yet, as we turn now (at last!) to an examination of the texts themselves in an attempt to define their intrinsic generic features, we can at least hope to arrive at a truer picture of the nature of naturalist fiction as a body of literature than can possibly be attained by merely investigating the often perplexing and always problematic relations of that literature with the history of the naturalist movement, or by reviewing the frequently deceptive theories of its practitioners.

3

THE FOUNDING TEXTS

In *Le Pacte autobiographique*, Philippe Lejeune makes a vigorous attack on what he considers to be the general drift of traditional and much modern genre theory: the tendency to devalue history, to search for norms, to reject the essential conditions of history, which are relativity and variability. At the heart of the notion of genre as it is usually conceived, he argues, is a desire for permanence, an illusion of eternity, a belief that there exists an immutable backcloth against which history unfolds, with historical facts on the one hand and perennial types on the other. 'Cet idéalisme anti-historique', he writes, 'projette dans le ciel des idées des "types" dont les genres historiques seraient des incarnations.'[1] He cites Northrop Frye's system in particular, based as it is on Platonic and Aristotelian principles and on what Lejeune calls 'la division trinitaire des anciens entre l'épique, le dramatique et le lyrique', as the most renowned example of this anti-historical idealism, which implies that there exists in literature an immanent structure of unchanging archetypes, all, as it were, so much 'Frye in the sky'. Thus Lejeune unequivocally asserts the historical nature of literary genres and defines the essential purpose of a modern approach to generic studies: 'Le travail de la théorie n'est donc pas de construire un classement des genres, mais de découvrir les lois de fonctionnement des systèmes historiques des genres.'[2] To fulfil this purpose, he proposes a workable, analytical method, drawing its inspiration from a number of sources: pioneering theoretical statements by the Russian Formalists (notably Tynyanov in his famous essay 'On literary evolution'), new linguistic models like communication theory, reception theory and a full use of Jauss's notion of 'horizons of expectation', along with a more extensive use of other arts in which equivalent problems are encountered. 'Cette méthode', he concludes, 'conduira non à l'élaboration hâtive de synthèses, mais au contraire à de minutieuses et analytiques études: celles-ci pourront utiliser avec profit le travail empirique et les observations accumulées par l'histoire littéraire traditionnelle, pour établir peu à peu des modèles de fonctionnement de la littérature comme système.'³

Other genre theorists, in recent times, have been equally as insistent in expressing a similar view. Jean-Marie Schaeffer, for example, stresses the importance of the dynamic relationship between texts and generic models as constituting 'la dimension temporelle de la généricité, son historicité'. He makes the important distinction between 'genre' and 'généricité', the former being 'une pure catégorie de classification' whereas the latter represents 'un facteur productif de la constitution de la textualité'.⁴ This historical sense derives in part from the Russian Formalists' recognition of the importance of generic factors in the processes of the historical development of literatures. Within the doctrines of this group there are two fundamental directions, the one focusing on the text as an architectural construct, as a 'cluster of compositional devices', the other sensitive to the shifts in the appreciation of a text or the evaluation of a genre from one period to another.⁵ Hans Robert Jauss, writing in their wake, gives the illuminating example of Feydeau's *Fanny* and Flaubert's *Madame Bovary*, two novels of adultery published contemporaneously, the former an instant success with its 'flowery style', its 'modish effects' and its 'lyrical confessional clichés' appealing to the public, the latter with its impersonal mode of narration disturbing the 'horizons of expectation' of the public but eventually creating a new 'canon of expectations' that eventually led to its prominence.⁶ By the time the naturalists came to write their own novels of adultery, such *impassibilité* had virtually become, at least for a substantial body of readers and writers, a matter of course − though it still remained to be fully motivated by reference to scientific theories − and Flaubert's innovative text became a model. It is this kind of inner dialectic of innovation and modelling which gives generic studies their vitality and which I shall try to demonstrate at work in the naturalist corpus. Such a study does not simply involve the tracing of sources, for antipositions, inversions, oppositions, transformations, parodies and modifications are usually far more significant than direct borrowings.

It is possible, nevertheless, to formalise and historicise notions of genre too much. The tendency to emphasise excessively the historicity of a genre leads to a failure to recognise its fundamental residuality. As Bakht in pointedly observes: 'The undying elements of the *archaic* are always preserved in the genre. True, these archaic elements are preserved in the genre only thanks to their constant *renewal*, and, so to speak, contemporization. Genre is always the same and not the

same, always old and new simultaneously.'[7] Thus our naturalist
'genre' will be shown as drawing upon an ancient fund of literary
structures and themes as much as upon contemporary systems of
discourse and meaning, whether literary or not. At the same time,
like other complex genres, it will be shown drawing upon other genres
with which it overlaps and establishes analogous, parallel or counter-
vailing relations. Like new wine in old bottles or old wine in new
bottles, the relationship among its elements is variable. If such a genre
can thus be shown as reaching back to draw upon the archetypical
and reaching out to draw upon contemporary determinants, it can
also reach up and down the prevailing scale of literary values,
appropriating prestigious forms for its purposes, parodying the
'noble' genres, or elevating sub-literary forms to a new status. Even
in a study of a literary genre belonging to an age when the rigid
hierarchies of the past were largely inoperative and generic barriers
were seemingly down (if not out), there remains to be taken into
account the inevitable retrospectiveness and sense of gradation that
are an integral part of generic development. These factors are not
necessarily constraining forces. On the contrary, they provide material
for innovative transformations and modulations. Fiction in particular, the mode in which most naturalist literature is written, lends
itself to such generic appropriations and adaptations, for it can
incorporate a whole variety of literary and non-literary forms of
discourse – myth, epic, romance, pastoral, memoirs, history,
biography and so on – almost without limitation. Hence its appro-
priateness for the varied purposes of naturalist writers, who, as we
shall see, also exploited its inherent propensity for satire and parody,
its potentiality for undermining official canons by virtue of its
versatility, its 'heteroglossia' or, more accurately – to torture
Bakhtin's famous expression – its 'heterogenericness'.

As for individual texts, from this point of view, they exemplify
in differing ways and with differing degrees of emphasis the varied
characteristics of such a complex genre, without being totally
subsumed by it. They may derive from a variety of generic traditions
themselves and transcend the limits imposed by their conventions,
though minor texts, of special interest to the genre critic because of
this fact, tend to articulate more straightforwardly the dominant
generic traits. Such traits, when they are not evinced in such meta-
textual and paratextual devices as prefaces, manifestos and interviews
(often misleadingly so, as we have seen in the case of naturalist
principles), manifest themselves transtextually, that is in the processes
of intertextual assimilations and transformations, particularly in

relation to certain exemplary works. 'Les archétypes de genre,' Laurent Jenny notes, 'pour abstraits qu'ils soient, n'en constituent pas moins des structures textuelles, toujours présentes à l'esprit de celui qui écrit ... On peut alors parler d'intertextualité entre telle œuvre précise et tel arché-texte de genre.'[8] Hence the particularly important inaugurating and mediating function of certain canonical texts. 'Pour les lecteurs d'une époque', Lejeune writes,

> il n'y a de 'genre' que là où il existe, d'une part, des textes canoniques qui font fonction d'archétypes, qui réalisent de manière presque idéale ce qu'on croit être l'essence du genre, et, d'autre part, la présomption d'une continuité d'écriture, la production d'un certain nombre de textes qui, sans être conformes au modèle, s'inscrivent dans la même problématique, comme autant de variations et d'écarts.[9]

Such texts fulfil the function of models, mediating between the abstract features of the genre and the texts that are generated by their example. They also fulfil an inceptive function, establishing the ground rules of the genre, bringing into play new combinations of features, admitting new (literary, sub-literary or non-literary) discursive traits, challenging prevailing horizons of expectation. The actual formation of literary genres remains a complex, even mysterious process. Claims have been made for several explanations: monogenesis, polygenesis, individual creative genius, external forces, etc. But the appearance of markedly original texts, whatever their own derivations, constitutes, if not a literary parthenogenesis, a decisive, inaugural, definable stage.

Germinie Lacerteux (1864), *Thérèse Raquin* (1867) and *L'Education sentimentale* (1869) form a troika of such founding works, whose choice is in no sense arbitrary, for they stand almost in a state of splendid historical isolation, appearing well before Yves Chevrel's first 'ground-swell' of the movement, as if their impact required some considerable time to assert itself. Gérard Delfau is a rare literary historian to have discerned the particular significance of their close appearance:

> Or il est curieux que les spécialistes n'aient jamais songé à souligner ce que la conjonction dans le temps de ces trois ouvrages apporte comme nouveauté à l'histoire du roman. Pour l'essentiel, la thématique, la sensibilité et la philosophie de ce que l'on ne nomme pas encore le Naturalisme s'y trouvent contenues; deux thèmes, appelés au ressassement: l'adultère et 'le mauvais ouvrier' avec sa constellation de sens: prostitution, alcoolisme et révolution; un milieu social caractéristique de la nouvelle école: la petite bourgeoisie,

volontiers provinciale, toujours en contact avec la classe ouvrière – le Peuple en somme selon la terminologie ambiguë d'alors; des personnages essayant d'en émerger: individus en rupture avec leur monde familier, comme Germinie Lacerteux, cas exemplaire, puisque son métier de servante la place dans le camp des exploités tout en en faisant la petite bourgeoise qui fréquente la boutique de madame Jupillon; enfin, plus profondément, au niveau du récit: le quotidien vécu sous le signe de l'échec, échec imputé souvent aux dérèglements d'une physiologie en conflit avec les normes sociales. Tel est bien le fond commun des trois romans.[10]

Despite the validity of the general point that Delfau is making, most of the characteristics that he enumerates apply more specifically in fact to *Germinie Lacerteux*, the Goncourt novel which traces the lapse into drunkenness, promiscuity, debt, illness and death of Mlle de Varandeuil's servant. In the novel, Germinie's double life of devoted service and dissipation is only revealed to her mistress after her death, just as the secret life of comparable excesses of the authors' own servant, Rose Malingre, on whose story the novel is based, only came to the attention of the brothers after her death in August 1862. It must therefore be counted as another of the oddities of our subject that this, the first acknowledged naturalist novel, with its sordid themes, should have come in this way from the pen(s) of two highly refined aristocratic aesthetes who prided themselves on their powers of observation, yet for years had been blind to the drinking, theft and sexual indulgences of their servant taking place right under their highly sensitive noses. Yet there is something wholly appropriate in the sense of shock that they record in the *Journal* (and in the terms of its expression) at this sudden revelation of life's sordid secrets: 'C'est affreux, ce déchirement de voile; c'est comme l'autopsie de quelque chose d'horrible dans une morte tout à coup ouverte' (21 August 1862). Such a casting off of veils, the veils of respectability, illusion or *maya*, will become a fundamental naturalist experience or gesture. At the time of the Rose Malingre revelations the brothers were in fact engaged upon the preparation of the novel about prostitution and prison life which they would never write together and which Edmond would complete as *La Fille Elisa* (1877), long after the death of Jules in 1870. But, after a trip to a women's prison on 28 October 1862, the *Journal* again records, on the same day, this essential naturalist reaction: 'J'ai encore froid de ce que j'ai vu. De temps en temps, quand on va au fond de la société et, pour ainsi dire, sous son théâtre, on y trouve de ces seconds dessous, machinés par la justice sociale, plus horribles que des abîmes, inconnus, ignorés, sans voix, pleins d'êtres et de supplices muets.' Perhaps il required this particular combination of revulsion and fascination, of disgust and attraction in the face of such harsh realities for the Goncourt brothers to launch into (and to launch) these naturalist themes. Once again, a few months later, are noted similar ambivalent reactions after a walk past a Paris hospital: 'Entre Lariboisière et l'Abattoir, ces deux *souffroirs*, je reste rêvant, à respirer un air chaud de viande. Des gémissements, de sourds mugissements viennent jusqu'à moi comme de lointaines musiques' (30 May 1863). Germinie Lacerteux comes to incarnate this funda-mental dialectic: 'De cette femme laide, s'échappait une âpre et mystérieuse séduction ... Tout en elle, sa bouche, ses yeux, sa laideur même, avait une provocation et une sollicitation. Un charme aphrodisiaque sortait d'elle, qui s'attaquait et s'attachait à l'autre sexe' (p. 53).[11] She is for the Goncourts that fascinatingly repulsive combination: Woman, People, Carnal Excess. The same kind of visceral response, whatever the justifying overlay of scientific investigation or sociological enquiry, is no doubt at the root of the naturalist project and it is the essential function of the literature to communicate it to the reader.

There have been several significant statements on the originality and importance of *Germinie Lacerteux* − and not only by Edmond de Goncourt himself! − that would bear out the ambitious claim made by Jules just before his death: 'On nous niera tant qu'on voudra, ... il faudra bien reconnaître un jour que nous avons fait *Germinie Lacerteux* et que *Germinie Lacerteux* est le livre type qui a servi de modèle à tout ce qui a été fabriqué, depuis nous, sous le nom de réalisme, naturalisme, etc.'[12] Edmond was of the same conviction, for, subsequently, the *Journal* is full of such claims, usually framed as complaints that the originality of the work has not been sufficiently acknowledged or that Zola has exploited it for his own gains. Even as late as 1891, he is still proclaiming and complaining: 'J'ai donné la formule complète du naturalisme dans *Germinie Lacerteux*, et *L'Assommoir* est fait absolument d'après la méthode enseignée par ce livre' (1 June 1891). It was Zola, in fact, who was the novel's earliest and most enthusiastic admirer, as he showed on 24 February 1865 in a review for *Le Salut Public* of Lyons (later published in *Mes Haines*), for which the Goncourts were most grateful at the time. He mainly interprets the novel as being the product of two febrile temperaments in an age of nervous erethism, but also gives a (proto) naturalist reading of the text. 'Il a l'intérêt puissant d'un problème physiologique et psychologique,' he writes, 'd'un cas de maladie physique et morale, d'une histoire qui doit être vraie' (X, 64). Daudet and Huysmans, in particular, came to admire it; Beuchat would see in it 'la première manifestation du *Naturalisme proprement dit*, tel que le concevra Zola';[13] and its direct influence has been traced, as well as more obviously on *Thérèse Raquin* and *L'Assommoir*, on Hennique's *La Dévouée, La Fin de Lucie Pellegrin* by Alexis, *Les Sœurs Vatard* by Huysmans, on works by Vallès, Descaves, Céard and Mirbeau, with George Moore's *Esther Waters* an obvious example of a foreign work inspired by the same text.[14] But a more telling testimony to the significance of the novel was the reaction of certain astute critics who, with an obvious distaste for the work, were nevertheless obliged to recognise its originality. Sainte-Beuve, the most influential critic of the time, though refraining from writing the article that the authors expected of him, did significantly observe in a guarded letter to them: 'Mais déjà je suis frappé d'une chose, c'est que pour bien juger de cet ouvrage et en parler, il faudrait une poétique tout autre que l'ancienne, une poétique appropriée aux productions d'un art nerveux, d'une recherche nouvelle.'[15] Flaubert, also in a letter and more enthusiastically, made a similar point: 'La grande question du réalisme n'a jamais été si carrément posée. On peut joliment disputer sur le but de l'Art à propos de votre livre.'[16] Such statements point to an awareness of the emergence of new generic patterns. Though, like any other text, the novel is derivative, most notably – to remain within the Flaubert canon – as the life of a fallen woman, like *Madame Bovary*, it was also written to counter a certain literary model, specifically the type of literature represented by Hugo's *Les Misérables* and its unreal picture of urban life.[17] But what is most significant is the manner in which this text established an innovative combination of features which would provide the basis and the model for a new generic development.

The preface to *Germinie Lacerteux*, with its (ironic?) Hugolian resonances, is the most obvious indicator of the novel's originality, for we see the authors boldly defying their readers' expectations as they openly declare that this new novel will inevitably violate them:

Le public aime les romans faux: ce roman est un roman vrai.

Il aime les livres qui font semblant d'aller dans le monde: ce livre vient de la rue.

Il aime les petites œuvres polissonnes, les mémoires de filles, les confessions d'alcôves, les saletés érotiques, le scandale qui se retrousse dans une image aux devantures des librairies: ce qu'il va lire est sévère et pur. Qu'il ne s'attende point à la photographie décolletée du plaisir: l'étude qui suit est la clinique de l'Amour.

Le public aime encore les lectures anodines et consolantes, les aventures qui finissent bien, les imaginations qui ne dérangent ni sa digestion ni sa sérénité: ce livre, avec sa triste et violente distraction, est fait pour contrarier ses habitudes et nuire à son hygiène. (pp. V–VI)

This challenging preface shows firstly that the naturalist text is directed, as it will continue to be, not only against the prestige of Romantic models, but also, even especially, against the generic conventions of popular bourgeois literature. Indeed, the whole preface may be read as an exercise in generic propagation.

One of the main arguments of the preface is the justification that it contains of the novel's subject and setting. In view of the authors' aristocratic conservatism which pervades the text, as a careful reading easily reveals, there is considerable irony, unintentional – one must presume – in their much-quoted declaration: 'Vivant au dix-neuvième siècle, dans un temps de suffrage universel, de démocratie, de libéralisme, nous nous sommes demandé si ce qu'on appelle "les basses classes" n'avait pas droit au Roman; si ce monde sous un monde, le peuple, devait rester sous le coup de l'interdit littéraire et des dédains d'auteurs qui ont fait jusqu'ici le silence sur l'âme et le cœur qu'il peut avoir' (p. VI). Apart from the palpably paternalistic tones, the bold impact of this innovation is significantly attenuated *generically* by being situated within the framework of the most prestigious and aristocratic of literary categories:

Il nous est venu la curiosité de savoir si cette forme conventionnelle d'une littérature oubliée et d'une société disparue, la Tragédie, était définitivement morte; si, dans un pays sans caste et sans aristocratie légale, les misères des petits et des pauvres parleraient à l'intérêt, à l'émotion, à la pitié, aussi haut que les misères des grands et des riches; si, en un mot, les larmes qu'on pleure en bas pourraient faire pleurer comme celles qu'on pleure en haut. (p. VII)

Just as Zola some years later will present *L'Assommoir* to his readers in a similar bold preface but with a similar compensatory, defensive strategy of compliance as 'un travail purement philologique', the Goncourts invite their readers to approach their original work as a new form of an ancient genre and, in so doing, create an exemplar for naturalist tragedy.

Germinie's life is in fact punctuated by a series of falls. There is the statutory rape (p. 39). Then she 'tomba dans une dévotion profonde' (p. 45) – an invariable sign of imminent disaster in naturalist works. Then she turns to drink and her mistress innocently enquires as she is stretched out in a stupor: 'Tu es tombée?' (p. 127). She falls for Jupillon, the son of a creamery proprietor, who 'tombe au sort', and is ruined buying him out of military service. She falls out of bed and has a miscarriage. 'Elle tombait à Gautruche', a vicious, drunken sign painter. Finally, as she breaks with him, 'Germinie tomba où elle devait tomber, au-dessous de la honte, au-dessous de la nature même. De chute en chute, la misérable et brûlante créature roula à la rue' (p. 228). Like Gervaise Macquart in Zola's later novel *L'Assommoir*, she sinks from humiliation to humiliation, dehumanised, depersonalised, desperately and aimlessly wandering the streets of Paris in scenes that set the pattern for future hopeless wanderings in filthy streets among dark shadows in the rain by the dim light of eery street lamps in naturalist novels, among the archetypal naturalist landmarks of despair, the *assommoirs*: 'Elle battait tout l'espace où la crapule soûle ses lundis et trouve ses amours, entre un hôpital, une tuerie et un cimetière: La Riboisière, l'Abattoir et Montmartre' (p. 214). These scenes in which the wretched woman prowls the streets bring about what will be typical experiences of engulfment by the night, by an insidious terreaqueous material environment which corrodes the character's sense of self and her whole being:

Quand la flamme des réverbères, tremblante dans une vapeur d'eau, allongeait et balançait, comme dans le miroitement d'une rivière, son reflet sur le sol mouillé; quand les pavés, les trottoirs, la terre, semblaient disparaître et mollir sous la pluie, et que rien ne paraissait plus solide dans la nuit noyée, la pauvre misérable, presque folle de fatigue, croyait voir se gonfler un déluge dans le ruisseau. Un mirage d'épouvante lui montrait tout à coup de l'eau tout autour d'elle, de l'eau qui marchait, de l'eau qui s'approchait de partout. (pp. 216–17)

Such a parodic baptism in fetid waters and mud, in the characteristic naturalist elements of disintegration, of loss of self, substance and humanity, precedes the ultimate fall into anonymity and death. The figures of misfortune (room number 21, bed number 14) give way in the end to a symbolic enumeration. Mlle de Varandeuil vainly seeks Germinie's grave 'entre deux croix dont l'une portait 9 novembre et l'autre 10 novembre … Sa tombe vague était ce terrain vague. Pour prier sur elle, il fallait prier au petit bonheur entre deux dates' (pp. 278–9).

In the naturalist scheme, the vengeful gods of ancient tragedy are replaced by a pervading sense of misfortune: 'Cette grande force du monde qui fait souffrir, la puissance mauvaise qui porte le nom d'un dieu sur le marbre des tragédies antiques, et qui s'appelle *Pas-de-Chance* sur le front tatoué des bagnes, la Fatalité l'écrasait, et Germinie baissait la tête sous son pied' (p. 193). As the novel develops more and more in the direction of allegory, a kind of literary

Schopenhauerism *avant la lettre* manifests itself in the presentation of Germinie's fate, a vision of evil and misfortune inherent in the very workings of life itself in its fundamental, instinctive aspects: 'Dans la flamme de son sang, l'appétit de ses organes, sa faiblesse ardente, ne sentait-elle point s'agiter la Fatalité de l'Amour, le mystère et la possession d'une maladie, plus forte que sa pudeur et sa raison, l'ayant déjà livrée aux hontes de la passion, et devant − elle le pressentait − l'y livrer encore?' (p. 194). The Goncourts' victim of nature's Will and of the metaphysics of 'love' even attains a rudimentary kind of *anagnorisis*: 'à force de ressasser en elle-même la continuité de son infortune et la succession de ses chagrins, elle arrivait à voir une persécution de sa malechance dans les plus petits malheurs de sa vie, de son service' (pp. 193−4). But the authors are clearly hampered by the lowly status and limited capabilities of their 'heroine', for, in one improbable scene, they have her eloquently declaiming her misfortunes in her sleep, like a professional tragedienne, before the astonished Mlle de Varandeuil: 'C'était comme une langue de peuple purifiée et transfigurée dans la passion' (p. 180).

Germinie Lacerteux, therefore, unequivocally establishes a pattern for naturalist tragedy, whilst steering a course between allegorical and disquisitional fiction as Germinie is at one time or another a human exemplar and a social type, a victim of both the forces of life and the injustices of society. In the first instance, with her instincts for life, pleasure and illusion, she is presented in significant contrast to her mistress, Mlle de Varandeuil, whose presence frames the story and who, as her name suggests, represents the ultimate naturalist truth and state: 'Des morts et de la Mort, elle avait un culte presque antique. La tombe lui était sacrée, chère, et amie' (p. 34). All abnegation, stoicism and austerity, in an almost perpetual state of immobile reflectiveness, Mlle de Varandeuil only leaves the sepulchral calm of her room once a week for a visit − to the Montmartre cemetery! The novel opens with a scene in which she is saved from a grave illness, but condemned to life, and closes with the death of Germinie, who was avid for life, with her mistress at her grave. Such ironies are an integral part of the naturalist vision. But, at the same time, Germinie is a representative of a social species and her fate illustrative of the plight of the 'people', so we are to understand, though the Goncourts' social concerns only surface explicitly again, after the preface, at the end of the novel in an extraordinary two-page apostrophe to Paris, 'le cœur du monde, la grande ville humaine, la grande ville charitable et fraternelle!' (pp. 275−6), to which a plea is addressed for a decent death and burial for the poor even if they cannot be given a decent life.

There is in naturalist works, at least when dealing with the life of the poor, a constant reformist strain, which is evident in Edmond de Goncourt's *La Fille Elisa*, for example, and in the works of certain other writers connected with the movement, like Gustave Geffroy, a close associate of Edmond de Goncourt, who wrote a preface to the 1890 edition of *Germinie Lacerteux* emphasising its authors' humanitarianism. Rarely, however, did the naturalists openly espouse causes in their fiction. But their works do tend to focus on a particular milieu with its social problems or on particular social types suffering their wrongs.

It was the Goncourt brothers who also firmly established a seemingly incongruous feature of naturalist fiction found in particular in texts by Huysmans and by certain minor writers like Lucien Descaves (another protégé of Edmond de Goncourt): a sordid or trivial topic treated with all the delicate grace of *le style artiste*. 'Personne', the *Journal* complains, 'n'a encore caractérisé notre talent de romanciers. Il se compose du mélange bizarre et unique, qui fait de nous à la fois des physiologistes et des poètes' (12 February 1869). A popular milieu like that of *Germinie Lacerteux* not only afforded opportunities to represent compelling human dramas, life in the raw, material for works 'sur le *vrai*, sur le *vif*, sur le *saignant*' (*Journal*, 18 December 1860), works that would disturb bourgeois readers, confront them with the scars of society, but also provided new sources of poetic inspiration. This dialectic of (realistic) involvement and (artistic) detachment, which we shall encounter again in a later chapter, is also characteristic of an even more extensive and fundamental feature of naturalist literature that the Goncourt brothers promoted in their works: the authentic detail, the human document, facts culled on site visits to hospitals, slums, back streets, prisons, brothels, as well as information researched in specialised books or provided by cooperative readers and friends. Such documentation, whatever its source, was incorporated into naturalist texts with varying degrees of integration within the narrative line. In *La Fille Elisa* (chapter 55), the prison canteen menu is 'reproduced' and the last chapter of Paul Adam's *Chair molle* (1885), another life of a prostitute, consists of nothing more than a hospital document that records details of the heroine's illness ('ostéite et hépatite syphilitique') and her date of discharge/death.[18] But, whether it takes the form of this kind of official record, or of a medical treatise, or of observations recorded 'on location', the naturalist document is more than just a guarantee of authenticity, an elaborate 'effet de réel', for it is invariably used for some literary effect, thematised as an ironic statement on heartless officialdom, elaborated into one of those compelling dramas of suffering and degradation, transformed into a decorous description. The naturalist's researches are never a total surrender to the real. Zola, riding through la Beauce in his carriage, notebook in hand, to 'document himself' for *La Terre*, epitomises this ambivalent position of immediate contact and preserved detachment, for he was able to observe the realities of peasant life that enrich his realistic novel, but maintain the distance and the vision that the peasants could never share and that went into the writing of what he called his 'poème de la terre'.

No less ambiguous − to return to *Germinie Lacerteux* − is the invocation of universal suffrage, democracy and liberalism in the preface, for nothing could have been further from the mind(s) of the Goncourts than to promote political reform. 'Il faut être aristocrate pour écrire *Germinie Lacerteux*', according to the *Journal* (10 September 1866). Zola, a man of the left, could write of this novel that it marked an important date, since, 'pour la première fois, le héros en casquette et l'héroïne en bonnet de linge y sont étudiés par des écrivains d'observation et de style' (XI, 170). But the People, to whom the Goncourt brothers invariably referred to as 'the rabble' ('la canaille') and whom they held more in disgust than in sympathy, represented for them some base and alien species on which they had happened to stumble. Why, Edmond asks himself, at a later date, does he choose such subjects?

Parce que c'est dans le bas qu'au milieu de l'effacement d'une civilisation, se conserve le caractère des choses, des personnes, de la langue, de tout ... Pourquoi encore? Peut-être parce que je suis un littérateur bien né, et que le peuple, la canaille, si vous voulez, a pour moi l'attrait de populations inconnues, et non découvertes, quelque chose de l'*exotique*, que les voyageurs vont chercher, avec mille souffrances, dans les pays lointains. (*Journal*, 3 December 1871)

There is thus both penetration into the essentials of life and withdrawal from them. If a legitimate claim can be made that the Goncourt brothers invented the novel *of* the people, dispelling the Romantic mythologisation of the class, they most certainly did not write *for* the people. In general, because of this kind of ambivalence, the naturalist novel, whether written by reactionaries like the Goncourts or socialists like Alexis, maintains a certain apolitical character − and was thus inevitably attacked from both the left and the right. Germinie is not even really a representative of the popular classes, for the narrator frequently underlines her singularity.

Nor are the events of her life situated with any degree of precision at a particular historico-political juncture. She is presented more as a specimen of some primitive and singular form of humanity, prone to certain physiological excesses. This novel, then, as the authors explain in their preface, once again adopting a generic point of view, is not history in the usual sense of the term (not, one might add, contemporary social history as Balzac conceived the function of the novel to be), but an example of a new development in the novel form, what they call 'l'Histoire morale contemporaine', with which 'le Roman s'est imposé les études et les devoirs de la Science' (p. VII). Zola also defined the originality of this work in similar, if somewhat more lurid terms, as not just a novel on the people but also a physiological novel:

En outre, je le répète, il ne s'agit pas d'une histoire plus ou moins intéressante, mais d'une véritable leçon d'anatomie morale et physique. Le romancier jette une femme sur la pierre de l'amphithéâtre, la première femme venue, la bonne qui traverse la rue en tablier; il la dissèque patiemment, montre chaque muscle, fait jouer les nerfs, cherche les causes et raconte les effets; et cela suffit pour étaler un coin saignant de l'humanité. (XI, 170)

The characterisation of the Goncourt novel in such violently charged terms by the future author of *La Bête humaine* may seem to the modern sensibility, not entirely improbably, to suggest fundamental links between naturalist narratology, physiology and (the sadistic fantasies of some kind of advanced form of) 'Ripperology'. Germinie, as well as being of the People, is also Woman, another unexplored territory, another 'coin saignant de l'humanité', probed by the fascinated scrutiny of the male naturalist cum physiologist, a hysterical woman with unrestrained sexual cravings — the two features were assumed naturally to go together — an inverted representative of the ideal female qualities that underpinned the social and moral order. In the naturalist age, dominated by masculine power and systems of explanation, pathological states were displayed with a considerable degree of theatricality and the naturalist novel became a vehicle for such displays. The naturalists themselves were exclusively male and their meetings had much about them of the all-male club. 'The woman', Terry Eagleton writes of her place in such a patriarchal setting, 'is both "inside" and "outside" male society, both a romantically idealized member of it and a victimized outcast. She is sometimes what stands between man and chaos, and sometimes the embodiment of chaos itself. This is why she troubles the neat categories of such a regime, blurring its well-defined boundaries.'[19] Much naturalist writing is about the threat of femininity, the dangers of feminisation. In *Germinie Lacerteux*, Mlle de Varandeuil, the stable presence, deprived of any trace of female sexuality, is first shown beneath a portrait of her father, and her features show 'je ne sais quelle flamme de mâle dévouement et de charité masculine' (p. 3). In adversity she displays 'un caractère de fer, une volonté d'homme' (p. 23) and her philosophy is 'un stoïcisme mâle, hautain, presque ironique' (p. 31). Despite her revolutionary name, Sempronie, the result of her father's precautions during the Republic, she represents the virtues of a stabler past: 'elle n'estimait plus les rois: mais elle détestait la canaille'. 'Ses dehors', the narrator adds, 'étaient tout masculins' (p. 32). By contrast, her servant is a creature of the modern age, all indulgence, a creature of the body, the instincts, the nerves, succumbing to 'les fièvres de son corps, et les irritations du dehors', 'les molles lâchetés de sa chair', 'toutes les sollicitations de nature qui l'assaillaient' (pp. 190–1). By the time she takes up with Gautruche, she has become hysterical, nymphomaniac, avid for 'des amours terribles, acharnés et funèbres, des ardeurs et des assouvissements sauvages, des voluptés furieuses, des caresses qui avaient les brutalités et les colères du vin, des baisers qui semblaient chercher le sang sous la peau comme la langue d'une bête féroce, des anéantissements qui les engloutissaient et ne leur laissaient que le cadavre de leur corps' (p. 221). Such a remarkable, mythical representation of proletarian 'love', frenzied, sadistic, animalistic, is obviously more a reflection of the overheated imagination of the authors than of their powers of realistic representation. But it also gives expression to certain deep-seated fantasies and fears of their age. Indeed, Zola described his whole generation in 1865 as 'esprits affolés et hystériques' living in an era characterised by the 'victoire des nerfs sur le sang' (X, 56) and frequently asserted that the works of the Goncourt brothers were the perfect expression of this new 'mal du siècle'. By the time *Germinie Lacerteux* appeared, Charcot had already been appointed to the Salpêtrière, the hospital and women's asylum, where he initiated clinical demonstrations in the pathology of neurotic hysteria. As we shall see later in more detail, the association of neurosis, female sexuality, nymphomania and female religiosity will form an essential component of naturalist thematics in certain major texts like Zola's *La Conquête de Plassans*, but also in a host of minor works like Jules Claretie's *Les Amours d'un interne* (1881) – a novel set in the Salpêtrière – or Gustave Toudouze's *La Baronne* (1883) – a novel on a higher class of neurotic nymphomania. If the main point is that *Germinie Lacerteux* inaugurated a type of novel that presents a pathological case study, documented by reference to current medical theories – the Goncourts read Brachet's *Traité de l'hystérie* – the frequency with which the naturalist writers themselves would refer to, even succumb to their own neurotic disorders, and their readiness to generalise from such instances to characterise the whole of contemporary life in such terms, suggests that their interest in these cases, whatever their pretensions, was rooted in more than a pure scientific disinterestedness and a curiosity for scientific investigation.[20]

The following analysis of one of the happier phases of Germinie Lacerteux's existence could well have been extracted from Zola's *Thérèse Raquin*: 'On aurait dit que la passion qui circulait en elle renouvelait et transformait son tempérament lymphatique. Il ne lui semblait plus puiser la vie comme autrefois, goutte à goutte, à une source avare: une force généreuse et pleine lui coulait dans les veines; le feu d'un sang riche lui courait dans le corps' (p. 71). Zola takes up the theme of female neurosis through Thérèse, 'troublée par des désordres nerveux', in whom, once again, the pathological drama of the age is played out, a 'victoire des nerfs sur le sang'. Her true nature lies dormant in the stifling atmosphere of the haberdasher's shop where she lives with her husband, the lymphatic Camille, until, with the appearance of the sanguinary Laurent, a railway employee and a not very talented painter, the chemistry literally works and sparks literally begin to fly: 'On eût dit que sa figure venait de s'éclairer en dedans, que des flammes s'échappaient de sa chair. Et, autour d'elle, son sang qui brûlait, ses nerfs qui se tendaient, jetaient ainsi des effluves chauds, un air pénétrant et âcre' (I, 548)! In his preface to the second edition of the novel (1868), in response to some outraged critical reactions, Zola sets forth his famous claims that his novel has a serious scientific purpose, studies the interactions of two temperaments, presents a rigorous demonstration of physiological laws that inevitably lead the lovers to murder the husband, then, as a natural consequence of the organic disorders that ensue from their remorse, to destroy each other:

Dans *Thérèse Raquin*, j'ai voulu étudier des tempéraments et non des caractères. Là est le livre entier. J'ai choisi des personnages souverainement dominés par leurs nerfs et leur sang, dépourvus de libre arbitre, entraînés à chaque acte de leur vie par les fatalités de leur chair. Thérèse et Laurent sont des brutes humaines, rien de plus ...
     On commence, j'espère, à comprendre que mon but a été un but scientifique avant tout ... En un mot, je n'ai eu qu'un désir: étant donné un homme puissant et une femme inassouvie, chercher en eux la bête, ne voir même que la

bête, les jeter dans un drame violent, et noter scrupuleusement les sensations et les actes de ces êtres. J'ai simplement fait sur deux corps vivants le travail analytique que les chirurgiens font sur des cadavres. (I, 519–20).

It is difficult to imagine how this overt purpose could possibly have escaped the attention of Zola's contemporaries (or even that it should have been largely passed over by more modern critics[21]), for the novel is overladen from beginning to end with long passages of physiological analysis which leave no doubt as to the author's intentions. *Thérèse Raquin* is an 'experimental novel' *avant la lettre* (or at least *avant la théorie*) by more than ten years, being Zola's most deliberate attempt to apply physiology to the novel. Zola directs the reader to believe that certain moral conditions and options (passion, remorse, homicide, suicide) are logically, fatally, determined according to the operation of certain general laws. 'Cette communauté', the narrator explains, 'cette pénétration mutuelle est un fait de psychologie et de physiologie qui a souvent lieu chez les êtres que de grandes secousses nerveuses heurtent violemment l'un à l'autre' (I, 592). The nub of the experiment is summarised in this typical passage which illustrates both the dogmatism of the theory and (by the emphasis that I have added) the degree of equivocation with which it is applied:

La nature sèche et nerveuse de Thérèse avait agi d'une façon bizarre sur la nature épaisse et sanguine de Laurent. Jadis, aux jours de passion, leur différence de tempérament avait fait de cet homme et de cette femme un couple puissamment lié, en établissant entre eux *une sorte* d'équilibre, en complétant *pour ainsi dire* leur organisme ... Mais un détraquement venait de se produire; les nerfs surexcités de Thérèse avaient dominé. Laurent s'était tout d'un coup jeté en plein éréthisme nerveux; ... Il serait *curieux* d'étudier les changements qui se produisent *parfois* dans *certains* organismes à la suite de circonstances déterminées. Ces changements, qui partent de la chair, ne tardent pas à se communiquer au cerveau, à tout l'individu. (I, 613)

In this, and in similar passages, the novel transmits an admixture – or, the more informed might say, a hotchpotch – of themes, a *bricolage* of theses and prejudices, culled from various undetermined sources:[22] female neurosis, the feminisation of man, the interaction of temperaments (according to the ancient categories, lymphatic Camille, sanguinary Laurent and nervous Thérèse), the influence of race, heredity and milieu on human behaviour (Thérèse's Algerian mother, Laurent's peasant blood), the transformation of physical into psychological states, the physical manifestations of moral conditions (Laurent's 'crispations nerveuses' and, more dramatically, the bite on his neck that never heals), all linked together by the narrative, such that one might even suggest that, in contrast to the way in which narratologists normally interpret such devices, it is the narrative itself that comes to 'motivate' the explanations. So conspicuous and recurrent are the passages of analysis that, for all the Gothic effects which have led critics to make comparisons with Hawthorne and Poe, the work reads like a psychological novel in which the psychology has been replaced by physiology and the moral issues by 'scientific' laws.

This is very much how Zola wished his novel to be read, as generic innovation, and his preface emphatically makes the point. There are only two or three readers, he claims, not 'les lecteurs de ces petits livres roses, de ces indiscrétions de boudoirs et de coulisses, qui se tirent à dix mille exemplaires', but the unnamed Taines of the age, who are capable of judging his novel, who 'y retrouveraient la méthode moderne, l'outil d'enquête universelle dont le siècle se sert avec tant de fièvre pour trouver l'avenir' (I, 521–2). But this tactical bravado merely makes more explicit the imperatives of the text, for already the hyperbolic encoding of a scientific discourse and the insistent repetitiveness of the long passages of analysis are themselves, to make the point again, the tactical signs of the emergence of a new generic form which the writer is seeking to impose. As E. D. Hirsch Jr points out, 'in a new genre, repetitions and tautologies may not indicate emphasis but may simply arise from the author's attempt to secure a meaning that might otherwise be missed or wrongly understood'.[23]

It was again the perceptive Sainte-Beuve who, despite his reservations about the novel's vulgar excesses and as guarded in his judgement of this work as he had been of *Germinie Lacerteux*, made a rare acknowledgment of its originality. 'Votre œuvre', he wrote to the author (on 10 June 1868), 'est remarquable, consciencieuse, et, à certains égards même, elle peut faire époque dans l'histoire du roman contemporain' (X, 680). More recently F. W. J. Hemmings has stated that '*Thérèse Raquin* may not be a great work of literature, but nothing quite like it had ever been written before'[24] and, for Furst and Skrine, it is 'the prototype of the Naturalist novel'.[25] To a considerable degree, Zola would continue in a similar vein with *Les Rougon-Macquart*, though happily sparing the reader most of the discursive theorising, basing his series of novels, as has been well documented, on certain scientific texts. At one level the whole series may be read as an elaborate continuation of the model of *Thérèse Raquin*, a vast fable of nerves and blood, harping back to the 'névrose originelle' of the family ancestor, Adélaïde Fouque, and to the chemistry of temperaments of the founding trio: Adélaïde, 'bizarre', 'le cerveau fêlé'; Rougon, 'lourd et placide'; Macquart, 'déséquilibré'. But the status of the science of naturalist fiction, even in a text like *Thérèse Raquin*, where it is so obtrusive, remains problematic, ambivalent and, in the final analysis, subject to literary constraints, myths, models, and conventions. When, to take a minor detail as an example, Thérèse and Laurent first meet, the woman feels 'de petits frissons lorsque ses yeux rencontrèrent son cou de taureau' and his penetrating gaze provokes in her 'une sorte de malaise'. There is a passage of scientific gloss on his 'nature sanguine' effecting in her 'une sorte d'angoisse nerveuse' (I, 541, 543). Here then is a naturalist version, with its physiological motivation, of the 'first-look scene' of long-standing literary ancestry.[26] In such instances the rationalist, authoritarian, scientific discourse reveals itself as a specious vehicle for the workings of more conventional literary structures, and of other generic determinants, that are no less an integral part of the naturalist manner.

There is, for example, in *Thérèse Raquin*, an element of social satire, particularly in the scenes of the Thursday night receptions in the Raquins' dining room, where the Michauds and the Grivets come for their weekly indulgences, a cup of tea and a game of dominoes, 'comme une orgie bourgeoise d'une gaieté folle' (I, 537). There are also the pictorial aspects of Zola's novel, the links with subjects and techniques of contemporary painting: the 'impressionism' of the 'partie de campagne' scene, the links with *Olympia*, for 1867 was the year of Zola's vigorous defence of Manet and his art. Then, less obviously, there are the ties between the novel and a journalistic genre, the *fait divers*. Had Zola written an epilogue to the novel, it could well have consisted of an imaginary snippet from one of the popular newspapers of the time, narrating the scandal (husband drowns in river – wife's secret affair – guilty lovers driven to suicide), not unlike Zola's story 'Un mariage d'amour' (I, 670–3) published in *Le Figaro* (24 December 1866), an earlier version of the novel. In fact the stock-in-trade of much naturalist fiction is precisely the type of felonies, misdemeanours and petty scandals that filled the gossipy *fait divers* columns of the press. As Paul Alexis pointed out in an article on Maupassant, his generation of writers was less scornful of journalistic activities than, say, Flaubert's had been, for in many cases they not only derived a living from the profession, but were able thereby to sharpen their skills and take up many of its themes: 'Outre que nous y gagnons plus ou moins l'existence de chaque jour, nous y assouplissons nos membres, nous y décuplons nos forces dans une hebdomadaire ou quotidienne gymnastique.'[27] The works of

Maupassant and Alexis, their short stories in particular, illustrate especially well the close affinities between naturalist fiction and the newspaper article of the gossipy kind in which bourgeois morality takes a tumble and the seamy side of life is revealed. It is not unusual in fact for naturalist fiction to revert back 'diegetically' to this sub-literary genre, as in Fontane's novel, *Effi Briest*, where the servants read of the heroine's affair and the ensuing duel as a *fait divers* in the appropriately named *Kleines Journal* (chapter 29). The journalistic *chronique, conte, vignette*, the *risqué* tale, accounts of domestic crimes, of incest and adultery, descriptions of oddities in human behaviour from the macabre to the titillating, formed a huge sub-literary generic stock of anecdotes on which naturalist fiction could draw and from which it is at times barely distinguishable. To take one or two examples from the collection of stories by Paul Alexis, *L'Education amoureuse* (1890), there is the tale of the devout and deformed spinster, Annette Leverdure, who is raped one night on her way home from church, but returns in hope in the spring to the same back alley ('A quoi rêvent les vieilles filles'); or the story of the café proprietor's pretty, but deranged daughter who resists the advances of a painter, yet stabs him to death when he finds a mistress ('La Chouette'); or another about the morbid narrator of 'Nuit à trois', with its echoes of *Thérèse Raquin*, who is obsessed with a desire to sleep with the widow of a *suicidé*; then there's the story of Octave Maublanc, an incorrigible punner, who beats his friend to death with a mallet in his wine cellar shouting 'Il ne l'est plus, s'il le fût' ('Dans l'arrière-cave'). In an article entitled 'De la moralité' (reprinted in *Le Roman expérimental*), Zola complains about the inconsistency of outraged critics of naturalist works who do not protest against the fact that mothers and daughters can read in the daily papers 'les épisodes épouvantables, les détails des crimes et des procès qui mettent cyniquement à nu toute l'ordure de l'homme' (X, 1329). After giving some salacious examples from accounts of trials in *Le Figaro*, he concludes: 'Que de brutalités et d'obscénités ensevelies! Un procès, c'est simplement un roman expérimental qui se déroule devant le public.' Indeed, such spicy dramas provide an indirect guarantee of the authenticity of naturalist works − and, clearly, a justification of their apparent excesses: 'Voilà la vérité, un drame vrai montre brusquement au grand jour le vrai mécanisme de la vie' (X, 1332).

It is not unusual for emergent literary genres to draw in this way upon such popular generic forms for their sustenance. 'While literature's innovatory thrust', writes Alastair Fowler, 'may draw strength from the past, it as often moves laterally and turns to popular

culture for its devices.'[28] Bakhtin wrote much about the regener-
ating function of popular forms and the Russian Formalist, Victor
Shklovsky, raised the same process to the status of a law of literary
evolution, according to which literature regularly renews itself by
deriving motifs and devices from sub-literary, 'non-canonised'
genres.[29] Precise sources of *Thérèse Raquin* have been traced in
popular literary works of Zola's and a previous age.[30] In general, as
we learn in the useful study by Yves Olivier-Martin, *Histoire du roman
populaire en France de 1840 à 1980* (1980), popular novels of the Third
Republic borrowed freely from naturalist themes, but there was
undoubtedly also a considerable reciprocal borrowing of popular
stock situations by the naturalist writers. The initial situation of
Thérèse Raquin: an energetic wife trapped in marriage to a dull
husband in a boring environment, languishingly looking through the
window, obviously recalls once again an already canonised novel of
adultery, as does the theme of the heroine's readings.[31] But, by the
time Thérèse takes to sentimental literature, the novel is almost half
over, the adultery and murder have already occurred under the
impulse of those physiological factors and the theme of her reading
almost seems like an afterthought. Yet, in its initial stages and
frequently beyond, in *Germinie Lacerteux*, in *Thérèse Raquin* – and,
as we shall later see, in *Une Belle Journée* and *A Mummer's Wife*
– the naturalist novel is obliged both to acknowledge its debt to
Madame Bovary and to distance itself from it.

Finally, moving further up the literary scale and into a broader
field, the theme of adultery in *Thérèse Raquin* leads us to consider
another fundamental naturalist trait. If we were to adopt a Fryean
perspective on this question, we would situate naturalism and myth
at the extreme points in the spectrum of literary design, myth being
a conventionalised narrative of superhuman accomplishments
unrelated to a plausible realistic context. Now, naturalism, like
realism, draws upon the same 'structural principles of literature' as
myth, according to Frye, but, in the low mimetic mode where it is
situated, the reappearance of myth is ironic.[32] Thus, if we were to
assume a similar but less holistic approach, we could suggest that
naturalist literature both recontextualises, transmotivates, parodies
idealistic literary constructs and creates its own mythical configur-
ations. If *Thérèse Raquin*, like *Germinie Lacerteux*, may be interpreted as a naturalist tragedy,[33] for all its (melo)dramatic intensity,
it may also be read, with its 'coup de foudre', its adulterous love, its
fatal 'amour-passion' and even its obstacle in the bed (the 'ghost' of
Camille) and its lethal philtre (an appropriately naturalist, chemical

version, 'un petit flacon de grès, contenant de l'acide prussique'), as a frenetic, downgraded version of an ill-starred love story of ancient romance, in which the naturalist lovers perform a parody of the *Liebestod* and its deliverance:

Une crise suprême les brisa, les jeta dans les bras l'un de l'autre, faibles comme des enfants. Il leur sembla que quelque chose de doux et d'attendri s'éveillait dans leur poitrine ... Thérèse prit le verre, le vida à moitié et le tendit à Laurent qui l'acheva d'un trait. Ce fut un éclair. Ils tombèrent l'un sur l'autre, foudroyés, trouvant enfin une consolation dans la mort. (I, 667)

Thérèse Raquin thus becomes a new Isolde, a naturalist Doña Sol, even in the dingy, sunless passage du Pont-Neuf.

The theme of adultery is an obvious link between *Thérèse Raquin* and our third 'founding text', Flaubert's *L'Education sentimentale*, though the differences between these two naturalist prototypes are just as obviously greater than the similarities. Whereas certain of Zola's novels, *Thérèse Raquin*, *L'Assommoir*, *Germinal*, were certainly more influential abroad, Flaubert's text was the most acclaimed model among the French naturalists themselves. As such, it exercised a particularly powerful influence as both a model and a 'hypotext', that is both as a work embodying approved general characteristics and as a specific text to be faithfully imitated, adapted, transformed.[34] For our purposes, therefore, far more important than an interpretation of the novel itself is a study of the prestige of this text, of its 'hypertextual' effects, of the esteem in which it was held (contrary to public opinion), of the 'myth' of *L'Education sentimentale*.

We have already noted Flaubert's sway over the French naturalist writers as a debunker of theoretical excesses, as a model of artistic integrity, as an almost intimidating presence. He also generated an undeniable 'anxiety of influence', for the most striking feature of homages to *L'Education sentimentale* by the naturalist writers is a sense of awe, of an achievement that could never be matched, of a work with which their own efforts would necessarily pale by comparison. We have already noted the great estime in which Zola held Flaubert's model text. 'La vérité est', he wrote in 1879, 'que ce livre trop vrai épouvante' (XI, 607). In 1891, J.-K. Huysmans declared: 'Le roman de l'être médiocre, de la majorité de gens, de l'électeur, l'analyse de M. Tout le monde me semble clos. Flaubert l'a fait de telle façon dans l'*Education sentimentale*, qui est le vrai, le seul livre naturaliste au sens exact du mot, car Zola n'a fait que le dévoyer, qu'après ce chef d'œuvre nous devrions nous taire.'[35] But it was particularly on the so-called 'petits naturalistes' that this 'Bible of naturalism' exercised its curiously inspiring and inhibiting effect. 'Je me rappelle le grand coup qu'il m'a porté alors que je le découvris en 1874', Céard writes to Zola in 1879, 'je l'ai depuis enseigné à bien du monde, faisant de bien rares conversions. Certaines de mes amitiés sont venues uniquement de là: les plus littéraires et les plus solides.'[36] It has even been claimed that certain of Céard's initiates committed the whole of Flaubert's text to memory and would recite passages from it to each other.[37] Such a feat is no doubt a part of naturalist mythology, but the novel was clearly a text which the younger writers, since they could not compete, were content to repeat, a text which, ironically, reduced them to a Flaubertian state of psittacism or to mere pastiche.[38]

The cult of *L'Education sentimentale* was not however entirely limited to Céard's coterie in France. In an article entitled 'A tragic novel' (1897), George Moore wrote perhaps the most laudatory commentary on Flaubert's text, long after he had given up being a naturalist himself, such was the lasting effect of Flaubert's work. It is, Moore emphatically writes, 'something wholly new in literature', a book, 'the like of which did not exist in the past, the like of which the future will not reproduce, a new thing come into human life; a new force, a new influence that was not there before, and will be there for ever'. Its impact is 'like that of a religion'; it 'forms the souls of at least thirty or forty readers in every generation'. With the advantage of hindsight – and with some considerable overstatement and fantasy – he testifies to the curiously invisible, yet all-pervasive (and clearly mythical) influence on the French naturalist writers:

While remaining itself obscure, this novel has given birth to a numerous literature. The *Rougon-Macquart* series is nothing but *L'Education sentimentale* re-written into twenty volumes by a prodigious journalist – twenty huge balloons which bob about the streets, sometimes getting clear of the house-tops. Maupassant cut it up into numberless walking sticks; Goncourt took the descriptive passages, and turned them into Passy rhapsodies. The book has been a treasure cavern known to forty thieves, whence all have found riches and fame.[39]

Unlike his erstwhile French associates, who tended to emphasise the formal innovations of the novel, Moore is more sensitive to its visionary aspect, calling it 'the tragedy of leisure' and comparing its author to the Hindu god Brahma, creating the passing spectacle of life to relieve his eternal ennui, sitting 'watching the generations rising out of the void and falling into the void'.[40] Thus, to the figure of the typical naturalist, the physiologist dissecting his specimens of human pathology in the amphitheatre of his writer's study, we must add the figure of the world-weary Magus, contemplating the futility of human existence. In the most general of terms, one could say that naturalism combines new knowledge with an old philosophy, the acquisitions of modern Western science with attitudes akin to ancient Eastern systems of thought, Charcot with Schopenhauer, Bernard with Brahma, Taine with the Theravāda.

L'Education sentimentale, Flaubert's 'epic of mediocrity' as Gide called it, established a pattern for naturalist thematics, both in the more abstract sense of the term, as a work in which all the most cherished of human values: love, art, morality, political ideals, are profaned in the daily commerce of life, but also in a more concrete sense, in the monotonous landscapes, the dismal skies, the images of liquidity and dissolution, that denote the essential erosion of life in time. Many a sentence from this novel, like the following, could have served as an epigraph for many a naturalist novel: 'Ainsi les jours s'écoulaient dans la répétition des mêmes ennuis et des habitudes contractées.'[41] The life of its hero, Frédéric Moreau, is not without its achievements and its periods of happiness, but, for Flaubert's followers, the predominant theme, as Zola came to describe it, was 'un continuel avortement, avortement d'une génération, avortement d'une époque historique' (XII, 607), for the essential message of this novel, in which so much occurs but so little seems to happen, could be summed up by the final, deflationary phrase of the penultimate chapter, the scene of Frédéric's last encounter with Mme Arnoux: 'Et ce fut tout.' But it was more the method of the novel than its message that disconcerted Flaubert's critics and inspired his future naturalist admirers. *L'Education sentimentale*, it has often been remarked, exploits in a masterly fashion the potentialities of the indissociable link between realistic representation and irony in the novel, where suggestive depiction is commentary enough and undermines the epic and Romantic expectations associated with the genre. But the expected moral and heroic purposefulness of the genre is especially contravened by the apparent artless lack of direction of the plot of *L'Education sentimentale*. The novelty of Flaubert's text, then, was precisely its apparent lack of *novel-ty*, seeming to represent, in Zola's phrase, 'la négation même de l'art du romancier' and going on to represent a model of structural experimentation in the genre, which Flaubert's naturalist followers would aspire to imitate as the perfect vehicle for the transmission of an 'anti-romanesque' vision of life.

The publication of *Thérèse Raquin* had been met with outrage and hostility, which at least drew attention to the work and contributed to a modicum of success. *L'Education sentimentale* was received with stony silence and incomprehension. But, whatever the response that our three texts evoked, there was at least a sense that a new type of literature was in the making, as in the virulent review of (mainly) *Thérèse Raquin* and *Germinie Lacerteux* which Louis Ulbach published in *Le Figaro* (23 January 1868), possibly on Zola's instigation.[42] The critic begins by asserting, with much sincere or fake indignation: 'Il s'est établi depuis quelques années une école monstrueuse de romanciers, qui prétend substituer l'éloquence du charnier à l'éloquence de la chair, qui fait appel aux curiosités les plus chirurgicales, qui groupe les pestiférés pour nous en faire admirer les marbrures, qui s'inspire directement du choléra, son maître, et qui fait jaillir le pus de la conscience' (I, 673). (*L'Education sentimentale*, which, in any case, could not be remotely described in such terms, had yet to appear.) It would take almost another decade before the new 'school' would emerge, before Flaubert's novel would find its imitators, before the novels of the Goncourt brothers would meet with approval, before a naturalist text, Zola's *L'Assommoir*, would have a major impact on critical opinion and reach a vast reading public. By then, the models had long been in place, three founding texts which belong to that category of works 'which break through the familiar horizon of literary expectations so completely that an audience can only gradually develop for them'.[43]

What then are the main characteristic features of the naturalist novel that we might deduce from a study of these three texts, features which would be taken up, developed and amplified by succeeding writers? Firstly, there will appear a scientific or sociological theme, posited and developed as the guiding principle of the novel, turning on a preoccupation with neurotic, pathological states or on the unmasking of the seamy side of life, establishing an intentionality which is opposed to the elaboration of a moral law, the basis of the bourgeois novel. Then, running counter to this utilitarian function, the naturalist novel will admit a more poetic, decorative kind of discourse, which aestheticises the often sordid and banal reality that is being represented. Indeed, as we shall later see, it is to a considerable degree the tension between, on the one hand, the imperious causality and directionality of the scientific thesis or the tragic model and, on the other hand, the disruptiveness and fragmentation of the descriptive set pieces that will give the naturalist novel its characteristic dynamics.

The plot, it is already clear, will be invariably dysphoric, deriving its action, in many cases, from the trivia of the popular press, relating a crime, a scandal, an adulterous affair, a fraud, but manifesting itself as the reversal or parody of a 'romanesque' or heroic action, subjecting man – or, more frequently, woman – to some ironic or degrading fate, displaying the emptiness of human existence, disclosing the veiled depravities of bourgeois life. In this respect, *L'Assommoir, Une Vie* and *En ménage* could serve as programmatic titles for the genre. The action will take place within the detailed, usually thoroughly documented representation of a particular milieu: a district of a large city, a country village, a maritime community, with its particular language and customs and with a topographical preciseness that is not usually matched by the vagueness with which the events of the narrative are dated. Finally, there is an often ferocious and uncompromising element of satire of bourgeois manners, a feature which (re)introduces morality into the novel, indirectly, by the back door or the servants' entrance, for it will often be the servants' point of view that will focus the satire of their masters. Such will be the diversity of the naturalist genre, as these early models have shown, that it will embrace a considerable range of fictional types, being at once, in varying combinations from text to text, the realistic novel of the (mis)fortunes of a central character, the thesis novel with a social or scientific purpose, (parodic) romance, the philosophical tale of man's subjection to an ironic fate.

Yet, despite this diversity, as I hope to show in the chapters that follow, there are recurrent features, procedures and themes. We shall see certain character types reappear: the martyred women, the hysterical mistresses and servants, the 'bourgeois épanouis' with their hidden vices, the dejected intellectuals, the 'fruits secs', who embody the main themes – altogether a motley crew of characters, men of inaction and women of lost virtue who form an obvious contrast to the heroes and heroines of romance and of sentimental fiction – but also other categories of characters, like the professional types (doctors, scientists, writers, artists) who observe, interpret, inform and even comment upon the main action and fulfil a metadiegetic function. Already, on the basis of the works that we have seen, we can propose a rudimentary taxonomy of plots and define two fundamental types of naturalist novel. There is firstly a Goncourtian type, to which Zola's works also sometimes adhere, that takes up the tragic model of the fall, presenting it as a process of deterioration, prolonged in time and deriving its causality from particular determining factors (hereditary taints, neurotic dispositions, adverse social conditions) rather than from transcendent forces, but a process which has its identifiable phases (hope, excess, struggle, degradation) and often its characteristic epiphany, as the wretched victims, like Germinie Lacerteux or Thérèse Raquin, come to some understanding of the socio-biological fate that is destroying them. Secondly, we can detect the outlines of a more Flaubertian type of novel, in which the determining factor is more generalised, a fundamental inadequacy in the human condition which traps the individual in the inextricable dilemmas, frustrations and disillusionment of daily existence. The process of disillusionment becomes the only dynamic element in these works, which seem plotless like *L'Education sentimentale*, following the repetitive course of biological needs and constant deceptions in which life is frittered away before its inevitable extinction. The first of these two types is more clinical, more objective; the second tends to be veiled autobiography. The first is more dynamic, the second static and repetitive. The first produces plots of submission, the second plots of resignation; the former go steadily downhill, the latter steadily nowhere. The coexistence of these two models in the naturalist canon explains the fact that Zola, in his critical writings, can both exalt the logic of the naturalist plot and praise Flaubert for the inconsequentiality and the discontinuities of the action of his exemplary text. My next two chapters will deal in turn with these two basic types.

4

THE TRAGIC MODEL

The use of one of the most bandied about and abused of terms, both in literary criticism and everyday life, to apply to a group of (mainly) late nineteenth-century (mainly) fictional texts clearly requires preliminary justification. As George Moore's article on *L'Education sentimentale* suggests, contemporary writers and critics were by no means loath to employ the term and to propose that the naturalist novel represented a new form of the tragic genre. The English 'naturalists' appear to have been particularly inclined to apply the term, even to the most mundane of misfortunes. In *A Drama in Muslin*, for example, George Moore's narrator even claims that, 'seen from afar, all things are of equal worth; and the nearest things, when viewed with the eyes of God, are raised to those heights of tragic awe which conventionality would limit to the death of kings or patriots'.[1] Arnold Bennett had a particular fondness for the term, writing, for instance, in *The Old Wives' Tale* (1908), of the 'tragedy of Sophia's life' and of the 'ineffable tragedy' of her sister's fate, even writing in the same novel that the 'clumsiness of children is sometimes tragic' or that Sophia's husband has nothing to show after four years of marriage but 'an enfeebled digestion and a tragic figure of a wife'. One suspects that, in such cases, the unfortunate term is being more ill-used than the unhappy characters. Hardy, as is well known, had a loftier view of tragedy, believed that the tragic spirit was very much in tune with modern times and sought to depict the desperate 'collision between the individual and the general' in the lives of humble folk. 'What Hardy describes', notes Anthony Winner, pointing to the same kind of incongruity that we have already met in *Germinie Lacerteux*, 'is something like the experience of a minor member of the chorus or of a walk-on player who must suddenly act the entire tragedy by himself.'[2] Yet the serious claim has been made that Hardy was the first great tragedian in the novel form and his later, more naturalistic fiction has been a point of reference on this issue.

The case against modern tragedy is a powerful one and it usually invokes the authority of George Steiner's famous study. According to *The Death of Tragedy*, the tragic vision is indelibly associated with an aristocratic society, for only regal and heroic figures can undergo a tragic fall. Modern ideologies, asserting the perfectibility of man and the possibility of social progress, attributing misfortunes to society's corruption, humanising or dispensing with the agents of divine retribution, 'relativise' guilt and destiny and are thereby incapable of generating a truly tragic vision: 'Tragedy speaks not of secular dilemmas which may be resolved by rational innovation, but of the unaltering bias toward inhumanity and destruction in the drift of the world.'[3] Thus Yves Chevrel, who addresses himself directly to the problem of naturalist tragedy in a whole chapter of his book, *Le Naturalisme*, refers back to Steiner's objections and raises some telling points of his own. Naturalism, he claims, rejects certain fundamental characteristics of tragedy: myth and destiny. In the naturalist scheme of things, 'l'homme se définit à partir de multiples composantes identifiables: le milieu, le métier, l'hérédité, ... et non pas à partir d'une relation mystérieuse à un destin incompréhensible et incommunicable'.[4] Nevertheless, in a discussion centring on the naturalist theatre of Strindberg, Hauptmann, Ibsen and Chekhov, the same critic is more inclined to entertain the notion of naturalist tragedy, noting, for instance, that naturalist theatre, like tragedy, manipulates tension and that Ibsen's *A Doll's House* evokes a tragic atmosphere in its denouement. 'Le naturalisme', he writes, 'rejette incontestablement les anciens modes de manifestation du tragique: les mythes, la transcendance, mais dans la mesure où le tragique est fondamentalement interrogation sur la destinée humaine, le naturalisme non seulement maintient, mais encore accentue cette interrogation.'[5] For him, in reasserting, like the naturalist theoreticians, the ageneric nature of naturalist literature, the tragic, inevitably a generic concept, takes on the most elusive of forms: 'Le tragique n'est plus limité à un genre, ou à une catégorie d'êtres: il est partout – et nulle part.' Or it becomes diffused, as George Moore argued above, into the fabric of everyday life in Chevrel's own interrogative conclusion: 'La mort de la tragédie, mort d'une certaine littérature, annonce-t-elle, ou appelle-t-elle, le retour d'un certain tragique, celui de la vie, celui de tous les jours?'[6]

One problem with this issue is the temptation to focus on the theories and intentions of the naturalist writers rather than on their actual practices, and to deal in metaphysical concepts rather than in concrete literary structures. Though the naturalists claimed to be representing life in all its diversity, their works, as we need to emphasise again, are patterned and coded like those of other literary genres. Though they belonged to an age of scientific progress and social reform, they invariably still wrote fables of abject misfortune and suffering about the bitter ironies of life. But the main problem is twofold: the degree to which the critic remains faithful to a particularly prestigious model of the genre belonging to the past or can accept the mutability of generic development; the degree to which the texts themselves conform to constant features of the genre, despite the tendency of modern literature to range freely over the boundaries of generic distinctions.

The pattern with which we are concerned in this chapter conforms to what one might reasonably accept as the transhistorical constants of the genre: an action centred upon the fall into misfortune of a somewhat typical protagonist whose nobility of character, if not of rank, engages the reader's sympathy, a sympathy which becomes pity, fear or a sense of outrage when the fall takes place; the cause of the misfortune must clearly be some insurmountable power, of more general import than mere accident, chance or caprice, and the state into which the character falls must be irremediable, whether it be the irrational, the immoral, the uncontrollable, the incomprehensible, or even the unsayable, a state which threatens the very basis of the human order. Like Aristotle's prescriptions, this is a mixed set of require-ments, mainly thematic and pragmatic, but, unlike its prestigious precedent, it relegates structural and formal features to a secondary status, requiring no more than a serried plot with its peripeteia through which the intended effect can be fulfilled. On this point, Gérard Genette makes a fundamental distinction:

En fait, bien sûr, il y a ici deux réalités distinctes: l'une à la fois modale et thématique, que posent les premières pages de la *Poétique*, et qui est le drame noble, ou sérieux, en opposition au récit noble (l'épopée) et au drame bas, ou gai (la comédie); cette réalité générique, qui englobe aussi bien *les Perses* qu'*Oedipe roi*, est alors traditionnellement baptisée *tragédie*, et Aristote ne songe évidemment pas à contester cette dénomination. L'autre est purement thématique, et d'ordre plutôt anthropologique que poétique: c'est le *tragique*, c'est-à-dire le sentiment de l'ironie du destin, ou de la cruauté des dieux.[7]

Clearly, certain texts would fulfil the requirements for both 'tragedy' and the 'tragic' according to Genette's definitions, whereas others would be called 'tragedies' without conforming to the thematic requirements. Then there are texts, like much of the naturalist fiction with which we are concerned, that obviously cannot be called 'tragedies', but which fit thematically within the tragic mode. With the final reservation that the specification *tragic* does not provide a total definition of the thematics of naturalist literature, since, as I have already argued, its generic composition is complex, this whole discussion may be summarised by reference to Genette's distinctions. Just as 'noble drama' combines with the thematic specification 'the tragic' to form 'tragedy', so too does naturalist fiction overlap with 'the tragic', without, of course, giving rise to a fresh birth of 'tragedy'.

By claiming, therefore, that naturalist literature, at least in one of its major directions, conforms thematically to the tragic model, I am not merely commandeering a prestigious literary term to apply to a set of realistic works which tend to tell of characters' undistinguished misfortunes. At a more fundamental level, as Northrop Frye argues, the sense of the tragic derives from 'an epiphany of law, of that which is and must be'. It is significant that, as Frye argues further, 'the two great developments of tragic drama, in fifth-century Athens and in seventeenth-century Europe, were contemporary with the rise of Ionian and of Renaissance science'.[8] Though the mythology of ancient tragedy with its *ananke* and *nemesis* was as obsolete as its noble protagonists, the new scientific age had its own inexorable laws to reveal, laws which threatened the very essence of the human condition, and naturalist writers explored their tragic potentialities. Thus ancient patterns, of necessity transformed within their new cultural context, do nevertheless recur.

To deal with this topic, one might consider it more appropriate to refer, as Yves Chevrel tends to do, to a corpus of naturalist plays rather than to naturalist fiction, to works like Strindberg's *Miss Julie* (1888), which would seem to be an ideal case in point, since it was written, according to the author, with both Zola's ideas in mind ('according to the experimental formula') and the Goncourt case history as a model.[9] The setting is characteristically naturalist, a kitchen, down into which sinks an aristocratic young lady in a brief affair with her father's valet, on a midsummer's night propitious for such orgiastic social levelling. But Strindberg's heroine is, so it seems, the victim of the complete catalogue of naturalist forces: Darwinian struggle, the hereditary burden of her mother's mental illness and irregular behaviour (arson and adultery), the environmental pressures of an unusual upbringing, her 'monthly indisposition', a somewhat perverse character, and, above all, the irresistible promptings of sexual desire which temporarily overcomes her hate of men ('when the weakness comes') and drives her to commit the indiscretion which will lead, we are to understand, to her suicide. As if all that motivation were not enough, the author describes her in his preface as a modern character type, who represents 'a retrogressive step in evolution, an inferior species who cannot endure' and, what is more, a tragic character:

The type is tragic, revealing the drama of a desperate struggle against Nature, tragic as the romantic heritage now being dissipated by naturalism, which has a contrary aim: happiness, and happiness belongs only to the strong and skillful species.

But Miss Julie is also: a relic of the old warrior nobility now giving way to a new nobility of nerve and intellect, a victim of her own flawed constitution, a victim of the discord caused in a family by a mother's 'crime', a victim of the delusions and conditions of her age — and together these are the equivalent of the concept of Destiny, or Universal Law, of antiquity.[10]

Equivalent structures and themes could be illustrated in less illustrious terms and works, in the naturalist short story, for example, on a much more trivial plane. We could take, as perhaps an extreme instance, one of the *Trente romans* (1895) by Alexis, a nine-page story called 'Le Lys dans les Modes'. Unlike Zola's Nana in similar circumstances, the heroine, a modest 'modiste', has resisted all the corrupting influences of her environment, determined not to follow the example of her drunken father and his mistress, whose antics she can hear through the thin partition in their sixth-floor rooms in (of course) the rue de la Goutte-d'Or. Solange is saving herself for a fine marriage, hubristically disdains a fine young cobbler's proposal, then *falls* in with a bohemian fellow named Camille Louvin, takes up his dissolute existence, then contracts a rare type of anaemia, which, curiously, though quite logically in the naturalist scheme of physical degeneration, leaves her constantly sweating and malodorous: 'Une mortelle odeur émanait sans cesse d'elle, traversait ses vêtements, empoisonnait autour d'elle, corrompait l'atmosphère, et, se glissant sous les portes, traversant les murs, empuantait les pièces voisines.'[11] As one can imagine, this ailment has a devastating effect on her social life. Camille abandons her. Starving, she wanders the streets in desperation until she is run over by a carriage, clutching the price of a loaf of bread. This unprepossessing story clearly does not deserve to be better known, but it does reveal, in stark relief, the typically naturalist 'tragic' scheme in its fundamental phases of development.

Much the same could be said, to pass on to an even narrower focus, of numerous passages within naturalist works, embryonic naturalist novels within naturalist novels, like the following extract from Bonnetain's *Charlot s'amuse* (1883), in which the wretched hero of the novel picks up an equally wretched creature near the Gare du Nord:

Charlot avait heureusement quelque argent, il commanda deux bocks, et alors la malheureuse lui dit son histoire. Histoire banale, vulgaire, mais qui intéressa comme un roman le malheureux pour qui Paris et ses mystères étaient encore un inconnu insondé. Elle s'appelait Fanny Méjean, et était fille de braves gens. Son père était chauffeur à la raffinerie Lebaudy, à la Villette, sa mère matelassière dans le même quartier. A seize ans, elle avait été séduite. De fait, elle n'accusait pas trop son premier amant. Elle s'était quasiment offerte. Elle aimait l'homme. C'était dans son sang, et les torgnoles que lui avait administrées son père n'avaient pu la guérir de sa passion. Elle avait fui la maison paternelle et roulé un peu partout, descendant de collage en collage jusqu'à une misère noire qui l'avait fait rouler, peu à peu, dans la boue. Ce n'était cependant pas entièrement sa faute. Si son premier homme avait été honnête, elle serait encore avec lui, mais il l'avait dépravée à plaisir, et devenu agent des mœurs, l'avait fait mettre en carte pour vivre à ses dépens, sans souci.

Elle racontait cela, tranquillement, d'une voix traînarde, avec des mots crus, des détails cyniques, comme ne comprenant pas l'horreur de ce qu'elle disait.[12]

In naturalist literature, such 'histoires banales, vulgaires' proliferate and generate narratives within narratives of varying length and detail, all of which, despite their evident differences, are variations on a single pattern of the fall into misfortune, each case being both realistic, particular, therefore ungeneric, and naturalistic, typical, therefore generic. Short stories, like the *Trente romans* of Alexis, tend to be novels in miniature. Plays, like *Miss Julie*, may concentrate on a crucial stage of a decline, but, if only because of the determining factors of the decline in the character's past that has to be *narrated*, they tend to be potential novels made for the stage or, as was frequently the case, novels adapted for the stage. The natural medium of naturalist literature remains the novel, for it requires the full span of the novel form to present the workings of the underlying, undermining processes with which the genre deals, to show their essential development in time, time which, for the hapless victims of the tragedies of everyday existence in this chapter (and for the hopeless brooders in the next), is itself the fatal agent of their undoing.

It will not have escaped notice that in the three examples that I have just given it is women that fall. 'And now you think I'm contemptible', screams Miss Julie to Jean, after the crucial and paradigmatic incident of the play. 'I'm falling, I'm falling!'[13] The motif of the 'falling' woman (for the text usually describes the process) is central to naturalist thematics, yet, as we have already had occasion to note in a more general way, it is almost entirely occulted in the aesthetics of the writers. As Henri Mitterand writes of Zola in this regard:

La censure que Zola fait peser sur son discours théorique (pas un mot sur l'*eros*, sauf à admettre que l'exigence affirmée d'"analyse exacte' implique que toutes les questions soient posées) disparaît du cycle romanesque, qui, au prix de quelques précautions de composition ou de langage, s'obstinera, du début à la fin, à faire entendre à des contemporains encore mal préparés à le recevoir le langage silencieux des fatalités charnelles.[14]

There is such a large corpus of naturalist literature that turns on the workings of such 'fatalities of the flesh' and conveys disaster through the woman's body with such an obsessive insistence that we are clearly dealing with a myth that is as imperious as any of the myths that fashioned ancient texts, the myth of catastrophic female sexuality. It was a myth fuelled by contemporary physiologists, doctors, psychiatrists, whose learned writings on heredity, hysteria and menstruation authenticated and sometimes directly inspired the literary dramas.[15] The fault was in the body, the woman's body, which was associated with the social body and the body politic in a society whose preapprehensions confined the woman to the role of gauge and guardian of its order, for her inviolability was to be preserved all the more vigilantly as its destructive potentiality became scientifically demonstrable. In a study of the theories of the Italian criminologist, Cesare Lombroso, author of the influential *L'Uomo deliquente* (1876) and the less famous *La Donna deliquente, la prostituta e la donna normale* (1893), Hilde Olrik demonstrates the prevalence and sometimes absurd manifestations of such prejudices: woman is closer to nature than man ('la femme est typique, l'homme est original'), more atavistic, endowed with a latent perversity which must be repressed by the holy trinity of feminine virtues, maternity—modesty—frigidity; prostitution is the unfettered manifestation of this inner perversity (tatooed ladies being particularly vicious!) and menstruation its stigma ('[pendant la menstruation] la femme est plus femme que d'ordinaire'); hysteria is 'spécialement la maladie de la femme', rooted as it is in her sexual organs. Lombroso's 'scientific' study of the fundamental erotico-hysterical perversity of woman leads him to a revealingly apocalyptic vision of the ravages of this impure blood, a 'vision catastrophique d'une masse souterraine de prostituées hystériques (= de femmes comme nous en voyons autour de nous), masse larvée, grouillante, encore invisible, mais explosive et prête à surgir, à envahir le monde'.[16]

Such an overcharged and in itself hysterical vision of the curse of female sexuality is conveyed in a far more restrained manner in the science of the age and, apparently, in its naturalist literature. A common explanation for the prevalence of the theme points to the fact that the naturalist writers (and the scientists, of course) were male and, in some cases, did not disguise their misogyny. In this (want of) respect, as in many others, the Goncourt brothers set the tone. Their *Journal* is replete with observations on women's fundamental inferiority, vanity, impressionability, sentimental religiosity. Their novels unequivocally affirm the theme that woman is closer to physical nature than man, 'beaucoup plus rivée à la matière que l'homme' (February 1854), and a constant threat to the artist, whose genius, quite naturally, is male. But generally, Zola's Nana notwithstanding, naturalist heroines are more victimised than victimising, for they are shown to bear the burden of nature's fundamental tendency to corrupt through the flesh.

There is something totally mysterious – to illustrate these various points with a brief look at the most significant work by Paul Alexis – in the illness of the heroine of *Madame Meuriot* (1891), a novel with an unmistakable Flaubertian title and subtitle (*Mœurs parisiennes*) and another hypertext of *Madame Bovary*, reworked in the naturalist, physiological mode. Juliette, whose Romeo is called (not altogether surprisingly) Gustave, was once 'active, volontaire, pratique, pondérée', but has become 'molle, sans énergie, lunatique, bizarre'.[17] Her fatal illness is characterised by swelling flesh and by an invasion of the mind by the lower parts of the body: 'Des régions basses de l'être, le désagrégement avait monté, altérant la sensibilité, atteignant les facultés affectives, viciant la volonté, creusant enfin ce fossé de désespoir et d'égoïsme derrière lequel se retirent les moribonds, comme s'ils craignaient d'être dérangés pendant le travail de mourir.'[18] In a sense, the character dies of her female body. These fallen women, with their hereditary taints, their neurotic disposition, their irrepressible sexuality, their physiological conditions, are victims, as it were, of their own flesh and blood. Middle class women, like Madame Meuriot, lapse into adultery; working class girls slip into promiscuity and prostitution; but they all lapse into an equivalent state of abandon, for they represent 'la chair molle', an expression and a condition which occur with extraordinary regularity in naturalist fiction.[19] The expression supplies the title of Paul Adam's novel on the life of a humble prostitute, a text which admirably illustrates a number of recurrent naturalist features.[20] There are scenes of life in a brothel, lesbian sex, treatments for venereal disease, orgies, beatings, soliciting in the streets, all leading to the inevitable decline and abjection of this once charming, sentimental girl, Lucie – called Nina in her professional capacity – who goes the way of all such soft flesh and ends like Zola's courtesan as a rotting, pox-ridden body, which the author, sparing the reader none of the details, describes: 'Et partout un pus suintait; elle sentait sur ses jambes dégouliner, en minces filets, une liqueur tiède et elle se vautrait dans des draps humides ... Le poignet avait perdu ses formes et présentait seulement une bouffissure rougeâtre, pâteuse, indécise de contours, sous laquelle un liquide pâle fluctuait. D'étroites fentes une liqueur livide sourdait, rubéfiée de fils sanglants.'[21] But, in its more general lineation, the novel is closer to *L'Assommoir* than to *Nana*, tracing the gradual moral and physical decline of the heroine in her sordid surroundings, with her poor woman's *hubris*, her pride, contributing to her downfall. As in *L'Assommoir*, and other texts like *Germinie Lacerteux*, the male characters are projections of the stages of the heroine's moral decline, leading to her lapse into complete indifference and to her desire to grasp desperately at the few pleasures that life can bring: the 'gourmandise' of a Gervaise Macquart and the frantic love-making, with its biting and scratching, of a Germinie Lacerteux: 'ses derniers scrupules fuyaient dans l'amollissement de cette vie commode'.[22] If the psycho-physiological core of the novel, the syndrome of neurosis, hysteria, religious fervour and violent eroticism, is more Goncourtian than Zolaesque, there is the same blurring of moral distinctions as in *L'Assommoir*, where the blame is shared between the heroine's weaknesses and her circumstances. But the last scenes of the novel derive from the common model, as the wretched woman wanders the streets in the bad weather of her degraded environment, in a 'torpeur abrutie', encountering in her despair nothing but the indifference of the world.

Thus a prevalent strain of the naturalist novel presents, often in agonising length and detail, the *spectacle* of the agony of the fallen woman, her decline, humiliations, her loss of self and identity after the catastrophic loss of her virginity or her honour. The originality of these novels lies in the treatment of the theme rather than in the theme itself, which is to be found *with an opposite effect*, within a propitiatory scheme, in much of the popular and bourgeois literature of the time.[23] In an age, then, when the 'new woman' was emerging, naturalist writers like Capuana in *Giacinta*, Verga in *Nedda*, Emilia Pardo Bazán in *La Tribuna*, Eça de Queirós in *O primo Bazilio*, to give some Latin examples, condemned her to an old and common dilemma. Whether it is the antique fetishism of chastity or a more modern fear of hereditary syphilis or a patriarchal appropriation of the woman's body that promoted the theme,[24] in the literary and symbolic order the heroine's fall marks the point of contact with the fatal forces of physiology, her irreversible commitment to the biological state that will bring her down. These heroines are representative figures in the sense that they are drawn from everyday life, but also in the sense that they represent their species. They may have exceptional beauty like Paul Adam's Lucie–Nina or Zola's Nana, a strong sense of moral integrity like the latter's mother, Gervaise Macquart, exceptional vitality like Liza of Lambeth in Somerset Maugham's naturalist novel of the same name, but these qualities, like the nobility of tragic kings and queens, only make their common(ers') lot more pathetic. They are drawn from life, but marked out for a literary fate.

The fatal forces which bring about the character's degeneration are both internalised in his (or usually her) physical constitution (blood, nerves, sexual organs) and externalised as symptoms of generalisable physiological laws that the character displays. One of the most significant paradigms of naturalist fiction is that of the (male) doctor – or his substitute, the narrator himself – observing and analysing the (female) patient's physiological plight and its devastating social consequences. Whether or not he has, in fact, received some medical training, like Céard, Chekhov or Somerset Maugham, or merely resorts to some *ad hoc* documentation for the occasion, the naturalist writer adopts the probing look of the doctor, as Jean Borie imagines it to have been in the case of a famous French psychiatrist:

Quand, sur le seuil de son asile, le docteur Moreau de Tours voit venir à lui le fou présenté par ses proches, il ne voit pas un malade entouré de gens sains, frappés dans leurs affections, torturés de douleur et de bonnes intentions. Non, il voit une tare, héréditaire certainement, dont la manifestation, unique apparemment pour l'instant, déteint déjà sur les comparses où son œil exercé la lit en filigrane, et scelle à jamais le destin de la famille entière: cette mère qui pleure trop et gesticule avec extravagance est hystérique sans doute, ce frère sombre et renfermé travaillé par le suicide, ce père vague et tremblant investi par l'alcoolisme, guetté par la paralysie générale.[25]

Naturalist families are indeed unhappy families: Mr Booze, Mrs Hysteria, Miss Vice and Master Crime – or some combination thereof in the shuffle of what were yet to be called their genes. So the intradiegetic chief doctor in the asylum of *L'Assommoir*, with his 'regards minces et perçants comme des vrilles' – 'Tous les marchands de mort subite', Gervaise remarks, 'vous ont de ces regards-là' (III, 933) – observes the symptoms of Coupeau's *delirium tremens* and utters dire warnings to the wife: 'Un jour ou l'autre, vous mourrez ainsi' (III, 934). On the grander scale of Zola's whole *Rougon-Macquart*, another discerning doctor plays this part, extradiegetically le docteur Prosper Lucas, author of Zola's principal source, the imposing *Traité philosophique et physiologique de l'hérédité naturelle dans les états de santé et de maladie du système nerveux* (1847–50), intradiegetically le docteur Pascal Rougon, who keeps records on the fatal effects of hereditary factors on his own far from happy family.

In naturalist novels, whether they are viewed in scientific terms as a series of case histories or in a more literary manner as a corpus of humble and often sordid 'tragic' tales, heredity is the invisible, deific force which provides a pattern of necessity revealed, of law unfolded. Zola has often been criticised for the rudimentary nature of his medical science as if it were a personal shortcoming. But other naturalist writers resort to even less credible hereditary principles to provide convincing motivation for their fables. One of the crudest and most obvious examples would be Paul Bonnetain's story 'Fille à soldats',[26] which, as its title suggests and as its dedication (to Edmond de Goncourt) and epigraph (a quotation from *La Fille Elisa*) make clear, derives from the older writer's fictional study of the prostitute's life. Maria is a startlingly beautiful girl whose father drinks, of course, and whose mother was raped by no less than twenty-three Bavarians in 1870. But, like all the girls in her family, 'fatalement d'incorrigibles gouges, de la chair à soldats et à matelots', she takes after her aunt, who teaches her the tricks of the trade: 'assoiffée d'amour, elle écoutait parler son instinct et gronder le sang de sa race'. Her loss of virginity is described with relish: 'Maria, vautrée sur le gazon, l'encourageait de son lascif regard et se tordait déjà avec l'animalité d'un bestial et voluptueux spasme.' Thereafter she follows 'la fatale tradition de sa famille', becomes inevitably pregnant, has an inevitable daughter whom an inevitable doctor examines to declare that the family tradition will be maintained – though, in an ironic twist to the pattern, Maria falls in love with the doctor!

Heredity has in these works a marked femininity. Hence, the implicit law dictates, its perverse virulence. When two conflicting, feminine determinants come into play, dominance, so it seems, is exercised by the earlier, more atavistic phase, as in Germaine, Lemonnier's female in *Un Mâle*:

C'étaient de brusques rappels de conscience, pendant lesquels la vertu ferme de sa mère semblait lui revenir et mettre un temps d'arrêt dans ses faiblesses. Mais un baiser du gars refoulait ses protestations au fond de sa chair lâche. Alors cet autre sang, celui de son aïeule, reprenait le dessus, et sa fierté s'en allait dans des besoins d'amour.[27]

The flesh is always weak before the all-powerful pulsations of the blood, for the drama of the lives of these characters is first played out in their veins. The immense advantage of presenting in this way what Zola calls in his preliminary notes to the *Rougon-Macquart* series 'luttes intestines produites par l'action fatale de l'hérédité', is that these determining forces remain mysterious and at the same time connote authenticity. Hereditary explanations can therefore present themselves as science and still function as myth. Within the authenticating framework of a modern, scientific discursive system of explanation, in the amphitheatres and the scripts of the doctors of physiology, primeval dramas of evil, guilt, crime, sex and violence find a new stage. As Françoise Gaillard writes of *Les Rougon-Macquart*:

Le silence de Zola, comme celui d'ailleurs des savants, sur la cause originelle de la tare/châtiment, l'assimile à une de ces grandes malédictions qui, dans les légendes de l'antiquité, frappent des familles entières. Il y a toujours dans ces récits un coupable par qui le mal arrive et se propage, comme il y a toujours dans l'histoire naturelle de l'hérédité un maudit par qui, et à cause de qui, la différence dont les généticiens observent les résultats concrets a fait irruption au sein de l'espèce théoriquement indifférenciée et utopiquement composée de frères égaux …

Associée à l'idée biblique de *Faute originelle*, l'hérédité apparaît comme une figure de l'expiation. Loin d'être absurdement inique, elle est la manifestation d'une justice immanente. Pour tout dire, l'hérédité c'est la nouvelle déesse du châtiment, la version positiviste des Euménides.[28]

Thus, in a large body of naturalist texts, a corps of ill-fated protagonists are elected to affliction. Their 'maladies' are but different forms of the same 'Mal'. The convulsions of *delirium tremens*, the throes of hysteria, the spasms of sexuality, the paroxysms of madness are the symptoms of their possession. A privileged site, therefore, for the naturalist novel is the hospital or the asylum into which, at some stage or other, the reader is usually admitted. Jules Claretie goes one stage further and situates a whole novel in such a place. In the preface to *Les Amours d'un interne*,[29] the author claims that his novel, 'un livre de vérité, de vérité âpre, aussi peu voilée que dans un mémoire scientifique', will study 'une des formes les plus étranges de la grande maladie du siècle'. With these sweeping and characteristic assumptions that the truth is contained in scientific studies, that the novel can present the same truths and, indeed, that his century is sick, he confidently asserts: 'L'hystérie est un peu partout à l'heure où nous sommes' and significantly adds: 'Il appartient donc au romancier d'étudier, après les savants, ces manifestations *inquiétantes, attirantes aussi*, et ces cas bizarres' [my emphasis]. The setting is, more precisely, the woman's hospital, la Salpêtrière, the area reserved for nervous illnesses, epilepsy and hysteria, which was under Charcot's supervision and which Claretie, in true naturalist fashion, had dutifully visited to witness the treatment. The hero of the novel writes to his father that 'la Salpêtrière, c'est comme l'embouchure d'un égoût où viennent se dégorger toutes les misères parisiennes, les plus sinistres des misères: les misères féminines'. To this, as we have already seen, obsessively recurrent and fascinating combination of themes (woman–hysteria–misfortune) is inevitably added the usual explanation: heredity. 'Les parents nerveux, le père alcoolique, et voilà une malheureuse créature vouée à l'hystérie.' The intern describes in detail the typical symptoms, their totally predictable, automatic development, 'qui, toujours, régulièrement, comme mécaniquement, se reproduisent avec les mêmes phénomènes'.[30] There are distressing descriptions in the novel of the effects of this infernal machinery of neurosis: the wild delirium, the shrieks from the insane, 'stridents comme des sifflets de machine', the violence of the horde of mad women tearing one another apart, 'des ongles plongeant dans les orbites, des bras tiraillant les membres, les morsures s'enfonçant, bestiales, en pleine chair', the religious fanatic with her ecstatic vision and terrible nightmares. Hysteria is thus both reassuring in its predictability but fascinatingly extravagant in its manifestations, the perfect female syndrome. There is the unusual case of a male hysteric, whom the disease, however, 'normalises' in its inevitable development by feminising the boy ('Il devenait fille – non pas au physique mais au moral – avec les goûts, les manières, les mines coquettes des fillettes'), much to his father's relief: 'parbleu! mais il savait bien que les femmes seules sont hystériques'![31] The novel's plot concerns the unhappy love story of Jeanne Barral, whose mother is a case of 'hystéro-épilepsie' and who therefore shrinks from a marriage proposal:

Elle entendait, comme un écho, des paroles tragiques du docteur Cadilhat:
– Les fous engendrent les fous!
– *Hérédité*!

Under the shadow of the dreaded curse that awaits her – 'Prédisposition – prédestination – hérédité! ... Tous ces mots tragiques grondaient dans le cerveau de Jeanne comme ces lointains orages qui roulent longuement, avec des répercussions de lointains tonnerres'[32] – she finds redemption in charity and escapes from our genre and its inflexible laws.

The same symptomatology – to complete the picture – applies

in the numerous works dealing with female religiosity, for not only has psychology become, as Zola frequently asserted, a branch of physiology; so too has religious devotion. The Goncourt brothers exploited this vein (*Madame Gervaisais*), as did Zola (*La Conquête de Plassans*), followed closely, as ever, by Alexis, who, in his story 'La Religion' (*Trente romans*), for example, crudely states the law: 'Quand la femme se voit à jamais privée de l'amour, paraît-il, il lui faut un exutoire. La religion succède à l'amour: la même chose peut-être au fond, mais renversée.' Alphonse Daudet's *L'Evangéliste* (1883) is a better known and more subtle treatment of the theme, significantly described by the author as his '*observation* de névrose' and dedicated 'A l'Eloquent et savant professeur J.-M. Charcot, Médecin de la Salpêtrière'. But the most revealingly extreme, if not canonical, text would undoubtedly be Camille Lemonnier's *L'Hystérique*. In this extraordinary novel, Sœur Humilité of the Sainte-Beggue community particularly impresses the tyrannical abbé Orlea, whose speciality is mortifications. Presumably by 'virtue' of Alexis's law, the priest's assiduousness, at least with Sœur Humilité, has a contrary effect: 'elle goûtait d'infinies mollesses, dans lesquelles elle crut que son corps allait se dissoudre et qui, coulant jusqu'en ses moelles, y chatouillaient délicieusement l'être, comme en un spasme voluptueux'.[33] The priest, to complicate matters, is subject to 'ferments humains qu'une hérédité complexe lui avait mis aux veines', his virility stirs 'comme une bête emprisonnée' and there is a double 'fall' from virginity and grace, which, fortunately for the shameful priest, the young sister takes to be a religious experience: 'il lui avait paru que Jésus était entré en elle sous la forme d'une grande lumière'![34] There follow further scenes of erotic, perverse practices, presented in similar religious terms, then a pregnancy, a lurid description of an aborted foetus – all of which the reader will, no doubt, be grateful to have been spared – until Sœur Humilité suffers the final naturalist humiliations of total degradation, animalisation, imbecility: 'Roulée aux iniquités honteuses, après avoir égalé en ferveur les pâles martyres de la légende catholique, elle croupissait à présent sur son fumier de misère, misérable charogne vivante qui ne se doutait pas de ses pourritures et qui, physiquement non moins que spirituellement, se décomposait chaque jour un peu plus.'[35]

The seriality of demonstrations of this kind and the exposure of the reader to ever more shocking details are, as we shall see in a later chapter, an essential part of the strategies of the individual naturalist text and of the movement itself. Consequently, the most excessive works become the best illustrations of the themes and patterns with which we are concerned. This is certainly true of one particular novel, Paul Bonnetain's *Charlot s'amuse*, a representative work for which Henry Céard – appropriately so, since he is the author of the equivalent text, *Une Belle Journée,* discussed in our next chapter – wrote a preface in defence of this much-scorned novel, presenting it as a serious scientific study, as moral as a treatise by Moreau de Tours.[36] Its most scandalous aspect is its hero's compulsive masturbation, a subject which, so it seems, earned the author the nickname Bonnemain. But its more serious and more naturalist theme is hereditary madness, one which was more than a literary interest of the author, since he is said to have written the novel at the bedside of his mother, a woman who went mad and committed suicide in a mental hospital. The author made repeated protestations about the seriousness of his intentions, particularly at his trial for obscenity, and the text's epigraph is a substantial extract from Zola's own statements of scientific purpose in his preface to *Thérèse Raquin.* Charlot is interestingly not only the perfect naturalist hero, but also an imperfect commentator on his own case history, a kind of amateur naturalist who accuses fate and weakly submits to his hereditary condition. He is thus both the victim of the classic scenario of the naturalist character and a response to its invariable recurrence:

Pour excuser sa déchéance, il se rappelait l'alcoolisme de son père et de son grand-père, l'hystérie de sa mère et l'épileptique folie de la mère de celle-ci. Il ne lui serait jamais venu à l'idée de supposer qu'il tenait d'eux seulement des prédispositions morbides surmontables par le vouloir et sans médication. Cela aurait entamé son système de défense, et il préférait pouvoir pleurer sur lui-même que d'avoir à se mépriser, – à se vaincre ... Ses terrifiantes lectures aidant, peut-être lui aussi se sentait-il perdu. (pp. 162–3)

In more senses than one, the novel could be called *Charlot s'abuse*, for we see that the other serious dimension to the text is its criticism of the very fatalism which characterises the naturalist novel, of the pseudo-scientific explanations which establish the literary pattern of inevitable degeneration. Bonnetain is both employing and indicating the limits of naturalist physiology. Therefore this novel, which was, and is, usually dismissed as a sensationalistic exploitation of naturalist themes, deserves some serious consideration.

Not that it is lacking in some of naturalism's most lurid special effects. It opens and closes with hyper-naturalist fatalities: Charlot's father drowns in a sewer; Charlot himself ends his days and, he hopes, his polluted lineage by drowning himself and his child, the product of his liaison with another heredity-burdened wretch whom we have already met, Fanny Méjean – but, as he goes down, he can see the child along with a dead dog or cat floating away: 'Et c'étaient l'enfant, surnageant, soutenu par ses langes, et la charogne roidie, qui se poursuivaient ainsi, dans une ronde incessante et monotone, sans pouvoir jamais s'atteindre' (p. 348). In the patent symbolism of these scenes, father and son clearly end up in their (naturalist) element, the fetid matter of disintegration, but the child, we must presume, will be rescued like a wretched naturalist Moses to perpetuate the fatal corruption.

With the father out of the way, in the early scenes, the focus turns to Charlot's mother, a woman of exemplary dissoluteness, who has a violent sexual encounter with one of the rescue party that brings her husband's body back home. She is a familiar case of 'chair molle' and religious hysteria, having lost her virginity to a priest, an event which prompted the necessary 'chemical' reaction: 'De l'épilepsie alcoolique de sa mère, elle gardait, d'ailleurs, une sensibilité nerveuse, une sensuelle lascivité et une religieuse exaltation qui, exaspérées par la rencontre du prêtre, la prédisposaient à l'hystérie' (p. 41). Prompted by a similar chain reaction, Charlot's masturbatory fervour is ignited by his mother's eroticism and his father's death: 'Dans une fatale hérédité, la folie épileptique dont était morte sa grand'mère semblait alors envahir son cerveau, tout d'un coup, comme si, latente jusque-là, elle éclatait en furieuse tempête, à cette heure, provoquée par les cruelles émotions sous lesquelles l'enfant succombait depuis deux jours, et qui, maintenant, débordaient' (p. 65). More interesting for our purposes than the character's particular complaint is the process of feminisation that it entails. At his religious boarding school he takes on feminine airs, 'd'étranges coquetteries d'une lascivité qui s'ignorait', 'tout un manège de fillette qui chatouillait' (p. 105). He has a grotesquely parodic love affair with one of the priests, with whom, fatally, like his mother, he loses his virginity, a decisive step in the direction of his decline which the narrator presents with the curious mixture of moral indignation, scientific jargon and bodeful expression that characterises his style at such moments:

Une demi-heure après, le crime irrémédiable était accompli; l'ignorantin avait fait un nouvel élève à qui les monstrueux mystères des pratiques unisexuelles seraient désormais familiers. A jamais, il était détraqué, le petit malheureux qui souriait maintenant, l'œil humide de plaisir. Fatale, la névrose héréditaire qui le prédisposait à la chute allait pouvoir éclater, le brisant pour la vie dans le dérèglement de son innervation génitale, et écouler dans un emportement effroyable les dispositions morbides transmises au pauvre être avec la vie. (pp. 102–3)

The rest of the novel presents with a demonstrative seriality the consequent manifestations of the character's intensifying 'folie génésiaque' and 'satyriasis': he has further homosexual affairs, dresses up as a woman, reads Octave Feuillet, visits brothels, turns to sadism and rape. One of his most innocent pleasures is to study the 'immondes pratiques' of the monkeys in the Jardin des Plantes, where, one day, he meets a certain docteur Jolly, who takes him to Charcot's lesson. The Master is lecturing, of course, on female hysteria. In what must qualify as one of the most emblematic scenes of naturalist literature, Charcot parades, with characteristic theatricality, a series of wretched women onto the stage of his amphitheatre, 'toutes présentant des cas différents, curieusement bizarres' (p. 292).[37] Now *Charcot s'amuse*, as, like a master naturalist, he *narrates* each life story, analyses the symptoms of each case, has the pitiful victims lift their skirts to show their trembling limbs. The last of the demonstrations is a particularly sad, but classic case, a woman who has been in the Salpêtrière for seven years, whose name is unknown:

Elle était un exemple des troubles morbides que transmet l'hérédité, son père étant mort du *delirium tremens*, et sa mère, qui était épileptique, s'étant volontairement noyé à l'hospice. Son cas était très curieux. Lorsqu'après la crise de la ménopause, elle s'était décidée à parler, on avait pu reconstituer sa vie. A dix-huit ans, elle était nymphomane et n'avait jamais pu se guérir. Avec l'âge, elle était devenue alcoolique, et l'hystérie avait remplacé la nymphomanie, pour faire place, à son tour, après la ménopause, à une paraplégie remarquable. (pp. 292–3)

Horrified, Charlot recognises his mother! In this epiphaneous scene he is thus faced with a mirror image of his own degenerate self, of her past that will be his future, of the biological fatality that is consuming him.

There is much that is absurdly hyperbolic in this novel, like the love scenes between Charlot and Fanny, two 'détraqués': he with his 'mal héréditaire', she with her 'utéromanie', in a marriage of two 'dissemblables névroses', locked in their convulsive, bestial, clinical embraces, lapsing into 'une sorte de folie postconnubiale entrecoupée d'accès semblables à des congestions épileptiformes' (pp. 307–8)! We are at the antipodes of Cythera, closer to Baudelaire's Cythère. Yet there is an engaging aspect to the novel in its sensitive depiction of the sufferings and loneliness of its erotomaniac hero, who, like other naturalist victims, comes to acquire a pathetic sense of doom: 'Le guignon ne l'abandonnerait donc jamais? ... C'était une fatalité. Il y avait quelqu'un dont la volonté s'opposait à ce qu'il sortît de ce

vice solitaire au bout duquel l'attendait la mort. Il était maudit!'
(p. 266).[38] But the novel is important as a stark instance of the
pattern of pathetic, naturalist tragedy with which we are concerned
in this chapter. It produces works that centre upon the misfortunes
of a single character (or, at times, of a family), in whom some fatal
physiological flaw contains the seeds of calamity. After an initial lapse
into some form of errant behaviour, usually sexual, a deceptive
period of prosperity, happiness or fulfilment follows, but, with the
inexorable force of the characters' physiological condition pitted
against them, the process of degradation sets in and in time, with the
complicity of unscrupulous characters ready to exploit them, often
after a phase of desperate indulgences in eating, drinking or sexual
excesses, our hero(in)es drift into madness, degeneracy or total
despair. Their decline has its marked phases, of hope, excess, struggle, degradation, and even, as we have seen, its epiphany, when the
victim is confronted with a ghastly image of his or her self-
degradation: Charlot before his mother, Renée Saccard (in Zola's *La
Curée*) before her mirror, Gervaise Macquart (in *L'Assommoir*)
before her grotesque reflection from the streetlights on the Paris
pavements. Like Charlot and Gervaise, the defeated character is left
to wander the dismal streets of the city, a wandering that epitomises
the ultimate loss of self, direction and purpose, or is left to live out
the final stages of degradation in some appropriate locale, the slum,
the brothel, the hospital, where the ultimate demotion occurs with
its dehumanisation and loss of spirit, usually leading to an insistently
physical, repulsive, lonely, anonymous death.

The type of naturalist novel which conforms to this pattern is
rigorously plotted, with devices of foreshadowing and recapitulation
that seal the character's fate in time. Space is just as rigorously
constrained, within the confined contexts that entrap the victims: like
Tess moving ever closer to the d'Urberville tombs, like Germinie
Lacerteux and Gervaise Macquart caught between the *abattoir* and
the hospital, like Charlot ending his days at the scene of his earliest
memories. Characteristically, as Gillian Beer notes, on the schemes
of Lyell, Bernard and Darwin on the one hand, and of Eliot, Hardy
and Zola on the other, deterministic organisations of plot 'emphasized
always the inevitable sacrifice of the individual'.[39] These are also
plots which not only take up essential features of the tragic scheme
within much degraded contexts, but also follow, and at the same time
invert, the initiatory scheme of an older romance tradition, tracing
the adventures of 'heroes' who, instead of achieving transcendence
and renewal in their contact with the sacred through their exploits,

become the exploited, undergo an ontological transformation in the direction of degradation, dragged down by a vile and desacralised reality. Uplifting trials and abnegation are replaced by orgies of indulgence; the process of purification becomes putrefaction; the symbols of transcendence, knowledge and power, symbols of gold and light, are replaced by irretrievable loss in the dark labyrinths of the fallen state, in the *materia prima* of putrescent matter and corrupting flesh, where the human spirit is eclipsed.

Compared to some of the texts that we have just seen, *L'Assommoir* seems to be a more temperate and less original work than when it is studied in isolation. Tragedy in Gervaise's laundry is no more uplifting than in Miss Julie's kitchen. But, like all great works, Zola's novel both conforms to and transcends generic conventions, even as it is in the process of establishing those same conventions. *L'Assommoir* fits neatly within the framework of the type of text that has been outlined in this chapter, but, at the same time, it draws upon the model to particular effect, exploits to the full its thematic, formal, technical and mythical potentialities, and may thus be interpreted as both a typical and exceptional example of the genre.

The plot of *L'Assommoir* follows the most rigorous of designs, punctuated by a series of 'falls': Coupeau's fall from the roof, the kiss of Gervaise and the drunken Coupeau in the laundry, the renewal of her relations with Lantier, her lapses into idleness and drunkenness, contained within a symmetrically regulated rising and falling action, with the famous birthday orgy providing the pivotal reversal scene as required by the traditional complex plot. *L'Assommoir* is also a useful example of the systematic way in which subsidiary characters tend to function in naturalist works dealing with the misfortunes of a central character. They fulfil either a reflective function, adumbrating, anticipating and illustrating some essential aspect of the protagonist's fate, or an 'actantial' function, serving as 'adjuvants' or 'opposants' (in Greimasian terminology) contributing to or arresting temporarily the hero(ine)'s decline. In the first category there is père Bru, a destitute housepainter (battling against dirt like the laundress Gervaise), who precedes her on the road to starvation and death in the sickly hovel of escalier B. Then there is Virginie Poisson, Gervaise's rival, who is clearly destined to follow her on the path of ruin as the next victim of Lantier's appetites.[40] In the second category there is Goujet, the ideal worker, platonic lover, abstainer, an Apollonian figure of order, progress and enlightenment, with his golden halo of blond hair and his purificatory mastery of the forge, set against his opposite number, Lantier, a dark and destructive

Dionysiac figure, Gervaise's first (therefore physiologically permanent and necessarily ruinous) lover, who is all indulgence and returns in the midst of the feast to sweep through the district and wreak his destruction. Thus, despite their variety and vividness, naturalist characters tend to be thoroughly functional and consistent in their behaviour, lacking the kind of complexity, unpredictability and gratuitous quaintness that certain critics require of believable fictional characters. Particularly in the type of text under scrutiny in this chapter, they are rigorously subservient to the plot.

But *L'Assommoir* has more than the external form, plot scheme and character profile of traditional tragedy in its fictional, naturalist manifestations. Gervaise is a Macquart, marked out for misfortune by her origins, by her name, one of a long line and a numerous company of 'assommées', for, as Oscar Wilde remarked, 'the scientific principle of heredity is Nemesis without her mask. It is the last of the Fates, and the most terrible.'[41] The character's fate is typically sealed at the stage of her conception, one night of 'assommage' when her drunken father beat her mother and sowed the seed of her misfortune, an event from which she derived her limp, the symbolic 'malheur de sa jambe', the stigma that she bears, the sign of her predestined calamity and of the corruption within her. She bravely resists her lot, attempting to rise against her debilitating weaknesses, against the hostility of her environment. If there is a certain *hubris* in her ambitions, there is an evident *hamartia* in the steps that she takes to realise them. Thus the main action of the novel occurs precisely in the interval which characterises tragedy according to Jean-Pierre Vernant, between human responsibility for evil and the inevitable order of things, between the logical outcome of character (or 'temperament' for the naturalists) and the manifestation of a noumenal power, between an *ethos* and a *daimôn*.[42] What is more, Gervaise is an evident scapegoat, admired, resented, scorned, then eventually expelled by her society. It has been noted that there is, in the famous birthday feast, something of a cannibalistic ritual in which Gervaise, in more senses than one, 'cooks her goose', with its 'peau fine et blanche, une peau de blonde'. It is evident also that, by virtue of her physical affliction, her links with the vegetative and her degraded tragic status, she is a lowly reincarnation of the 'limping hero', the figure of myth and tragedy whose history Peter Hays has traced from its mythical and ritual origins to the host of maimed and deformed characters in modern literature.[43] Gervaise is doubly ill-favoured, for she is not only of the fated Macquart line, but she is also of the race of ancient pariahs, a *pharmakos*, royally treated in the feast before a ritual death. In an unusual passage from the novel, which occurs at the lowest point in the character's misfortunes, wracked by hunger, she recalls the feasts of yore. The passage, curiously unrelated to any previous event in the novel, functions like the *mise en abyme*, as a microcosmic, generic reading of the heroine's fate, but also, like the soliloquy of Germinie Lacerteux, it serves to promote the heroine to a higher literary status. Gervaise remembers having been, in a single day (within 'one revolution of the sun', as it were), a queen, a parodic, carnivalesque queen, decked out in garlands like Kore, celebrated '*malgré sa jambe*', all the more tragically to fall:

Une fois surtout, par un froid de chien, un jeudi de la mi-carême, elle avait joliment nocé. Elle était bien gentille, blonde et fraîche, en ce temps-là. Son lavoir, rue Neuve, l'avait nommée reine, malgré sa jambe. Alors, on s'était baladé sur les boulevards, dans des chars ornés de verdure, au milieu du beau monde qui la reluquait joliment. Des messieurs mettaient leurs lorgnons comme pour une vraie reine. Puis, le soir, on avait fichu un balthazar à tout casser, et jusqu'au jour on avait joué des guibolles. Reine, oui, reine! avec une couronne et une écharpe, pendant vingt-quatre heures, deux fois le tour du cadran! Et, alourdie, dans les tortures de sa faim, elle regardait par terre, comme si elle eût cherché le ruisseau où elle avait laissé choir sa majesté tombée. (III, 917–18)

Indeed, as René Girard remarks, tragedy is 'la fête qui tourne mal'.[44]

We could go on tracking down this pattern, if not indefinitely, certainly insufferably, in the charnel houses of fiction, where many a critic of the past would gladly have dispatched any naturalist text. Or we could travel beyond France, to, say, the banks of the Thames with *Nell Horn de l'Armée du Salut* (1886) by J.-H. Rosny and watch the pure and zealous girl with a limp like Gervaise dragged down into prostitution. Or, in the same city, we could see how Liza Kemp in Somerset Maugham's *Liza of Lambeth* (1897) spurns her Goujet, Tom, and to her shame, misfortune and death (from a miscarriage), goes off with the unscrupulous Lantier figure, Jim Blakeston, a roguish married man. We could then move on to a tobacco factory in Galicia, with Emilia Pardo Bazán's *La Tribuna* (1883), the work of our only female naturalist writer (and an aristocratic Catholic as well), in which Amparo similarly spurns the faithful country boy, Chinto, only to be seduced by the wicked army captain, Baltasar Sobrado, ending her story, if not her days, in another obstetrical scene. Across the Atlantic we would come across *Maggie: A Girl of the Streets (A Story of New York)* (1893), by Stephen Crane, a work that has frequently been compared to *L'Assommoir* for its street scenes, tenement buildings, drunken violence, popular speech and equivalent plot, and in which William Dean Howells discerned 'that quality of fatal necessity which dominates Greek tragedy'.[45] In novels by Frank Norris, for a change, we could watch male protagonists fall: the upright Vandover (in *Vandover and the Brute*, 1914), lapsing into debauchery, drunkenness and gambling, a victim of *lycanthropy-mathesis*, a form of nervous disorder, until he ends up, like Gervaise, scrubbing the floors of the property he once owned; the dentist in *McTeague. A Story of San Francisco* (1899), who loses his practice, his money, his scruples and his reason; Hurstwood in *Sister Carrie* (1900), a prosperous businessman who falls on hard times and can barely afford the fifteen cents to rent a sordid little room in which to gas himself, brought down by 'certain poisons in the blood, called katastates'.

But I would much prefer to conclude this chapter – as we shall conclude this book – with a more significant juxtaposition of texts: two English novels which belong to the type that has been defined, but which we may briefly set in opposition to each other in telling contrast. Several features of *Tess of the d'Urbervilles* (1891) bring us back to our first naturalist paradigm: the fateful heredity that afflicts the heroine, the degeneration of the noble d'Urberville family into the Durbeyfields, the ancestral curse that Tess is destined to relive, the catastrophic sexuality of the maiden's 'fall' in the Chase, her 'corporeal blight' that becomes her 'mental harvest' but the immediate source of her misfortunes, the depiction of a particular popular milieu with its scenes of men and women at work, milking cows or harvesting swedes, the use that Hardy made of themes from popular genres like the ballad, the melodrama, the romance, the vestigial nobility of the heroine whose spirit is broken by a combination of destiny, nature, man and circumstances such that her fate belongs to the 'best tragedy', to the 'highest tragedy', as the author defines it in relation to *Jude the Obscure*: 'that of the WORTHY encompassed by the INEVITABLE'.[46] Thus, with its doubly ironic subtitle ('A Pure Woman'), this novel closely follows the fundamental naturalist scheme: the story of a humble girl in whom beats, to use Hardy's expression, 'the great passionate pulse of existence' and who is plunged, after an initial moral lapse, into a struggle against the evil side of her nature, which is, in a way, nature's evil working within her. There is the now familiar structure of two male characters in her life, Alec d'Urberville, the rogue and first lover who returns, like Lantier, to torment her, opposed to Angel Clare, an intellectual pessimist, who belongs more in his own person to our next chapter, but who forms with Alec contrasting projections of the contending forces in the heroine's struggle between the moral and the instinctive. Finally, Tess, like her fellow naturalist victims, is left, as misfortune pursues her and the inextricable relatedness of events conspires for her downfall, to wander, apparently at the whim of circumstance, but is fatefully drawn back into her predetermined degradation to share the lot of the humiliated naturalist protagonist, beaten by the greater strength of nature, society, the Will and lost in the ultimate undifferentiated state of the natural(ist) universe.

In 1894 George Moore published a novel which also closely follows the naturalist scheme. In fact, as Jean Noël points out,[47] *Esther Waters* has often been interpreted as a return by Moore to the naturalist mode after his defection, and has been compared to *Germinie Lacerteux, L'Assommoir* and Flaubert's story 'Un cœur simple'. But Moore's intention in writing this novel, so it seems, was quite the opposite, for he sought not to acquiesce to but to repudiate naturalism so that no one, as he put it, would ever link his name again with Zola's. It is the familiar story of a servant girl seduced and made pregnant by a footman, William Latch, the cause of her misfortunes, the gambling man who (yet again) returns to her life, like Lantier in *L'Assommoir*, and prevents her from marrying the good Fred Parsons, a Plymouth Brother, her Goujet. Gambling on racehorses, as the text makes clear, plays an equivalent role to drinking in Zola's novel. There is a typical confinement scene and no lack of harsh realities. But the novel was spared the typical naturalist reception, no doubt because of Esther's unshakeable religious faith and William Latch's deathbed conversion, such that at the finish morality wins by a nose. Gladstone defended the novel, W. H. Smith was obliged to sell it and the critics reviewed it with approval − all evident signs that, despite its conformity to our scheme, *Esther Waters* represents a naturalist palinode. Now we know that in writing this novel Moore deliberately took *Tess of the d'Urbervilles* as a model, determined, as he later explained, that his heroine should systematically make the opposite decisions to those of Tess in similar circumstances.[48] We are thus presented with the curious situation in which a text that is traditionally considered to be one of the rare examples of English naturalism, *Esther Waters*, was written in opposition to the genre, whereas another text, *Tess*, whose naturalism is rarely acknowledged, reveals itself to be a more authentic naturalist work. But what these texts show above all is the vigour of the naturalist model, for, in order to break with it, Moore was compelled to conform to it.

5

COMIC STRAINS

In a study of the fundamental principles of narrative – 'succession' and 'transformation' in his view – Tzvetan Todorov argues that there are consequently two fundamental types of narrative organisation. The first, which he calls 'mythologique', combines a logical development of succession with the most straightforward kind of transformation, from one state to another, or, as he succinctly puts it, from A to non-A. In the second type, the emphasis is less on the transformation than on the apprehension of that change: 'la logique de succession est secondée par le deuxième genre de transformations, récits où l'importance de l'événement est moindre que celle de la perception que nous en avons, du degré de connaissance que nous en possédons'. He calls this second type 'gnoséologique' (or 'épistémique').[1]

These very general categories are a useful guide to the essential differences between the model described in the previous chapter and a second type of naturalist work to which I wish now to turn. In the first, as we have seen, *mythos*, plot, the fortunes of a *protagonist*, of an active participant in life's struggles, are the directing features in a set of 'romances' that go terribly wrong (if indeed it could ever be said that they had a chance of going otherwise). In the second type, the protagonist is more a spectator on life who draws back from any active – and thereby potentially 'tragic' – commitment into a more reflective posture of refusal, resignation, cynicism, despondency. There is thus a shift from action to attitude, from physiology to philosophy, from the dynamic, teleological kind of plot to a less decisive, repetitive, unresolved organisation. Whereas the first type presents typical examples of life's misfortunes rooted in biological or social conditions, the second type communicates more directly the novelist's own sense of despair at the fundamental inadequacy of human experience through, as it were, a spokes(wo)man rather than through the fated speci(wo)men. While the two types remain distinguishable, they frequently combine in the works of the same writer or even in the same text. There is thus a difference of emphasis rather than an absolute divide. If Zola's more naturalist texts, like *L'Assommoir*, tend to illustrate the first kind, a work like *La Joie de vivre* clearly belongs to the second category. Indeed, if we take the latter to be ironic, Zola's two titles are suggestive of the essential nature of these two kinds: 'myths' of submission to overwhelming forces, fictionalised reflexions on the ironies of life. Alexis, who produced a typical example of the first type with *Madame Meuriot*, typically failed to complete what would have been a fine example of the second, a novel which he was planning in 1881 and which he describes in a letter to his mentor, Zola: 'Comme fond, en réalité, une sorte de confession générale et passionnée d'un homme de lettres, où je me cacherai tel que je suis – *avec une sincérité cynique.*'[2]

To illustrate the distinction further with a clear example, we might turn to the *roman militaire* of Lucien Descaves, *Sous-Offs* (1889), a text which combines the two tendencies. It could be more accurately described as an anti-military novel, in the tradition of *Les Soirées de Médan* and of lesser-known naturalist studies of the servitudes and lack of grandeur of military life, like *Le Cavalier Miserey* by Abel Hermant, *Au port d'arme* by Henry Fèvre and another text by Descaves, *Misères du sabre*, all published in 1887, a bad year for the literary image of the French army. The novel takes up the Goncourt thesis of *La Fille Elisa*, that there is a fundamental equivalence between the soldier and the prostitute, between the barracks and the brothel. On the one hand, the novel traces the declining fortunes of the 'fille à soldats', Généreuse Couturier, whose name, as Henri Mitterand remarks in a recent edition of the text, 'est tout un programme'.[3] Her degradation is measured by the progressive drop in rank of her clients until she has nothing left of her 'chair molle' to offer the privates who frequent the 'Corbeille fleurie' but 'son misérable accoutrement et sa pauvre chair talée, les goussets fatigués de ses yeux, les gris épis de ses tempes, les vacances visibles dans la denture, derrière l'ocre craquelé des commissures, le tassement du buste, enfin … sa passivité fataliste' (p. 367). The other aspect of the novel is provided by Généreuse's frequent lover, André Favières, a bored, pessimistic, intellectual, autobiographical observer of the tawdry existence of military life. 'Dans la veine huysmansienne cette fois', writes Henri Mitterand, 'c'est plutôt un itinéraire nauséeux à travers une quotidienneté dont le rituel militaire ne suffit sûrement pas à épuiser les ressources de laideur et de bêtise' (p. vi). In a manner typical of our new naturalist hero, Favières 's'enlisait dans une boue d'ennui' (p. 29) and characteristically complains: 'Comme la vie se recommence!' (p. 297). The joys of parenthood are typically demystified as he reacts with disgust before the fruits of his jaded passion: the scrofulous, syphilis-ridden pile of flesh to which Généreuse gives birth (p. 214). The last meeting of Favières and Généreuse, which takes place in the brothel, when the totally spent woman pathetically tries to offer herself one final time to her former lover, is like a grotesque parody of the famous parting scene of *L'Education sentimentale*. One could even suggest that the whole novel, with its seemingly endless round of sordid scenes and empty routines, of gratuitous violence and squalid sexuality, with its meandering plot that follows the aimless manœuvrings of the regiment, betrays the same 'défaut de ligne droite' of the earlier work and, more generally, of the naturalist texts of our second type.

The experience of disillusionment is clearly the thematic centre of this second model, a banal enough theme, but one which acquires a certain specificity in naturalist texts. It is no longer, as in the earlier Romantic and realist tradition, the problem of the nobility of the protagonist's inner life and aspirations that must remain unfulfilled in the real world, the Hegelian model of the inner poetry of the character trapped in prosaic surroundings, but rather a device for perceiving and heightening the discovery of the essential nature of that world. The problem is not so much, as in *Madame Bovary*, the gap between the vastness of the heroine's dreams and the narrowness of her house, but rather the woodworm eating away the foundations of the house. Thus, more than ever before, in the naturalist genre, the novel turns away from its heroic past, undermines its origins in the adventures of epic and romance, taking on the character of the anti-novel. In an article on 'Les petits naturalistes' (Céard, Huysmans, Hennique and Maupassant), Brunetière astutely emphasises (and, naturally, deplores) this tendency of naturalist works, which, he argues, are in the process of expelling from the novel 'l'intérêt romanesque d'abord, et ensuite, autant qu'il se pourra, toute espèce d'intérêt généralement quelconque'. Flaubert – the now familiar argument states – despite his inherent Romanticism, set the tone in his later works, while Zola, despite his theories and because of his 'fougue d'imagination méridionale', has not succeeded in imitating the platitudes of human existence. But the latter's disciples, aided by 'la stérilité de leur génie naturel', have immediately found their touch. Alongside the obvious candidate, Céard's *Une Belle Journée*, Brunetière cites Hennique's *L'Accident de Monsieur Hébert* for special dishonourable mention: 'Voilà le vrai roman naturaliste, le roman selon la formule, le roman enfin sans incidents, péripéties ni dénouement, reproduction fidèle de la nature, exacte imitation de la vie dans la simplicité de sa "nullité crasse" – comme ils disent – et la réalité de sa "platitude nauséeuse".[4]

Already by 1878 a new naturalist canon was thus emerging with its models and its exclusions. Not surprisingly Brunetière bans from the group of texts conforming to the new style Hennique's recent first novel, *La Dévouée* (1878) – whose dedication reads 'Aux frères d'armes Henry Céard et J.-K. Huysmans, j'offre ce roman naturaliste' – the story of a fanatical inventor, the clockmaker Jeoffrin, who poisons one of his daughters and has the other one guillotined for the crime in order to get his hands on their inheritance to finance his scheme to build a navigable balloon! As Brunetière dryly remarks: 'Cette façon de se remettre en fonds ne m'étonne pas autrement, mais elle est relativement rare.'[5] Despite his reservations about the subject, Zola was, no doubt for tactical reasons, more flexible. He included Hennique's novel, along with *La Fin de Lucie Pellegrin* (1880) of Paul Alexis and, in particular, *Les Sœurs Vatard* (1879) by Huysmans, in the emerging corpus of naturalist works characterised by the rejection of plot, in terms reminiscent of his views on *L'Education sentimentale* and similar to Brunetière's remarks:

Notre roman contemporain se simplifie de plus en plus, par haine des intrigues compliquées et mensongères; il y a là une revanche contre les aventures, le romanesque, les fables à dormir debout ... On finira par donner de simples études, sans péripéties ni dénouement, l'analyse d'une année d'existence, l'histoire d'une passion, la biographie d'un personnage, les notes prises sur la vie et logiquement classées. (X, 1307–8)

Louis Desprez made similar comments about the Goncourt brothers' novels, Brunetière about those of Daudet, and Lafcadio Hearn about Maupassant's works, all suggesting that, in naturalist fiction, the classical plot was in the process of elimination.[6] Indeed, as André Vial has noted, whereas Flaubert, the Goncourt brothers and Zola merely played down the importance of 'invention' in the elaboration of their plots, certain writers of the second naturalist generation took to an extreme this tendency to minimise plot, to strain the limits of narrativity, to focus their works less on what happens than on what never happens in their characters' lives. 'Aux environs de 1880', he observes,

se précise ainsi une sorte de Jansénisme de l'Art; un rêve hante les cerveaux créateurs, le rêve d'une perfection aride, ascétique: l'idée d'un roman où il ne se passerait rien, où il n'arriverait rien, d'une œuvre blanche qui ne s'accommoderait même plus du nom de roman et ne se soumettrait à aucune des catégories traditionnelles, qui, sans cesser d'emprunter sa matière à la réalité, s'imposerait cent contraintes appauvrissantes et limiterait de la façon la plus étroite, en durée, en volume, en qualité, la substance dont elle se nourrit. C'est à qui, par une sorte de gageure, saura isoler la parcelle de vérité la plus banale, la plus navrante, la plus stérile, pour en faire surgir un sens accessible seulement à quelques initiés. Le roman, à défaut d'un autre terme qui, de l'aveu même d'E. de Goncourt, n'a point encore été trouvé, veut être l'envers absolu de la rhétorique, de l'épique, du tragique, du lyrique.[7]

In the second type of naturalist texts with which we are dealing in this chapter, texts which subscribed to this banal orthodoxy and which remained usually unappreciated, sometimes unpublished – or even unwritten! – an evident shift away from the traditional linear plot occurred, if not to an ideal plotlessness or to an ideal non-generic state, at least to the elaboration of alternative constructs which emerged, not only in the interests of mimetic veracity, but as a natural expression of a view of life that they were given to represent. Within this second category of texts, one could further define three different kinds of plot formation, all rejecting implicitly the narrative purposefulness associated with the very notion of plot. There is firstly the *circular* scheme, which brings the characters back to an initial situation and exposes the uselessness of their efforts, the type of plot which seems to have led nowhere or, in Todorov's terms, to have progressed from A to non-A then back to A again. Secondly, there is what might be called the *para-plot*, made up of a series of aborted adventures, of events that never really take place, romance and adventure that never occur, frustrating expectations in character and (perhaps) reader alike. A third type could be called the *recurrent plot*, structured (at one level at least) by the periodicity of physical needs rather than by purposive action and determined by the repetitiveness of events and a cynical view of the motivating factors of human endeavour. All three of these types clearly convey a view of human life that is problematic, characterised by inertia, lassitude, dejection, disgust or resignation. Characters, even those with heroic aspirations, are caught up in the treadmill of the daily grind, their hopes trammelled by their circumstances, their ambitions eroded by the fundamental drift of life into a drab repetitiveness. If the common denominator of certain genres is the search for the exceptional, the extreme, the excessive, in these naturalist texts it is the common denominators of life. It is the poetry of the trivial round and common task, the epic of undistinguished lives, the drama of routine sexuality, the adventures of alimentary habits, sagas of sordidness and meanness. The drudgery of domestic life plays a large part in these texts, which frequently dwell upon the tribulations of marriage, as, typically, if somewhat immoderately, in Léon Gandillot's *Entre Conjoints!* (1888). Sidonie finds marriage 'un long baillement', resorts to literature of escape – 'Le genre naturaliste, lui ramenant devant les yeux l'image du monde réel, lui déplût' – and works herself into a prolonged state of nervous crisis, whilst her husband runs through a veritable legion of prostitutes, 'toute l'infernale série', to relieve his boredom, until inevitably 'il se résigna' and the couple lapses back unenthusiastically after all their frantic, futile efforts into their matrimonial routines: 'Et, désormais conformes, et l'un à l'autre idoines, ces deux êtres, mâle et femelle, purent subsister harmoniquement, dans ce parallélisme infiniment rapproché, qui donne à la conscience humaine, pour son repos, la bienheureuse illusion de l'intangible absolue communion des adéquates personnalités.'[8]

There is the same reductive, cynical attitude to social and political success in these texts, which expose the pettiness, hypocrisy and shams of public life, and clearly derive their inspiration from Flaubert's *L'Education sentimentale*, texts like Céard's story 'Mal Eclos' (1881), in which the most mediocre of characters, the ironically named Martial Moaclar, rises to the rank of Major General in the National Guard, founds left wing newspapers and becomes a fanatical leader in the Commune.[9] But love remains the supreme illusion that naturalist literature submits to its 'cruel analysis', reducing it to physiological urgings and obstetric consequences, dwelling upon the vast gulf of selfishness and deception that separates lovers, whether they seek romance in adulterous liaisons or relief from their periodic lusts in more sordid entanglements. The catastrophic sexuality of the female protagonists of our first novel type tends to be replaced by the serial gratifications of jaded male appetites in the texts of the second type.

Another major unifying principle of these texts, again reminiscent of *L'Education sentimentale*, is the problem of passing time, for time in naturalist literature has irretrievably lost the inherent purposiveness of the epic or romance. It has all the immediacy of represented time, but it is never enjoyed in its existential fullness, merely perceived in its corrosive potential. If the fundamental function of narrative, as Ricoeur has argued, is to appropriate time, in naturalist literature narrative merely serves to record its inexorable, unrestrained power, whether in the interiority of the processes of disruption and decay or in the exteriority of a general levelling of all human activities. Hence the frequent scenes in which the course of time is highlighted and its ravages displayed, often in the spectacle of the faded beauty of a woman or the retrospective survey of desert years, as, once again, in the concluding scenes of *L'Education sentimentale*. The narrator of Alexis's 'Journal de Monsieur Mure' (in *La Fin de Lucie Pellegrin*), who, in yet another patent borrowing from Flaubert, has harboured a secret love over many years for a certain Mme Moreau, sums up the problem: 'Rien ne dure. Tout s'arrange et se nivelle. Le choc des passions et les catastrophes ont beau accidenter la vie, produire des déchirements et des brisures; peu à peu une poudre fine, impalpable, retombe sur les choses, émousse les angles, veloute les nouvelles situations, étend partout l'uniformité d'une patine salutaire.'[10]

Not surprisingly, with the erosion of human values, energies and prerogatives in these texts, there is an equivalent crisis in human language, reduced to repetition, inarticulateness, cliché. There is a general tendency within the naturalist movement, as we have already seen in the study of the first category of texts, to take up such typical Flaubertian themes and exploit them to the point of parody, self-parody, or even to absurdist limits. At the opposite extreme in our corpus to the works with serious scientific purposes, the earnest case histories, are texts of a resolutely anarchical, ironical, savagely satirical strain. Here too there are myths and mystifications. There is even in France a distinct group of writers, overlapping with, and in reality as amorphous as, the Médan group, consisting of Huysmans, Hennique, Céard, Pol Neveux, Ludovic de Francmesnil, a group of friends sharing a passion for Flaubert and Schopenhauer, a profound pessimism, and, by way of compensation, a mordant sense of humour. But, because of the mythical aura that surrounded him, perhaps the most significant figure of the group was Gabriel Thyébaut, a man with several claims to his obscure fame.[11] He was, not surprisingly, a devoted civil servant, working in the prefectorial administration of Paris, remarkably intelligent, so it seems, and endowed with the prodigious memory required to commit the 'Bible of Naturalism' to memory.[12] Furthermore, he had the curious distinction of being a writer of some (local) repute who never published a single word, though he was the author of a legendary text, *Le Vin en bouteilles*, which his family insisted remain unpublished and whose manuscript Céard, so it appears, jealously guarded. C. A. Burns has edited this text,[13] which, disappointing as its readers will inevitably find it, represents, in his view, 'la formule naturaliste poussée à l'extrême; c'est le naturalisme réduit à l'absurde, au grotesque'.[14]

Le Vin en bouteilles is a one-act play of no more than three published pages. In scene I a husband and wife, delighted to be able to save on the wages of a cooper, introduce into their cellar L'Homme des Choses Médiocres who habitually bottles their wine for them. Scene II consists of this character's soliloquy, his claim to have had a brilliant academic career and to know everything. Amongst his intellectual accomplishments, he states: 'J'ai eu l'idée de ces théories récentes grâce auxquelles la science moderne destructive de l'âme explique les choses de l'esprit par des considérations physiques, combat les présomptions des théodicées, et, plus divine que la foi, plus impérieuse que la révélation, conclut despotiquement à l'éternelle vacuité des cieux.' The upshot of all this knowledge is that he has returned to 'les choses médiocres, convaincu ... de leur permanence et de leur incommutabilité', to the repetitive task before him. In scene III a mediocre maid comes down to help him and, after some lewd gestures with a bottle and a cork, he takes her 'médiocrely' on a pile of coke. In the final scene the husband and wife return to check that all is in order, then, along with the maid, leave the now silent Homme des Choses Médiocres to his humble task.

Not the most stirring of literary texts! But one that admirably illustrates the naturalist's Flaubertian investiture of the banal. Deffoux and Zavie suggest a comparison with *La Tentation de Saint Antoine*,[15] but an analogy with *Bouvard et Pécuchet* would be more appropriate. Even Flaubert's title, or at least the first and last syllables, suggest the link between the work with a hero who corks bottles (*boucher*), 'stuffs' the maid and seems to advocate, if not exemplify, dull-wittedness (*l'esprit bouché*). More generally, the themes of this slender text – the repetitiveness of human action, unromantic sex, the insignificance of human life, the impasse of knowledge and thought, ultimate silence – are thoroughly character- istic of the 'comic' strain of naturalist literature with which we are dealing. So too is the strain that these works impose on their readers, who might still expect to be amused, intrigued, enlightened by a literary work. Inevitably such texts remained in obscurity, if indeed they were ever published. Some were never even written, like the novel planned by Huysmans which Remy de Gourmont described in 1912 (with further mysterious and, as it proves, largely inaccurate allusions to Thyébaut's text):

Un monsieur sort de chez lui pour aller à son bureau, s'aperçoit que ses souliers n'ont pas été cirés, les livre à un décrotteur, pendant l'opération songe à ses petites affaires, puis continue son chemin. Le problème était de tirer de cela trois cents pages. C'est sans doute la même difficulté qui arrêta M. Th... dans la rédaction d'une comédie qu'il avait pourtant méditée plus de dix ans. Il paraît que c'était très drôle. Je n'ai pas eu le bonheur de l'ouïr, mais j'en connais la substance, qui est brève. Un boutiquier s'en va un dimanche à sa maison de campagne mettre du vin en bouteilles. Incidents de l'opération. Rentrée à Paris. Voilà tout.[16]

The modern reader is not unfamiliar with works which exploit the vein of absurd triviality, and with the cynical comments that they contain on human existence, but it is still not at all surprising that Henry Céard and his colleagues, with their particular taste for such 'livres de désenchantement spéculatif', for 'des romans sans la moindre intrigue apparente', should have had no chance of commercial success with their attempts at the genre.[17] Nor is it surprising that Céard himself should have left several texts uncompleted and unpublished, like the novel *Mademoiselle 24*, in which the heroine, Aline Sertisson, was to remain on her back in a hospital bed throughout the 'action' of the novel until she died, with the medical student that she loved becoming the lover of the girl in the next bed![18]

I have dwelt at some length on such marginalia, trivia and *disjecta membra* of the French naturalist movement firstly, of course, to make the point, once again, that in such lesser texts the stereotypes of the genre are more evident, but also to show that, in this second type of work, failure, incompleteness, triviality and mediocrity are an integral part of the thematics *and* the aesthetics of the naturalist text. Better known works by better known writers present analogous features, but are more compromising with their readers' expectation of some degree of novelistic interest.

The title of the journal which characteristically Huysmans and his associates failed to found, *La Comédie humaine*, is both a tribute to Balzac and a generic comment on the fiction of the group. Paradoxically, in texts which are often autobiographical in many of their details, the authors have achieved the detachment of comic art, presenting the spectacle of human life to a degree of typicality that agonisingly insists upon its ordinariness. The case histories of our first group of texts were, as we saw, not only representations of social types, but were also illustrative of generalisable laws, presented in the realistic guise of the particular. Similarly, our second group of texts not only fulfils the requirements of realism − being, in a famous definition by Engels, 'the truthful representation of typical characters under typical circumstances'[19] − but tends to deal with even more general themes, adopting the *generic* view of man that characterises naturalism. Indeed, one could generalise to the extent of suggesting that naturalism is the genre of the human genre, a body of literature that views man generically, as a (threatened) species. Hence the lack of importance of history in these texts. Zola's series is presented in its subtitle as the *Histoire naturelle et sociale d'une famille sous le Second Empire*, and certain of its episodes are historical novels, like *Son Excellence Eugène Rougon* and *La Débâcle*, but the most naturalist texts (*L'Assommoir, Pot-Bouille, La Joie de vivre, La Terre, La Bête humaine*) are the least dependent on their historical context. Marxist criticism has seized upon the biological vision of naturalism to condemn it by comparison with the more historicised realism of an earlier age, as does Lukács in an important essay on Zola:

Here we have the new realism, *recte* naturalism, in concentrated essence and in sharp opposition to the traditions of the old realism; a mechanical average takes the place of the dialectic unity of type and individual; description and analysis is [*sic*] substituted for epic situations and epic plots. The tension of the old-type story, the co-operation and clashing of human beings who are both individuals and at the same time representatives of important class tendencies – all these are eliminated and their place is taken by 'average' characters whose individual traits are accidents from the artistic point of view ...[20]

Yet what for the Marxist are mere biological 'accidents' are for the Naturalist the essential conditions of human nature, just as what for the Marxist are indispensable historical factors are for the Naturalist incidental circumstances.

Maupassant's novel *Une Vie* (1883) is an excellent illustration of this problem. In fact, in *The Historical Novel*, Lukács refers to this text in particular as the paradigm of the naturalist tendency to 'make history private'. He is bemused by the fact that Maupassant sets the events of the novel back into an earlier age. Even so, he observes, 'the essential action of the novel is quite "timeless"; the Restoration, the July Revolution, the July Monarchy, etc., events which objectively must make an extremely deep impression upon the daily life of an aristocratic *milieu*, play practically no part at all in Maupassant'.[21] The plot of this novel is ordinary and typical enough. Jeanne returns from her convent school to the family manor, full of hopes, dreams and vitality, all of which are progressively quashed by her subsequent life, in particular by her marriage to the mediocre and selfish vicomte Julien de Lamar, who deceives his wife with the maid and with a countess, called Gilberte. After her husband's dramatic death (at the hands of the jealous count), after the death of her parents, indeed after the death of all that she loves, she is left with her memories, with the relics of her past life, with a son who exploits her but who at least provides her with a last ray of hope for happiness by confiding his child to her care. Monotony is the prevailing mood of the novel as the heroine's life simply slips away: 'Et la journée s'écoula comme celle de la veille, froide, au lieu d'être humide. Et les autres jours de la semaine ressemblèrent à ces deux-là; et toutes les semaines du mois ressemblèrent à la première' (p. 96).[22] The whole novel has the structure and tone of any undistinguished life: a lot of hopes and dreams, a few brief moments of happiness, some painful crises, the trials of coping with the malevolence of others, long and monotonous periods of routine existence, physical suffering and death. It has the sea-like rhythm of the bovaresque adventure, surges of hope and illusion, lapses into despondency and disillusionment, with long spells of becalmement. The novel's obvious debts to Flaubert have been traced to the earlier writer's more naturalist texts. As André Vial writes: '*Une Vie* combine visiblement la formule et la tonalité d'*Un Cœur simple* et celle de *L'Education sentimentale*, réduite à l'élément strictement individuel, à l'exclusion de toute préoccupation historique.'[23] Jeanne ends up physically immobile like her corpulent mother and morally paralysed by inaction such that her life (all life) is reduced to the stark emptiness of passing time. Even the exceptional moments, like her courting days or her honeymoon in Corsica, are presented in the reductive mode of the cliché and the repetitive. Even the great drama of her existence, the revelation of her husband's infidelities, becomes a commonplace event as she discovers other adulteries all around her; 'tout le monde en fait autant', as the worldly-wise abbé Picot observes (p. 124). Her love is presented in the perspective of her species and set against discreet references to copulating insects; her pregnancy is deprived of its distinctive character, for, all about her, 'à tout moment on apprenait une grossesse nouvelle, ou bien quelque fredaine d'une fille ... Ce printemps ardent semblait remuer les sèves chez les hommes comme les plantes' (p. 147). Even the requisite naturalist parturition scene is *repeated* in this book.[24]

Like all the principal characters of the novel, as the initial letter of their names phonetically suggests (*J*eanne, *J*ulien, *G*ilberte), the heroine is imprisoned in the solipsism of her illusions, in the egocentric vision, as her limited point of view directs the narrative. With the character's failure to transform the 'mythological' plot of her existence, the novel constantly shifts to the 'gnoseological' (or 'epistemic') mode. Indeed, the text combines the various formations of the problematic plot indicated above, in the abortive 'para-plots' of Jeanne's hopes, in the recurrent pattern of her disillusionment and in the circular nature of her experience, as she goes back to Les Peuples

in the final scenes, to where the novel began, obsessively intent upon
reliving her past – her last defence against time. There is in fact much
in *Une Vie* that reminds one of the 'conte philosophique', for
Jeanne is a Candide-like figure, caught between her father with his
Rousseauesque, pantheistic adoration of nature and the new priest,
l'abbé Tolbiac, with his ranting against the evils of nature, the former,
at least in name (baron Simon-Jacques Le Perhuis des Vauds) bringing
to mind le baron de Thunder-ten-tronckh and the fulminations of the
latter recalling frère Archangias in Zola's *La Faute de l'abbé Mouret*,
a text which may also be read as a novelised philosophical tale. Like
M. Homais and l'abbé Bournisien in *Madame Bovary*, these two
characters (or caricatures) provide the elements of a fundamental
ideological debate out of which the (dia)gnosis of the novel emerges:
by combining the natural religion of the first with the ethical negation
of nature of the second, one arrives at a Schopenhauerian vision of
man's subjection to nature's laws (or Will), of the illusion of our
separateness from the phenomenal world, combined with a sense of
the futility of hope, of love as a delusion wrought by nature's
procreative volition, of the inevitability of human suffering. But in
this text, written no less than Voltaire's under the shadow of a German
philosopher, but in an age less confident in the power of reason, the
protagonist acquires no wisdom, only inklings of the truth when one
corner of the veil of *maya* is lifted, as when she is confronted with
the finality of death and hears her dead mother's watch symbolically
go ticking on: 'Tout n'était donc que misère, chagrin, malheur et
mort. Tout trompait, tout mentait, tout faisait souffrir et pleurer'
(p. 155). In typically naturalist fashion – as in Zola's own 'conte
philosophique' on the theme of Schopenhauerism, *La Joie de vivre*,
published the same year as and, no doubt, in many respects in response
to *Une Vie* – it is left to the servant, Rosalie, to convey the wisdom
of the work in the final phrase: 'La vie, voyez-vous, ça n'est jamais
si bon ni si mauvais qu'on croit.'

Arnold Bennett, who, among English writers and with the usual
English mitigations, is closest to the manner under review in this
chapter, wrote in the preface to the 1911 edition of his own derivative
novel, *The Old Wives' Tale* – a story of *two* lives – that *Une Vie*
was 'the summit of achievement in fiction'. He also wrote admiringly
of Huysmans' *En ménage* (1881), of its 'unique charm' despite 'the
sordid ugliness of commonplace life' that it contains.[25] There is in
truth very little charm in the novel, absolutely no excitement, but at
least it contains, for our purposes, a perfect example of the circular
plot: the novelist André returns unexpectedly one evening, finds his

wife *en flagrant délit*, leaves home and, for three hundred pages, seeks alternative domestic arrangements, wandering the streets, frequenting filthy restaurants, encountering stupid people, drifting from one sordid encounter to another, as the plot, if such is the appropriate term, is supplied by his 'crises juponnières', before he finally accepts a reconciliation with his wife and returns home. Beneath the apparent aimlessness of André's frequentations is a systematic arrangement, for the novel reads like a bachelor's handbook, or, in more Balzacian terms, a 'Physiology of Alternatives to Marriage', a kind of typology of available females, as André explores the possibilities. There is, for example, the 'obscène candeur des pubertés qui poussent' or the 'hystérie sympathique des femmes de quarante ans' or the 'vice compliqué des bourgeoises plus mûres'.[26] For a while the housekeeper, Mélanie, seems to provide the solution, until he turns to Blanche, the prostitute, 'la femme hebdomadaire qui n'est pas une maîtresse et qui n'est déjà plus une passante' (p. 215), then to Jeanne, a former mistress, who moves in for a while. His friend Cyprien seems to have the ideal arrangement, a concubine, Mélie, 'une vache puissante et pacifique' who provides for his needs. But, in the end, it's back to Berthe, whom he embraces as he did Jeanne, 'en égalant ainsi sa femme à une maîtresse, en les rapprochant, en les mettant sur le même niveau, sur le même plan' (p. 363). For André, as for Flaubert's Frédéric Moreau, his women end up as interchangeable, as all experience is levelled in the general ennui that afflicts him: 'il s'affaissa sous l'écroulement d'une vie qui, à peine reconstruite, s'abattait de nouveau, ensevelissant ses dernières espérances sous un bruyant monceau de dégâts et de ruines' (p. 299). Both André and Cyprien finish up as 'hommes des choses médiocres' and arrive at the familiar jaundiced quietism of the typical defeated naturalist intellectual: 'Ce n'est pas mauvais d'être vidés comme nous le sommes, car maintenant que toutes les concessions sont faites, peut-être bien que l'éternelle bêtise de l'humanité voudra de nous, et que, semblables à nos concitoyens, nous aurons ainsi qu'eux le droit de vivre enfin respectés et stupides!' (p. 375).

If *En ménage* could be concisely defined as a travesty of romance, its sequel, *A vau-l'eau* (1882), is a travesty of the epic: the heroic quest for a decent meal. Henry Fouquier, writing in the Paris paper *Gil Blas*, included Huysmans' 'nouvelle' in a review of some recent novels in the following terms:

'Pour être ému, dit-il [Maupassant], il faut que je trouve dans un livre de l'humanité saignante; il faut que les personnages soient mes voisins, mes égaux, passent par les joies et les souffrances que je connais, aient tous un peu de moi, etc.' A merveille! Cette formule est excellente ...

Voyons donc ce roman, tel qu'il l'analyse lui-même, car je ne veux tenir que de lui cet exposé fidèle du sujet. 'C'est l'histoire d'un employé à la recherche d'un bifteck. Rien de plus. Un pauvre diable d'homme, forçat de ministère, n'ayant que trente sous à dépenser à chaque repas, erre de gargote en gargote, écœuré par la fadeur des sauces, l'insipide coriacité des viandes inférieures, les douteuses senteurs de la raie au beurre noir et la saveur acide des liquides frelatés.' Voilà tout! voilà ce que M. de Maupassant appelle la recherche de 'l'humanité saignante'. C'est la recherche du beefsteak saignant qu'il aurait dû dire![27]

The suggestion has been made, rather charitably, it would seem, that the quest of this pathetic little clerk, M. Folantin, is symbolic, a search 'in his very humble way for spiritual satisfaction'.[28] It is true that the narrator frames the story in religious terms. When a new 'pâtisserie' opens nearby with a home dinner delivery service, the little man exultantly exclaims: 'je suis sauvé' (p. 430). He is, it is also true, *Jean* Folantin, saint of the Unsated, martyr of Mandication, who lives in the rue des Saints-Pères and underwent a most appropriate baptism at birth: wiped down with butter and powdered with flour! But the story belongs far more to burlesque than to religious allegory and the character's torments are most decidedly *crises de foie*. He is another perfect anti-hero, an ultimate 'homme des choses médiocres', engulfed by the repetitive pattern of his routine existence and his compulsive bachelor needs. The text takes up the familiar naturalist theme of the equivalence of our appetites in recalling how, in M. Folantin's youth, 'dans ces gargotes où son bel appétit lui faisait dévorer de basses viandes, sa faim charnelle lui permettait d'accepter les rebuts de l'amour'(p. 387). Nowadays, unlike André in the previous text, he has largely suppressed his sexual desires, that is until the final, comic episode in which a prostitute lures him back to her room, where 'une bouffée de jeunesse lui revint' (p. 445). Even more disgusted by this sentimental adventure than by his usual epicurean frustrations, he is left to provide the usual retrospective view and philosophical conclusion that are characteristic features of this category of texts:

M. Folantin descendit de chez cette fille, profondément écœuré et, tout en s'acheminant vers son domicile, il embrassa d'un coup d'œil l'horizon désolé de la vie; il comprit l'inutilité des changements de routes, la stérilité des élans et des efforts; il faut se laisser aller à vau-l'eau; Schopenhauer a raison, se dit-il, 'la vie de l'homme oscille comme une pendule entre la douleur et l'ennui'. (p. 445)

Inevitably he adopts the attitude of resignation that we have come to expect at the conclusion of these works: 'il n'y a qu'à se croiser les bras et à tâcher de dormir'. In his frigid bedroom without any matches, he sententiously concludes: 'Allons, décidément, le mieux n'existe pas pour les gens sans le sou; seul, le pire arrive' (p. 446).

Pessimism, Bertrand Russell remarks in a chapter on Schopenhauer, assumes that the universe exists to displease us,[29] a common naturalist attitude. It is entirely appropriate that M. Folantin should be prompted to such 'profound' reflexions as he emerges from the prostitute's embraces. Schopenhauer notes that on the door of the *fornix* in Pompeii, adorned with a phallus, was written the inscription *Heic habitat felicitas*; 'for those going in this was naïve, for those coming out ironical'.[30] In the ironic naturalist universe, post-coïtal *taedium* is a privileged state of divination. Frédéric Moreau, it will be recalled, refrained from the experience in a famous scene of *L'Education sentimentale*, but his illusions were only temporarily preserved from profanation, for, as Victor Brombert observes, the bordello motif would be closely bound up with Flaubert's character's essential apprenticeship to life,[31] as it would be for characters in later naturalist fiction, subject to the tyranny of the Will and its concomitant illusions.

Such a splenetic view in naturalist literature cannot be solely attributed to Schopenhauer's influence, extensive though it was in certain circles in the 1880s. In 1886 Albert Wolff observed: 'A cette heure, Paris est plein de Schopenhauer en herbes qui rongent les lettres françaises comme le phylloxera dévore les vignes de Bordeaux.'[32] The degree to which Schopenhauerism really became in France an 'epidemic' or a new 'mal du siècle' remains open to interpretation, but, as far as the naturalist writers were concerned, they were already much predisposed to pessimistic ideas and found in the doctrine of the German philosopher confirmation of these tendencies and some compelling arguments to justify their views. Significantly, as A. Baillot observes, the borrowing was selective, for it was only Schopenhauer's pessimism that claimed the attention of the French and not his whole doctrine.[33] Thus, for the authors of the texts of the kind with which we are concerned in this chapter, Schopenhauer would seem to have provided an external source of authoritative reference similar to the medical treatises invoked in the previous chapter. In any case, well before the date of publication of the first works to bring Schopenhauer's ideas to the attention of a wider public, the mentors of the naturalist movement, Flaubert and the Goncourt brothers, had expressed similar views. Albert Thibaudet has called Schopenhauer a 'Flaubert de la philosophie'; and Flaubert, when he came to read the philosopher's views in 1879, recognised in him a kindred spirit.[34] The Goncourt *Journal* abounds in pessimistic views with a Schopenhauerian ring to them. In any case too, the naturalists responded in different ways to the philosopher's ideas and availed themselves of his views for their own purposes. 'Les médanistes', writes René-Pierre Colin, 's'étaient forgé chacun une image différente de celui qu'ils nommaient parfois respectueusement "le vieux": pour Céard, c'était un positiviste dont le pragmatisme était capable de corriger les maux du monde; pour Huysmans, ce sceptique avait d'abord offert par la lucidité désespérée de ses vues une consolation aux âmes d'élite; pour Maupassant, ce destructeur de chimères avait dressé crûment le tableau de l'existence.'[35] Zola, again, appears to be the exception of the group in vigorously seeking to negate the great negator's views, notably in the positive attitudes of Pauline of *La Joie de vivre* set in opposition to the popular pessimism of Lazare – though, as Huysmans was quick to point out, she is the more truly Schopenhauerian with her acceptance of the human condition and her altruism.[36] In general, Schopenhauerian themes provide suggestive correlatives in the fiction of the naturalist writers, like Ixion's wheel, the symbol of time, and the eternal round in which naturalist characters and plots are entrapped, or the 'metaphysics of love' and the inevitable disillusionments that befall naturalist lovers. In this group of texts, the intradiegetic commentator of the previous type, usually a doctor or physiologist, is replaced by the pessimistic thinker, like Norbert de Varenne in Maupassant's *Bel Ami*, who keeps the hero's worldly successes in perspective.

The French writer who most thoroughly drew lessons from Schopenhauer's ideas, and in whose works the various threads of my demonstration in this chapter seem best to converge, is Henry Céard. He saw beyond the popular image of the German philosopher as a pure negator and was more responsive than most to his more positive prescriptions, elaborating, despite some apparent misinterpretations, a similar doctrine of resignation. Furthermore, he established a link between the fashionable philosopher and the obscure 'writer' Thyébaut, arguing that they shared the view that 'le devoir de tout être pensant était de réparer vaille que vaille les malfaçons d'un univers construit sans soin, remis à la conduite de l'instinct et de corriger à force d'intelligence les inconvénients de la nature et des individus'.[37] But, above all, Céard's work illustrates the obsessive reworking of Flaubertian themes, most obviously in certain minor texts, like 'La Tentation de Pécuchet', published in *L'Evénement* in 1891 (6

September), or the unpublished 'final chapter' of *L'Education sentimentale* that he wrote to amuse Thyébaut in which Frédéric and Deslauriers read that their brothel, the maison de la Turque, has just burnt down![38]

But *Une Belle Journée* (1881), Céard's major achievement – and the most representative work of this rather sour comic strain of texts – a novel that, not surprisingly, the author dedicated to Thyébaut and one which illustrates his doctrine of resignation, also shows a marked influence by Flaubert, or, more precisely and more significantly, represents an attempt to rewrite *Madame Bovary* in the mode of *L'Education sentimentale*. It is a key naturalist text, not only because it illustrates these various tendencies but also because, despite its obscurity, it represents a considerable literary achievement. As Murray Sachs has argued, Céard's novel 'deserves our attention for its intrinsic artistry as well as for what it can tell us about the esthetics of Naturalism'.[39] Unlike the plot of Flaubert's text, however, which stretches over a considerable expanse of time, the (in)action of *Une Belle Journée*, as the ironic title implies, is concentrated into a single day. But, as Deffoux and Zavie describe the work – 'un modèle accompli de l'esthétique naturaliste', 'trois cent quarante-six pages où rien ne se passe'[40] – it seems to have fulfilled as far as possible the Flaubertian ideal of a novel about nothing. The plot is indeed barren in the extreme, one which most writers would consider suitable for the shortest of short stories: one Sunday the wife of an upstanding architect, Mme Duhamain, has a rendez-vous with an upstairs neighbour, M. Trudon, with whom she recently danced at a ball. They plan to spend a 'perfect day' in the country; they stop off at a restaurant on the way, become rapidly bored by each other's company, are trapped in their private room in the restaurant by the rain, eventually take a cab and return home separately, she to her husband, he to a woman that he brings back in frustration at the abortive adultery. 'Voilà tout!' The art of this novel resides, clearly not in its plot, but in its depiction of bourgeois life and attitudes; in its masterly study of obsessive economy, order, hypocrisy and repressed sexuality; in its fine descriptive passages, with their typically livid naturalist tones, depressing landscapes and skyscapes rendered with an unquestionable poetic sense, indeterminate hues of twilight in the rain, with a symbolic fading of the contours of reality; in its uncompromising analysis of the fundamentally gross and banal motivations that human beings disguise with grandiose notions of love; and, above all, in the skilled manipulation of different levels of discourse and shifts of point of view, which constantly bring out the vast gulf between the two characters, the contrast between their brutal, selfish, frank and scornful inner discourse and the polite, decorous and banal nature of their conversation, the misunderstandings between them, the conventionality and emptiness of their language, the poverty of their thought. C. A. Burns has suggestively related this novel to the whole tradition of the classical *roman d'analyse*, extending from *La Princesse de Clèves* to *L'Immoraliste*.[41] More precisely perhaps, the novel invites comparison (and more revealing contrasts) with *Les Liaisons dangereuses* – Céard had a particular fondness for Laclos. It is a novel of the (*failed*) seduction of a respectable, married woman, of the most harmless of liaisons, a novel in which language proves to be as ineffective as it is effective in the earlier work and in which the variations of discourse provide an equivalent device to the epistolary fracturings of the diegesis. 'Quel Lovelace!', Trudon remarks of the wayward husband of his companion's friend, 'essayant d'insinuer par ce blâme hypocrite qu'il était un cœur d'or, incapable d'une mauvaise action' (p. 101),[42] referring the reader back to the genre of the successful seducer, of whom he represents a pathetic parody.

By the time the couple leave the restaurant after a visit to the privy, all vestiges of romance have been stripped away from their relationship, which ends, as the narrator makes clear, in vulgar pisses not ardent kisses. All the veils of illusion have been lifted; the naturalist 'epiphany' takes place. Trudon sees a different person in his companion and, in the very nullity of their experiences, they achieve for the first time a sense of communion, an 'inerte sympathie'. Somewhat improbably – for the limits of her intelligence have previously been emphasised – Mme Duhamain becomes the vehicle of the standard philosophical conclusion of this type of text, presenting through her 'obscure consciousness' the philosophy of resignation of the Schopenhauerian author of (the play) *Les Résignés*[43] and friend of Thyébaut:

Pendant qu'elle coiffait son filet de nuit où ses cheveux tout blonds tombaient retenus par les larges mailles blanches, des philosophies s'éveillèrent dont elle eut obscurément conscience. Elle comprit que la misère des cœurs résulte non pas de la douleur continue qui les poigne, mais de l'effort qu'ils font pour échapper à leur condition. L'idéal qu'ils réclament ainsi qu'une délivrance se montrait plus meurtrier encore que les vulgarités auxquelles ils tentaient de se soustraire, et puis, il y avait en plus les dangers, les craintes, les pertes d'habitudes, et aussi, et invariablement, les retours plus douloureux, après les aspirations non réalisées. Elle devina quelle ampleur de sottise se manifeste dans les continuelles révoltes contre cette loi de la médiocrité universelle qui, pareille à la gravitation et despotique autant que la pesanteur, ploie le monde et le soumet à son ordonnance: cette nécessité lui apparut qu'il fallait se tenir à sa place et tâcher de s'y faire tout petit pour diminuer les risques d'aventures et provoquer le moins possible les déconcertants déclenchements de la fatalité. (pp. 338–9)

This unheroic, quietist ideal is the wisdom attained by Céard's new Emma Bovary, lacking the rebellious spirit to defy her 'fate', resisting the blandishments of her (pale imitation of) Rodolphe and deciding to stick it out with Charles. The 'plot' of *Une Belle Journée* brings the 'hero' and 'heroine' — if such terms can still be said to apply to such a work — back to their initial situation, whilst the real 'belle journée', the para-plot, the idyllic romp in the countryside, that they both imagined (pp. 88–90), never comes about. But this is not a novel in which nothing happens, so much as a novel in which what one expects to happen does not. At the beginning of the text, the narrator teasingly presents the story as 'un petit roman tout court', one which Mme Duhamain recalls, smiling 'ironiquement avec une sorte de pitié aiguë' (p. 3), and frames it with an almost identical closing statement, thus confining the 'adventure' to the security of the definite past, to the impregnability of the character's unshakeable habits and resolve. M. and Mme Duhamain are safely tucked up in the conjugal bed: 'Et le ménage sans caresses, le ménage sans désirs s'assoupit doucement, mêlant ses souffles, tandis que le balancier de la pendule, avec son va et vient raccourci, emplissait l'ombre de la chambre du battement continu des heures monotones' (p. 345). The ironic naturalist clock, ever present, still goes ticking on, for all that essentially happens in this 'comic' naturalist world, where habit inevitably prevails, is the passing of time. But there has been a gain in this 'gnostic' text. The value of habit has been discovered, habit which, at least, is human activity in tune with time and not engaged upon a futile rebellion against it. The value of resignation has been discovered too, along with an essential tenet of the naturalist view: the fundamental sameness and tedium of human experience. Mme Duhamain's resolution in the affairs of the heart echoes the resigned attitude of André in *En ménage*, published the same year as *Une Belle Journée*:

Ainsi de quelque côté qu'elle se tournait, le mariage ou l'adultère ouvraient devant elle un égal horizon de sottise, et l'adultère avait, en plus, l'inconvénient de compromettre et de déconsidérer. Désormais, son parti fut pris. Comme ces malades accablés qui renoncent à se retourner dans leur lit parce que le changement de position ne leur procure qu'un changement de douleur, elle se résigna. Banalité pour banalité, elle préférait la platitude légale; ennui pour ennui, elle acceptait plus volontiers celui-là qui ne l'empêcherait pas d'être respectée et qui n'aiguiserait pas contre elle les médisants commérages du quartier. (pp. 153–4)

Not the most eloquent of defences of the matrimonial state! But, more to the point, the passage confirms the fact that, if Céard, Thyébaut and the other naturalist writers liked to *recite* and *re-cite L'Education sentimentale*, they were no less impelled to *rewrite Madame Bovary*.

A critic of the *Revue bleue*, commenting on Céard's novel, sardonically imagines a conversation between Zola and his 'disciple':

Et le grand Zola dit au jeune Céard: tu es le bien-aimé dans la foule de mes disciples, qui sont quatre. A toi mes préférences, car aucun des autres n'a montré une soumission si complète ... *Une belle journée* réalise ma formule dans sa simplicité et son intégrité. Ni poésie, ni sentiment, ni intérêt, rien, rien, absolument rien! Bravo! Embrasse-moi, jeune Céard! Et rien, pas dans une nouvelle de quelques pages, mais rien dans tout un volume, voilà le beau, le magnifique, le triomphant.[44]

In fact, this assessment contains more error than irony. Zola's own review of the novel in *Le Figaro* (11 April 1881), for example, though laudatory, contains certain reservations and certain telling turns of phrase with which Zola tended to express his tacit disapproval: 'note extrême', 'amour de la mécanique', 'rhétorique' (XIV, 584–5). There is, of course, nothing resembling *Une Belle Journée* in Zola's works. For the younger writer this novel represented, already in 1878, when it was first written, a departure from Zola's manner. As Céard later explained in a letter to René Dumesnil (13 July 1916): 'Je me suis détaché des procédés de Goncourt et de Zola; *Une Belle Journée* fut le symptôme de ma transformation.'[45] Once again we can discern at the heart of the French naturalist movement, even before its heyday in the early 1880s, a considerable shift in emphasis from our first model, dramas of catastrophic degeneration motivated by scientific theories, towards the Flaubertian model, the 'comedy' of human illusions and of the trivialities of bourgeois existence, now seemingly ratified by a philosophy of resignation. Once again one becomes aware of the extent to which much naturalist literature was written, in fact, in reaction to Zola's manner. It was not just a question of Goncourt's own jealous reaction in breaking publicly with Zola in his attack on what he called the *canaille littéraire* in his preface to *Les Frères Zemganno* (1879). It was rather a growing impatience with the conventions of the first naturalist manner even at this relatively early stage, a sense of its flagging relevance, as Maupassant explains in his study of Zola, situating the problem in relation to the inevitable

decline into monotonous repetitiveness and loss of appeal of any
literary tendency:

Quelque belle qu'elle soit, une forme devient monotone, surtout pour les gens
qui ne s'occupent que de littérature, et qui en font du matin jusqu'au soir,
qui en vivent ... Les plus grandes merveilles mêmes, que nous admirions
passionnément, nous écœurent parce que nous connaissons trop les procédés
de production, parce que nous sommes du bâtiment, comme on dit.[46]

The advantage of the Flaubertian model was that it 'thematised' this
very process of banalisation. Thus, if one is condemned to repeat
oneself, one might as well repeat oneself repeating that life repeats
itself. Hence, in the works of the more rigorous naturalist writers,
the tendency to abandon clinical analyses and evolve towards more
ironical and parodic modes of representation.

Huysmans is undoubtedly the writer who best exemplifies this
trend, for he wrote significant examples of the two models: *Marthe,
histoire d'une fille* (1876) for the first; *En ménage* and *A vau-l'eau*,
as we have seen, for the second. *Marthe* presents the thoroughly
documented case of the degradation of a young girl, charting her series
of falls into abject prostitution, along with the story of the decline
into alcoholism of one of her lovers, Ginginet, who ends up in the
'salle des autopsies' of – where else? – the Lariboisière hospital as
a demonstration model for the instruction of the interns. But the novel
also recounts the disillusionments and ennui of Léo, another of
Marthe's lovers and an autobiographical figure, of course. With
Marthe back in the brothel and the demonstrating surgeon about to
make his first incision on the second victim of heredity, Léo, the
disabused intellectual, unenthusiastically, resignedly, speaks of his
forthcoming bourgeois marriage: 'Ce sera terre à terre que de la
regarder, le soir, ravauder mes chaussettes et que de me faire assourdir
par les cris de mes galopins, d'accord; mais comme, malgré toutes
nos théories, nous n'avons pu trouver mieux, je me contenterai de
cette vie, si banale qu'elle te puisse sembler.'[47] The two trajectories
are also evident in Huysmans' next novel, *Les Sœurs Vatard* (1879),
dedicated to Zola by 'son fervent admirateur et dévoué ami' – a
dedication that the author was later to regret. This work has the
makings of an *Assommoir* with a double plot, along with grim slums,
sweat shops, seedy bars, popular language extensively used in
narrative sections, and two dramas of corruption and degradation:
one sister, Céline, all animal appetites, 'névralgies', 'chaleurs',
'persécutions de la chair'; the other, Désirée, like Gervaise, with the
same kind of ambitions for an ordered, honest life that are normally

the sign of imminent disasters in naturalist texts. But, significantly, the two potential tragedies drift into inconsequentiality, as one sister returns to a former lover and the other marries a better prospect than the poor fellow that she has been courting for most of the novel. Zola publicly complimented Huysmans on the novel's characters and progressive lack of plot (X, 1307–10). Flaubert, in a letter to the author (February–March 1879), was less impressed, criticising the novel for its plotlessness, for its lack of *la fausseté de la perspective*, for its structural resemblance to *L'Education sentimentale*. More important than the paradoxical nature of these views – Flaubert advising against a formula that he had inspired, Zola praising a formula that he never espoused himself nor recommended – they illustrate the shift in kind taking place within the naturalist scheme and the atrophying of plot that it entailed. For the writers like Huysmans and Céard who best represent this tendency, as we have seen, narrative itself takes on the repetitiveness, circularity and banality of the bourgeois discourse that in the manner of Flaubert they would satirise. In fact, as we shall see, apart from the pleasures and distractions of description – for the naturalists, in France in particular, had the painter's tastes and eye – there only remained for them, still within the naturalist genre and beyond the wry representations of this comic strain, a fuller indulgence in the malign joys of satire and the liberating exercises of parody.

6

IN THE IRONIC MODES: NATURALIST SATIRE AND PARODY

In the days when it was held, as Boileau states in *L'Art poétique* (II, 130), that 'tout poème est brillant de sa propre beauté', those impertinent genres, satire and parody, knew their place, but the tendency is now to regard them as transgeneric 'modes', ranging over a wide variety of texts. 'Diversity of form', as Alastair Fowler notes, 'is paradoxically the "fixed" form of satire', which 'catalyzes generic mix', as the etymology of the term [*satura*, mixture] implies.[1] Parody, too, in a literary context, rather than being a particular type of 'poem', includes works or parts of works created in opposition to texts of any possible literary kind or any set of conventions. 'La parodie', writes Jean-Marie Schaeffer, 'est une relation textuelle possible (elle est de tous les temps et de tous les lieux), alors qu'un genre est toujours une configuration historique concrète et unique.'[2] Like the world of antimatter in its relation to the material world, parody opens up the possibility of counterforms, usually with a devalorising effect, any time a literary work comes into being. Satire is more precisely focused – on the vices and follies of men – but is similarly universal in its application. Both involve some degree of imitation (of the text or the world) and both freely employ irony for their effects. As Linda Hutcheon observes:

L'ironie est essentielle au fonctionnement de la parodie et de la satire, bien que ce soit de manière différente. Autrement dit, l'ironie jouit d'une spécificité double – sémantique et pragmatique ... Il faudrait scruter les rapports du trope avec les genres d'un point de vue pragmatique (et non seulement antiphrastique) dans le but d'une différenciation générique plus précise.[3]

Whatever the strategies of representation of the text might be, parody and satire serve to 'rhetoricise' the fiction, implying, in Linda Hutcheon's terms, 'une attitude de l'auteur–encodeur à l'égard du texte lui-même', 'attitude qui permet et demande au lecteur–décodeur d'interpréter et d'évaluer le texte qu'il est en train de lire'.[4]

The interrelatedness of irony, satire and parody has led to some confusion of terminology or, in the other direction, to excessively precise and exclusive definitions. This indeterminacy is further complicated by the close but problematic historical association that is usually made between these modes and realist fiction. The origins of the realist novel have been traced to the mock epic (Fielding's 'comic epic in prose'), to mock romance (from Sorel's *Berger extravagant* on) or as an ironic response to the romance of a previous age. For Northrop Frye, ironic literature is an even vaster category situated at the 'realistic level of experience', 'taking the form of parody or contrasting analogue to romance', tragic or comic 'in its main emphasis', and including a large body of literature that deals with an 'unidealized existence' in which heroic values are lacking and which tends towards the demonic.

In order to attempt some more precise definitions and distinctions, one would first of all have to make the obvious points that irony is a trope, that satire (in literature) is directed against certain extratextual realities, whereas parody is aimed at other texts or literary conventions. Another useful distinction would be made between the *verbal* and the *situational* aspects of these modes.[5] Due to the more obvious and immediate presence of the (signs of the) voice of the ironist—satirist—parodist and to a lower level of ambiguity in the discourse, the 'verbal' forms are more distinct: verbal irony as antiphrasis, verbal satire as diatribe, verbal parody as pastiche. In the 'situational' aspect, however, the forms tend to coalesce, for the same narrative situation, particularly in realist works where the narrator is conventionally 'absent', can be at once ironical, satirical and parodic. Since, in their situational aspect, all three of these modes have in common the effect of reducing, deflating and degrading with a convenient implicitness, they are admirably suited as devices for maintaining the pretence of impartiality whilst fulfilling the less overt purposes of naturalist literature, in short, for reconciling the theory and the practice, the aesthetics and the pragmatics. In a sense, everything in the naturalist world tends in time towards degraded repetition, which is the essence of satire and parody. These modes, then, are at the core of the ironic, naturalist vision, which captures the very processes whereby art satirises life and life itself parodies art. It is perhaps above all in this ironic dimension that naturalist literature can most truly be said to represent an extreme form of realism, for its irony is more mordant, its satire more virulent, its parody more defiant – and, despite the connections, each of these aspects deserves separate treatment.

Critics have long recognised the extent to which naturalist literature relies upon irony. That energetic Victorian polymath, Havelock Ellis, wrote in 1896 that 'Irony may be called the soul of Zola's work, the embodiment of his moral attitude towards life.'[6] Ellis had no doubt discussed Zola's works with the Scottish philosopher, Thomas Davidson, with whom he had worked to found in 1883 the Fellowship of the New Life (later the Fabian Society) and who caused a stir in the United States when, at the Concord summer school in 1886, he placed Zola in the exalted company of Aristotle, Plato and Christ, declaring that, in the whole range of literature, he knew of 'no more cool, calm, terrible irony than that of Zola'. 'It is', he added, 'the very irony of truth itself.'[7] But critics, especially when they take at their face value the writer's claims of impartiality, do not always recognise that this irony is an evaluative, rhetorical strategy. In fact, naturalist literature provides an almost inexhaustible mine of examples for the detectors of those strategies of complicity that constitute in fiction 'a rhetoric of irony'.[8] Verbal and situational irony depend, of course, on the reader sharing the values that seem to be implied by the ironic statement or situation, the most elusive being the kind in which Flaubert delighted and which challenges the implied reader's beliefs. The appeal of naturalist irony is to that cynical side of the reader's convictions which always expects the worst in life to prevail. But most naturalist irony is directed against the unscrupulous practices or the naïve beliefs of characters themselves, who only indirectly represent the beliefs and institutions that are being satirised or the literature that is being parodied. The following description of l'abbé Picot in *Une Vie*, a randomly chosen passage, illustrates the discreet operation of the narrator's ironic voice:

D'une inflexible sévérité pour lui-même, il se montrait pour les autres d'une implacable intolérance. Une chose surtout le soulevait de colère et d'indignation, l'amour. Il en parlait dans ses prêches avec emportement, en termes crus, selon l'usage ecclésiastique, jetant sur cet auditoire de rustres des périodes tonnantes contre la concupiscence; et il tremblait de fureur, trépignait, l'esprit hanté des images qu'il évoquait dans ses fureurs. (p. 168)

There is the ironic frustration of an expected antithesis at the end of the first sentence, then the unexpected apposition 'l'amour' strategically placed at the end of the next sentence, a shocking complement of the priest's indignation. There is the ironically located 'selon l'usage ecclésiastique', followed by the ironic situation of the priest's eloquence cast before his rustic audience, before the final ironic effect of the exposure of the priest's own vicarious involvement in the proceedings. In other cases, the ironic voice takes on a more jaunty tone and its mocking purpose is more in evidence. Much of *L'Assommoir* is written in this tone, as is the ribald *Autour d'un clocher (mœurs rurales)* (1884) by Fèvre-Desprez, which provides us with an extreme, outrageous example, a passage which describes in ecclesiastical terms one of the many encounters between the village priest (less verbally restrained than l'abbé Picot, but more actively involved) and the school mistress: 'Puis, tout d'un coup, en affamé, l'abbé, se dressant à moitié, troussa la dame, leva le voile du tabernacle, fourrageant en affolé dans les linges qui sentaient la femme à pleine gorge, lui équarquilla les cuisses et la goupillonna en conscience.'[9]

As one would expect, however, from a type of literature firmly established in the realist tradition in many of its procedures, most naturalist irony is purely situational, depending for its effects on the contrast between a character's hopes, ideals, aspirations and ensuing plight. Every text is in itself an example and illustrates the point. Some, like *Tess*, with its heroine as the helpless 'sport' of the 'President of the Immortals', rise to a sense of cosmic irony; others merely present characters as victims of some irremedial misfortune. Thus the naturalist narrative invariably functions as a mediator between the idealistic discourse of characters, society, tradition, and the ironic discourse of the seemingly absent narrator, for the narrative purports to be a neutral form of discourse, limited to an account of facts and events, yet operates as a vehicle for the frustration of idealistic expectations and the justification of tacit ironic responses. Into the apparent innocence of the mimetic representation and the historicity of narrated events is introduced a subversive element, the derisive or cynical intentionality of the ironist, engaging the reader in the veiled complicity of his deceptions and his indignation. Irony in naturalist literature is therefore an ideal medium for, on the one hand, satire, a disarming weapon that penetrates the armoury of the bourgeois ideology and institutions against which it is invariably directed, and, on the other hand, parody, for, as its function as a trope suggests – as a response to hyperbole[10] – by merely asserting the ways of the world it casts down the flights of fancy of idealistic literature.

The use of irony in the direction of satire in naturalist literature can be demonstrated in its diversity and at its best in a collection of short stories, in fact in the work which is supposed to have typified the French movement. We know that *Les Soirées de Médan* had a double purpose: to reaffirm the solidarity of the Médan group in the public eye and also to attack what Maupassant called, in his fanciful explanation of the genesis of the collection, the 'sentimentalité ronflante des romantiques', the hollow chauvinism of the literature of the day dealing with the Franco-Prussian War.[11] These two tendencies are not by any means irreconcilable, for to attack one's adversaries is a way of consolidating a sense of communion, and any declaration of principles serves to exclude those who do not share them. Even the elements of fantasy in Maupassant's presentation belong to this strategy of inclusion–exclusion and reveal what interests us here: the spirit of irony and raillery. The precise butt of the satire of the collection was in fact a diverse phenomenon, a whole set of entrenched and rarely disputed public attitudes towards the 1870 disaster that were as prevalent in the press, in the songs of the 'café-concert' and in school text books as in literary works, attitudes that gave rise to such organisations as the Ligue des Patriotes which sought to inspire in the new generations of France a spirit of heroic vengeance. For the young naturalists, the surest way to dispel such illusions was to demystify war and to present the public with an opposite diet to the jingoistic anecdotes with which it was being fed and in which it so delighted. Claude Digeon has noted the great similarity that existed amongst writings on the war of 1870 in France at this time, a common tendency to afford less importance to the imperial war and the major battles than to 'la seconde partie de la campagne, à la résistance nationale des francs-tireurs, ou aux petites luttes menées sur des points isolés'.[12] Deprived of a great military triumph to depict, writers relived the little victories: the heroic defence of a house, the courageous resistance of a group of civilians, adventures of the fearless 'turcos', skirmishes that illustrate the bravery and sublime spirit of sacrifice of the oppressed.

Paradoxically, with its idyllic setting, its sentimental, then pathetic plot, its worthy peasants and noble youths ready to sacrifice themselves for love or duty, Zola's contribution to the collection, the anthology piece 'L'attaque du moulin', seems to belong fully to the type of narrative that has just been described, a fact which explains the warm reception that it was given by critics generally hostile to the collection. In Zola's story, the Prussian invasion destroys the solidly established social order which, at the beginning of the story, associates the bourgeois values of work, economy and deferred sexuality with eternal nature, as the young Belgian, Dominique, is shown to have earned his place in this order of things and the right to marry Françoise, the daughter of the miller, le père Merlier. But, after the mill has been battered in a succession of raids by both contending forces, the story takes an ironic turn and is integrated into the dominant spirit of the collection at the very end, where the French officer, having recaptured the mill, bursts in amongst the pile of corpses which includes Dominique and le père Merlier and cries out in triumph before the bemused figure of Françoise: 'Victoire! Victoire!' With a single stroke the whole set of motifs of the narrative is transformed into rhetorical 'motivation' through the rebounding effect of this final touch, which reveals the manipulation of ironic contrasts contained in the story. This shock tactic is thoroughly consonant with the general effects of the collection, for all the stories are in different ways assaults on the reader's received ideas and heroic conception of war, provocative, outrageous statements like the 'para-texts' that accompanied the publication of the texts: Maupassant's article or the preface.

Zola's story, like the others in the collection, illustrates, therefore, the process by which representation in satire becomes instrumental, for, as Ronald Paulson remarks, 'however much mimesis and rep-resentation is involved, the generic end is rhetorical'.[13] The mimetic is one aspect of the double strategy of situational satire: to convince the reader of the reality of the fiction, but, at the same time, to devise significant contrasts of a derisive nature that are meant to provoke reactions in the reader. The mode thus combines the authority of narrative with an oblique form of discourse, as in the model of the ironic trope (a single 'signifier' referring to two 'signified', manifest and latent[14]), and works into the text contrasts between pretence and reality, between creed and conduct, between principles and practice, or, to give precise examples from Maupassant's famous story, 'Boule de suif', between the ideal morality of the citizens of Rouen, 'qui ont de la Religion et des Principes' (p. 85), and their abject behaviour – between, as the narrator observes on the intellectually most pro-gressive occupant of the carriage, Cornudet, 'les deux grandes passions qui occupaient toute sa vie: le Pale Ale et la Révolution' (p. 96).[15] Such contrasts may set in opposition the narrator's and the character's discourse, or the narrative events and an implicit system of values, or different parts of the diegesis of the same text. There is a particularly ironic effect obtained when the characters in these stories directly employ noble and heroic language in the interests of baser motives. Thus the bourgeois of Rouen in Maupassant's story invoke examples of heroic devotion – the exploits of Judith, Lucretia, Cleopatra, 'toutes les femmes qui ont arrêté des conquérants, fait de leurs corps un champ de bataille, un moyen de dominer, une arme, qui ont vaincu par leurs caresses héroïques des êtres hideux ou détestés, et sacrifié leur chasteté à la vengeance et au dévouement' (p. 109) – to persuade Mlle Rousset, alias Boule de suif, to yield to the Prussian officer so that they may continue their journey. Similarly, in Céard's story, 'La Saignée', the general-in-chief in charge of the defence of Paris during the siege is shown to be under siege himself to the tyranny of his elegant, voluptuous and fickle mistress, Mme de Pahauën, whom 'les imaginations militaires déréglées par de vieux souvenirs de romans-feuilletons' compare to 'quelque Jeanne d'Arc ou Jeanne Hachette', conjuring up 'les souvenirs des femmes romaines, les dévouements des épouses de Lacédémone' (p. 180), while the courtisan herself imagines that one day 'elle tiendrait sa place, dans l'histoire, à côté des héroïnes célèbres dont le courage et la volonté avaient affranchi des peuples et délivré des patries' (p. 198). The heroic sortie itself proves to be a humiliating defeat, a sordid bloodletting.

In the satirical world of *Les Soirées de Médan*, heroism has no effective role. In these 'Scènes de la vie militaire', all the action takes place in the wings of the theatre of war and, except again in Zola's story, the only combats that are described are either comic or grotesque, like the 'manœuvres' and the 'plan des attaques' of the little squadron of Rouannais preparing the 'blocus, comme pour une forteresse investie', to lay siege to Boule de suif's virtue (p. 108). Descriptions of battles in these texts are rare and are presented in a Stendhalian manner from the confused perspective of the simple soldier, ignorant and afraid. The army is a rabble, given to drunkenness, gratuitous violence, idleness, indiscipline and pillage, most dramatically in Hennique's 'L'affaire du Grand 7', where, to avenge the death of a comrade shot in a brothel, a whole company runs amok, destroying the brothel, killing all inside, then disposing of the officer who tries to stop them. Even in Zola's story, military action is an absurd toing and froing as each side takes over the mill.

Back at headquarters, as 'La Saignée' shows, things are little better. Maupassant observed in his article that his colleague's story was not to be judged according to historical accuracy, but according to a broader truth, for the story is 'toujours vraisemblable sinon vraie, mais toujours réelle depuis le vieux poème d'Homère'. Whether or not Céard had in mind the burlesque episodes of the *Iliad*, he certainly took up the old satirical theme of the warrior in the thrall of woman, the 'Omphale archetype' as Frye calls it, 'the man bullied or dominated by woman, which has been prominent in satire all through history'.[16] Thus, as he censures the weakness and indecision of the

leaders in the struggles of 1870, Céard links up with the antifeminine
tradition of satire through the flippancy, cynicism, cold ambition,
sphinx-like airs and inexhaustible sexuality of Mme de Pahauën,
who becomes a mythical figure, reminiscent of Zola's Nana, a symbol
of the fallen Empire, 'la courtisane éclatante que maudissaient
les Juvénals' (p. 188), crossing 'la Seine ensanglantée' with her
'apothéotique allure' (p. 207), like a modern Cleopatra, deploying
'l'obscure puissance' of her sexuality to direct the course of History.
Similarly, Alexis, in 'Après la bataille', reworks an ancient satirical
theme, combining the antifeminine with the anticlerical as in the
medieval *fabliaux*. La baronne de Plémoran transports the body of
her husband from the field of battle, picks up a young priest lying
wounded by the roadside and makes love with him before the night
is out. Despite the long passages of naturalist explanation on heredity,
past history and temperaments, there emerge in this story of a priest
and a faithless wife the contours of the old fable of the Widow
of Ephesus from the *Satyricon*[17] – a theme to which we shall
come back – illustrating the fragility of codes of honour in such
circumstances.

Unmasking the frailty of bourgeois principles and the sexuality of
respectable people is manifestly one of the major objectives of 'Boule
de suif' – to return to Maupassant's tale. The narrator indulges in
the satirist's malicious pleasure of exposing the capers of the upright
wine merchant, nicely named Loiseau, along with the prurience of
the bourgeois gentlemen (as Boule de suif, finally, does her 'duty')
and the barely disguised desires of the bourgeois ladies who secretly
envy the manner of her humiliation. But Maupassant's story, it could
be argued, turns upon other appetites, more ritualised but no less
inherent in the satirical vision. From the beginning to the end of the
story, the travellers think of little else but eating, their appetites
particularly keen at the time of the 'sacrifice' of Boule de suif, whose
provisions they have already consumed on the road. The girl herself
is described unequivocally as a 'tasty dish': 'Petite, ronde de partout,
grasse à lard, avec des doigts bouffis, étranglés aux phalanges, pareils
à des chapelets de courtes saucisses, avec une peau luisante et tendue,
une gorge énorme qui saillait sous sa robe, elle restait cependant
appétissante et courue, tant sa fraîcheur faisait plaisir à voir' (p. 86).
In short, Loiseau's little joke – 'il proposa de faire comme sur le
petit navire de la chanson: de manger le plus gras des voyageurs' (p. 88)
– becomes ironically an exact gloss on the instinctive cannibalism
of this microcosm of society.

'O sainte joie des bâfres!', declares the narrator of 'Sac au dos', the Huysmans text, in which the alimentary instinct also plays a dominant role. The war memories of Eugène Lejantel, who spends the whole campaign in the barracks, in hospital with dysentery or in a train being transported from one place to another then back again, form perhaps the most iconoclastic text of the collection, for the narrator's irony is turned upon all aspects of society, educational institutions, the law, political life, the army and the medical corps. But what Huysmans describes with particular insistence is the un-aesthetic side of military life: the promiscuities and bodily privations, the filth and the lice, the smell of sweaty feet and the bloodstained bandages, the sickness and the rudimentary needs, reminding us that in the often ultra-realist world of satire, humanity is reduced to its most animal aspects. So Eugène's dysentery – not to put too fine a point on it – has a double significance: both as a sign of the protagonist's contamination by this repugnant reality and as a kind of correlative to the narrator's unrestrained choler. At the same time, this character, despite the artistic sensitivity that he naturally derives from his status as a Huysmansian hero, lives by ruse, expediency and deception, becoming a kind of naturalist picaro, or, to use Frye's terminology, a 'low-norm *eiron*', 'irony's substitute for the hero'.[18] Particularly at the end of the story, he illustrates the fundamentally regressive nature of the *eiron*'s dubious accomplishments, the very opposite of those brought about by the true hero's ascensional powers, as he takes refuge at home 'pour savourer la solitude des endroits où l'on met culotte bas, à l'aise' (p. 151).

Les Soirées de Médan is thus a collection of texts rich in mock effects, ranging from the most implicit diegetic arrangements to the most explicit intradiegetic comments. One could even suggest that their very form is an integral part of their rhetoric of irony, for they combine an amplitude conducive to realistic representation with a concision appropriate to the revelation of significant contrasts and parallels, incorporating aspects of traditional ironic genres (the picaresque adventure, the *fabliau*, even the convention of the 'ship of fools' in 'Boule de suif') into a series of short, varied works in implicit defiance and rejection of the epic expansiveness and con-tinuity of the noble genre of war. As Vladimir Jankélévitch argues, 'l'ironie non seulement abrège, mais encore morcelle'; whereas 'la continuité est sérieuse', irony 'désagrège et futilise la totalité destinale'.[19] In this collection of terse, ironic tales, epic *élan* is impossible and the 'disillusionists' of Médan (to adapt the expression of one of the group) have presented (to return to the supposed etymology of the term) a true mixture, a harvest of the bitterest of fruits to be served up to what one critic calls the 'Cankered Muse of Satire'.[20]

The antimilitarism of *Les Soirées de Médan*, though it set the pattern, as we have already noted, for a whole series of such works, is only one aspect of a more general satirical tendency in naturalist fiction, which normally grew out of the journalistic activities of naturalist writers. An obvious example is Paul Alexis, who cut his teeth with a home town journal *Le Grognon provençal* before becoming Trublot, the mordant contributor to *Le Cri du Peuple*. A more obvious example would be Zola himself, according to Louis Desprez. '*Les Rougon-Macquart*', he writes, 'sont imprégnés d'une morosité forte. Toutes les pages vibrent d'une sourde colère. Sous le naturaliste couve un satirique contenu.'[21] In any case, satire, however destructive its intentions, does derive from a desire, albeit frustrated and latent, 'to mend the world with a sense of publick Spirit', as Swift put it. But, in the naturalists, any sense of public spirit is hard to trace in political life, for they shared a common disdain for the political institutions and politicians of their age, whether or not they tended in their own views to the right, like Edmond de Goncourt and Daudet, or to the left, like Zola and Alexis. The naturalists held in equal contempt those in power and those that sought it. Edmond de Goncourt prided himself on never having voted in his life, and the *Journal* contains such cynical, Olympian and dismissive comments as the view that 'il n'y a que deux grands courants dans l'histoire de l'humanité: la bassesse qui fait les conservateurs et l'envie qui fait les révolutionnaires' (12 July 1867). Zola's political activities predated and post-dated his main naturalist period, confirming Yves Chevrel's observation that naturalist writers played an essentially critical role in political life,[22] that is when they did not treat the whole business with complete disdain. Zola poured as much scorn on the heads of politicians of the Third Republic as on the leaders of the previous régime. 'Prenez-moi un scrofuleux, un crétin, un cerveau mal conformé,' he wrote in an article for *Le Voltaire* (17 August 1880), 'et vous trouverez quand même dans le personnage l'étoffe d'un homme politique. J'en connais que je ne voudrais pas pour domestiques' (X, 1372).

There is little doubt, then, that naturalist satire is more moral than political. As a body of literature, it represents a major assault on bourgeois morality and institutions. Naturalist fiction takes an unmitigated delight – where it does not see the process as a serious duty – in revealing the vices, follies and corruption behind the respectable façade, in exposing the 'other Victorians' and their

counterparts elsewhere, in uncovering the 'worm in the bud'. Along
with the host of adulterous respectable women and husbands seducing
servants or frequenting brothels, there is the recurrent figure of the
upright middle class gentleman with secret vices, like Alexis's M.
Murand, a model of punctuality, reliability and polite reticence, a
devoted card player, whose 'pot aux roses' is unearthed at the end
of the novel: 'plusieurs liaisons, aussi clandestines que dangereuses:
des femmes mariées ... des mineures encore chez leurs parents ... la
propre fille de la servante-maîtresse, par lui retirée du couvent et
rendue enceinte ...'.[23] There is venality along with the venery in texts
which satirise bourgeois greed and corruption, like the particular
string of plays that deal with vicious struggles over a will: Zola's *Les
Héritiers Rabourdin* (1874), inspired by Ben Jonson's *Volpone*; the
most famous French naturalist play, Henry Becque's *Les Corbeaux*
(1882); and Hennique's *Esther Brandès* (1888), in which a young
Jewess hastens the death of her brother-in-law to share her sister's
inheritance. But the ultimate and most rudimentary example of a
naturalist text in this vein must be *Une Vieille Rate* (1883) by Lucien
Descaves, another of those works, published by Kistemaeckers in
Brussels, which take naturalist tendencies to the extreme. The novel
consists of nothing more than a series of episodes in the struggle to
the death between a rich old lecher, Gamard, and his housekeeper,
the 'vieille rate' in question, which only ends when a final victory costs
the former his ultimate defeat and the latter triumphantly inherits.
Such texts have recourse to the most familiar procedure of satire, that
of animalising human behaviour and analogising human beings in
relation to the less endearing species of the animal kingdom, like
crows, foxes and rats.

Another frequent device of satire exploited to the full in naturalist
fiction is the use of the servant's perspective to expose the hidden
baseness of a bourgeois household: chambermaids' gossip become
literature, the goings-on upstairs, particularly in the lady's chamber,
seen from downstairs. The canonical text would be *Le Journal d'une
femme de chambre* (1900) by Octave Mirbeau, who, if he had shared
his colleagues' disdain for politics and had not been away at the time
on political business in his subprefecture, would have been one of the
contributors to *Les Soirées de Médan*. The novel purports to be the
authentic diary of Mlle Célestine R..., touched up by the author –
we are asked to believe – against his will.[24] It is a catalogue of
revelations of the secret life of the bourgeoisie, a fund of anecdotes
ranging from the most scabrous to the mildly comic, the whole tenor
of which is summed up in a scene in which a group of servants gossip

away at the grocer's shop: 'Une odeur de saumure, de légumes fermentés, de harengs saurs, persiste autour de nous, imprègne nos vêtements ... C'est intolérable ... Alors, chacune de ces créatures, tassées sur leur chaise comme des paquets de linge sale, s'acharne à raconter une vilenie, un scandale, un crime ...'[25] The view from the kitchen degrades, levels, assimilates and presupposes that what remains hidden is shameful, sordid and rotten. It leads to works that are plotless, episodic, a series of exposures loosely linked by an inquisitive eye or a loose tongue or an indiscreet pen. Even though the satirist, as Gilbert Highet points out, presents his fiction as a continuous story with a single title, the workings and development of a plot are his least concerns. 'Therefore gaps and interruptions, even inconsistencies, in the story scarcely concern him. His characters flit from one amusing humiliation to another with scarcely any intervals of time and reflection.'[26]

Pot Bouille (1882), or 'Zola's Stink-Pot' as an American reviewer dubbed the novel,[27] is the masterwork of naturalist satire, typifying its themes and procedures. As F. W. J. Hemmings has observed, there is only 'the ghost of a plot in this book',[28] merely a series of furtive adulteries, wrangles over dowries and wills, a merry-go-round of sordid philanderings in a Parisian apartment house of supposedly impeccable respectability. The 'hero' of the 'novel', Octave Mouret, an inveterate womaniser, a kind of degraded Rastignac, a salesman who has given up travelling and decided to 'conquer Paris' from the counters of a department store, provides the link amongst the various episodes as he moves from ménage to ménage, seducing the ladies whilst his friend Trublot concentrates on the maids. The basic procedure of his novel is exposure. Each chapter begins with a pretence of respectability and moves to sordid revelations, just as the novel opens with Octave's arrival at the apartment house and his impressions of its luxurious façades, its 'abîmes d'honnêteté', then proceeds to penetrate into the ignoble secrets beyond appearances. As well as being endowed with the convenient virtues of mobility and irresistible charm conducive to revealing situations, Octave is invested with a penetrating, indiscreet look, which constantly gives him access to secrets hidden behind half-closed doors and to any woman's 'heart'. Scenes of peeping, prying, surprising proliferate in this text. In *Pot-Bouille* the spectacle of the human comedy develops into farce. The patron saint of the naturalist writer in this satirical vein is clearly the mythical character Asmodeus, the limping devil who raised the roofs of houses to reveal the household secrets beneath.[29]

Zola skilfully employs for his satirical purposes the device of gossiping servants notably in the famous scene in which Octave and his mistress, Berthe, during their rendezvous in a maid's room, are forced to overhear the tittle-tattle of the maids from the kitchen yard as they uninhibitedly comment on the 'affairs' of each household, for in this novel the omniscient narrator lives in the kitchen: 'Maintenant, leurs amours, si soigneusement cachés, traînaient au milieu des épluchures et des eaux grasses. Ces filles savaient tout, sans que personne eût parlé' (IV, 589). Degrading, levelling and debased repetition are the basic processes at work in this as in any satire, as shown in the concluding statement of the novel, whereby Julie is given the authority of the last word: 'celle-ci ou celle-là, toutes les baraques se ressemblent. Au jour d'aujourd'hui, qui a fait l'une a fait l'autre. C'est cochon et compagnie' (IV, 683). Scenes are repeated in the novel's constant round of furtive encounters. Berthe performs the same practised ploys to get her man, any man, and the women for Octave are all the same. At the end of the novel, Octave has 'une singulière sensation de recommencement' (IV, 680). The treadmill of ruttishness and petty exploitation, with its pretence of honesty and finery, grinds on. Zola called *Pot-Bouille* his *Education sentimentale*.[30] The comparison is strained, but there is at least in Zola's novel, as in Flaubert's, a certain jaded promiscuity, a sense that in bourgeois society there is a permanent adulteration of values and ideals and that action is inevitably and inherently degraded, repetitive, indiscriminate. 'There is a systematic animalization of everything connected with sex', as F.W.J. Hemmings notes, 'not excluding maternity', for the novel contains, of course, a confinement scene in all its gory details.[31]

Certain modern critics have expressed admiration for *Pot-Bouille*, somewhat surprisingly, since it is not normally recognised as one of Zola's major works. Brian Nelson admires in this novel 'an assured and controlled art, revealing an unfamiliar Zola with no small talent for incisive satirical comedy', quoting George Steiner's claim that it 'is one of the best novels of the nineteenth century – great in its comic ferocity and tightness of design', as well as Lionel Trilling's assessment that the novel is 'in the tradition of massive comic morality' alongside works by Breughel, Ben Jonson, Swift, Hogarth, Heine, the later Dickens and Flaubert.[32] Yet, when the novel first appeared, it met with an onslaught of attacks. In reply Zola insisted upon the serious moral purpose behind it. 'Pas une page, pas une ligne de *Pot-Bouille*', he wrote in *Le Gaulois*, 'n'a été écrite par moi sans que ma volonté fût d'y mettre une intention morale.'[33] Such a claim may seem like a mere defensive strategy conjured up for the occasion, for it clearly contradicts the more usual statements about the moral impartiality of naturalist fiction. But it clearly confirms the view that, in adopting the satirical mode, naturalist literature does inevitably moralise, however obliquely. Less convincing, however, was Zola's further claim that his novel is realistic. When Henry Fouquier listed thirty-one improbabilities in *Pot-Bouille* in an article in *Gil Blas*, Zola replied point by point, though conceding that his novel 'prend parfois un ton aigu de satire' and that 'l'accumulation des faits en un même cadre lui donne souvent une intensité que le train-train réel de la vie n'a pas'.[34] But such improbabilities are also an inevitable feature of satire, which imposes a strain on the mimetic art. As Gilbert Highet remarks, 'few long satiric stories can be enjoyed unless we suspend disbelief'.[35] Interestingly, Brunetière, who was delighted with the excesses of *Pot-Bouille*, which seemed to justify all that he had ever said in depreciation of Zola's art, compared the novel, along with much other naturalist fiction, to a different, but allied genre: 'Jusque dans les œuvres des maîtres, et, plusieurs fois déjà, nous avons signalé cette remarquable affinité du roman naturaliste pour le vaudeville et la grosse farce.'[36] This was meant as obloquy more than as generic definition, but, as Gilbert Highet reminds us, the Romans enjoyed a type of entertainment on the stage consisting of variety shows with 'no continuity and no sustained plots' and involving 'turns', 'skits', dancing and 'the imitation of real-life situations', which were called *saturae* and were the forerunners of literary satire.[37]

The fact that *Pot-Bouille* could equally serve as an example of naturalist parody as well as satire is hardly surprising, since the two modes are so closely linked. It is a novel directed almost as much against bourgeois literature (or the literature favoured by the bourgeois reader) as it is against bourgeois morals. To a considerable degree it is the novelist's settling of accounts with his detractors and their moralistic rejection of his fiction from *L'Assommoir* to *Nana*. There are, for this effect, suitable foils built into the novel: an honest working class victim of bourgeois hypocrisy, a pregnant girl hounded out of her apartment for her immorality, and a despised author of naturalist novels who leads a perfectly respectable life with his happy family. When preparing the novel, Zola had Alexis obtain for him a copy of *Paul et Virginie*, the pre-Romantic novel of chaste love which became an obvious and frequent butt of naturalist parody. The texts by Bernardin de Saint-Pierre and Zola clearly belong to opposite orders of literature, but nowhere in *Pot-Bouille* is the parodic relationship between them made at all explicit. Whereas naturalist satire is very much in evidence, naturalist parody remains much more discreet and requires some preliminary theoretical consideration.

The realist aesthetic of naturalism would seem to preclude parodic effects from the mimetic naturalist text, for the respective devices of parody and realism are apparently incongruent. In plain terms, parody does not imitate actions and phenomena in life, but imitates and distorts another text or set of literary practices. The impulse of realism is to disguise literary conventions, whereas the mainspring of parody is to expose them. In creating an ironic hiatus between itself and the target text(s) and drawing the readers' attention to literariness and artifice, the parody clearly undermines the mimetic conventions. It would be tempting, therefore, to conclude that the two modes are irreconcilable, limit our interest to the single direction of travesties *on* naturalist texts and, in the manner of Archibald Shepperson's delightful survey of the burlesque novel in English, look at French equivalents of *Muddlemarsh, Beerjester Brewers* or *Twenty Thousand Tweaks Sundered the Flea*.[38] Nevertheless, the notion of parody *in* naturalist works is not as inconceivable as one might at first assume. Realist literature, as Harry Levin has shown, often has its origins in parody and many realist novelists have started out as parodists.[39] The problem is not the exclusiveness of the two modes, but rather the degree of explicitness that parody can enjoy in realist or naturalist literature. Naturalist texts would clearly avoid flagrant travesty and the more obvious parodying of a single text, preferring effects of debased recontextualisation directed at more general features in the target literature like generic conventions or typical characters and situations. Thus many of the same 'paratextual' procedures that can be seen openly displayed in more obviously parodic works are evident in naturalist texts, even though they may not normally be thought to function within the context of parody. Though compliance with the strategies of realistic representation precludes the more patent rhetorical devices of parody, they continue to function in ways that can be accommodated without undermining the mimetic illusion, through implication, allusion, irony. Incongruous analogies may be implied to actions, situations or other characteristics associated with the conventions of a genre, normally some form of romance, presented in the inner discourse of characters and opposed to the stark realities of their lives. Any direct evocation of the target literature, usually, in French texts, the works of Lamartine, George Sand and Walter Scott, as well as *Paul et Virginie*, appears as references to the characters' readings. Such literature is thereby deprived of the status of mimetic representation and its conventions are discredited as they are contrasted with the representational force of the degraded realities.

Just as *Madame Bovary* exploits the topos of the heroine's Romantic readings – *Paul et Virginie* again and 'Le Lac', 'choses historiques' in Walter Scott – the humble whore of *La Fille Elisa* reads and succumbs to the lure of the kind of literature that the author denounces in his preface. The hero of *L'Education sentimentale*, who, typically, 'ambitionnait d'être un jour le Walter Scott de la France', starts to write (and, just as typically, fails to complete) the type of romance that he would have liked to have lived with Mme Arnoux if he had not been a character in a realist or naturalist novel (I, chapters 2 and 3). In *Une Vie*, significantly the first novel of an amateur parodist, it is curiously the heroine's mother who is an avid reader of *Corinne*, the *Méditations* of Lamartine, 'romances langoureuses' and the inevitable 'livres de Walter Scott', but, in a naturalist fashion, she passes on to her daughter 'une sorte d'instinct héréditaire de sentimentalité rêveuse' (pp. 149–50). The mere mention of a text belonging to an incongruous order of conventions has a distinct parodic effect, for it acts as a kind of generic foil and prompts the reader to make contrastive associations between two text-worlds. More comic in their effects are examples of the same procedure in *Pot-Bouille*. The shrewish Mme Josserand is, ironically, a devoted reader of Lamartine's *Jocelyn*, while the naïve and blushing Mme Pichon, a voracious reader of romances, yields in a most unromantic scene to the sudden advances of Octave on the dining-room table between a plate of radishes and a copy of George Sand's *André*: 'et elle se soumit, il la posséda, entre l'assiette oubliée et le roman, qu'une secousse fit tomber par terre' (III, 76). In addition to such well-known Romantic texts, the naturalist novel constantly encodes mimetically its opposition to more popular forms of romance, compared to which its own harsh realities constitute a parodic gesture, works belonging to a typology that Maupassant neatly sketched in one of his articles:

C'est toujours la jeune fille pauvre qu'épouse un jeune ingénieur riche et plein d'avenir; des cousins qui s'aiment et se marient, ou bien un jeune homme ruiné qui choisit une riche héritière, et cela se passe avec des surprises, des héritages inattendus, pour équilibrer les situations, et des aventures dramatiquement attendrissantes dans le parc d'un vieux château breton. Il y a la scène de la tour, la scène de la chasse, la scène du duel et la scène de l'aïeule, invariablement ... De cette littérature 'sirop' à l'usage des *dames*, on tombe bien vite dans la littérature mélasse à l'usage des petites bourgeoises; et de la littérature mélasse on dégringole dans la littérature tord-boyaux (pardon) à l'usage des portières.[40]

Such an awareness of the stereotypes of bourgeois and popular fiction of their day lends weight to the view that naturalist works invite a reading that goes beyond the purely referential into the decoding of ironic effects directed against idealistic and noble genres that are *in absentia*, but implicitly present in the characters' expectations, which the reader may or may not share. To return to *Pot-Bouille*, there are certain standard anti-heroic episodes, like the duel that Octave and the cuckolded Auguste never get around to fighting or the bungled suicide scene in which Duveyrier, having failed to find a more 'romanesque' site, shoots himself in the toilet. At least, Zola writes, 'c'était un endroit tranquille, personne ne viendrait l'y déranger' (IV, 659). When his wife discovers him sitting there with a bullet hole in his cheek, somewhat insensitive to his heroic gesture, she cries: 'Eh! tuez-vous dehors!' (IV, 660). Indeed, in more formal terms, just as the servants' gossip that we have noted implicitly parodies the moralising (meta)discourse of the traditional narrator of romance, the monotonous repetitiousness of scenes in *Pot-Bouille*, which we have also observed, stands in defiance of the inexhausible inventiveness of the plot of romance.

Thus the naturalist text deploys its disconcerting effects at all levels of the novelistic structure, admitting shocking *subjects*, likely to shake its bourgeois readers into a reaction of indignation and disgust. It employs a *technique* that subverts the moral finality of the bourgeois novel and, at the level of the narration, yields the authority of narrative voice and commentary to a variety of sources likely to be disconcerting to the reader of such conventional works: to the language of servants in *Pot-Bouille*, to the slang of the Parisian worker in *L'Assommoir*, to the speech of Sicilian fishermen in Verga's *I Malavoglia*. The naturalist text constantly parodies the myths, plots, idealised situations and heroic character types of the institutionalised literature that it implicitly combats. As we shall see more fully in the following chapter, these parodic effects contribute to the 'pragmatics of rejection' that characterises naturalist literature.

Naturalist parody, therefore, tends to operate between a text and a genre and, paradoxically, tends to perpetuate the hierarchical differentiation between noble and inverted forms that is an essential feature of classical genre theory. The inversions that it brings about may be shown to exist even with genres other than romance that are seemingly remote from the modern world of naturalist fiction. In Zola's *La Curée*, for example, frequent allusions have been noted to *The Thousand and One Nights* and to the code of the fairy tale.[41] One could go on and establish more fundamental links between the genre and Zola's story of Renée Saccard's corruption, her affair with her effeminate stepson, Maxime, in the setting of extravagant dissipation during the Second Empire. Zola's demonic, inverted fairy tale begins with the beauty (Renée) marrying the beast (Saccard), then living it up licentiously ever after. It opens in a wood (the Bois de Boulogne), with the languid, if not sleeping, beauty riding in her carriage. There are, as in all fairy tales, interdictions and even a kind of magic potion: the 'plante maudite' which Renée bites in one of the steamy hot-house scenes of the novel (II, 345). There is a fairy godmother (of sorts), Mme Sidonie, Saccard's sister, the energetic 'entremetteuse', the indomitable 'magicienne', whose financial dealings unfailingly conjure up good fortune. Then, of the innumerable mirrors that appear in this novel of specularity as well as of speculation, there is the large looking-glass in Renée's mansion, which constantly reassures her that she is the most voluptuous of them all. But, in the penultimate chapter, in the midst of the orgy of masquerading and nudity of the *bal travesti*, on 'le jeudi de la mi-carême', in the perfect ambience for parodic reversal, Renée in her most daring *décolleté* sees the image of her degradation in the same mirror: 'Elle en était arrivée à cela, à être une grande poupée dont la poitrine déchirée ne laisse échapper qu'un filet de son' (II, 521). In such scenes, parody unmasks and tends to focus its effects upon the person of certain parodic figures, phantom heroes and heroines who embody the demotion. This grotesque mirror reflection of Renée, 'la déchirée', recalls the similar reflection of another fallen 'queen', the defeated Gervaise Macquart of *L'Assommoir*, whose shadow in the light of the street lamp is 'énorme, trapue, grotesque': 'un vrai guignol' (III, 922).

A form of divestment and travesty is also a feature of Zola's *La Débâcle* – to turn briefly to a different genre – the novel of the defeat of Sedan and the fall of the Second Empire. In some respects, this massive, almost Tolstoian text contains many genuine epic strains: rhapsodic passages, the famous Homeric leitmotiv and the equally Homeric scenes in which, high on 'la Marfée' like an ancient *theologeion*, the ruling forces of history manifest themselves to the King of Prussia as he contemplates the imbroglio of the battle below. But the novel also contains a parodic undermining of its own epic trends. It is, for example, narrated mostly from the far from heroic perspective of the simple troopers. 'Des héros peut-être', the narrator observes, 'mais des ventres avant tout' (VI, 846). Such a trivialisation of war, along with the frequent scenes of confusion and disorder in the ranks, adds to the ironic contrast with past Napoleonic glories. 'Hier la Grande Armée', as Hugo wrote in 'L'expiation' (*Les Contemplations*), 'et maintenant troupeau.' The dual perspective, the dialogic contrast which is so much a part of the parodic vision, is conveyed throughout this text by the Cervantic couple, the two protagonists, Jean Macquart, with his practical sense, and the Quixotic Maurice Levasseur, the intellectual seeker after military glory. But it is the Emperor himself who becomes, as Marx also saw him, the truly parodic figure, the very antithesis of the epic hero, reduced to a shadow of his Napoleonic self. He invariably appears as a vacuous presence, an 'ombre d'empereur, indéfinie et vague' (VI, 723). In one desperate expedient he makes up his face with rouge, like the victorious Roman generals, and emerges onto the field of honour to die. But the masquerade fails: 'La mort n'avait pas voulu de lui, décidément. Sous la sueur d'angoisse de cette marche au travers de la défaite, le fard s'en était allé des joues, les moustaches cirées s'étaient amollies, pendantes, la face terreuse avait pris l'hébétement douloureux d'une agonie' (VI, 874).

In Zola's earlier novel *La Terre* (1887), Jean Macquart's 'grand besoin de repos' after Solferino and before Sedan, his 'envie de s'allonger et de s'oublier dans l'herbe' (V, 827), introduces the basic framework of pastoral, as Eleanor Lincoln defines it, 'an interlude in epic or active endeavour when the hero faces the crossroads of choice'.[42] But, inevitably, following the tendency of naturalist literature to parody the noble genres, Zola's 'King Lear of the Beauce', with its realistic presentation of rural life, has the literary corollary of the anti-pastoral. Both in the story of how old Fouan divides up his land amongst his three children to be cast out into exile until the main pretender, Buteau, brutally kills him, and in the parallel development of Jean Macquart's retreat to the land, a number of pastoral themes are taken up and reversed. Instead of peace, tranquillity and innocence, Jean Macquart encounters violent disputes, rapaciousness and villainy on Zola's 'Cold Comfort Farm'. Instead of bountiful nature in harmony with man, bucolic *otium* and the lyrical celebration of love, in Zola's anti-Arcadia there is the constant battle of brutalising labour against the capricious elements, brutish rape and fornication. In *this* version of the pastoral, the myth that informs the lives of the peasants is not the legend of the 'golden race', but the litany of 'les malheurs de Jacques Bonhomme' (V, 812–13). Their present condition is beset with an agricultural crisis undreamt of in Arden. There is, however, romance of a kind in *La Terre*. Jean falls for Françoise in the opening scene – the one that was read out in a Victorian court and led to Vizetelly's prosecution – the scene in which, contrapuntally, he helps her mount a bull on her cow. Françoise is shown at her most resplendent somewhat later in the text, perched on a cart full of manure: 'elle avait l'air très grande, saine et forte, comme si elle eût poussé là' (V, 1066). There is even a complicated love intrigue, the familiar 'cross-eyed Cupid' situation of the pastoral: Jean loves Françoise who really loves Buteau who lusts after Françoise though married to her sister. But it ends in a brutal rape on an exposed hayrick, the very opposite of the enclosed and gentle *locus amoenus* where pastoral love is conventionally consummated.

Rape is a constant of the anti-pastoral, as it was of the medieval *pastourelle*.[43] Much of the dynamic tension of *Tess of the d'Urbervilles* derives from a naturalistic undermining of the novel's pastoral potentiality, as the consequences of the initial rape–seduction are played out deterministically against a Rousseauesque view of nature or, to put it more symbolically, in Hardy's words, as 'the serpent hisses where the sweet birds sing' (chapter XII). But the novel which invites the closest of comparisons with Zola's text is Ringuet's *Trente arpents* (1938). This work continually evokes the reassuring, recurrent patterns and rhythms of rural life in Quebec: 'D'un mouvement égal et continu le fil des jours s'enroule sur le fuseau de l'année; chaque aujourd'hui recouvrant un hier.'[44] As in *La Terre*, the passing of the seasons, the processes of ageing and death, are presented 'suivant l'ordre établi depuis les millénaires', and the four parts of the novel correspond to the four seasons in the life of the central character Euchariste Moisan. But the pattern of the character's gratitude for the harvests is blighted by historical disruptions: migration from Quebec to the United States, the strains of the First World War, an economic crisis. He loses his land in a lawsuit; and the once proud peasant becomes the victim of the more exacting pattern of naturalist degeneration, a pathetic, exiled figure, like Zola's le père Fouan, cut off in the appropriately named White Falls, USA, from his language, his culture, his land and his reason for living: another martyr to what he also calls 'la guigne', a fallen 'King Lear of the New Beauce', who has lost his kingdom, his 'thirty acres'. Just as Zola's novel was written against the tradition of the rustic idyll which George Sand had made popular, Ringuet's text is a response to the idealities of the Quebec 'roman de la terre', with its 'sentimentalité intempestive', its 'mièvrerie pastorale' and its 'faux lyrisme',[45] of which the harsh realities of the novel are an implicit indictment.

But, in Ringuet's serious text, there is no character who could be truly said to typify the more irreverent aspect of the spirit of the anti-pastoral. For this we must return to Zola's novel, to the figure of old Fouan's profligate son, Hyacinthe, nicknamed Jésus-Christ, a lazy drunkard, a veritable buffoon, whose vulgar antics enliven the pages of this often grim text. Significantly, he inhabits a dilapidated house called le Château; his best friend is a vagrant revolutionary named Leroi; and he feels a particular sense of affection and affinity for Buteau's jackass (a common parodic figure), Gédéon, which, in the lively grape-harvesting scene, drinks a bucket of wine and staggers drunkenly about (V, 1024). Hyacinthe's special capacity is his irrepressible flatulency. 'Jésus-Christ était très venteux', the narrator informs us, 'de continuels vents soufflaient dans la maison et la tenaient en joie' (IV, 634). With this, his version of the oaten flute of pastoral − Zola insists on the musicality of his talent − he is indeed the only character of this eclogue with the leisure to sing and pipe. But this character's particular art is also, in a vulgar sense, the expression of the essence of naturalist parody, which may be defined − if the reader will pardon the puns − as deflating *re-pètition* or *contrepèterie*.

Titles are amongst the most obvious of generic signals and titles of novels are usually indicative of the fictional types to which individual works belong: two abstract nouns, like *Pride and Prejudice*, for the novel of moral analysis; the riddling title, like *Under the Net*, for the novel of ideas; the figured title, *1984*, *Fahrenheit 451*, for the dystopia.[46] Like generic typologies, systems of classification of titles vary considerably in their degree of complexity. Using as a basis Yves Chevrel's mixed scheme,[47] one could suggest more simply that naturalist titles tend to fall into overall categories which reflect the different types of texts that I have defined. There are firstly the monograph titles, indicating usually the name of a character, a group or even a place: *La Fille Elisa*, *Marthe*, *Thérèse Raquin*, *Pierre et Jean* or *Les Frères Zemganno*, *Sous-Offs* or *Un Mâle*, *Trente arpents*, works which recount 'tragic' physiological destinies. Then there are the thematic titles, which refer to a more general situation or problem, *L'Education sentimentale*, *En ménage*, *Une Vie*, corresponding to the works of the more philosophical kind that has been defined. These categories are obviously not hard and fast, but the general validity of this division is suggested by the hesitance of certain writers over their titles, a fact which is also indicative of the general drift that we have noted among the French naturalists from the monograph to the problem novel. Zola's titles for the earlier novels of the *Rougon-Macquart* series tend to belong to the first category, then, after *Nana*, move into the second. The fact that *L'Assommoir* was originally to be called *La Simple Vie de Gervaise Macquart* points to this shift of emphasis. Similarly, Huysmans moved from *Marthe* and *Les Sœurs Vatard* to *En ménage* and *A vau-l'eau*, this last work bearing a different title, *M. Folantin*, down to the last stages of publication.[48]

There is, however, a third category of naturalist titles belonging to the works, or to aspects of the works with which we have been dealing in this chapter: ironic, satirical, provocative titles: *Pot-Bouille*, *Une Belle Journée*, *Charlot s'amuse*, even *La Joie de vivre*. As in the last case, or in the case of the subtitle to *Tess of the d'Urbervilles: A Pure Woman*, the irony is not always evident because it remains problematic. In one significant case − to return to the texts with which this chapter began − it was suppressed, for the Médan group intended to call their collection *L'Invasion comique*, thought better of it with so provocative a theme and substituted *Les Soirées de Médan*. Such compromises show that the naturalists were involved in artful strategies in presenting their works for publication within the context of certain reader expectations and also that their texts have a performative intentionality beyond the declared mimetic and demonstrative functions. The following chapter explores more fully these extrinsic and intrinsic aspects of the pragmatics of naturalist fiction.

7

THE 'SCANDAL'
OF NATURALISM

Parody is perhaps not normally considered to be an aspect of the reception of literary texts. But parodies *of* naturalist works, unlike the parodic dimension of naturalist texts themselves that was explored in the previous chapter, being more overtly derisive, critical and corrective, clearly form part of the multifaceted process of reception. They could be said to fall into two distinct categories: on the one hand, those that are part of the polemical rejection of the genre in its incipient and successful stages, representing a counteractive commentary in a literary, derivative form directed against the themes and procedures of the literature under attack; on the other hand, those which occur at the declining stage in the evolution of the genre, exposing these same themes and procedures to ridicule as mere conventions and stereotypes or, as we shall see in the conclusion of this book, incorporating them negatively into works written according to new conventions.

Clearly parodies of the first type are useful pointers to the precise nature of the literary, social and ideological codes that the innovative literature has violated. One rather elaborate example may suffice to illustrate the point. *Nana*, like any significant work, is, as we know, a complex 'hypertext' arising from the imitation, adaptation, transformation and exploitation of a variety of previous works and models, ranging from burlesque works to more prestigious texts in the tradition of the literature on the life of the courtesan, 'les Marion Delorme, les Dame aux Camélias, les Marco, les Musette'.[1] But it was also an important 'hypotext', inspiring, so it seems, as many 'hypertexts' as its heroine has lovers, of all shapes and sizes: pirate versions, stage adaptations, caricatures, pastiches, 'vignettes nanaturalistes' and 'nanatomiques', and parodies. One such work, *La Fille de Nana. Roman de mœurs parisiennes* by Alfred Sirven and Henri Leverdier,[2] deserves more than a passing reference, for it enjoyed considerable success, went through at least twenty-five editions and was translated into several languages. In this novel,

Nana is miraculously restored to life (or, more precisely, her death in Zola's novel is ignored) and she has in addition a daughter, little Andrée, or Nanette, conceived significantly in the courtesan's 'cinq minutes de béguin' with the only man she ever really loved. Thus, whilst her mother, the 'mangeuse d'hommes', goes rampaging on, Nanette, her spitting image, is protected from nefarious naturalist influences and from the typical naturalist fate worse than death by her 'sang tranquille et fort', by the Naviels, 'braves ouvriers' who bring her up, by her impeccable chastity, by her honourable fiancé and even by her supposedly lost, but still solicitous, father who makes numerous appearances in the novel in various disguises up to the inevitable recognition scene at the end of the work. In this way *ANdrée NAviel* is meant both to reflect and reverse her mother's destiny. Not, however, without a struggle, or a series of struggles involving her virtue, which form the major interest and suspense of the plot, as this 'frêle Andrée', 'la résultante de deux natures antipodiques', has to resist the 'fermentation impure' that emanates from her mother's world, in a kind of anti-naturalist experimental novel. She escapes the advances of her boss, not inappropriately called Paillardin, then turns down her mother's offer of, as it were, a partnership in the family business. Further close calls occur in a work that, in contrast with *Nana* itself, is all plot, with the ordered manipulation of surprise and suspense providing the providential scheme of this reversal of what the authors took to be the point of Zola's novel. There are gambling scenes, a duel, an English lord and a dying raja, and two rescues from fire before all comes to light and to order in a final courtroom scene where Nana's evil is exposed, the demon of heredity exorcised and Nanette consigned to blissful marriage. Thus Nana's daughter's role is not only to be a foil to Nana herself but to negate her by the active, redemptive power of her virtue. *La Fille de Nana*, as a work based on a moral law of providential retribution pitted against a work based on the naturalist law of catastrophic excess, serves to cleanse, replace, efface the earlier text, to wipe the slate clean – a veritable palimpsest. Indeed, the whole process is (melo-) dramatically reinforced in the denouement of the novel. A redeemed prostitute, Margot, throws vitriol in Nana's face. The evil courtesan, deprived now of all her possessions, of her beauty and of her sight, staggers down into the streets – where happy throngs of families are joyfully singing 'La Marseillaise' to celebrate the fourteenth of July (and, no doubt, the new 'Ordre Moral') – and falls through an open manhole into the sewers. Slowly, the character described as 'la pourriture des générations énervées qui coulait dans la puanteur du bourbier' is engulfed by the 'boue engluante' and is plunged 'à plein cours dans l'horreur de l'infection': 'Et son cadavre continua de rouler, noir de vase, gonflé de boue, et faisant parmi les tourbillons des culbutes hideuses sous les clartés livides qui tombaient des regards d'égout!'[3] Sirven and Leverdier have clearly defied the castigating closure of Zola's text (the scene of Nana's horrible disfigurement by smallpox) all the more horrifically to close it in their own *mud*-slinging version, resurrecting the heroine all the more effectively, and with a revealing insistence, to immolate the woman, the whore, the plebeian in her unfettered state. The stain on society has been effaced. The slut is back in her element, the snipe back in her gutter, the 'mouche d'or' back on the dunghill and, like some sordid excretion, Nana, with her threatening carnality, has been liquidated, liquified and literally flushed away.

Similar and, in their way, no less drastic corrections of Zola's texts were made in England. Angus Wilson has noted that the combined forces of Puritanism and the English law handed Zola's work over to the tract vendors, particularly after the Vizetelly trials:

Charles Reade's dramatisation of *L'Assommoir* was the only serious approach for the next ten years. For the rest Zola's novels were boiled down into twenty-page tracts of which 'Gervaise Coupeau. A story of drink' is a good example. The travesty of Zola's work may be judged from the following passage with which the work ends. Gervaise, widowed after the drunken death of Coupeau, is reformed and married to Goujet. Dear little Nana, a saved child, sits beside them. 'May mamma have some of this dish, Papa Goujet?' said Nana. 'And then, me, a little. I am *so* hungry, but don't give her any wine – no wine, papa, for my other papa was killed by wine.' 'I'll try to live again!', said Gervaise. 'And a happy life this time', Goujet added, 'for Drink *shall* not enter our home.'[4]

Even Reade's adaptation (of the French adaptation) of *L'Assommoir*, called simply and significantly *Drink*, which, according to Eileen Pryme,[5] enjoyed considerable success on the London stage and in the provinces, goes a long way in the direction of the temperance tract. Reade's Gouget [i.e. Goujet], who is an ardent temperance advocate, denounces the evils of drink, persuades Parisian workers to sign the pledge, takes Coupeau under his protection until the bigamous traitor Lantier and the wicked Virginie drive him mad with drink. Nana dies of misery (at least preserved from her fate in Zola's novel), but a new character appears, called Phoebe Sage, a 'café-concert' singer, who, true to her name, is the antithesis of the wayward Gervaise. Fortunately, the heroine is saved by Gouget's love, of course, while Virginie and Lantier are duly stabbed to death. The indefatigable Gouget has the last word: 'There is a Providence. Severe but just.'[6]

In all of these works we can see how Zola's texts have been appropriated to different, even opposite ends. Such appropriations were part of a process of active, corrective, parodic criticism aimed at redressing the improprieties of naturalist texts, tempering their audacity, recuperating them into the prevailing social and ideological order that they threatened to disrupt. In a broader context they were also part of a sometimes impassioned dialectic of effect and response, of purpose and resistance that this chapter aims to explore.

In the general drift of criticism in recent times towards an interest in the reading process and reception of literary texts, critics have looked for inspiration to the linguistic discipline of pragmatics, which rejects the priority traditionally given to the descriptive and representative use of language in favour of its performative functions. As Terry Eagleton has written on this trend: 'Literature may appear to be describing the world, and sometimes actually does so, but its real function is performative: it uses language within certain conventions in order to bring about certain effects in a reader.'[7] From this perspective, however, fiction seems to be a special and somewhat problematic case. In Rainer Warning's words, 'pour caractériser le discours fictionnel, l'on peut recourir au mode illocutoire du faire semblant. Ce faire semblant est une action ludique. Et l'essence même de la situation ludique, c'est son exclusion spécifique du monde environnant des actions, c'est-à-dire de la continuité des séquences d'actions qui la constituent.'[8] There appears, then, to be in fiction, with its 'pretending', a dissociation from the pragmatic situation, a break between the enunciation and the use or effect of the discourse. Nonetheless, Warning argues, the pragmatic model still remains operative, 'car le discours fictionnel lui aussi est utilisé, lui aussi se trouve, selon la définition de Morris, en relation avec des interprètes'.[9]

Naturalist works, which have recourse not only to the 'pretending' ('faire semblant') of fiction but also to the 'resembling' ('faire ressemblant') of mimetic literature and whose authors tend to define their purpose as descriptive and representational, place their readers in a particular dilemma. Their response may be either to accept the representation (and agree or disagree that it is representative) or see the text as (scandalous) perlocution, for there will always exist between writer and reader a contractual relationship of shared conventional expectations that the text either confirms or violates. These two responses are of necessity mutually exclusive, but the reader may be led into hesitance prompted by the ambiguity of the effects: finding the fiction representative enough or literary ('ludique') enough to be acceptable or to give offence. Naturalist fiction presents readers with both an imitative model of the reality in which they recognise their own historical situation, and a textual artifact which evokes a response according to preconceptions about the nature of realist representation. 'La fiction offre à la fois', adds Rainer Warning,

l'habituel et l'inhabituel, le normal et l'anormal, la positivité de l'autorisé et la négativité de l'exclu, la construction d'un monde et le combat contre cette construction, et de cette façon elle oblige le destinataire à intervenir, à prendre position, à prendre parti. Pour saisir pleinement tout ce qu'une telle prise de position implique comme processus négateur, conservateur ou même fondateur de normes, il faudrait certainement avoir recours à une analyse empirique de la réception.[10]

In *Le Naturalisme*, Yves Chevrel devotes a useful chapter to the problem of the reception of naturalist works ('La part du public', chapter X), which tends to focus on the theatre and on the situation in Germany, but which makes a number of important general points. There is the fact that each country, of course, has its history of controversy surrounding the publication of naturalist texts and the production of naturalist plays, a history of expressions of outrage by critics, public figures and indignant readers, as we saw to be the case in France and England, with polemics, censorship, prosecutions, petitions, and even earnest rewritings. The total picture of the reception of naturalist literature would be monumental in scale and has so far been drawn only in part. But what interests us more than the historical aspect of the question is the fact that, as Yves Chevrel reminds us, critical reactions to naturalist literature inevitably reveal the canonical models against which readers judged it, usually models of a literature designed to reassure them. The impact of naturalist literature was in all respects a 'succès de scandale', promoted by certain writers but even more so by critics always disposed 'à s'effaroucher et, par là même, à signaler aux lecteurs potentiels que quelque chose de nouveau est en train de se passer dans la littérature qui pourrait bien être résumé par l'adjectif "brutal".' Indeed, Chevrel adds, 'le public se sent agressé, soumis à des chocs répétés'.[11]

The shock factor of naturalist texts can be measured on the Richter scale of the vehemence of critics' counterattacks against this feeling of aggression. These were usually made on moral grounds, but frequently reveal a political dimension, for behind the outcries in the daily press in France were gathered the more formidable and powerful opponents of this new literature, the representatives of France's literary Establishment, the arbiters of taste associated with both literary and political officialdom. As Brunetière's prolonged campaign shows, naturalist works clearly provoked reactionary fears. Thus, in a sample of hostile reactions quoted by Louis Desprez,[12] we read Armand de Pontmartin's revealing claim that 'une littérature infecte s'est produite à la faveur des triomphes de la démocratie et du radicalisme comme ces couches d'insectes puants et malfaisants qui pullulent dans la vase, et en augmentent la pestilence, après les débordements'. For many years Zola entertained the notion of collecting together under the title *Leurs Injures* an anthology of the insulting articles, the 'crapauds', that he had accumulated. In an article in *Le Figaro* (28 February 1896), he claimed to have an attic full of them, 'toute une mare, la crapaudière elle-même, dans son affreux pullulement' (XIV, 730). He claimed to welcome the putrid flow of invective as a perverse proof of his vitality and distinction: 'on m'attaque toujours, donc je suis encore' (XIV, 733). Zola's heavy-handed irony is clearly a measure of the ferocity of the attacks that his works had provoked and, reciprocally, of the aggravation and exasperation that he had provoked by his works. 'A tout homme qui ouvre un roman de Zola', writes Yves Chevrel on the perils of reading naturalist texts, 'il faut une condition toutefois: qu'il soit, ou qu'il devienne fort, capable de supporter le choc d'un texte qui ne le ménage pas.'[13] Paul Lindau, it seems, was man enough for the task. Chevrel quotes his reactions on reading *Nana*: 'Avant qu'on se soit remis de son étonnement, on reçoit un deuxième coup en plein visage, encore plus cynique et brutal cette fois. On s'indigne, on veut rejeter le livre, mais l'intérêt est éveillé … On continue à lire.'[14] Most readers of naturalist texts, however, were much less compliant and the writers themselves regularly complained that their works were being judged as if they were addressed to young girls or to ladies of delicate sensibility. 'The novel', wrote Henry James in an article on *Nana* which touches upon the problem of the English reading public, 'is almost always addressed to young unmarried ladies, or at least always assumes them to be a large part of the novelist's public. This fact, to a French storyteller, appears, of course, a damnable restriction, and M. Zola would probably decline to take *au sérieux* any work produced under such unnatural conditions. Half of life is a sealed book to young unmarried ladies, and how can a novel be worth anything that deals only with half of life?'[15]

The situation was not in fact all that different in France, where the naturalist text was also held to be a *violation* and the expectations of a feminine reading public were kept constantly in mind. The author of *Germinal*, for example, made the following surprising declaration to a Viennese critic, Ernst Ziegler: 'Je crois pouvoir vous promettre que mon prochain roman n'effarouchera pas les dames.'[16] His *Une Page d'amour* was advertised in *Le Bien public* as 'une page intime qui s'adressera surtout à la sensibilité des lectrices, et dans une note absolument opposée à celle de *L'Assommoir*. Ce roman pourra être laissé sans crainte sur la table de famille.'[17] One of the standard defences of naturalist writers against charges of immorality was that, contrary to the prevailing view, it was idealist, Romantic literature that was responsible for the corruption of the 'fair sex'. 'De pareilles lectures et de pareils spectacles', Zola wrote (in an article entitled 'De la moralité dans la littérature'), 'encouragent les débauches solitaires, les réserves jésuitiques, les compromis et les détours du cœur. Walter Scott a fait plus de filles coupables et de femmes adultères que Balzac. George Sand a créé toute une génération de rêveuses et de raisonneuses insupportables' (XII, 511). In any case, the naturalist's argument goes, art has its own morality, as does the naturalist search for truth. 'Nos analyses ne sauraient être obscènes', wrote Zola, 'du moment où elles sont scientifiques et où elles apportent un document' (XII, 507). He boldly claims the moral high ground against 'les impuissants et les hypocrites': 'Le monument ne s'en élève pas moins pierre à pierre, et il vient un jour où, devant cette masse superbe, la postérité, qui en comprend enfin la grandeur logique, s'incline d'admiration' (XII, 512).

The problem of the reception of naturalist works cannot, however, be explained entirely by their readers' misreadings, their critic's misrepresentations and by the lack of an enlightened public, for there was undoubtedly an element of provocation on the part of the naturalist writers. 'Nous ne chatouillons pas', Zola revealingly wrote in the same article, 'nous terrifions, et une partie de notre moralité est là' (XII, 502). Consequently, they were compelled to deal circumspectly not only with their public's likely responses, but also with the reactions of the public authorities. Despite a few scares, the major French naturalists remained largely unscathed, but a number of minor writers, bolder in their effects, ran foul of the authorities. Indeed, the history of French naturalism is marked by a number of trials.[18] If it is undoubtedly true, as George Steiner argues, that the 'consolidation of middle class taste' and 'bourgeois criteria of allowed sensibility' in the mid-nineteenth century led to the famous prosecution of *Madame Bovary*, a work which in the area of sexual explicitness is very tame compared with the libertine fiction of the previous century,[19] there had nonetheless been a considerable easing of constraints in France since the date of Flaubert's *cause célèbre* (January and February 1857). Even in the later stages of the Second Empire, as the examples of *Germinie Lacerteux* and *Thérèse Raquin* show, there was a greater degree of tolerance of sexually explicit material. The early years of the Third Republic were considerably more tolerant than the previous age. As Alexandre Zévaès explains, with the eventual abrogation of the censorship laws of 1819, to which Baudelaire and Flaubert had famously fallen victim and which were replaced by the law of 29 July 1881 on the freedom of the press, a flood of obscene literature appeared, though it was quickly stemmed by the law of 2 August 1882 that brought books into the purview of the earlier legislation (article 28), incriminating 'l'outrage aux bonnes mœurs', bringing delinquents before a jury and raising penalties to a maximum of two years of prison and a two thousand franc fine.[20] But even during the so-called 'liberal' Empire and particularly during the regime of 'l'Ordre Moral', there were real risks of prosecution. When Huysmans sent Edmond de Goncourt a copy of *Marthe*, published in Brussels, and told him that the book had been stopped at the border from entering France, the elder writer, who was just finishing his own life of a prostitute, spent a restless night, dreaming of prosecution.[21]

On 20 December 1884, Goncourt's nightmare became a reality for a young disciple, Louis Desprez, who had published that year in collaboration with an even younger disciple, Henry Fèvre, his *Autour d'un clocher*, with the Belgian firm of Kistemaeckers. Despite his eloquent plea in court and a letter of support from Zola that was read out, he was condemned to a month in prison and a thousand franc fine; a young man of delicate health, whose condition was aggravated by the deplorable state of the Sainte-Pélagie prison, he died within a year (6 December 1885).[22] The following passage, another encounter between l'abbé Chalindre, the vicar of Vicq, and the schoolmistress, Irma Delafosse, around whose relationship the plot turns, usually within the confines of the obviously phallic clock tower, around which, in turn, the anti-pastoral action revolves, gives an idea of the very playful nature of the text, to which, so it seems, the jury was insensitive:

Le clocher, dans un échafaudage de poutres, se rétrécissait en pointe, comme un fond d'éteignoir. Dehors, des oiseaux pépiaient en se pourchassant.
Ils se mirent en posture commode, sous les cloches pansues dont la gueule

ronde s'évasait, la grosse larme du battant pendante. Le curé se déboutonna, comme quand on a trop bien dîné, et se coucha tout du long, avec une moue gourmande (1) ...

(1) Ici, lacune. Notre manuscrit est resté si longtemps dans les cartons qu'une corne de page y a été grignotée par les souris. O toi qui voudrais savoir, ouvre Brantôme, livre IV, page 380.[23]

The whole novel, clearly an interesting intertext between Zola's *La Faute de l'abbé Mouret* and *La Terre*, is written in a colloquial, lighthearted style, exposing rural manners (or the lack thereof) in a comic mode, outrageously exploiting its anticlerical theme, and containing such typical naturalist scenes as battles over inheritances and a childbirth. With curious inconsistency, the prosecutors of this text failed to indict a passage about l'abbé Bouleux and his vigorous masturbation. Strangely too, just a week after the Desprez trial (27 December 1884), Paul Bonnetain was acquitted by the same jury in the same court of the same charges for publishing *Charlot s'amuse* (1883), a novel, it will be recalled, on that theme, thanks, no doubt, to the public outcry over the previous verdict, to the author's more compliant attitude in court, to his repeated claim to have written a scientific work and to consideration for his care of his widowed mother.[24] Paul Adam, eight months later (on 10 August 1885), was less fortunate; *Chair molle* earned him a verdict of fifteen months in prison and a thousand franc fine. Though he avoided the prison term, the experience ruined him and he became a symbolist![25] When Lucien Descaves and the publishers of *Sous-Offs* (Veuve Tresse and Pierre-Victor Stock) were dragged before the courts on 15 March 1890 on forty-five counts of offence to the army and seven to morality in response to the intervention of General Boulanger and the Ministry of War, no less than fifty-four writers, including Zola, Edmond de Goncourt, Daudet and Céard, published a protest and a petition in *Le Figaro* (24 December 1889). Interestingly, at the trial, *Charlot s'amuse* and Zola's novels were invoked as a standard of licence. Descaves was acquitted, but was stripped of his military rank.[26] Clearly the links between the naturalist campaign and the Dreyfus Affair were not as remote as one might at first assume. Clearly too, the ploy by certain of the more audacious naturalists of having their novels published in Belgium did not render them immune to prosecution. Kistemaeckers himself, a kind of Belgian Vizetelly, though more political in his motivations than his English counterpart, was eventually ruined as a result of his own numerous court appearances.[27]

These various brushes with the legal authorities have considerable significance not only for the history of the naturalist movement but, in a broader context, for the study of literary censorship and the progress towards tolerance of explicitness in literature. As George Steiner notes: 'The work of Zola and Maupassant marked a deliberate expansion of sexual designation. In so far as it addressed itself to the physicality of man, to society as biologically determined, the entire naturalistic movement – Gorky, Dreiser, Hauptmann – tended to a new erotic frankness.'[28] But the fact that, as we have seen, the works that were most vigorously prosecuted were not only erotic, but anticlerical, antimilitary and more than implicitly critical of social and political institutions, suggests that much more was at stake than the delicate sensibilities of female readers. The naturalist text not only admitted more explicit sexual matter into its range of reference and attacked the modes of representation of bourgeois culture, especially its reassuring, edifying literature. In a more fundamental way, it also appropriated that culture's favourite genre, the novel, the genre of moral, social, political and intellectual consolidation and distraction in order to shock with it, disturb with it and defy the bourgeois myths of order, decency and permanence. By dealing with certain forbidden topics and by employing strategies, as we shall see, to implicate the reader in its disconcerting enterprise, naturalist literature rode roughshod over the carefully maintained barriers between the literature of the drawing room and the literature from under the counter. It incorporated into fiction matters that were more safely confined to the studies and the specialised libraries of the doctor, the politician and the sociologist, matters that were held to be better kept in their place. Like a Trojan horse of fiction, the naturalist text was a dangerous intruder, penetrating into the protected domains of bourgeois proprieties. It was an importunate, a troublesome kind of literature.

Asmodeus is a truly prying spirit and all corners of society are his province. 'Si nous sommes curieux', Zola wrote in 1880, 'si nous regardons par les fentes, je soupçonne que nous verrons, dans les classes distinguées, ce que nous avons vu dans le peuple, car la bête humaine est la même partout, le vêtement seul diffère' (X, 1331). The naturalist aesthetic may be essentially defined as a set of strategies appropriate to unearthing this human beast lurking beneath the political, moral and social order. The naturalist novel marks an extreme stage in the evolution of literature as revelation rather than as decorum, going beyond the stage of the Balzacian project of penetrating into the dramas of every household. As we have already seen, the purposes of observation and scientific investigation did not always hide a tremulous excitement and fascination at exposing the hideous and the scandalous aspects of society: 'le *vrai*', 'le *vif*' and 'le *saignant*'. So extensive is the latitude that a realist art allows, in the depiction of the unpleasant, that the repugnant comes to be equated with the truth. 'A la limite', writes Gérard Genette, 'pour "faire vrai", il suffit de faire laid.'[29] Thus the sordid secrets of the barracks, the brothel, the battlefield and the boarding school are exposed, along with the so-called 'bas-fondmanie' of naturalist literature. In a revealing portrait of Alexis, Zola's son-in-law, Maurice Le Blond, illustrates this dynamic of intention and pretension, as a *passion* for sordid subjects is transformed by an aesthetic *formula* into a search for the *document*: 'Passionnément épris de la formule naturaliste, et l'ayant adoptée trop à la lettre, il ne goûtait que le peuple, qu'il se plaisait à étudier surtout dans ses tares, ses déchéances morales. Un instinct à la fois brutal et raffiné le portait à rechercher le document vécu parmi les bouges, les tripots, les lieux de débauche, dans les endroits équivoques où les odeurs du vice s'assaisonnent et s'encaillent des relents âcres de la misère.'[30] The strange appeal that working class life held for these writers (who usually had never really lived it) did not preclude a sincere concern for the plight of the poor, particularly in the case of such English naturalists as Morrison and Gissing. But working class dramas had the distinct advantage of being all at once intriguingly exotic, convincingly real and outrageously disturbing to the reader, thereby satisfying the conditions of the naturalist aesthetics, poetics and pragmatics.

The naturalist, then, is endowed with an insatiable curiosity. 'Je suis terriblement indiscret et j'écoute aux portes' (X, 346), wrote the young journalist, Zola, announcing a life's programme that would turn indiscretion into a virtue. In a typical negative assessment of Zola's method containing the usual charges (bad style, filthy content, superfluous description), Arthur Symons seizes upon this supposedly prying and prurient aspect of the novelist's work, the 'worrying way in which *la derrière* [*sic*] and *le ventre* are constantly kept in view'. 'Nothing is more charming', he adds, 'than a frankly sensuous description of things which appeal to the senses; but can one imagine anything less charming, less like art, than this prying eye glued to the peephole in the Gingerbread Fair.'[31] The tendency is by no means limited to Zola: *vide* a street scene in *En ménage*, with its ragged, scrofulous kids, three girls playing in the mud, who 'se levaient et s'abaissaient, en mesure, découvrant des petits derrières bien fendus au milieu et blancs' (p. 78). But the masterwork of the genre is the story of Zola's street urchin, Nana, his 'poème du *cul*', as he called it in his notes, a novel in which the motifs of unveiling and disclosure are omnipresent. From the display of Nana's voluptuous body in chapter one to the revelation, on the final page, of her rotting flesh, 'we might define *Nana*', Janet Beizer observes, 'as a prolonged *strip-tease*'. The same critic relates this theme to problems of narrative representation, to what she calls 'the nexus of sexuality and textuality, body and narrative, showing and telling'. If it is true, as she argues, in a Barthesian perspective, that *texte* is *tissu*, that *Nana* is more *tease* than *strip*, that there is no ultimate showing because Nana's sex is text and the veil of language cannot be broken, the novel is remarkable for its dynamic of voyeurism and exhibitionism, and for its use of devices of focalisation for what advertisers call 'display purposes'. 'We watch Muffat', as Janet Beizer notes, for instance, 'like a child spying on his parents, peeking through curtain peep-holes, squinting through wall-cracks, peering around half-opened doors, and averting his eyes from their too-avid focus upon Nana's nominally veiled nakedness.'[32] But we also 'watch' what Muffat watches and the text's telling inveigles the reader into sharing in the indiscreet showing.

Studies of point of view or 'focalisation' in naturalist fiction tend to view the technique mainly as a device of realism or verisimilitude. Thus Philippe Hamon analyses the function of the 'regardeur–voyeur' in Zola's works, as one of the three types of 'personnages-prétextes' or '*fonctionnaires* de l'énonciation réaliste', along with 'le bavard volubile' and 'le technicien affairé', who serve as inter-mediaries in presenting and 'motivating' description. Scenes with characters at windows (as in the opening episode of *L'Assommoir*) or ambulatory descriptions (as in *Germinal*) are familiar techniques that are related back to the aesthetics of the screen, the mirror or the 'fenêtre ouverte sur la création'. Philippe Hamon writes: 'Le regardeur, le bavard, le technicien sont les délégués, les truchements, sur la scène du texte, du narrateur; ils sont des agents de transmission de l'information.'[33] Yet, if the naturalist text has more than a mimetic function, as I am arguing here again, another purpose is served by this technique of 'pseudo-focalisation', as Genette calls it.[34] To dwell a little on these narratological questions (and, in so doing, to employ somewhat freely Genette's terminology), we might suggest that the two fundamental types of naturalist texts that have been defined tend to use focalisation in a different way. In the 'Flaubertian model', as in *Une Vie*, for example, 'external focal-isation' (what the character sees) tends to develop into 'internal focalisation', a presentation of the character's inner thoughts, emotions, deceptions. In the 'Goncourtian model' there is a much more extensive use of external focalisation, which tends inevitably to become pseudo-focalisation, for the narrative can only briefly describe the character looking before describing directly what the character sees. In the first case the protagonist–witness and his or her experience are likely to be of a type to belong to the range of experience of the virtual reader. In the second case the virtual reader is led to witness unfamiliar and even shocking events. Thus the technique of focalisation, along with the controlling presence of the (absent) narrator and his ironic voice, serve not only to authenticate the narrative, but also to engage the reader in the pragmatic effects of the text. By the mediation of the intradiegetic witness, the reader becomes the watcher, the voyeur, aghast at the truths that are revealed. If the naturalist work postulates, like all texts, an ideal reader (the dispassionate observer of the truth), its virtual reader remains the bourgeois creature with a taste for fictions of a distracting and reassuring kind, the narratee that the strategies of the text are most likely to disturb.

Naturalist literature sets out therefore to shock and discompose the reader while pretending not to do so by being a mere representation of reality. There was naturally the constant danger of overstepping the mark and lapsing into the excessive, as certain minor texts so clearly do. We see Zola in certain private statements openly articulating this pragmatic effect. In August 1886, for example, he urged George Moore to write a novel on Ireland, 'un roman social, vrai, audacieux, révolutionnaire'; England would be 'bouleversée'; 'jamais occasion pareille ne s'est offerte de remuer un peuple. Songez-y. De l'audace, de l'audace, encore de l'audace!'[35] There is little doubt that Zola constantly had in mind the effect of his texts on his readers, though such considerations are largely absent from his theoretical writings. In a revealing incidental comment in the *ébauche* of *Germinal*, he both defines the nature of the pragmatic effect and the type of reader for whom it is intended: 'Les ouvriers lâchés vont jusqu'au crime: il faut que le lecteur bourgeois ait un frisson de terreur.'[36] The idea will lead to the impressive scenes of part five of the novel presented, significantly, in the most dramatic parts, in the mode of external focalisation when the bourgeois of Montsou witness the rampaging mob of striking miners. Zola notes again in his plans: 'Il me faut un cresendo [*sic*] d'effet terrible qui fasse passer un frisson, dans tous les lecteurs.'[37]

Naturalist writers, despite certain hesitations – the Goncourt brothers withdrew a description of a Caesarian operation witnessed at the Maternité hospital from *Germinie Lacerteux* as being 'trop vrai' (*Journal*, 13 and 23 October 1864) – present life in the raw, no more so than in those recurrent obstetrical descriptions that have been noted, scenes of painful and bloody childbirth, abortion and miscarriage. 'Très bonnes pages chez la sage-femme', Zola wrote to congratulate his Swiss colleague, Edouard Rod, on one such scene in *Les Protestants. Côte à côte* (1882).[38] Given a certain neutral tone or some surrounding scientific justification, descriptions of lascivious acts were also drawn into the realm of serious literature, as in the veritable catalogue of such scenes in the delirious visions of the dying Madame Meuriot:

Comme une chienne en folie, accepter le premier venu. Par un doux soir de mai, déniaiser un innocent; une heure après, galvaniser un octogénaire! Puis être battue et violentée par un goujat, débaucher un prêtre, payer un Alphonse, soutirer de l'or à un millionnaire, vivre une journée dans une maison publique! Même passer une heure avec un condamné à mort, en tête à tête, le matin de l'exécution! Dans cette voie des aberrations, ne s'arrêtant plus, elle en vint à rêver des accouplements avec des hommes de toutes races, de chaque peuple; même avec des singes et d'autres animaux; avec deux hommes à la fois. Et s'attaquer à son propre sexe? 'Oui, connaître une femme ... Pourquoi pas? ... Qui sait? ...'[39]

Naturalist texts openly violated taboos to scandalous effect, as did *Charlot s'amuse*, in an age when what Henri Guerrand calls 'cette folie antimasturbatoire née au siècle des Lumières' was still rampant and Charlot's habit was still considered likely to produce retributive effects ranging from heart failure, cancer, blindness to premature ageing.[40] They function to some degree like popular genres, taking up many of the fundamental fears, taboos and repressed desires of a society (violence in the thriller, miscegenation in the nineteenth-century American romance, sexual promiscuity in ghost stories[41]), but, instead of veiling these dreads in literary conventions, they bring them starkly to the reader's attention with shocking directness. Working class brutality and bestiality in slum novels work out similar repressions, with considerable ambiguity, as Jean Borie points out: 'Chez Zola, par exemple, la violence des misérables est à la fois réactionnelle: la grève de *Germinal* – et originelle: Nana, germe de pourriture et de destruction, issu des taudis de la Goutte-d'Or pour empoisonner la ville.'[42] But naturalist realities are more frequently biological than political: corpses and coffins, bodily evacuations, the emaciated body of a dead prostitute and her ill-fitting box (in 'Les

Funérailles de Francine Cloarec' by Hennique), the body of Charlot's father and his oversize coffin that comes crashing down, 'avec d'atroces émanations' (in *Charlot s'amuse*, p. 64) – for there is no dignity in naturalist deaths – vile liquids, corrupt flesh, decaying interiors, Lucie Pellegrin vomiting blood in Alexis's story, an incontinent old lady in the same writer's 'Une ruine' (*Le Collage*), 'des morceaux de cervelle et des fragments de la calotte du crâne' from Tétrelle's suicide in *Sous-Offs*, the 'flot ininterrompu d'ordures vomies' of which the maids tell in *Le Journal d'une femme de chambre*, or that 'chose sacrée qui doit toujours rester voilée', 'le sexe de Sidonie', which is finally revealed to her wayward husband, Marcel, in the bed of a sordid prostitute, a woman remarkably resembling Sidonie: 'C'etait là cette porte des entrailles féminines, ouvrant sa plaie béante, malsaine, dans sa disgrâce anatomique et son entrebaille-ment de cloaque.'[43] Life stripped of its veils, its illusions, its pretensions, its poetry. Life in its monstrous, demystifying nakedness.

By describing the pragmatics of naturalism in this way, I seem to be endorsing the familiar view of the genre as a brutal and outrageous form of realism. But a more complex process of generic action and reader reaction is in fact involved. It is now a commonplace of criticism that a literary text establishes at the outset an understanding with the reader, then either conforms to the latter's expectations or proceeds to manipulate and even thwart them. One theorist describes the process in blatantly economic terms: 'avant d'entreprendre sa narration, le narrateur tente de passer un marché avec celui (ou celle) à qui il est en train de s'adresser. Le récit est un objet d'échange, narrer équivaut à marchander.'[44] This exchange, or pact, clearly occurs within the framework of generic conventions to which the submissive writer adheres and which the submissive reader accepts. There is, thus, a generic contract between writers and readers according to which the practitioners of the genre either commit their works to provide the kind of effects and satisfactions that conform to the recipient's expectancies or institute transgressive practices to confound them. Traditional genre theorists have tended to attribute single emotional or intellectual effects to particular genres, but there is no reason why a work belonging to a particular genre should not evoke complex or contradictory responses. In any case, the novel, as Tony Tanner points out, has always been by its very nature 'a transgressive mode, inasmuch as it seemed to break, or mix, or adulterate the existing genre expectations of the time'.[45] By its very nature also it can establish varying patterns of feeling within the prolonged process of its temporal development.

Now, if naturalist literature is considered to be no more than an intemperate form of realism, it can be held to do no more than seek to engage the reader in what Philippe Lejeune has called 'le pacte référentiel',[46] purporting to deny its fictionality and to provide, in a similar way to biography, autobiography, scientific or historical discourse, information about a reality external to the text. But we know that realism is more a discourse of verisimilitude than one of referentiality, determined more by accepted concepts of appropriate fictional representations, by an image of reality rather than by images *from* reality. As Philippe Hamon writes: 'Ce n'est jamais, en effet, le "réel" que l'on atteint dans un texte, mais une rationalisation, une textualisation du réel, une reconstruction *a posteriori* encodée dans et par le texte, qui n'a pas d'ancrage, et qui est entraînée dans la circularité sans clôture des "interprétants", des clichés, des copies ou des stéréotypes de la culture.'[47] Once again it becomes clear that we need to interpret naturalist literature not on the basis of the avowed aesthetic principles of its creators, but rather, in this case, from the point of view of the effects brought about by their creations, according to *pragmatic* considerations, 'l'hypothèse étant, selon une formule que l'on peut emprunter à K. Stierle, que "l'usage projeté d'un texte donne les règles de sa constitution"'.[48] From this point of view, naturalist literature can be defined, not as a continuation of, but in opposition to, the realist enterprise.

An evident way to illustrate this crucial point would be to examine in naturalist novels what have come to be called (again mainly by Philippe Hamon) the 'lieux stratégiques' of a text, especially its beginning and its ending. As far as naturalist fiction is concerned, these determinants have always been viewed as *realistic* strategies, as a series of procedures relating to the contact between the world of the fiction and the world of the reality that it is supposed to represent. Yet these 'strategic sites' are also indicators of genre specific to naturalist literature in the way that they function in opposition to each other. Thus the *incipit* of the naturalist text introduces readers into the familiar world of their mimetic literature, into the reassuring reflection of their own reality by the mirror aesthetics. But the conclusion of the text certainly does not fulfil this same familiarising function. Whereas the naturalist *incipit* tends to derive from the realist project, the ending is more particular to the genre. Between these two 'ensemble-limites' of the text, as Barthes calls them,[49] and through the transformations that the world of the text has undergone along the way, the naturalist work takes on its own 'genericness', under-mining the realist 'contract' with the reader's expectations and instigating a new (dis)order. Having led its readers into the universe of the mimetic order and still maintaining the mimetic illusion, the naturalist text subjects them to the scandal of its thematics. They are caught up in the dynamics of attraction and repulsion that the *incipit* has set in motion and that the conclusion completes. Thus naturalist endings provide the finishing touch to these effects, in various ways, but in accordance with the basic types that have been defined. There is the deprivation ending, in which the victim, like Gervaise Macquart in *L'Assommoir*, sinks down into her or his ultimate misfortune. There is the banal ending, which frustrates the reader's expectation of closure and prolongs the trivialities of the story beyond the conclusion of the plot. Finally, in some cases, there is the sententious ending which summarises the satire of the baseness that has gone before, as at the conclusion of *Pot-Bouille*.

The naturalist text, therefore, may appropriately be called a 'scandal', not only in the sense of an outrageous action or of the refined sort of gossip that it often resembles, but also in the etymological sense of the term, as a snare or trap, which involves its readers in secure expectations and offers them the pleasures of the 'readable' text, all the better to provoke them with its disturbing content. Texts of the first kind that I have defined tend to shock, as does *L'Assommoir* by its graduated disconcerting effects, or, more obviously, *La Terre*, in which, as Roger Ripoll observes, 'la recherche de l'excès se découvre dans tous les domaines; Zola éprouve le besoin d'aller toujours plus loin, de montrer toujours plus nettement ce qui est le moins supportable.'[50] Texts of the second kind tend less to shock than to disappoint, as does *Une Belle Journée*, disappointing the reader's expectation that a piquant adultery will take place, but burying the prospect in the trivialities of the narrative that follows. Indeed, in all types of naturalist text, the 'realism' added a further dimension to this problem of reception, disturbing, by the very representative nature of the fiction, to readers who would be doubly shocked that life is as it is represented and that literature should represent it so.

None of this, however, detracted from the resounding commercial success of naturalist literature, at least in France, where the 'groundswell' of texts coincided with a tremendous boom in the publishing industry in the late 1870s and early 1880s. After 1875, for example, more than ten times as many novels were published in Paris than under the July Monarchy. Whereas few of Hugo's works before 1870 had sold more than ten editions, more than thirty-eight editions of *L'Assommoir* and fifty editions of an illustrated version had appeared by the end of its year of publication (1877). It is tempting to consider that the serious crisis in the book publishing industry in France after 1885 directly contributed to the decline of the naturalist movement there, at precisely the time when, as Zola's correspondence clearly shows, it was extending its influence abroad. During the last decade of the century, in fact, numerous publishers went out of business. Undoubtedly, as Christophe Charle has shown, this situation did have considerable consequences for writers associated with the movement. Various literary factions were competing for a shrinking market. Of the second, younger generation of naturalist writers in France, Charle writes: 'Leur situation objective les poussait à traiter certains sujets de type scandaleux. Le scandale, à la lumière des succès des médaniens, était connu comme payant.'[51] The 'Manifeste des Cinq', as we have noted, could be viewed in this light as a symptom of the competitive and contradictory situation in which the younger writers found themselves, imitating Zola's formulas, taking them to extremes, yet denouncing him for practising them himself.

Such economic and social factors are clearly not without relevance to the loss of dominance that naturalist literature suffered and that was evident at the time of the Huret enquiry, when Alexis sent his famous telegram. They must be added to the traditional explanations, like the so-called 'bankruptcy of science', the reaction against positivism, the emergence of the psychological and religious novel. But, to be consistent in our approach, we must also take into account more intrinsic factors, endemic to the processes of generic development as a whole and to the evolution of the naturalist genre in particular. There is, first of all, the fact that genres, like people, as they mature, tend to repeat themselves. As Martino writes about the 1890s in France, 'la matière du roman naturaliste est épuisée; on a tenté tout ce qui se pouvait tenter; on ne saurait, désormais, que se répéter'. He quotes from Huysmans' retrospective preface to the 1903 edition of *A rebours*: the naturalist school 'était condamnée à se rabâcher, en piétinant sur place'; naturalism 's'essoufflait à tourner la meule dans le même cercle. La somme d'observations que chacun avait emmagasinée, en les prenant sur soi-même et sur les autres, commençait à s'épuiser.'[52] Other commentators have made the same point. 'Le pittoresque des sujets ne se renouvela point', writes Léon Deffoux. 'Les hontes secrètes de la bourgeoisie et du peuple, les misères des militaires et des filles furent décrites à satiété. En un mot, on *pratiqua* le naturalisme et, le pratiquant, on acheva d'user la formule.'[53] Then there is the fact that in the mere practice of a literature that sought to shock, successive writers were inevitably obliged to outdo previous audacities and to seek more shocking effects. Thus the very pragmatics of the genre contained within it its own tendencies to excess and the seeds of its own eventual discredit. Writers seized upon the tendency to scandalise to such a degree that their works, by over-systematically exploiting naturalist themes, already read like parodies of the genre. Consider the relatively early example, *Vices parisiens: Madame Bécart* (1879) by Vast-Ricouard, who claimed to be naturalists: the once virtuous, bourgeois heroine, 'qui eût voulu se saoûler de matière', but is married to a docile poet, lusts after the family tutor, rolls around in his bed, 'les yeux brillants, les narines gonflées', 'haletante', much taken by 'cette puissante bestialité d'homme', whilst her nephew, Georges, 'ses veines brûlantes', lusts after the maid and takes to smelling her underwear. There are hothouse love episodes (with hunting scenes, pictures of 'la curée' in the dining room!) leading to the culminating incident in which the lady, bare breasted in her peignoir to await her lover, is locked in a tower, where she starves to death after trying to chew the bed linen, providing an occasion for a description of her rotting body. (Monsieur, by the way, to complete the story, falls down the stairs and dies of grief.)[54]

'Tout genre dépassé', Laurent Jenny writes – as we turn briefly to the second kind of parody mentioned at the beginning of this chapter – 'n'apparaît-il pas automatiquement comme surcodé pour la simple raison que son codage devient apparent?'[55] Naturalist fiction in France inevitably became 'overcoded', overloaded, repetitive, excessive – easy prey for the parodists. Writers in succeeding generations would incorporate and overturn naturalist themes and procedures in their works.[56] More obviously revealing, however, was the appearance of a type of text in which the naturalist writer himself was satirised and his practices parodied. In *Le Termite* by J.-H. Rosny, for example, a work full of pastiches of naturalist descriptions and parodies of naturalist mannerisms, a naturalist novelist, Servaise, is represented with his 'pauvre philosophie de documentaire': 'Sa minutie d'arrivée coïncida avec le surmenage de la méthode: le but, pour lui et cent autres, fut de descendre dans les boyaux de la basse vie, de disséquer les microbes sociaux, d'assécher la phrase et de fuir avec horreur la finalité du but. Ce travail, qui pouvait prêter à des développements infinis, ils le bornèrent à la hâte, refusant toute enquête qui dépassât la surface, tout fait absconse, toute induction.'[57] In a more comic vein is Hippolyte Parigot's short satirical play, 'Dialogue des morts',[58] in which the naturalist novelist, Pierre, is preparing a novel about a grocer, M. Juponneau,

whose wife is about to yield to the attentions of a municipal guard.
It will be a study of two temperaments. 'Voilà la vie; là voilà bien,
la vie!', the novelist affirms. He is helped by his wife, Sabine, and
at a difficult moment in the creation of the work, they turn to a
portrait of Zola and intone: 'Maître, inspirez-nous!' (p. 296). Pierre
proposes that Sabine put herself in the place of Mme Juponneau 'et
faisons parler la nature' (p. 301), but she rebels against her husband's
naturalist view of woman and complains to his friend, Lieutenant
Robert, who is not a naturalist, of the lack of poetry in her life. Pierre
comes in and reads from his latest chapter, on Bichette Juponneau:

A son entour frémit une gaîté mâle; dans l'air épaissi de la chambre et la
chaleur sèche du choubersky, parmi le fade relent des plats à peine desservis
et des sauces figées, avec, sous ses narines, l'odeur forte des bottes de cuir,
Bichette ressent une trouble indéfinissable, maladif, contre lequel elle est
impuissante à lutter. Au cerveau lui montent les effluves d'un tempérament
héréditaire. (p. 326)

Both Robert and Sabine proceed to denounce Pierre and the
naturalists, always ready to 'fourrager dans les choses sales, pour
déclamer scientifiquement que voilà la vie, le tout de la vie', 'romantiques à rebours, pédants de l'ordure', with their 'intuitions
malpropres' and their 'audaces qui puent' (p. 328). Robert defends
Sabine: 'Elle est honnête, et elle est nature, elle aussi' (p. 328), though,
no doubt, the further to confound the confused writer, there are hints
that she might indeed imitate Bichette with the officer. Pierre is left
alone in the brief final scene:

SCENE IX

PIERRE, *assis devant son bureau, la tête dans les mains.*

Nature???

8
NATURALIST DESCRIPTION

We must leave Parigot's parodic novelist, at least for the time being, pondering upon the crucial question of the nature of nature in the naturalist scheme, and observe that, in certain theoretical statements, 'nature', 'naturalism' and 'description' became almost interchangeable terms. In the opening section of his article 'De la description', reproduced in *Le Roman expérimental*, Zola writes: 'sous cette question littéraire de la description, il n'y a pas autre chose que le retour à la nature, ce grand courant naturaliste qui a produit nos croyances et nos connaissances actuelles' (X, 1299). The naturalist, in the image of Zola, is popularly represented as a zealous observer, assiduously frequenting the sites of his future novel, notebook in hand, filling it with notations that will provide passages of authentic description in the work under preparation. The naturalist mode is regularly considered to be one which gives primacy to description, not lavish, emotionally charged Romantic raptures nor Parnassian gems, but concrete, material delineations, inspired by the belief that an accumulation of 'petits faits vrais' would give a sufficient representation of the truth.[1] According to Northrop Frye, 'in the documentary naturalism generally associated with such names as Zola and Dreiser, literature goes about as far as a representation of life, to be judged by its accuracy of description rather than by its integrity as a structure of words, as it could go and still remain literature'.[2] Indeed, beneath Zola's portrait, Parigot's novelist, Pierre, solemnly declares: 'la description est la formule de l'Art, le dernier mot de notre Ecole'.[3]

Zola's essay provides, in a convenient form, the main arguments of the orthodox naturalist doctrine on the question of description. Contrary to the descriptive 'orgies' of Romantic writers, a scientific, anthropological purpose is ascribed to the mode in naturalist works:

... nous ne décrivons plus pour décrire, par un caprice et un plaisir de rhétoricien. Nous estimons que l'homme ne peut être séparé de son milieu,

184

qu'il est complété par son vêtement, par sa maison, par sa ville, par sa province; et, dès lors, nous ne noterons pas un seul phénomène de son cerveau ou de son cœur, sans en chercher les causes ou le contrecoup dans le milieu. De là ce qu'on appelle nos éternelles descriptions. (X, 1299)

This Balzacian or Tainean perspective, encapsulated in an appropriate formula – 'Je définirai donc la description: un état du milieu qui détermine et complète l'homme' (X, 1300) – is designed, however, not only to justify naturalist description but to keep it in check. There is something of a penitent aspect to Zola's essay and, like all his theorising, as we have noted, it is largely prompted by attacks on his works, more precisely, in this particular case, by criticism of the five descriptive panoramas of Paris in *Une Page d'amour* (1878). Flaubert's sober use of description is set up as a model against Gautier's excesses, though Zola acknowledges more than once his own intemperate tendencies: 'J'ai assez péché pour avoir le droit de reconnaître la vérité' (X, 1302). But he defends his fellow naturalists against the charge that their 'fureur de description' is gratuitous: 'cela se complique toujours en nous d'intentions symphoniques et humaines' (X, 1302).

Zola's essay, though short, is of interest in a number of respects for what it shows, what it denies and what it ignores. Even whilst arguing to some degree against it, the essay illustrates an ingrained suspicion of the descriptive mode, what Philippe Hamon calls 'la culpabilisation que le discours théorique classique sur la description a attachée à cette pratique textuelle'.[4] But, even up to modern times – the *nouveau roman* notwithstanding – description, as Philippe Hamon further explains, has held a subservient place in the craft of fiction:

Le descriptif semble n'être qu'une sorte de repoussoir universel, de degré zéro général et commode servant à discriminer des catégories plus 'marquées' ou des objets théoriques plus dignes d'intérêt: tantôt en effet le descriptif est opposé au narratif, au récit; tantôt il est opposé aux 'actions', ou à la 'psychologie' des personnages, par opposition aux objets ou aux paysages; tantôt il est une partie (subordonnée) du récit; tantôt (Valéry) on l'oppose à l'énoncé poétique; tantôt le descriptif est opposé au performatif (Searle, Austin), au 'littéral' (N. Frye), ou au prescriptif et au normatif, tantôt il est opposé à l'explicatif.[5]

With such an inglorious status, it is hardly surprising that Zola should wish to 'functionalise' description, not only as a continuation of his scientific view of literature but as a defence against the accusation of descriptiveness with which his works and those of his fellow naturalists were being taxed. The charge was not new and had been vigorously levelled against those realists who were considered to be the forebears of the naturalist movement, in, for instance, Duranty's attack on Balzac's 'système de description obstinée' or in reviews of *Madame Bovary*.[6] In fact, descriptive excess became, and has remained, a particularly convenient issue on which to attack naturalist literature and on which to pin dismissive and reductive attitudes. Brunetière, attacking from the right in his essay on 'Le roman expérimental', is particularly scathing about the naturalists' 'useless' description: 'Vous me montrez un tapis dans une chambre, un lit sur un tapis, une courte-pointe sur ce lit, un édredon sur cette courte-pointe ... quoi encore? Ce qui fatigue ici, c'est bien un peu l'insignifiance du détail, comme ailleurs c'en sera la bassesse, mais c'est bien plus encore la continuité de la description. Il y a des détails bas; il y a surtout des détails inutiles.'[7] At a later time, Lukács, attacking from the left, denounces Zola's 'obsession with monographic detail', the divorce from 'epic significance' in his descriptive works, the trivialisation, the fetishisation of objects and the debasement of character to the state of inanimate things that this process entails. Description, Lukács argues, levels everything, creates lifeless artifacts deprived of human significance, leads to 'a series of static pictures, of still lives connected only through the relations of objects arrayed one beside the other according to their inner logic'. Realist art loses its capacity to represent the true dynamics of life.[8]

Such disapprobation, whatever elements of truth it contains, brings us back into the arena of polemical reductions and defensive theorising, back to the dismissive arguments and swift generalisations, which gloss over the precise nature and varied functions of naturalist description.

Narratologists, in recent times, have convincingly demonstrated that the traditional distinction between narration and description, from an analytical point of view, is largely invalid, for there is always an element of description in narration and a degree of narrativity in description. Genette especially argues against the traditional demotion of description: 'On peut ... dire que la description est plus indispensable que la narration, puisqu'il est plus facile de décrire sans raconter que de raconter sans décrire (peut-être parce que les objets peuvent exister sans mouvement, mais non le mouvement sans objet).'[9] Narration and description are equivalent operations, the one developing the temporal delineations of narrative, the other its spatial vectors, but both constituting, not distinct 'modes' (to use Genette's terms) but 'aspects' of fictional representation. Peter Klaus, to take another example, defines description as 'any moment in a text, at which a property of someone or something is mentioned'. Even the pronoun 'he' is descriptive of maleness. Thus, he argues, description should be viewed as a '*function* present in *any* part of a text' and not as a '*quality* of *particular* parts of a text', as a basic element of the narrative and not as 'a kind of "ballast"'.[10]

This kind of minimal, analytical definition does attribute to description an unaccustomed importance, even a certain primacy, but it tends to subsume much that is not perceived of as description by the reader into that category and leave open the question of the distribution, functions and role of apparently static, descriptive passages in the economy of the fictional world. It would be more useful, therefore, to review the question in terms of the 'descriptive', as Philippe Hamon prefers to call it, as a type of dominant mode or aspect that texts draw upon from amongst the available resources of their techniques. In this way, as Hamon observes, the essence of the descriptive consists of an effort 'pour résister à la linéarité contraignante du texte, au *post hoc ergo propter hoc* des algorithmes narratifs'.[11] In so far as the naturalist writer generally considered complex plot development to be a fundamental characteristic of types of literature that he rejected (Romantic, escapist, 'feuilleton' novels), of 'literature' as opposed to 'life', then the descriptive is most decidedly opposed to plot.[12] Descriptive passages thereby tend to take on a certain autonomy and develop their own aesthetic forms. The functions of plot are apparently suspended and, as Martino remarks of the typical Goncourt text, 'le roman semble renoncer délibérément à son caractère romanesque'.[13] For an unsympathetic critic like Lukács, this tendency is evidence of a 'decadent style', of the 'strained artificiality of a synthetic art' which 'makes everything episodic'.[14] Yet it may also be more reasonably viewed as part of an essential dialectic of naturalist texts, a feature of an inherent dynamic, to which, in varying degrees, all individual texts subscribe and which offsets the rigorous 'logic' of the deterministic or repetitive plot of our two standard models with more disruptive, discontinuous procedures, for naturalist fiction cannot be reduced to its most evident descriptive indulgences. Such apparently conflicting tendencies are an integral part of the essential conflation of logic and discontinuity, of integration and disintegration, which is at the heart of the naturalist vision (and of the thesis of this book), of a 'chronotopic' tension which the varied but interrelated functions of the descriptive in naturalist texts allow us to explore.

If we combine the more general perspectives of Genette and Hamon (with due acknowledgment to Barthes and Ricardou), we can define three functions of the descriptive. Firstly, there is its denominative, referential role, common to all fictional forms, according to which the descriptive denotes and informs, creating a representational effect which may extend in realist texts to a purely asemantic guarantee of authenticity, the famous 'effets de réel'. Secondly, a decorative function, what Genette calls a 'récréation dans le récit, de rôle purement esthétique'. Thirdly, an explicative, symbolic function, which makes of description 'ce qu'elle n'était pas à l'époque classique, un élément majeur de l'exposition',[15] including the forms of 'la description créatrice' that Ricardou has recommended or allegorical description in which the semantic charge is at its most prominent. Since description fulfilling any one of these functions can constitute a threat to narrative action, each of these modes would involve a particular kind of excess: encyclopaedic ostentation for the first, elaborate ornamentation for the second, and abstract schematisation for the third. Though the same description may fulfil more than one or all of these functions in a text, they would appear to be independent rather than interdependent, even contradictory, certainly differing fundamentally in their degree of significance and their degree of integration into the narrative scheme. In naturalist texts, however, as I wish to show, these various functions are more closely integrated than these abstract definitions seem to imply.

The mimetic effect sought by naturalist descriptions may appear to need no explanation or illustration because it seems such a simple and obvious fact. But a number of recent studies, in particular Philippe Hamon's work, have shown that the externalia of descriptions have more profound implications. Hamon has suggested, for example, that the descriptive tendency derives from an implicit, utopian theory of language, 'celle de la langue comme nomenclature, celle d'une langue dont les fonctions se limiteraient à dénommer ou à désigner terme à terme le monde, d''une langue monopolisée par sa fonction référentielle d'étiquetage d'un monde lui-même "discret", découpé en "unités"'.[16] It derives also from an attempt to align language with the fundamental condition of material reality itself, which is considered to be outside the realm of the semiotic. Yet it may do no more than signify the real, connote reality rather than denote realities, as Barthes argued, producing 'un *effet de réel*, fondement de ce vraisemblable inavoué qui forme l'esthétique de toutes les œuvres courantes de la modernité'.[17] Indeed, there is a residual effect of authentification in any coherent descriptive segment of the narrative, even when 'focalised' through the character's look or memory, for, if point of view subjectivises the descriptive, the subject's presence acts also as a further guarantee of authenticity, according, no doubt, to the principle that reading about seeing is believing.

Philippe Hamon also makes the point that the reader of realist or naturalist works may be naïvely led to believe that descriptive passages give direct access to the real, whereas in fact the description frequently constitutes a rewriting of textual sources, which again serve to provide a basis of apparent authenticity: 'Dans le descriptif, un savoir semble toujours quelque part mis en réserve, ou en jeu, un certain capital de savoir, caché ou asséné, déjà archivé ou en cours d'archivation, posé ou présupposé, est à faire fructifier, et doit en même temps être validé, se valider soi-même.'[18] The point, however, can be overstated. Henri Mitterand's edition of Zola's 'carnets d'enquêtes', the mass of notes taken by Zola for a number of his novels, the result of direct observation, like a painter's sketches, on Paris, the stock exchange, the department store, the theatre, the mine and so on, show that what the novelist saw and heard directly has a massive and varied presence in his works. 'Aucun intermédiaire entre le monde et le texte', writes Henri Mitterand, 'sinon les catégories de pensée qui filtrent tout naturellement les faits chez un observateur issu de la petite-bourgeoisie intellectuelle.'[19] These notes belong to a different category from those taken more systematically from published sources. There is no doubt, for instance, that *Les Sœurs Vatard* by Huysmans, a work which, as Zola was the first to point out, is remarkable for its descriptive richness (if for little else), owed much to the author's own experiences of its setting, the 'maison de satinage et de brochure' like the one that he inherited and where for a brief time he worked, providing for an impressive range of descriptions, from the technicalities of the trade, the squalid sites of the district, to subtle and impressive light effects. However predictable naturalist plots tend to be, the range of naturalist description seems inexhaustible, encyclopaedic, in its dimensions. Mimetic naturalist descriptions seem, thus, impelled by an inner energy towards both autonomy and exhaustiveness. 'Même si elles servent à documenter et à nourrir la fiction,' Henri Mitterand notes, 'si elles sont la plupart du temps postérieures à l'ébauche du roman, et si elles résultent d'un choix thématique qui est lui-même tributaire de la fiction, les notes d'enquêtes [of Zola] échappent dans une grande mesure à cette dernière et tendent à devenir un texte autonome.'[20] Frequently, like a conscientious realist in this respect, the naturalist describer accumulates facts and features, draws upon a broad range of nomenclatures, revelling in the copious referentiality that describing the ambient world entails. Hence, what Philippe Hamon calls his 'esthétique du "fragment", du "morceau", de la "tranche de vie", du "tableau"'.[21]

There is, nevertheless, more to this propensity for description than the desire to imitate the massive profusion of objects that characterise modern industrial life, with a professional concern for thoroughness and a scrupulous attention to detail. There is a revealing urgency in the task, a desire not only to model the novelist on the scientist or the encyclopaedist, but also to partake in the same eagerness – or, some would say, rage – to name, classify, fix, stabilise, dominate the external order and impose a verbal system on the phenomenal world. Writing on one of Zola's most descriptive texts, *La Faute de l'abbé Mouret*, with its lavish descriptions of plants, Philippe Bonnefis observes that botany is not an innocent pastime, for 'le botaniste s'unit à l'architecte, au géomètre, au législateur et au prince, dans le même désir absolu de rendre la nature conforme à la lisibilité d'un Ordre. Les flores naturalistes, de même, sont l'instrument d'un pouvoir.'[22] This far-from-innocent brand of flower-power may be seen to derive from the imposition of 'the order of mimesis', as Christopher Prendergast defines it, an order that is repressive and constraining, a part of the 'fabric of mystification and bad faith from which the dominant forms of our culture are woven' and which occults the ideological infrastructure of representation. 'The authoritarian gesture of mimesis', Prendergast argues, 'is to imprison us in a world which, by virtue of its familiarity, is closed to analysis and criticism, in which the "prescriptive" and the "normative" (themselves tacit) ensure that the "descriptive" remains at the level of the undiscussed, in the taken-for-grantedness of the familiar.'[23] Thus the formal, surface nature of the mimetic project has profounder implications and could be seen as an aspect of the ideology of 'purposive-rational action', as Habermas characterises the legitimisation of domination in the scientific age. The invocation of a scientific method by naturalist writers would, therefore, not just be a rhetorical device and a strategy of motivation, but would constitute telling evidence of their *apparent* adherence to the 'purposive-rational imperatives' of an era of science and technology with its 'rationality of domination'.[24] Zola's theorising would seem to bear this out, for, in *Le Roman expérimental*, he links the naturalist novelist's purpose with the fundamental project of the scientific age, quoting with approval Claude Bernard's assertion that it is the experimenter's task to 'maîtriser les phénomènes qui l'entourent' and 'étendre sa puissance sur la nature' (X, 1188). Naturalist literature, like experimental medicine, describes because it fundamentally prescribes.

But, once again, we must guard against two long-standing assumptions: the equation of naturalism with Zola's ideas and the subsumption of naturalism and realism. We shall see that naturalist description cannot by any means be totally attributed to the zeal of the scientific spirit or the will to master the world with the descriptive Verb. We shall see also that the view expressed by Leo Bersani, for example, that both realist and naturalist literature offer society 'le confort d'une vision systématique d'elle-même et la sécurité d'un sens structuré' is very much open to question as far as naturalist literature is concerned. Whereas it may be true, as the same critic claims, that 'le romancier réaliste tente désespérément de maintenir la cohésion de ce dont il perçoit très bien la désagrégation',[25] naturalist literature, no more so than in its descriptions, depicts that very process of disruption, the disintegrating order of mimesis itself.

Henry James, writing on the Goncourt brothers, remarked on the curious disparity between the baseness of the subjects of their works and the sophistication with which they treated them. 'There is something ineffably odd', he wrote, 'in seeing these elegant erudites bring their highly complex and artificial method − the fruit of culture, and leisure, and luxury − to bear upon the crudities and maladies of life, and pick out choice morsels of available misery upon their gold pen-points.'[26] This contradiction applies in some degree to a number, if not to all, of the naturalist writers who were aesthetes treating most unaesthetic themes. Some, like Hennique and George Moore, tried their hand at painting; others, like Zola and Alexis, lived for part of their lives amongst painters, wrote about their works and defended them in the process. They regularly transposed artistic, particularly impressionist techniques into their works: the nominal syntax, the reproduction of sense impressions, juxtapositions of colours, vague contours, weak predicates, a general tendency towards abstractness. Under the influence of the Goncourt brothers, *l'écriture artiste* was widely practised amongst the French naturalists. Huysmans wrote *transpositions d'art* and perfected the literary *croquis*. Certain naturalist writers, like Zola and Maupassant, became impatient with the stylistic affectations of the disciples of the Goncourt brothers, but the often drab and dismal fabric of their works is nonetheless marked by purple passages of description.

Naturalist discourse, then, frequently tends towards the picturesque,

towards *ekphrasis*, in passages that seem all the more detached from
the main development of the plot by the contrast with the surrounding
inartistic realities. It has already been noted that the descriptive in
literature, as Philippe Hamon emphatically points out, normally
displays itself in the form of relatively autonomous descriptions, as
detachable units with all kinds of framing and signalling devices –
punctuation, interventions by the narrator, the use of terms like
'portrait', 'landscape' – which serve to indicate that the text is about
to embark upon the descriptive manner: 'une des obsessions du texte
descriptif sera, bien souvent, d'hypertrophier son système démarcatif,
de souligner au maximum, par divers procédés, l'encadrement de
l'unité descriptive elle-même, d'accentuer en particulier son début et sa
fin'.[27] The most common device for integrating artistic descriptions
into the fiction is the use of external focalisation, usually through the
eyes of an artist, a device which is typically ambivalent in that it both
authenticates the description as reality and signals to readers that they
should adjust their attitudes accordingly to an appreciation of the
'visual' effects.

In the opening chapter of Hennique's *La Dévouée*, the artist
Aristide Poupelart, who, for some curious reason, has a wooden leg
painted red, white and blue, seems to debunk the device by scornfully
dismissing the beauty of a Parisian twilight: 'Pouf! fit Aristide,
ça n'a qu'un défaut: celui de se reproduire un peu souvent. Les
romanciers en ont abusé, les poètes encore plus.' But, a few pages
later, mellowed, no doubt, by dinner, he lends his gaze, along with
those of his companions, to the beauty of a typical naturalist Paris-
scape:

Maintenant, les regards se promenaient aux portes de la ville morne, sur Passy,
sur Auteuil. Au fond du tableau, les buttes Montmartre se dessinaient presque
roses sous un rayon attardé. Devant elles, le dôme des Invalides paraissait
un morceau d'astre mourant, et la frise de l'arc de triomphe perceptible
au-dessus de la houle bleuâtre des toits ressemblait à une luxueuse nacelle
prête à sombrer.

Juste en face du plateau où Aristide piétinait, ... la Seine apparaissait,
luisante comme un lac glacé, et derrière la Seine, Paris, avec ses entassements
de maisons et de monuments noyés dans une obscurité naissante, parsemée
d'étoiles que des mains allumaient; enfin, lourd sur le colosse dont l'agitation
faiblissait, un ciel sans nuages, d'une blancheur obscurcie et compacte.[28]

As in the more famous artistic descriptions of Paris in Zola's *Une
Page d'amour*, the monuments of Paris provide a framing structure
for the tableau. The scene is fixed, set apart, and its hues lend it
characteristic, pictorial qualities. The reader's 'eye' follows the

characters' focalising exploration of the various planes of the composition, which transpose the aestheticised objects into a compositional framework.

In 'Le Retour de Jacques Clouard', a story by Paul Alexis, the aesthetic suddenly irrupts into the sordid: 'Au milieu de la courte ruelle, une crémerie—fruiterie, dont les bottes de radis, les salades, choux-fleurs et carottes, les piles de fromages, font une grande tache gaie au milieu de la banalité des masures voisines. Le regard, accroché par cette sorte de nature morte claire, s'y arrête avec complaisance.'[29] This brief example clearly derives from the better known descriptions of *Le Ventre de Paris*, the symphonies of vegetables, cheeses, fish and *charcuterie*. In Zola's novel, significantly, there are two protagonists. The painter, Claude Lantier, provides the aesthetic *distance* and is the vehicle for the presentation of each *nature morte*. For Florent, who is more *involved*, nature is very much alive in the Paris market, a constant material presence that threatens to engulf him. The two characters represent opposite reactions to the material world, both characteristically naturalist, and reveal the underlying function of the aesthetic descriptions in naturalist works. Claude, at least in this novel, joyously aestheticises, sublimates, distances, orders, contains, recomposes this superabundance of matter. Florent is repelled and overwhelmed by it. As the two of them contemplate a growing mountain of provisions set against a landscape of Paris: 'Il [Claude] força son compagnon à admirer le jour se levant sur les légumes. C'était une mer. Elle s'étendait de la pointe Sainte-Eustache à la rue des Halles, entre les deux groupes de pavillons. Et, aux deux bouts, dans les deux carrefours, le flot grandissait encore, les légumes submergeaient les pavés. Le jour se levait lentement, d'un gris très doux, lavant toutes choses d'une teinte claire d'aquarelle' (II, 587). Before the same spectacle his companion has the opposite reaction: 'Florent souffrait. Il croyait à quelque tentation surhumaine. Il ne voulait plus voir ... il voulut se secouer, secouer ce rêve intolérable de nourritures gigantesques dont il se sentait poursuivi' (II, 589—90). Significantly, in this novel, Florent is incapable of adopting a serene, panoramic, ordering vision over the market scene, for he must always see beyond the surfaces, like a precursor of Sartre's Roquentin, into the nauseating, corruptible *en soi* of the substantive order: 'Elles étaient sans cesse là. Il ne pouvait ouvrir la fenêtre, s'accouder à la rampe, sans les avoir devant lui, emplissant l'horizon ... Son malheur était là, dans ces Halles chaudes de la journée. Il poussa violemment la fenêtre, les laissa vautrées au fond de l'ombre, toutes nues, en sueur encore, dépoitraillées, montrant leur ventre ballonné et se soulageant sous les étoiles' (II, 789–90).

The contrasting attitudes of Claude and Florent suggest that naturalist description in its more artistic aspects, the *style artiste* evocations of a milieu, the impressionist sketches, the urban scenes, is part of a dialectal process of abstraction and submission to a vision of the natural order, part of a more general aesthetic response, common perhaps to decadentism, impressionism, aestheticism. 'Or, la fin du XIXe siècle', writes René Huyghe, 'a tendu à créer un antimatérialisme, réaction naturelle après l'excès de matérialisme qu'entraîna à sa suite la Science, positive, vouée au concret, et dont le corollaire en art et en littérature fut le naturalisme.'[30] But naturalism itself was no less an artistic meditation on the transcience, the fluidity, the impalpability of the concrete world and an attempt to transpose, fix, exorcise its inexorable solubility and corruptibility. In naturalist works also, 'un sens nouveau de la nature apparaît alors: tout ce qui en elle évoquait l'immobilité, la stabilité s'efface; elle est sollicitée de plus en plus par le fluide et l'impalpable'.[31] The Symbolist constructs against this desubstantiation an essentialist universe of Ideas. The Naturalist has an ambivalent response. Whereas Claude rejoices at and depicts the *sea* of vegetables, Florent recoils from the vaporisation of matter. In a similar way, the description of the Paradou in *La Faute de l'abbé Mouret*, as Philippe Bonnefis pointedly observes, 'est l'apiècement de deux discours, un discours adjectif (délicieux), un discours substantif (nauséeux)'.[32] Thus, the naturalist novelist–scientist seeks to dominate this threatening materiality with his categorisations; the novelist–artist, with his pictorial descriptions; but the novelist *tout court* submits the human spirit to its invasive contamination.

In Céard's *Une Belle Journée*, to take a less obvious example, Mme Duhamain 'focalises' a typical description: 'Elle leva les yeux. De tous côtés, sur leurs têtes, le ciel se déployait, bleu indéfiniment. Seuls, au-dessus des toitures de la gare d'Orléans, dont les vitres criblées de soleil étincelaient en l'air comme les flots d'argent d'un fleuve féerique, de légers nuages, un peu jaunâtres sur les bords, voltigeaient, pareils à des flocons de laine sale' (pp. 87–8). Descriptively, in this novel, it really *is* a fine day, despite the menacing clouds. In such naturalist works, nature provides for the eye a temporary deliverance from the violence that it is doing to the body and the spirit. Description is thus a reprieve: composition elaborated upon decomposition. Hence the ambivalent attitude of the describer, his exultation and his melancholy. There is an evident nervous tension in naturalist descriptions, not only because, like impressionism, as Arnold Hauser characterises it, 'it is an urban style, because it describes the change-ability, the nervous rhythm, the sudden sharp but always ephemeral impressions of the city',[33] but also because it betrays a deeper malaise. In his *Essais de psychologie contemporaine* (1883), Paul Bourget comments upon the fundamental pessimism, melancholy and neuroticism of the literature of his age, founded on observation: '*Observer, n'est-ce pas sortir de la vie inconsciente et féconde pour entrer dans l'analyse, dans la réflexion et dans la critique, signe certain que la poussée instinctive diminue?*' André Vial, who quotes this passage, adds that the attitude is common to what are apparently the most conflicting aesthetics, from the obsessively detailed naturalist observation of the lives of the Vatard sisters − to use Huysmans' work as an appropriate illustration − to the extravagant hypersensitivity of des Esseintes (in *A rebours*), such that the latter has an apparently contradictory cult for both Mallarmé and Zola. 'Ce malaise', Vial writes,

dont nous dirons seulement ici, résumant mille inquiets témoignages, qu'il naissait du spectacle de la laideur physique et morale présente, a selon les tempéraments et les vocations, appelé deux remèdes et suggéré deux exorcismes: les uns cherchèrent refuge et salut dans un exil à la fois spirituel et temporel, l'absence poétique, célébrant, sur un mode voulu artificiel à l'extrême, irrecevable, et offensant au commun, un ordre de sensations et d'émotions qui n'emprunteraient plus rien aux couleurs et aux accidents du monde ...; d'autres préférèrent approfondir leur souffrance en appliquant à leurs semblables et à eux-mêmes les exigences les plus impérieuses de l'observation et de la sincérité, pour libérer ensuite en *objets* d'art les images dont ils étaient obsédés.[34]

If it is the work of Huysmans that, as usual, exemplifies all the facets of this disquiet, it is the Goncourt brothers who, as usual, best give direct expression to its manifestations. 'Tous les observateurs sont tristes.' Genius is a nervous state. 'L'épithète rare' is the true mark of the artist. 'Tout pourrit et finit sans l'art. C'est l'embaumeur de la vie morte et rien n'a un peu d'immortalité que ce qu'il a touché, décrit, peint ou sculpté.'[35] At his brother's funeral, Edmond had all the roses in their garden cut and placed 'dans le creux autour de son corps' in the coffin 'sur un lit de poussière odoriférante'.[36] Like those roses, the artistry of the Goncourt brothers, and of other naturalists too, is offered up as a fragile, prophylactic defence against the encroachment of the material world, even as the lucid depicter of naturalist realities records its inevitable contamination.

The aestheticism contained in naturalist fiction represents an attempt to aestheticise the ugly, material world itself rather than to escape it. The most characteristic naturalist descriptions are not those which provide an artistic distraction from the rigours of the plot and the grave vision that impels it, but those in which the sordid and the visceral coalesce with the decorative. In *Sous-Offs*, as the troops leave Paris for Le Havre, we read this rapid evocation of the décor in which the technique of *écriture artiste* is mobilised by Descaves into a brief, but typical description: 'C'était, d'abord, la porte de Vanves, évoquant une rumeur de marché, le piétinement moutonnier des recrues, vaguant sous la pourriture d'un ciel dont les violets gangréneux, en dépit de copieuses ponctions, publiaient la décomposition hivernale' (p. 2). Such typically naturalist descriptive passages combine in varying degrees three fundamental components: a precise realist concern for detail, even to the extent of a mannered technicality; impressionistic effects of light and colour; an evocation of the ever-present process of disintegration or the state of putrescence. Here, from another Descaves text, *Une vieille rate*, is an extreme case in which the scene of the battered body of a murder victim, along with her mutilated dog and some rabbits huddled in a corner, is transformed into a colourful picture:

Et ils faisaient là comme un bouquet tiède et frissonnant, un bouquet où se fondaient et harmonisaient les nuances des robes: les gris, les pommelé, les café-au-lait, les blanc-crasseux et les blanc immaculé, les roux éteint et les châtain-clair; au milieu, jetant dans cette grisaille tonale sa note éclatante, deux fleurs rouges déchiraient le cœur du bouquet, saignaient dans une hermine qu'une pluie horrible avait éclaboussée. (pp. 179–80)

Such a scene is an inevitable strain on the reader's aesthetic sensibilities.

Even as he is about to commit suicide, Bonnetain's hero in *Charlot s'amuse* takes the time to look around and 'focalise' a picture:

Le soleil se couchait. Le ciel semblait saigner au-dessus de la Villette et le canal filant au loin, entre les quais déjà presque obscurs sous l'ombre des maisons, faisait comme une coulée d'or en fusion, au milieu de laquelle les chalands et les péniches tremblotaient, pareils à de noires épaves qu'aurait agitées un roulis. A droite, au contraire, le ciel s'éteignait dans une nuance de lilas tendre, vaporeuse, et, sur ce fond clair, les hautes cheminées d'usines se profilaient, nettes et rigides, semblables à des couleuvrines rose braquées sur les nuages ...

Et dans cette débauche de tons pourpres et indigo, dans cette orgie de flocons d'étamine pavoisant Paris, on eût dit, du haut de la passerelle, qu'un pinceau monstrueux et invisible promenait partout une aspersion de couleurs puisées dans vingt godets dont les gouttes éclatantes criblaient la ville de taches splendides, arlequinant l'espace, ainsi qu'un écolier barbouille, en un gâchis ruisselant, une aquarelle mal réussie. (pp. 337–9)

Such disturbing associations or juxtapositions of the sordid and the ornate, of the grim and the resplendent, place readers again in an ambivalent position, evoke contradictory responses, assault their sense of beauty and propriety, form part of the disturbing pragmatic effects characteristic of naturalist fiction, as we have seen. The reader's attention is divided between the beauty of the landscape and the horror of the scene. 'Les Funérailles de Francine Cloarec', Léon Hennique's naturalist novel in miniature, allegorises this problem. In a filthy Paris backstreet, in 'une puanteur d'égoût, une odeur de graillon rance et de charnier', as the girl's wasted body is taken away, her former lover, the painter Joseph Ricard, embarks upon a discussion of the winter scene with its 'tons roses', its 'finesses bleutées', its 'jaunes exquis', its 'phénomènes d'irisation parmi les ombres pâles' – and misses the funeral! Such is the reader's dilemma: to follow the corpse or admire the scenery. Or, perhaps, to be doubly shocked by the scenes of human suffering and degradation and by the indifference of the aesthetic response to them. Naturalist aestheticism presents the obverse of the natural process, fixing and transmuting a world in decay. The subject of naturalist fiction becomes an aesthetic object, material for the writer's palette, a procedure totally unpalatable for the politically conscious critic.[37] Lives become still lives. This aesthetic appropriation of the real world is thus the commonest reprieve within the naturalist vision from the lucid apprehension of life's corruptibility. Each naturalist had particular enthusiasms, ranging from the lyrical, epic and idyllic interludes of a Zola or a Hardy to the consolations of cynical resignation of a Céard or a Maupassant, but the aesthetic response, conveyed in these descriptions, is the most frequent recourse, part of that fundamental dialectic, even a solution to it, for it involves both a submission to and a dominance of the real. Science and art are therefore complementary processes of this dialectic. Art submits to the materiality, even to the essential corruptibility of life, but, by de-ontologising it, abstracts a fragile beauty from it.

The novels of Huysmans offer a casebook of the various types of the 'descriptive' in naturalist works that we have so far reviewed, just as his ancillary works like *Le Drageoir à épices* (1874) and *Croquis parisiens* (1880) contain a wealth of sketches that constitute fascinating exercises in the descriptive art, detached from a fictional context, but, in many cases, intertextually related to it. But, to stay with the novels, *Marthe* and *Les Sœurs Vatard* cover the full range of descriptive modes. There are the technical facts, how imitation pearls are made in *Marthe*, for example. There are Balzacian, encyclopaedic, accumulative descriptions of furniture and houses, usually with the author's characteristic stamp of extreme sordid, malodorous dilapidation, or of the vulgar glitz of the brothel. There are Zolaesque shop fronts, with similar but less enthusiastic displays of colour and, above all, substance, overabundant matter oozing and overflowing on the page. Naturalist description in general differs from realist denomination in its emphasis not only on the oddity of things but on their iddity, their oppressive 'Dasein'. But what makes the descriptive in Huysmans particularly representative is the irretrievably solvent nature of the reality that he depicts. Even the most colourful scenes take on a dull etiolation, a grubby liquefaction. His Paris landscape, more than most, must embrace the river, the rain and the clouds, as in this view of the city, focalised (somewhat distractedly) by Marthe:

La Seine charriait ce soir-là des eaux couleur de plomb, rayées çà et là par le reflètement des réverbères. A droite, dans un bateau de charbon, amarré à un rond de fer grand comme un cerveau, des ombres d'hommes et de femmes se mouvaient confusément; à gauche, se dressait le terre-plein du pont avec la statue du Roi. Planté au bas, près d'un concert, un arbre déchiquetait ses linéaments frêles sur le gris ardoisé du ciel. Plus loin enfin, le pont des Arts s'estompait dans la brume avec sa couronne de becs de gaz et l'ombre de ses piliers se mourait dans le fleuve en une longue tache noire. Une mouche fila sous l'arcade du pont, jetant une bouffée de vapeur tiède au visage de Marthe, laissant derrière elle un long sillage de mousse blanche qui s'éteignit peu à peu dans la suie des eaux. Une pluie fine commençait à tomber.[38]

As in much naturalist writing, but for Huysmans in particular, grimy water seems to be the elemental analogon that essentially defines the external world. Rain, then, in filthy city streets gives rise to almost lyrical promptings: 'L'eau clapotait, sortant en blanche écume par ses fissures, bouillonnant en bulles savonneuses, s'épanouissant en roses blanches, puis toutes ces fleurs de l'eau crevèrent et tombèrent en une nappe d'une saleté ignoble, tandis que d'autres éclosaient à nouveau et s'effeuillaient encore en des crachats troubles.'[39]

Edmond de Goncourt wrote in the *Journal* (27 February 1881) that another text by the same author, *En ménage*, 'possède une qualité incontestable: l'intensité dans le gris'. This was a compliment, for 'le gris' is a constant tonality of the vision of life of the Goncourt brothers and of the naturalists in general. It is not merely a realist reflection of drab existences in dreary cities in an industrial age, the scene of so much naturalist fiction, but an imaginative choice, for, as Bachelard remarks in *La Poétique de l'espace*, when philosophers look to poets for guidance on how the world should be characterised, they soon discover that 'le monde n'est pas de l'ordre du substantif mais bien de l'ordre de l'adjectif' and that 'on pourrait donner ce conseil: pour trouver l'essence d'une philosophie du monde, cherchez-en l'adjectif'.[40] Quite naturally, the same is true of the inclement weather in naturalist fiction, which is not a comment on the climatic conditions of the places in which the action of these works takes place, but is rather the projection of a view of life's general inclemency, of its unwelcome subjection to the elemental. As Deffoux and Zavie write of the naturalists, 'un paysage de pluie les attire plus qu'un décor ensoleillé; il pleut beaucoup dans les romans naturalistes'.[41] Not surprisingly, *A vau-l'eau* starts off in the rain, as does *Charlot s'amuse*, *Une Vie*, *L'Œuvre*, to name a few key texts. In *Une Belle Journée*, rain comes to play a significant role in the action, confining the 'lovers' to the restaurant where they bore themselves into inaction. In *Sous-Offs*, it rains with the same monotony and regularity with which the soldiers perform their barrack routines and the prostitutes service the regiment. It rains also (though not surprisingly either) in the English naturalist novel: ominously Tess agrees to marry Angel as it rains and Jude's worst days and decline take place in the rain. It rains in the North American naturalist novel too: as the fortunes of McTeague the dentist and his wife decline, the rain sets in and 'all the filth of the alley invaded their quarters like a rising, muddy tide'[42] – though the hero does end up in Death Valley without a drop to drink! Similarly, in Ringuet's *Trente arpents*, the whole environment degenerates with the protagonist's hold on life, as Euchariste Moisan's decline is marked by the Quebec equivalent to the rain of despair, what French Canadians picturesquely call 'la slush'.[43]

Such banal observations do suggest, however, that such passages fulfil more than the function of 'fillers' or 'mood setters' or mimetic décors. One could even suggest that they derive not from the 'horizontal', purely mimetic tendency of much fictional description, but from what Philippe Hamon calls the 'tendance "verticale"', *décryptive plutôt que descriptive*' of certain passages of description, 'une tendance plus qualitative que quantitative, de compréhension plus que d'extension du référent, de la volonté d'aller *sous* le réel, *derrière* le réel, chercher un sens, une vérité fondamentale derrière les apparences trompeuses ou accessoires d'une surface'.[44] Not that one could make claims for the primacy of description in naturalist fiction, as one can for the 'description créatrice' of the 'nouveau roman', which 'invente en toute cohérence un univers et tend à susciter un sens avec lequel elle entre en lutte'.[45] Still totally subject to the referential project of the realist tradition, naturalist description cannot therefore be 'protodiegetic' or 'antidiegetic' in these ways. But it can nevertheless, I would claim, be in a real sense 'metadiegetic', inscribing into the fiction a certain reflective narrativity, not the narrativity of agents and actions, but of the fundamental ontological processes that the agents and actions themselves represent. It becomes in a sense allegorical, but in a concrete form, representing the more basic 'action', in the physiological meaning of the term (action and reaction), that the fiction depicts. It may more accurately be defined less as 'de-scription' than as the 'in-scription' of a fundamental drama of the material world, analogous to the human dramas of the plot, involving the dissolution of the forms of the environment which decompose before the eyes of the reader or of the intradiegetic observer. This second order action, inscribed into the narrative by the descriptive, constitutes, therefore, a further function of a mode which reveals itself to be far more complex than one might at first suppose: it names and categorises that which ultimately lies beyond the naming process; it highlights the forms and colours of a reality that is in the process of losing such distinctions to become formless and colourless; it transposes into the material environment of the fiction a graphic, intensified, substantialist version of the essential naturalist action that is being depicted more diffusely in the full extent of the text.

Goncourt texts, from which we might take one or two brief examples, would provide perhaps the most comprehensive illustrations of this poetics of dissolution, which in the very act of representing a concrete reality condemns it to effacement. Even a spring day is marked by this potential erosion, 'un jour qui a des clartés de cristal et des blancheurs d'argent, un jour froid, virginal et doux, qui s'éteint dans le rose du soleil avec des pâleurs de limbes'.[46] In the same text, Germinie and Jupillon walk in a Paris street, 'dans le vague, l'infini, l'inconnu d'une rue qui suit toujours le même mur, les mêmes arbres, les mêmes réverbères, et conduit toujours à la même nuit' (p. 143). In Vincennes, nature is already 'morte': 'rien ne remuait; les verdures avec leurs petites ombres sèches ne bougeaient pas, le bois était las et comme accablé sous le ciel pesant' (p. 198). Germinie's whole being is fused into the desubstantialised, rain-swept décor: 'quand les pavés, les trottoirs, la terre, semblaient disparaître et mollir sous la pluie, et que rien ne paraissait plus solide dans la nuit noyée, la pauvre misérable, presque folle de fatigue, croyait voir se gonfler un déluge dans le ruisseau' (p. 217). All the heroine's human strivings lead to the inevitable ambience of the cemetery with its grey walls, its leaden sky, its bare trees, its dead cypresses, its pell-mell of rotting crosses (pp. 273–5). In naturalist novels human destinies are distilled into disintegrating decors.

Such fading tableaux are to be found in other Goncourt texts and in other naturalist works, betokening a more general imaginative response. Two such descriptions frame Edmond de Goncourt's *Les Frères Zemganno* (1879):

De ce ciel défaillant tombait, imperceptiblement, ce voile grisâtre qui dans le jour encore existant apporte l'incertitude à l'apparence des choses, les fait douteuses et vagues, noie les formes et les contours de la nature qui s'endort dans l'effacement du crépuscule: cette triste et douce et insensible agonie de la vie de la lumière. (p. 8)[47]

C'était un jour de la fin d'octobre, pendant lequel il avait plu toute la journée, et à la fin duquel on ne savait pas bien s'il ne pleuvait pas encore; de ces jours d'automne de Paris, où son ciel, sa terre, ses murailles semblent se fondre en eau, et où, à la nuit, les lueurs du gaz sur les trottoirs sont comme des flammes promenées sur des rivières. (p. 377)

Darkness, liquefaction, livid skies, shadowy forms, rain, fading lights, all partake of this poetics of decomposition of naturalist texts. The calvary of Héloïse Pajadou is a common, essential naturalist fate: to be cast out into a world of dank putrescence, to be engulfed by liquid filth, to be subject to a process of dissolution:

Héloïse perdit pied et tomba sur les genoux. Tout de suite un grand froid la saisit et une petite pluie fine comme un brouillard lui glaça les moëlles. Un silence régnait, la campagne, au-delà de la Bièvre, s'étendait triste et nue, barrée par une rangée d'arbres maigres, chevelus au faîte et qui semblaient de longs plumeaux que la terre poussait vers le vaste plafond de nuages lourds et noirs. Le hurlement d'un chien s'éleva, au loin. C'était une plainte profonde, un sanglot prolongé d'enfant qui souffre. Héloïse l'écoutait, la tête penchée ... Mais une trépidation la secoua, et elle comprit vaguement que ses pieds baignaient dans une flaque. Une fraîcheur entrait en elle, lui courait sous la peau, de la nuque aux talons.[48]

Only in naturalist texts, no doubt, could standing in a puddle have any special significance, but such scenes are part of a pattern, the recurrent theme of the invasion of character by the décor, of spirit by matter. This is the fate of Gervaise Macquart, who, after *her* night in the snow – 'sa promenade dernière, des cours sanglantes où l'on assommait, aux salles blafardes où la mort raidissait les gens dans les draps de tout le monde' (III, 922) – becomes that matter, the rotting flesh in the corridor. In that typical state of uncertain substantiality that characterises such threshold poetics, darkness takes on a material presence as it overtakes the naturalist character, like Liza of Lambeth, an East End London Gervaise, as her young life is spent: 'And the darkness was awful; it was a heavy, ghastly blackness, that seemed palpable.' Then, at the end, 'a heaviness seemed to fill the air like a grey blight, cold and suffocating; and the heaviness was Death'.[49]

The effect itself is somewhat cumbersome, but it illustrates the fundamental disposition of the naturalist imagination to imagery of tainted fluidity, a kind of descriptive correlative to the tarnished blood that urges naturalist characters on in their plots in their course towards degradation. This association is far from arbitrary. As Michel Guiomar argues, 'tout élément fluide acquiert donc la tendance à se transformer en sang ... Toute métamorphose eau–sang et vice versa serait donc signe de Mort même quand celle-ci n'est pas évidente ... A l'insu parfois de l'auteur, cette présence d'une pluie quelconque accompagne souvent l'approche de la Mort.'[50] This drama of the material imagination, actively played out in the mode of naturalist description, is again a reminder that the essential matter of the naturalist novel is the destiny of matter. Naturalist plots become exhausted, characters spent in the hopeless dynamics of the degenerative struggle, merging into the description of a fading light and of a dissolvent materiality. Despite the assertive posture of realistic description, despite the abstracting transformations of the *instantéiste* aesthetic, the tragic time of the narrative peters out, yields inexorably to the spatial state, which is not in the usual state of stasis of description, but is caught up in the dynamics of disintegration. Naturalist description has only the most tenuous of holds, phenomenological and aesthetic, on the ontological state of a reality which it seeks to represent, but which, paradoxically, eludes its power, for it cannot determine the indeterminate, compose the decomposing, describe that which is in the process of escaping description.

There is perhaps no better illustration of these various points than the five elaborate descriptions of Paris in Zola's *Une Page d'amour*, to which I alluded at the beginning of this chapter. With their 'intentions symphoniques et humaines', they are fully 'mimeticised' (and authenticated) descriptions, reflecting human passions, focalised by the *dramatis personae*, just as they are fully aestheticised, framed, colourful, impressionistic pictures in prose, captivating to the mind's eye. Yet they describe a Paris that is fading away, dying, disappearing in a series of encounters with the natural elements: transformed into a seascape, in Part I, where 'cette ville fut engloutie sous le débordement d'une inondation' (III, 1007); burning out like a spent fire in Part II; erupting like a volcano in Part III; swallowed up by a storm in Part IV; disappearing under a sea of ice and into the blankness of a shroud of snow in Part V. Thus we must reject the standard view of critics who, like Terry Eagleton, echo the traditional charge and equate the naturalist world with the naturalised, the given, the verisimilitudinous, itemised, familiar and reassuringly *described* world.[51] On the contrary, it might more accurately be termed, as we have seen by its various disjunctions, dissolutions and dissociations, a world, not of description, but of *dis-scription*.

9

THE ENTROPIC VISION

Thematic criticism has now long been out of favour and is often dismissed as an outmoded or unsophisticated, uninventive process of inventorying, as modern theories of literature have apparently evolved at the expense of thematic studies. Formalist critics, poeticians and semioticians, it has been recently argued in an attempt to remedy the situation, 'ont mis en relief la grammaire et non le message, la langue et non la parole, l'articulation et non le référent'.[1] In practice, though, forms of thematic criticism have been and still are far more extensively applied than is usually considered to be the case. There was, of course, within the French context the prestigious and highly influential spate of psychoanalytical and phenomenological studies in the 1960s, by Roland Barthes, Charles Mauron, Jean-Paul Weber, Jean-Pierre Richard, Georges Poulet, Jean Rousset, Jean Starobinski, which, despite their diversity, are usually grouped together as representing a form of thematic criticism.[2] There is also, among comparatists, the lasting tradition of *Stoffgeschichte*, studying legendary figures and myths through the ages and across national boundaries, along with the various forms of archetypal criticism which study significant thematic recurrences and relate them to structures of the unconscious, the subconscious, the transhistorical imagination or the ideologies of a particular age.[3] Even deconstruction, though theoretically opposed to the synthesising function of thematic criticism – yet, as Derrida points out in *De la Grammatologie*, always being prey in a certain way to its own work – can often fall paradoxically, despite itself, as Shlomith Rimmon-Kenan writes, 'dans le "piège" de la suggestion d'un thème – celui ne serait-il que le thème de l'absence de thème ou celui de l'impossibilité de dégager une signification stable'.[4] Furthermore, leading formalist and structuralist critics have commonly paid far more attention to thematic questions than we tend to suppose. In his *Introduction à la littérature fantastique*, for instance, Todorov notes that 'dans les études littéraires on accepte une approche théorique des éléments "formels" de l'œuvre, tels que le rythme et la composition, mais on la refuse dès qu'il est question des "contenus"' (p. 150). Yet a good half of his generic study of fantastic literature is devoted to themes. Indeed, generic criticism must inevitably lead into thematics, for generic categories, whatever the modal or formal modulations that they take on, are inextricably linked to thematic specifications.

A persistent problem besetting thematic studies is one of terminology. Any survey of usages of the term 'theme' would inevitably lead to considerable confusion: Yet, in the usual sense of the term, there are probably present, with varying degrees of emphasis, three fundamental attributes: recurrence, coalescence, abstraction. Where one of these attributes significantly dominates, another term usually applies (respectively): (leit)motif, subject or *topos*, message. The relationship between these and allied concepts, whatever the fluctuations of usage, is normally hierarchical and dependent upon a differing level of abstraction from the narrative events (or 'diegesis'). Thus the 'theme' is regularly considered to be a more abstract and a more general determination than the 'motif', as motifs in a text or a body of texts combine to form a theme.[5] Quite naturally, what is held to be a mere motif in one study may become a theme in another as the focus of attention of the critic shifts. In this study I shall continue to follow a direction of interpretation which abstracts from the particular and concrete events of the diegesis in roughly the following manner: motifs (e.g. the fallen woman) → themes (e.g. disintegration) → (the entropic) vision. Other types of thematic study might remain closer to the narrative dynamics of the texts, in perhaps the following way: motifs → *topoi* → myth(s). But, particularly in the case of mimetic literature, the thematic order tends to remain implicit and requires explicit formulation, an abstraction of disparate textual elements into a coherent structure.[6] The essential movement is, as Claude Bremond defines it, between theme and concept, the former qualifying the latter, the latter unifying the former: 'Libéré du corset définitionnel, plongé dans un bain de contaminations empiriques, le concept devient thème; mais, aussitôt repris par la réflexion et asservi à la nécessité de se figer dans une appellation commode, le thème tend à se résorber dans le concept.'[7]

Even in a body of literature as apparently varied as naturalist fiction, different texts clearly exhibit different, though allied themes, from which may be abstracted a conceptual core deriving from a common vision. In dealing with such a variety of texts, however interrelated they are by influences, intertextual links, common strategies, common aesthetic goals, the process is necessarily selective and reductive, for the texts themselves remain, in many cases, sufficiently complex to have attributes belonging to other thematic fields and other generic structures. But, as Michel Potet notes, 'le thème peut à lui seul fonctionner comme un genre, en ce que sa réception s'opère selon les servitudes imposées par la re-connaissance d'une continuité'.[8]

So far, mainly through a study of the fiction, I have attempted largely to 'decompose' the naturalist 'genre' into its different components and we have seen that there is considerable diversity even though certain consistent patterns are quite evident. No doubt this diversity explains the comparative rarity of thematic studies of naturalist literature. Even Yves Chevrel is somewhat awed at the prospect of defining a naturalist thematics, which 'comprise comme la mise en ordre des sujets traités risquerait d'être impossible à dresser, sauf à répertorier la quasi-totalité des milieux traités'.[9] The problem lies both in the diversity of the material and in the elasticity of the concept, a problem which is complicated even further by the suggestion that 'le terrain de la thématique littéraire conduit tout droit à l'étude de l'univers propre à chaque écrivain', which precludes the possibility of there being any common vision. Then there is the equally problematic claim that 'le grand thème, l'unique thème de l'écrivain naturaliste est donc le monde', which has the same effect but by an excess of comprehensiveness.[10] Naturalist thematics would appear to be both too particular and too general. On the same topic, in an earlier study, Raymond Pouilliart attempts to define a naturalist thematics under a series of rubrics: 'modernité', 'physiologie', 'le peuple', 'le regard', 'le communard', 'la passivité', 'l'artiste', 'la dissolution', 'l'objet';[11] but, however important and recurrent these traits may be, their excessive disparity is clearly evident.[12] But the essential problem lies perhaps in the resistance of the literature itself to thematic interpretation, its pretence at being a representation of life in all its diversity rather than literature with its formal and thematic constraints. For those who tend to view naturalist literature as a method, or as a set of mimetic procedures, or as scientific investigation, or as detailed description of the external world, it will have no specific thematic determinants, but, potentially at least, will draw into its purview the whole of modern life. Thus, paradoxically, it has tended to be the detractors of naturalism, with their scandalised rejection of naturalist themes, who have been more inclined to focus on its specific content and to see that it represents less a mirroring of reality than a vision of reality, less the rendering of the truth than the rendering of a vision of the truth. In his early study of naturalism, the hostile critic, Charles Bigot, writes: 'le naturalisme sort bien moins de la nature elle-même que de l'esprit de messieurs les naturalistes. Plus que l'expression de la réalité, il est l'expression de leur esthétique, de leur éducation, de leur philosophie, de leur tempérament, de la constitution de leurs organes.'[13] Unlike the famous five of the manifesto against *La Terre*, I shall refrain from speculation about 'la constitution de leurs organes'. But from a thematic standpoint, we might be able to discern a certain unity in the naturalist project, a common vision, one which, in many respects – morally, socially, aesthetically, philosophically – represented an impasse for naturalist writers, but one to which they unremittingly gave expression.

Let us begin with the theme of adultery, an eminently literary theme, of course, which goes back to Sir Lancelot's 'adventures' and which is particularly frequent in the nineteenth-century novel. It occurs in naturalist literature with an extraordinary persistence, deprived quite naturally of any heroic or romantic potentialities, for, as we have seen, such values are unknown and even parodied in these works. Here adultery is invariably catastrophic or banalised. *Madame Meuriot* by Alexis is an excellent example of the former; *En ménage* by Huysmans or *Une Belle Journée* by Céard are significant instances of the latter. It runs through Zola's novels, notably *Pot-Bouille*, during the preparation of which the author wrote a systematic commentary on the theme of bourgeois adultery.[14] It is an obsessive theme in the works of Maupassant, who also wrote an article on the topic, prompted by Zola's novel.[15] In fact, for at least one contemporary commentator at this time, the theme came to be almost indissociable from the French novel. Mark Twain claimed that 'all a person had to do to write a French novel was concoct thirty-seven cases of adultery and have everyone live happily to the end'.[16] The naturalist novel at least seemed original in giving the theme a disastrous turn and, as *Madame Meuriot* in particular shows, in suggesting that profounder disorders were at stake.

The prevalence of the theme could be explained to some degree as a reflection of contemporary mores in an age marked, as Alain Corbin explains, by a fascination for adultery, by 'l'ascension du modèle de la maîtresse, telle que la popularisera le vaudeville de la Belle Epoque', by the fact that 'le caractère majeur de la sexualité fin de siècle est bien le brouillage qui s'opère, la confusion des modèles. L'épouse bourgeoise s'érotise lentement tandis que nombre de prostituées se mettent à ressembler à des femmes respectables.'[17] In works as famous as *Nana*, where the heroine plays all the rôles and demolishes all such distinctions, or in works as obscure as *Entre Conjoints!*, as we saw in previous chapters, naturalist writers were quick to record the trend. It is certainly not enough to argue, as does Brunetière in his review of *Pot-Bouille*, that the naturalists are reacting against the Romantic idealisation of adultery.[18]

More to the point, no doubt, is the fact that in naturalist novels as varied as *L'Assommoir, Effi Briest, L'Accident de M. Hébert, Une Page d'amour*, adultery is presented, whatever her precise circumstances, as a drama of the fall of the woman. Now, as Tony Tanner remarks in a study of the same theme, 'the woman in the marriage situation becomes a paradigm for the problems of interrelating patterns'. The action of adultery, he adds, 'portends the possible breakdown of all the mediations on which society itself depends, and demonstrates the latent impossibility of participating in the interrelated patterns that comprise its structure'.[19] Adultery is thus the violation of a code, the transgression of boundaries, provoking dissolution in the precarious stability of the social order. But it is also the 'natural', the instinctive, the primordial, the sexual, asserting themselves to subvert that order. Adultery is therefore both typical and symptomatic, denoting a whole body of themes, for, in a more general way, the naturalist text recounts the passage from order to disorder, from mental stability to hysteria and madness, from sobriety to intemperance, from integrity to corruption. Heredity, illness, obsession, sexuality, are disruptive factors which break up the fragile balance of differences, of structures, of codes. The characteristic movement of the naturalist novel is in the direction of disintegration and confusion. A process of adulteration is endemic to the naturalist vision.

Zola, in typical fashion, mythologised this process in the *Rougon-Macquart* series, endowed it with an obscure mythical past conveyed across the generations in the tainted blood of his accursed fictional family. As it manifests itself in its most violently explosive form through the mania of Zola's Jacques-the-Ripper, the narrator of *La Bête humaine* glosses in indirect discourse on the origins of Lantier's destructive instinct:

Puisqu'il ne les connaissait pas, quelle fureur pouvait-il avoir contre elles? car, chaque fois, c'était comme une soudaine crise de rage aveugle, une soif toujours renaissante de venger des offenses très anciennes, dont il aurait perdu l'exacte mémoire. Cela venait-il donc de si loin, du mal que les femmes avaient fait à sa race, de la rancune amassée de mâle en mâle, depuis la première tromperie au fond des cavernes? (VI, 62)

The primordial scenario is played out in the blood and in the fading memory of Tante Dide, the forebear(er) of the family, the rotten stump of Zola's family tree. As Françoise Gaillard pointedly observes on *Le Docteur Pascal*, the last volume of the series, in which this character reappears:

Les crimes qui se sont gravés dans l'esprit désormais éteint de tante Dide, ne sont jamais que la conséquence et la répétition d'un crime antérieur, jamais vraiment nommé, tout au plus vaguement désigné comme étant l'adultère dont elle s'est rendue coupable autrefois, aux temps presque légendaires de la naissance de la famille Rougon-Macquart ... Tous les crimes qui éclaboussent de sang la famille maudite, ne sont que la répétition de cet événement primitif qui est resté fixé dans la mémoire collective.[20]

Thus, even a novel like *Une Page d'amour*, infinitely more sober than the pages of lust, rape, perversion, fornication and murder of other novels in the series, may be linked to a central theme 'which runs through nearly all of Zola's fiction: the disruptive nature of a sexuality seen as an irresistible fatality'.[21]

In preparing *La Bête humaine*, as we saw earlier, Zola consulted Cesar Lombroso's *L'Uomo deliquente* (1876) − *L'Homme criminel* (1887) in the French translation − a work which articulated a commonly held belief in atavistic criminality. Then there was the later text by the same author, *La Donna deliquente, la prostituta e la donna normale* (1893) − *La Femme criminelle et la prostitution* (1896) − which, as we also saw, argued that the prostitute is the female equivalent to the criminal, that, being closer to nature, woman is more susceptible to atavistic and hereditary tendencies, and that she has a natural, latent perversity. Against the background of such commonly held views, fantasies and fears, presented with the authority of scientific investigation, there is an evident continuity of significance between the more moderate forms of sexual impropriety and its more evidently devastating, pathological manifestations in prostitutes and criminals as in Zola's half-brother/-sister pair, Jacques Lantier and Anna Coupeau. Protestations about the untruth of naturalist exposés of the 'bas-fonds' of human nature as well as the 'bas-fonds' of society clearly betrayed a private conviction that they were true. Naturalist thematics is obsessively engaged upon an exploration of the frontier between the normal and the pathological, probing the breakdown of distinctions in the biological and social order. In the most thorough thematic study of the *Rougon-Macquart* series, Auguste Dezalay has shown that Zola's novels most heavily charged with sexual themes, works like *La Curée* and *Nana*, deal fundamentally with such disappearing discriminations, recounting the assimilation of men and women with machines, plants, animals, and are characterised by mixture, mobility, flux, a promiscuity of states and forms.[22] Princes and paupers sleep in Nana's bed; the 'demi-monde' absorbs and becomes the 'monde'; in *Pot-Bouille*, 'toutes les baraques se ressemblent'. Incest in *La Curée* and sapphic love in *Nana*, for example, become 'deux manières, en cherchant la différence, d'exalter la passion de l'Identique, dans la fusion des mêmes sangs ou des mêmes sexes'.[23] Inversions, reversions, perversions become the norms. Money as well as sex, 'la note de la chair et de l'or', as Zola liked to state the problem, runs rampage over social barriers, circulating like a raging ferment in the social body.

There are two particular naturalist motifs that, in different ways, illustrate this crisis of forms and distinctions, this contamination of the social by the biological, with which we are dealing. Firstly, the Widow of Ephesus motif, with its multiple variants in different traditions from Chinese literature to Breton folklore and its most familiar manifestations in (sections 111–12 of) *The Satyricon*: the motif of the mourning widow 'consoled' by a soldier, which G. Hainsworth has traced in a number of naturalist texts.[24] Bakhtin has commented on this tale and interpreted its tightly structured set of elements (the tomb, youth, food and drink, death, love, the conception of new life, laughter) as a narrative of the triumph of life over death.[25] The naturalist versions, however, are more morbid and cynical, less 'carnivalesque', a kind of retroactive adultery that parodies the more prestigious *Liebestod* myth. But if, as Jean Borie argues, 'un fantasme de la société bourgeoise ... donne à la veuve la mission profonde de représenter la continuité sacrée de la famille et du patrimoine',[26] it is another instance of violated codes, subverted taboos, a further breakdown of the distinctive by the instinctive.

A second, not unrelated, motif (death in sex as opposed to sex in death) is the prevalence of venereal disease in naturalist works. It is not merely a case of scrupulous realists recording the ravages of a social disease on the lives of prostitutes, or, in the novels of Lucien Descaves, an addition to the 'misères du sabre'. It is more a disease of society, symptomatic of the corruption of 'the social body', a visible reminder of the corruptibility of the flesh, an 'allegorical representation', as Jean Borie suggests, of 'damnation'.[27] In a sense it is the naturalist malady *par excellence*, not the wages of sin, but the price of illusion, nature's ever menacing and fearful revenge, the putrid fruits of 'love', the corruptibility of the flesh made manifest, and very much a part of the recurrent symptomatology and mythology of an age against whose values it constituted an insidious defiance. 'Le siècle de la Science et du Progrès', writes Patrick Wald Lasowski, 'se trouve confronté à la toute-puissance d'une maladie folle, baroque, incontrôlée.'[28] Zola again gives the most dramatic expression to the motif in *Nana*, drawing upon a whole thematic range in his allegorical myth of the 'mouche d'or', as Nana is described by the journalist Faucherey, a myth that links the courtesan's final putrid state to her hereditary past, to her origins, her tainted blood and nervous derangement producing this ferment of destruction, this 'force de la nature', which corrupts and disorganises all in her wake. 'Nana corruptrice,' as Wald Lasowski writes, 'en qui s'incarne le mal, c'est aussi le Peuple, la Nature et la Femme, forces effrayantes, fascinantes et incontrôlées, qui trouvent dans la mouche leur expression la plus menaçante.' The fly, he argues, is 'le défi à la structure: "remontant" du peuple à l'aristocratie en une fermentation puissante digne de tout germinal, la mouche dénonce la division des classes, et passe allégrement toutes les barrières, faisant communiquer en son vol innocent les charognes abjectes aux palais protégés, se revêtant de soleil à partir de l'ordure, disséminant le poison dans l'éclat des pierreries et des cuisses de neige.'[29] By having Nana die, disfigured, of the 'petite' rather than the 'Grande Vérole', Zola maintains the allegorical potentiality of the myth and its role in a broader thematic complex, that of the 'bourgeois' order, submitting ultimately to the biological order of corruption, as it generally does in naturalist texts. This is why death, putridity, fetid matter, illness, filth, venereal disease, have such prominence. In the cycles of continuous creation, the naturalist imagination invariably seizes upon the phases of disintegration. Commenting on the innumerable descriptions of deaths and burials in naturalist works, Colin Burns notes that Henry Céard became something of a specialist in what he calls 'la documentation putride', providing Zola with information for Nana's death and conducting Huysmans to the autopsy room in the Lariboisière hospital for *Marthe*.[30] But Céard had no hand in the description of the dying Darius Clayhanger, whose 'body seemed to have that vague appearance of general movement which a multitude of insects will give to a piece of decaying matter',[31] nor in the even more graphic end of Paul Adam's Lucie Thirache, that I have already quoted, the rotting flesh of the pathetic prostitute of *Chair molle*, a much cheaper moll than Nana, but one who dies of the genuine thing.

Paul Adam's novel also provides an impressive example, not only of physical corruption, but of mental derangement, the familiar condition of hysteria and delirium into which the heroine lapses in the final pages (part III, chapter 7). The naturalist novel in general, not just *La Bête humaine*, tends to go off the rails, as the novelist pushes his heroines and heroes beyond the rational order. Brian Nelson has remarked, for example, that 'the characteristic narrative rhythm of a Zola novel is one of accelerating movement', and Barthes points out that in *Nana* 'le récit s'accélère, les mois de la fin sont comme des minutes du commencement: la désagrégation est emportée dans un mouvement progressif, qui rend d'une façon hallucinante son caractère implacable'.[32] There is, to take *Nana* as a typical case, a mounting effect of disruption and catastrophe marked not only by Nana's sudden physical collapse, but also by the frantic destructiveness, the capriciousness and lasciviousness that characterise the latter stages of her career. In the dynamics of the naturalist novel, there usually occurs a point at which the subversive forces break through the resistant social and biological order when the collapse occurs. The process may be more gradual, as in *Charlot s'amuse*, where 'chaque jour plus profonde, cette consomption, qu'accélérait une exagération primitivement vicieuse et héréditaire du système nerveux de l'enfant, se traduisait déjà par un détraquement physique et par une déchéance des facultés morales et intellectuelles' (p. 123). This 'déchéance', this universal degeneration at all levels of life, the *Entartung* of Max Nordau's influential book, is inscribed into the very structure of naturalist fiction. Major characters, minor characters, rich and poor, all seem affected by this general drift of life. Charlot notes in Fanny, his pathetic mistress, whose sad tale has already been told, 'quelque chose des traits de sa mère, et cette apathie abrutie du regard qu'il lui avait vue, l'autre jour, à la Salpêtrière' (p. 303). There is a certain interchangeability in naturalist fates, a certain family air amongst naturalist characters, all Rougon-Macquart in a way, as in different manners, at different rates, with differing degrees of resignation and understanding of their common fate, they submit to the same process of dissolution of their bodies or of their illusions.

It seems that this immoderate literature corresponds to a real crisis in human values. Insistently the human spirit is shown defeated by the appetites, the instincts, by nature itself, for there is a constant assimilation of man (and particularly woman) to the natural order. Hence the common tendency, against which many a critic protested, to reduce human behaviour to the determining action of the body, the nerves, the blood, the sexual organs, the stomach. In naturalist works, however willing the spirit, the flesh is far too strong, for there is a kind of primitive 'nature', an irresistible, universal, depersonalised, instinctive (Schopenhauerian) Will that rises to the surface, saps the individual's sense of human values and brings about the decline.

Two further naturalist motifs illustrate the pathetic and the fearful aspects of this theme. Firstly the figure of the ugly, deformed or pre-formed child. Whether it is the foetus flushed away, as in *Pot-Bouille*, or the scaly pile of flesh, the 'plaie', in *Sous-Offs*, or the sickly child in *Misères du sabre*, or Jeanlin, the vicious throwback in the Maheu family in *Germinal*, or Nana's Louiset, or even Little Father Time, Jude's ill-fated son in Hardy's novel, to name but a few, the naturalist child incarnates the essential naturalist condition by its marginally human aspect, its brief, tenuous hold on human existence, its evident biological nature. The second motif is no less common, the figure of the 'human beast' − a fine oxymoron which sums up the dynamics of the naturalist vision − springing up from its lair to wreak destruction. It may take the form of the beast in man, as in Zola's *La Bête humaine*, an atavistic regression to a primordial state of the species marked by uninhibited violence and brutish murder, whose constant readiness to emerge is signified by certain stigmata like the prominent jaw, the mass of hair, the penetrating look. Or it may be the beast in woman, the beast that is woman in Nana's case, particularly as we see her through Muffat's enthralled gaze: 'Il songeait à son ancienne horreur de la femme, au monstre de l'Ecriture, lubrique, sentant le fauve. Nana était toute velue, un duvet de rousse faisait de son corps un velours; tandis que, dans sa croupe et ses cuisses de cavale, dans les renflements charnus creusés de plis profonds, qui donnaient au sexe le voile troublant de leur ombre, il y avait de la bête' (IV, 173). Such a bestial reversion may characterise a whole community. In his preface to a recent edition of *La Terre*, Emmanuel Le Roy Ladurie notes that Zola's peasant is a kind of Neanderthal man: 'On en revient à l'animal, à une sorte de pithécanthrope rural, non plus végétarien, ni fructivore. Le voilà ce primate agraire, cet ogre, qui se met à aimer la chair fraîche.'[33] Or, to take less obvious examples, the disruptive force may take a more symbolic and more allusive form, a myth perhaps, like the legend of the d'Urberville Coach that condemns Tess to re-commit ancestral crimes, or even a ghost, as in *Effi Briest*, where the heroine's life is haunted by the spirit of the mysterious dead Chinaman. Whatever its form or formlessness, there is frequently in the naturalist text a sense of an all-powerful other self, which reaches back to an unbridled, libidinal past ready to invade the present, an irresistible fount of unquelled rage, of ungoverned energy, which the present moral order can barely hold in check and which breaks loose in the novel.

The American naturalist novel seems to have been particularly disposed to this theme and to the motif of the human beast. The narrator of Dreiser's *Sister Carrie* (1900), for example, interrupts the narrative to present a portentous lesson in the popular Darwinism from which the theme and the motif derive in order to explain his heroine's fall:

Among the forces which sweep and play throughout the universe, untutored man is but a wisp in the wind. Our civilization is still in a middle stage – scarcely beast, in that it is no longer wholly guided by instinct; scarcely human, in that it is not yet wholly guided by reason. On the tiger no responsibility rests. We see him aligned by nature with the forces of life ... He will not forever balance thus between good and evil. When this jangle of free will and instinct shall have been adjusted, when perfect understanding has given the former the power to replace the latter entirely, man will no longer vary. The needle of understanding will yet point steadfast and unwavering to the distant pole of truth.[34]

Of the outcome of this great battle between, in Tennyson's words, 'Evolution ever climbing after some ideal good and Reversion ever dragging evolution in the mud', others were less confident and, like Frank Norris, dwelt more on the Lombrosian themes of atavism and degeneracy. It is *McTeague* and *Vandover and the Brute* again which most graphically and somewhat bluntly illustrate this motif, both works showing evident signs of the influence of *Thérèse Raquin* and *La Bête humaine* as well as of *L'Assommoir*. McTeague, the salient jawed dentist, is given to 'fits of atavism', especially when Trina is in his chair: 'Suddenly the animal in the man stirred and woke; the evil instincts that in him were so close to the surface leaped to life, shouting and clamoring.' In this early instance of the battle with the human beast, the brute is cowed, but the outcome is inevitable: 'Below the fine fabric of all that was good in him ran the foul stream of hereditary evil, like a sewer. The vices and sins of his father and of his father's father, to the third and fourth and five hundredth generation, tainted him. The evil of an entire race flowed in his veins.'[35] Not surprisingly, as the beast takes over, he murders Trina (in whom, incidentally, an equivalent second self, bestial Woman, has also arisen) and he is tracked down like a beast in Death Valley. Such rudimentary naturalist psychology is even more evident in the dualism of *Vandover and the Brute*, where a rather ordinary character is relegated several notches on the evolutionary scale. In Vandover too, the 'animal in him, the perverse evil brute, awoke and stirred'. He holds the creature in check at first, but Flossie brings out the worst in him and the brute takes over, 'raging, more insatiable, more irresistible than ever', leading him to a life of gambling, drunkenness and debauchery: 'It was Nature inexorably exacting. It was the vast fearful engine riding him down beneath its myriad spinning wheels, remorselessly, irresistibly.' This 'inexorable law of nature', as the narrator insists, drives Vandover into the hysterical state called *lycanthropy-mathesis* to the extent that he ends up crawling on all fours growling 'Wolf-wolf-wolf' and barking like a dog![36] A lengthy description of Vandover standing before a mirror and being transformed into the brute (pp. 271–3) shows how close naturalism came to Gothic conventions. But the naturalist beast in man is no transcendent being, but the elemental self itself, reaching back into the distant reaches of the supposed origins of the human species and out into those marginal states in which the human identity breaks down.

Thus naturalist literature represents the drama, the tragedy, the comedy and, at times, even the farce – for generic distinctions themselves tend to break down – of the human being subjected to a *natural* condition. There is a traditional tendency, that derives, no doubt, from hasty generalisations based on certain pronouncements by Zola, to ascribe to naturalists a veneration for nature. Charles Beuchat, for instance, claims that Huysmans, with his legendary aversion to nature, 'a beau se dire naturaliste, alors: il en emploie les termes et l'audace, mais l'esprit n'y est pas'; Huysmans 'ne relève pas du bon naturalisme'.[37] But on the basis of their works, it would be difficult to ascribe to the naturalists, Zola's pantheistic tendencies notwithstanding, a belief in the beneficence of nature. At the very least one could say that the naturalists' attitude to nature was ambivalent. Even Maupassant, for all his love of the countryside and healthy exercise, was too much a Schopenhauerian to disagree with his character Roger de Salins in *L'Inutile Beauté* (1890), who declares: 'Je dis que la nature est notre ennemie, qu'il faut toujours lutter contre la nature, car elle nous ramène sans cesse à l'animal.'[38] The Goncourt brothers' view, expressed more crudely in the privacy of their journal, is similar: 'Rien n'est moins poétique que la nature et que les choses naturelles: c'est l'homme qui leur a trouvé une poésie. La naissance, la vie, la mort, ces trois accidents de l'être, symbolisés par l'homme, sont des opérations chimiques et cyniques. L'homme pisse l'enfant et la femme le chie. La mort est une décomposition' (4 February 1861). The countryside itself has little appeal for the diarist: 'La nature, pour moi, est ennemie; la campagne me semble mortuaire. Cette terre verte me semble un grand cimetière qui attend.

Cette herbe paît l'homme' (8 June 1862). As for Huysmans, Françoise Gaillard relates his attitude to a general *fin de siècle* malaise. For the author of *En rade*, she writes, nature is 'une machine déchaînée en proie à l'entropie la plus folle. Rien ne va plus! Le dérèglement sort de la régulation, le désordre de l'ordre.' Nature is fundamentally pathological: 'Elle n'est plus que carie, pourriture, souillure, rouille, croûte, plaie, eczéma, chancre, corruption, fermentation, décomposition, infection. Vision morbide d'une nature senescente, victime d'une fatalité interne. La maladie n'est nullement une anormalité scandaleuse, la maladie est inscrite dans la normalité.'[39]

In the naturalist vision, therefore, nature may be aesthetically good, but it is ontologically evil, for, however decorous and comforting it is in its place, it threatens the human order, draws man into an essential compliance with its laws, abolishes his distinct humanity. Zola too, in his most characteristically naturalist works, shows the ravages of nature's lethal and disruptive purposes at work in human life. These attitudes are clearly, to some considerable degree, a legacy of the Darwinian age, conclusions drawn from interpretations of Darwin's views as much as from what Darwin himself actually wrote. Though the naturalists refrained from the more hysterical responses of popular Darwinism, which saw an ape crouching in every family tree, and though they were far from unanimous in their adherence to what may be vaguely called a Darwinist vision – even as *La Bête humaine* was being published (in March 1890), Zola was busy preparing *L'Argent* in which he was to give expression to a far more positive Darwinian view – they did equate human life with the prevailing view of the natural order of things. Naturalist literature unhesitatingly sees man as essentially formed by, and explained in terms of, the biological model: birth, life, decline, death, developing within the broader framework of evolution, destined to struggle and eventual waste. It has been frequently noted that, whilst scientists, philosophers and historians tended to give an optimistic turn to Darwinism, and the popular imagination saw in the theory of evolution fresh justification for an optimistic belief in the progress of mankind, novelists took a dimmer view.[40] They tended to seize upon a view of man subjected to irrepressible drives, reacting mechanistically to biological urges, motivated by the basic instincts for food, sex, violence, ruled by environmental, hereditary and even primeval impulses, spurred on or defeated in the ruthless competitiveness of life. For the naturalists the human species itself was being subsumed into the animal species. Marxist and Spencerian concepts of social and economic determinism, deduced from the work of Darwin, reinforced these views.[41] As Jacques Barzun has pointed out, at each stage in the progress of science, whether it be the displacement of the earth from the centre of the universe by Copernicus and Galileo or the contemplation of distant worlds or the hint of the fact that man is but an animal, there is an initial inclination to believe that man has been degraded by such discoveries.[42] Like psychoanalysis for later novelists, the suggestively plausible scientific, naturalistic account of dark forces impelling human action presented convincing justification for novelists intent upon dispelling traditional illusions and myths in this most critical and iconoclastic of literary forms. It complemented Schopenhauer's philosophy, which, based also on earlier physiological presuppositions, asserted in an equivalent manner a belief in all-powerful, subterranean forces.

This combination of Schopenhauerism and Darwinism – if a whole intellectual climate may be reduced for convenience's sake to such a formulaic mould – the passive resignation of the one blunting the potential dynamism of the other, is suggestive of the fundamental pattern of naturalist fiction where there is much change, flux, development, evolution, but where all ends in the same predicament. The more Darwinian texts (model one) emphasise the struggle and strife; the more Schopenhauerian texts (model two) bring out the futile repetitiveness of it all. Whether there is grief or boredom, it all amounts to the same in the end. Schopenhauer's fundamental tenet, the illusion of the 'principle of individuation', reinforces the 'uniformitarianism' of philosophical Darwinism, its fundamental climatic principle.

Naturalist literature is, therefore, bold enough to expose the anguishing other side of the lessons of contemporary science in defiance of an ideology which constantly asserted its belief in the happy collaboration of society and of nature suitably controlled by science for the benefit and progress of humanity. Literary genres cannot be dissociated from their social, political, historical and ideological context. Naturalist literature is regularly considered to be a product of the scientific age, a view which makes too easy an association. But, as Fredric Jameson argues, the 'ideologeme' may be grasped 'not as a mere reflex or reduplication of its situational context, but as the imaginary resolution of the objective contradictions to which it thus constitutes an active response'.[43] Naturalist writers assume the prevalent scientific vision of man, but demonstrate the degrading, dehumanising implications of that vision. They appropriate for their works the most progressive theories of their age, but relentlessly display in their fiction the subjugation of intellectual, moral and

spiritual values to the tyranny of the natural processes. In their
mimetic texts, they elaborately represent the ostentatious materialism
and materiality of their age, but dwell upon its underlying shams,
hypocrisy, tyranny and injustices. Their work was attacked by their
contemporaries, not because it was sordid and corrupt, but because
it undermined the myths that disguised the sordid and the corrupt.
It offered images of disruption to an age that desperately sought
continuity, failure to an age bent on success, disorder and atrophy
instead of regularity and progress, chinks in the chains of cause and
effect, the rotting foundations of proudly constructed edifices. As
Yves Chevrel notes: 'La cruauté du naturalisme ne réside pas, en
définitive, dans le traitement pessimiste de tel ou tel thème, même si
certains écrivains, par goût ou par tendance personnelle (Maupassant,
par exemple), paraissent tentés par un désespoir fondamental: elle est
dans la mise en évidence des forces qui animent la société et qui ne sont
jamais "neutres", et surtout pas du point de vue moral.'[44] It is a
literature which, intellectually, takes into account the new science and
the new realities of its age, but offers an implicit, humanistic protest
against them for the loss of human dignity and integrity that they
entail in the hospitals, brothels, taverns, slums, barracks, cemeteries,
salons, parlours, bedrooms, in which they irreverently situate their
representations. Too incredulous to fall back upon old beliefs, too
sceptical to take fully to the new dogmas, it only remained for the
naturalists to confound the illusions of their contemporaries and
unmask the truths, the shame, the disorder that the latter wished to
ignore. In the age when man discovered the origin of species, they
uncovered a crisis in the human species, tracing the descent of Man
and the fall of Woman. In the age, too, when Darwinism seemed to
threaten to abolish distinctions of species and Marxism distinctions
of class, they exposed the spectre of a universal levelling.

Hence, in the works of the naturalists, the uncompromising
reductionism of their satire, parody and irony, which are often veiled
and subtle, which can often be crude and shocking, but which are
always devastating, abolishing differences, hierarchies, pretensions,
with no respect for rank, class or status. Beneath the unremitting
opposition to naturalist works may be discerned the fundamental fear
that they constituted a threat to the very foundations of the literary
institution itself with its 'discriminations', its conventions. In
Brunetière's opposition to the naturalist novel there is not only a
defence of generic distinctions, of 'les moyens d'expression propres
et spéciaux à chaque forme de l'art', but a vigorous opposition to the
language – or rather languages – of the naturalist text, its mixture

of styles, what we now would call, after Bakhtin, its 'heteroglossia', that agglomeration of discourses that characterises the novel and, as here, breaks down the stability and the authority of an official literary discourse. But if, politically (and somewhat charitably), one could interpret this process as a democratisation of the literary institution, it is more fundamentally the appropriate discursive and formal equivalence to the thematics of indifferenciation, of trivialisation, of repetition and substitution at the level of human existence, that we are exploring in this chapter.

Philippe Hamon has noted in Maupassant's work the frequency of the 'theme' (or, for us, 'motif') of 'la fille qui copie la femme du monde' and 'la femme du monde qui copie la fille', part of a more general 'thématique de la ressemblance'. He points out how, in Zola's novels, 'la copie, la ressemblance (l'hérédité, la persistance du même) introduit une redondance et une lisibilité entre des espaces disjoints' and how, in Maupassant's texts, 'elle transgresse les espaces sociaux, normatifs, juridiques et sexuels'.[45] It is as if the very art of mimesis, normally called upon to record the diversity and multiplicity of the real, is condemned to represent incessantly a universal mimeticism, as all differences fade and fail. In Zola's *La Curée*, to take another example, as Anne Belgrand has shown, all oppositions, antitheses and contrasts dissolve: 'Et tout, finalement, est plongé dans une morne uniformité; le mouvement cède devant l'immobilité'; 'tout parcours contient en soi sa propre annulation', 'tout dynamisme est vain'.[46] Another Zola text gives vivid allegorical expression to this theme: in the opposition between le Paradou and les Artaud in *La Faute de l'abbé Mouret*. Zola's mythical garden is for the naturalist–botanist a paradise, as Philippe Bonnefis observes, not only for its abundant flora but because its species are distinct and nameable: 'Les signes qu'y recueille le botaniste sont, partout, ceux de la différence.' In this ideal place where differences abound, the scientist's fear is repressed, the fear of 'l'amalgame, l'homogène, la confusion. Obsession au XIXe siècle, on craint que les espèces ne dégénèrent, on craint surtout que les différences ne s'estompent.' But outside the walls of le Paradou is the domain of the naturalist–novelist, les Artaud, 'là où, tous noms de lieux et de personnes mêlés, le pluriel inscrit moins la marque du nombreux qu'en fait de l'innombrable … Le retour au même: animaliser, c'est uniformiser. Danger toujours menaçant de l'uniformité.'[47] Thus Zola's novel, which rewrites the Christian myth of the Fall, recounts the naturalist myth which, in a sense, naturalist texts are fundamentally called upon to repeat and recall: the fall into the anonymous, indiscriminate, formless, depersonalised biological state. Once again we see that naturalism, reputedly the literature of science and of descriptive detail, both enterprises that seek to define and preserve differences, distinctions and thresholds, is rather the literature that insistently bears witness to their threatening abolition.

If the key moral attitude in *Une Belle Journée*, to return to Céard's model naturalist text, is one of resignation, the key ontological experience that is narrated is this same sense of uniformity, of levelling, of ultimate confusion. As Mme Duhamain's desires are confounded, in the décor of the restaurant, '*tout se confondait*' and, as the daylight fades, she contemplates the bright tones of the wallpaper which 'unissaient leurs couleurs, s'effaçaient dans un ton gris, *uniforme*'. Outside, 'la ligne des maisons tremblait dans le lointain, comme prête à disparaître, les arbres prenaient la teinte *confuse* particulière aux images négatives des plaques photographiques, et le Pont National, perdu dans la brume, *confondait* ses arches grises avec le gris mélancolisant du ciel'. In the same scene, the river Seine, 'toute verte ainsi qu'un fleuve de pus, coulait jusqu'à l'horizon où *tout se confondait*'.[48] She reads the newspapers for distraction, but, 'à la fin, *tous se confondaient* dans une égale sottise, l'admiration du dernier livre de Victor Hugo, l'exaltation de la *même* chanteuse d'opérette, la réclame pour les *mêmes* remèdes, l'éloge du *même* sympathique confrère qui venait de terminer une pièce en cinq actes'. Then, on Trudon's side, all the women in his life become confused in his mind: 'Et reconnaissant, pour la première fois, *l'uniformité* des manifestations du plaisir, l'éternelle médiocrité des effusions, il préférait toutes ses maîtresses passées à Mme Duhamain.'[49] The 'uniform' is the characteristic design of Céard's naturalist texts. 'Tout se confond dans le même néant', as he wrote in one of his (typically unpublished) poems, his 'Ballade de la parfaite inutilité de tout et spécialement de ces ballades', with its subversive refrain: 'Rien ne mérite un refrain de ballade.' Indeed, Céard's despondent little ditty not only points, in its simple way, to the author's profound pessimism, but also interestingly contains essential naturalist themes and generic features: the lack of discrimination in nature's laws, the destructive, reductive effect of time and process in life ('Dans l'infini du Temps, tout équivaut'), a satirical view of human activity (of 'l'humaine bousculade'), the illusions of love ('Plus d'un baiser s'achève en engueulade'), the ultimate tendency of naturalism towards ironic lament and even a questioning of language itself which breaks down into useless refrains, futile repetition and empty clichés.[50] In general, in the Flaubertian type of text of our corpus like *Une Belle Journée*, oppositions and differences that are themselves generators of purpose, meaning and thematic readings collapse into indeterminacy. In the more Goncourtian type of text, characters are driven gradually or precipitously by the inexorable workings of their biological fate into a state of dehumanising dissolution. Whether it is in the fate of the descendants of Flaubert's anti-hero, Frédéric Moreau, contemplating the spectacle of the empty repetition of his days, or in the degrading death of a pathetic heroine like Gervaise Macquart, reduced to the state of formless, anonymous flesh, there is in naturalist texts the same traumatism of the Same.

Naturalist literature could, therefore, be defined as a genre which calls upon the strategies of realist art to represent in its human aspects this entropic, this 'lysomorphic' vision of life. Gillian Beer has remarked that, in the latter half of the nineteenth century, fiction had particular recourse to analogies with the scientific method and scientific theories, indeed that science itself became less concerned with the analysis of fixed forms than with 'the narrative of process': 'The *methods* of scientists become the methods of emplotment and scientific theories suggest new organizations of fiction.'[51] The usual view is that naturalist literature developed to a considerable degree in the rearguard of scientific enquiry, mobilising for its purpose some convenient scientific principles and procedures, importing especially into fiction some of its outmoded physiological laws, quaint theories of heredity, treatises on hysteria or criminality, prejudices inherited from, or confirmed by, an amateurish familiarity with recent scientific developments, recycling its myths in the name of truth. However, this complicity between science and literature, as I have sought to show on the basis of a study of the naturalist genre, also manifested itself at a profounder level, where literature presents a challenging, even progressive vision of reality in the vanguard of scientific speculation, a vision that corresponds not to the old pseudo-certainties but to the newer, often tacit and, by comparison, deeply disturbing conceits. Writing on significantly parallel developments between science and the arts in this age, René Huyghe observes:

Progressivement, la Science, volontairement cantonnée jusque-là dans le mesurable, domaine positif des sens, et dans la logique, domaine rationnel de l'esprit, va rejoindre les réalités déroutantes et impondérables de la vie, réservées en principe aux armes suggestives et intuitives de la pensée 'littéraire'. Elle va quitter ses deux points d'appui: la réalité dense, décomposable, divisible de la 'matière', et l'immuabilité de code légal du raisonnement.[52]

The contours of the organisation of material reality fade; its ordered arrangements are perceived to degenerate into disorder; the continuity of the laws regulating it breaks down; matter becomes energy — and the spectre of its dissipation looms. Far from scorning Zola's science, Michel Serres sees the novelist's work as articulating imaginatively the essential epistemological issues of his age. 'Il faut faire gloire à Zola, fils d'ingénieur', he writes,

d'avoir vu clair parmi les choses. Ou d'avoir écrit et produit une œuvre comme s'il voyait clair. Ou d'avoir été là, d'où la vue était bonne. Rien ne dit mieux que les Rougon-Macquart l'écrasement, le gaspillage, la dissémination, la perte, l'irréversible jusant vers la mort–désordre; la déchéance, l'épuisement, la dégénérescence. Ils le disent: ça brûle trop vite. Epopée d'entropie ... Le naturalisme, contrairement à ce que disent les ignorants, est exactement à l'heure de sa science et précède la philosophie.[53]

At the heart of the naturalist vision, then, there is a poetics of disintegration, dissipation, death, with its endless repertory of wasted lives, of destructive forces, of spent energies, of crumbling moral and social structures, with its promiscuity, humiliations, degradation, its decomposing bodies, its invasive materialism, its scenes of mania, excess, destruction, the hovels and brothels, the 'assommoirs' and the 'abattoirs', the hospitals and the cemeteries, the mud and the blood, the rain and the pain, along with all the 'theriomorphic', 'nyctomorphic' and 'catamorphic' images (in the system of Gilbert Durand) belonging to the 'régime multiforme de l'angoisse devant le temps'.[54] Indeed, it is a literature in which time is fundamentally problematic, for time is presented as a process of constant erosion. 'Tel est, malgré leurs efforts pour donner à leur représentation du monde une solidité formelle ou objective, le temps des parnassiens et des naturalistes', writes Georges Poulet. 'Un monde de causes et d'effets devient un monde illusoire, un monde qui se dissipe, comme le brouillard, en lambeaux de durée, dont certains, plus hallucinatoires, survivent un peu plus longtemps que d'autres.' The passage of time is 'comme une genèse de mort', writes the same critic, who asks: 'Combien fréquemment le roman naturaliste ne décrit-il pas le phénomène de dissolution des images dans une conscience?'[55] Or rather: the dissolution of a consciousness. Poulet takes as an example *La Fille Elisa*, the loss of memory and of a sense of self in Edmond de Goncourt's heroine, a character who, in more general terms, is reduced to a state of imbecile animality typical of the disintegrating humanity of the naturalist character. But to conclude more appropriately perhaps — yet still according to the well-tried practice of thematic criticism in focusing on the literary hero for all that he incarnates traditionally: the values of a society, spiritual aspirations, ironic truths, possibilities of regeneration, tragic falls, personal, social, national, cosmic destinies, mythical schemes − let us return to the origins of the French naturalist movement, to an earlier Goncourt text, one which presents a striking 'specimen' of the disintegrating hero and illustrates the themes that have been traced in this chapter. 'Il se faisait lentement en lui', the brothers write of Charles Demailly, a man of letters, 'le travail sourd d'une existence qui se décomplète, et où, dans une résolution indéfinissable de la constitution vitale, dans la disjonction des organes, chacun des sens, chaque partie du *moi*, désagrégée et isolée de l'être, semble perdre le pouvoir de se correspondre et de réagir de l'une à l'autre.' It is as if the very substance of this character is being undermined. He is eventually taken to Charenton and there this creature undergoes all at once the familiar naturalist dehumanisation, animalisation, loss of linguistic control, the degradation of his species:

Et il vécut. Il vit, comme s'il avait été dévoué à épuiser jusqu'à l'horreur les expiations et les humiliations de la pensée humaine. Il vit pour n'être plus, aux mains de la vie, que l'effroyable exemple des extrémités de nos misères et du néant de nos orgueils ... Tout, jusqu'aux noms dont on nomme, dans le langage humain, les choses nécessaires à la vie, tout a quitté sa mémoire. Plus de passé, plus de souvenir, plus de temps, plus d'idées! Plus rien de survivant à la mort, qu'une masse de chair d'où sortent des petits cris, des grimaces, des pleurs, des rires, des syllabes inarticulées, les manifestations que les hasards de l'idiotisme poussent sans motif au dehors d'un être! Plus rien d'humain que ce corps, n'appartenant plus à l'humanité que par la digestion! ce corps lié sur un fauteuil, balbutiant les monosyllabes de l'enfant dans ses langes, immobile et remuant avec un mouvement incessant d'élévation et d'abaissement des épaules, jetant dans l'air, à la vue du soleil ce cri animal: *coc ... coc*, ouvrant la bouche à la nourriture qu'on apporte, et se frottant contre l'homme qui lui donne à manger avec la caresse et la reconnaissance de la bête.[56]

Traditionally, we know, the hero is solar. But the sun that is reflected by the naturalist hero in the fallen, subverted order of nature is clearly on the eclipse. The ultimate scandal of naturalist fiction is that life is its own negation.

10

BY WAY OF CONCLUSION: TWO ENGLISH EXAMPLES

It may well seem totally inappropriate to raise once again the question of the *origins* of genres in the *conclusion* of a book which has been dealing with genre all along. Yet, unless one denies the reality of their interrelatedness, the problem of the formation of genres is essentially the same as that of their so-called demise. In each case, of course, the circumstances are different, but the process is no doubt equivalent, for − to take the simplest possible scenario − as one genre loses its prestigious hold on the literary scene, another genre emerges into prominence. For two of the most conventional views of genre the problem never arises: if genres are considered to be permanent archetypal structures, then they lie outside the pale of historical development; if they are examined exclusively as historical events, as has often been the case in studies of the naturalist movement, then their origins are merely dated by some historical occurrence like the Trapp dinner or the 'Manifeste des Cinq'.

The question remains a thorny one. 'This is not an easy question to handle', writes Christopher Prendergast. 'One of the most sophisticated attempts to answer it (Todorov's) comes up with the perhaps somewhat unenlightening conclusion that the origin of genres is genres. There is indeed a chicken-and-egg dimension to the problem.'[1] Or indeed, if one genre does in fact produce a different genre, how does the chicken produce a duck egg? Certainly, if taken individually, the standard explanations of the origin of genres − from prototypical, simple forms, from the 'canonisation' of non-literary types of discourse, from the promotion of sub-literary forms or the encoding into literature of contextual ideological principles, from the stamp of an individual writer's creative genius, from natural transformations of literary systems, from the imitation of foreign models, or, indeed, from other genres − may not in fact seem sufficient to account for the complexity of the process. But this does not mean that certain explanations, or, more likely, a combination of explanations, cannot account for some. The example of naturalist literature, as the various chapters of this book have shown, suggests that a number of these explanations can apply in combination: the canonisation of the popular novel or of the *fait divers*, the application to literature of extra-literary scientific knowledge and principles, of contemporary ideological and epistemological models, the fictional treatment of certain social issues, the energetic initiatives of Zola to name, promote, defend and impose the new forms, the imitation, transformation and parodying of the themes and practices of Romantic and bourgeois literature, and, no doubt, others beside which have escaped our attention. This assortment of attributions is not intended as a model for other generic developments, which may be simpler or more complex in their elaboration, but it does seem to bear out Alastair Fowler's confident assertion: 'Of all the codes of our literary *langue*, I have no hesitation in proposing genre as the most important, not least because it incorporates and organizes many others ... It is an instrument not of classification or prescription, but of meaning.'[2]

In dealing with questions of genre, one is easily led, as here, to think (however rudimentarily) in terms of communication theory. Generic conventions, though they do not constitute an obligation, are nevertheless like codes, regulatory and prescriptive constraints which direct the reading process, part of the contractual relationship between encoder (writer) and decoder (reader) through the sharing of literary codes in what Linda Hutcheon calls a state of 'amicable communality'.[3] These conventions are consciously or unconsciously encoded into texts, setting up patterns of expectation for the reader, who recognises the appropriate 'signals' and reads according to the generic scheme. As Terry Eagleton writes on this matter:

Even the *absence* of certain devices may produce meaning: if the codes which the work has generated lead us to expect a rhyme or a happy ending which does not materialize, this 'minus device', as Lotman terms it, may be as effective a unit of meaning as any other. The literary work, indeed, is a continual generating and violating of expectations, a complex interplay of the regular and the random, norms and deviations, routinized patterns and dramatic defamiliarizations.[4]

As we saw in the chapter on the 'founding texts' of the naturalist canon, in the early stages of the onset of a genre writers not only purposefully programme their texts with new generic attributes, but, I would suggest, forcibly impose them on the reader's attention while maintaining the framework of the established generic system. Innovative texts 'reprogramme' the authoritative texts of the prevailing system with new generic features, then, in turn, the authoritative conventions of the new generic system are used in the process of 'deprogramming' that occurs when a new system intervenes. Transformations may be thematic or formal, introducing, in the first instance, new principles of 'motivation' for familiar plot situations or, in the second instance, undermining familiar procedures with defamiliarising formal experimentation.

This process, which I have somewhat awkwardly called the 'programming' and 'deprogramming' of generic conventions, would no doubt be most conveniently demonstrated if I were to remain with French examples, by taking, for instance, early works by Zola and Gide, the former aggressively asserting the new principles of deterministic motivation, the uncompromising depiction of shocking scenes, the 'tragic' impetus, the oppressive presence of description, with the latter parodying such (by then) familiar naturalist devices and situations. We have already seen that *Thérèse Raquin* dramatically establishes its originality in relation to the moralising prescriptions of the bourgeois novel (by 'scientifically' reformulating the bases of vice and virtue) and, in relation to the model realist text *Madame Bovary*, revealing a kind of generic 'anxiety of counter-influence' in its restatement of the Bovary situation, along with the heroine's Romantic readings, and in the frenetic and Tainean plot that derives from it. The relationship of Gide's to Zola's works shows a comparable authority to be acknowledged and defused. As Emily S. Apter goes so far as to claim: 'Marked at each moment by entries in the *Journal*, Zola's insistent presence for Gide seems to take on the character of a fetish: avowed and disavowed, negated and de-negated, displaced, like a prosthesis affixed to Gide's literary anatomy, from one modality of his writing to another.'[5] Thus *Les Caves du Vatican*, to take a single episode as an example, parodies the *fait divers* of *Thérèse Raquin* through the famous 'acte gratuit', the unmotivated murder in the train, travestying the hypermotivated murder of Camille, down to the detail of the neck wound that the victim, Fleurissoire, inflicts on Lafcadio's neck, just as Camille bites Laurent before drowning.[6]

Zola's and Gide's texts would more neatly stake out the phase of emergence and the more protracted phase of decline in a historical study of the naturalist movement in France (even though, as we have seen, it had long been proclaimed dead by 1914, the date of publication of *Les Caves du Vatican*). But the two English examples that I wish briefly to present are more appropriate for the type of generic study that has been attempted in this book, not only because they illustrate well the processes of generic incipiency and decline that I have just outlined. They also justify the claim that the models, themes and procedures that have been analysed throughout this book functioned beyond the boundaries of France, yet kept in view the French prototypes. But, above all, they provide an excellent summary in themselves of the essential characteristics of the naturalist genre with which we have been dealing.

George Moore's *A Mummer's Wife* (1885), English scholars would unanimously agree, has not borne out in time the wildly enthusiastic assessment made of it by Arnold Bennett as 'one of the supreme novels of the century, a work which stands out, original, daring, severe, ruthless, and resplendent, even amongst the finest'.[7] But it admirably suits our present purpose as an inaugurating text of at least a potential English naturalist tradition and as, arguably, the most character- istically naturalist novel of English literature. The epigraph of this work is an appropriate statement of deterministic principles taken from a *French* source, *L'Introduction générale à l'histoire de France* by Victor Duroy: 'Change the surroundings in which man lives, and, in two or three generations, you will have changed his physical constitution, his habits of life, and a goodly number of his ideas.'[8] The novel is, in Zola's sense, 'experimental', transposing the heroine- specimen, Kate Ede, out of her stifling, routine-bound life as the wife of an asthmatic shopkeeper in the Potteries town of Hanley, into the loose-living, wayward, uncertain mode of existence of a travelling theatrical company, when its manager, the lusty Dick Lennox, a lodger at the Ede household, elopes with the dissatisfied wife. Despite her resolution to remain an honest woman, 'touches of Bohemianism' appear in her character (p. 183). She takes to drink. The company falls on hard times. There is, naturally, a confinement scene. Kate neglects her child for the brandy bottle and, at this stage, the demonstrative naturalist narrator ponderously summarises her 'case':

She had met Dick in her seven-and-twentieth year, when the sap of her slowly-developing nature was rising to its highest point, when it was burning and forcing to blossom the fancies and passions of a dreamy youth. A few more years would have killed those desires, as the October winds the flowers, and Kate would have lived and died an honest workwoman. But Dick had passed in time for the harvesting, and the flower had fallen into his hands ... – the febrile, emotional, dissolute life she had since led had worn out her lymphatic temperament, and to her existence was now no more than a nervous erethism; and the gentle imagination had become morose, cynical, and dissatisfied.

We have, therefore, arrived at the period of decadence of Kate's character. (p. 264).

Her fate is sealed in a typically naturalist way by the determinism of the theory of temperaments. Like Gervaise Macquart in Paris, Kate wanders the streets of London. Demon drink has released her demonic self and the characteristically naturalist dehumanising process sets in. The reader is treated to the spectacle of the disordered female, in an appropriate setting, as 'more like a demon than a woman', she screams hysterically at Dick in a theatre. Her words become, through the familiar upgrading process that we have already met, 'like the cry of the chorus in the Greek tragedy against the mystery and inflexibility of fate' (p. 321). Typically, a doctor intervenes to pronounce sentence: 'I have never known a case of a woman who cured herself of the vice of intemperance. A man sometimes, a woman never' (p. 333). Kate takes the one step that remains 'between her and the lowest depths' one night near Charing Cross. Like a 'worn-out machine, from which all rivets and screws had fallen' and 'miserable as a homeless dog' (p. 348), she succumbs, shrivelled, dishevelled, yellow, haggard and delirious, in an exemplary naturalist demise.

Milton Chaikin has enumerated what he calls the 'Zolaesque features' of this novel: the announced experiment in environmental influence, the documented presentation of particular settings, the alcoholic and hysterical woman, the sordid décor, the 'frankness with which unpleasantness is laid bare'.[9] There is also the obvious similarity between the initial situation of this novel and that of *Thérèse Raquin*: the sickly husband, the neurotic wife, the shopkeeper environment, the lusty lover, even an interfering mother-in-law.[10] Several of these features are, as we have had occasion to note, recurrent naturalist traits which *Thérèse Raquin* itself introduced into the generic canon. *A Mummer's Wife* was clearly intended to fulfil a similar purpose. But this novel is representative of the naturalist genre not only by virtue of the Tainean, deterministic experiment that it contains. There are also typical scenes involving the implicit parodying of Romantic situations, as in the episode of the (for Kate) agonisingly delayed elopement whilst Dick heartily tucks in to a breakfast of chops, crumpets, fried eggs and bacon. But there is above all the characteristic fall into disintegration, excess, delirium, as Kate's life, like Gervaise Macquart's, takes on the grotesque disorders that are the very antithesis of the strict bourgeois order with which the novel begins. Through her theatricals, the bourgeois wife of the *incipit* becomes herself a kind of mummer, again like Gervaise Macquart,

whose own bizarre imitations of her husband's *delirium tremens* seem
to mock, violate and undermine the very 'order of mimesis' itself.

There is the further relevant theme of the heroine's readings, the
romances, not surprisingly, for she has the inevitable sentimental
disposition. One text in particular appeals to her: 'It concerned a
beautiful young woman with a lovely oval face, who was married to
a very tiresome country doctor.' The allusion is not difficult to grasp!
The narrator goes on: 'This lady was in the habit of reading Byron
and Shelley in a rich, sweet-scented meadow, down by the river which
flowed dreamily through smiling pasturelands adorned by spreading
trees.' Unfortunately, one day, 'in her poetical dreamings', she falls
into the river! Fortunately, a broad-shouldered young squire, who
has been secretly observing her daily musings, is on hand to rescue
her and, emboldened by the incident, proceeds to court her when the
doctor is off curing the country folk. But she refuses to leave 'poor
Arthur' and the broken-hearted squire withdraws to foreign parts for
thirty years waiting for 'poor Arthur' to die: 'Then he came back with
a light heart to his first and only love, who had never ceased to think
of him, and lived with her happily forever afterwards' (pp. 38–9).
C. Heywood has shown that Kate's favourite novel derives from a
real text, *The Doctor's Wife* (1864) by Miss (Mary Elizabeth)
Braddon, reputedly the earliest borrowing from *Madame Bovary* in
English literature.[11] Though there are important differences between
this text and Moore's, Miss Braddon's work constitutes an interesting
intertext (in more than one sense of the term), being both an intermediary work between the novels of Flaubert and Moore and, at the
same time, the direct source of this *mise en abyme* in *A Mummer's
Wife*. Moore thereby 'diegetically' and 'metadiegetically' distances
his text not only from the traditional English romance in both its
moralistic and escapist forms, but also from Flaubert's realist model,
by introducing the familiar motif of the heroine's Romantic readings
and by relegating it to a decidedly secondary symptom of her dilemma.

Moore's novel is thus of interest to us as an illustration of the ways
in which a single text can fulfil a mediating function in the process
of generic development. Recognisable features of the romance are
radically transformed and parodied. Deferential acknowledgment
is made to the masterpiece of realist fiction. But, in both instances,
new principles of motivation and new themes are introduced. Moore's
text thereby realises in fiction the author's campaign of detraction
against the conventional Victorian novel, his overt support of French
naturalist literature and his ambition to introduce naturalism into the
resolutely resistant English tradition. *A Mummer's Wife* clearly

qualifies, therefore, as one of a category of works that Thomas Kent calls 'de-formed texts', that is works in which the predictable elements that constitute the formulas of popular, conventional texts (or what he calls 'automatized texts') are 'deformed' or 'recombined' with different generic features.[12] This procedure, I would add, clearly serves also to 'programme' new generic conventions and to institute generic change.

Now, the naturalist text, as we have already noted, brings about such changes from within the mimetic conventions of the realist literature to which it is related. A more modern strategy for subverting generic predictability is, as Kent points out, 'the transformation of generic conventions into the subject matter of the text', a characteristic of the 'meta-fictional narrative'.[13] *The French Lieutenant's Woman* (1969) by John Fowles is an exemplary novel in this respect, not only as a work of rich and complex intertextual relations which parodies the conventions of the Victorian novel, or, indeed, the conventions of any antiquated fictional system, but also as a work that deals in an original way with the fundamental presuppositions of the relationship between fiction and reality. 'In a sense', William J. Palmer writes, 'it is the most creative kind of literary criticism. It personifies the past of the novel as genre while simultaneously probing the modern atrophy of the genre. It examines the style and tradition of the genre's past, not in imitation of that past, but rather as a means of breaking the bonds of tradition.'[14] To present this novel therefore in its parodic relationship to a single generic fictional kind is necessarily a restriction. Nevertheless, though the link may seem surprising, there are in fact several features of *The French Lieutenant's Woman* that justify our relating it 'critically' to the naturalist novel.

The action of the novel is set, as the narrator reminds us, in a crucial year, a date of considerable significance for the history of Communism, female emancipation and Thomas Hardy's love-life.[15] But 1867 was an important date also in the history of naturalism, the year of publication of *Thérèse Raquin* and of some of Zola's important early theoretical texts. However, more importantly, *The French Lieutenant's Woman* takes up and combines the two central naturalist model situations that I have defined: the disenchantment of the male intellectual, and the fall of a woman. Despite his firm scientific interests and convictions, Charles is afflicted with a thoroughly Flaubertian ennui, for, in his reflective moments, he sees beyond the powers, pleasures and certainties of his taxonomies, 'all his arrogance dowsed by a sudden breach of Nature's profoundest secret: the universal parity of existence' (p. 191). Charles, the palaeontologist, the *naturalist* (in the scientific sense of the term), comes to perceive the precariousness of the scientific order; he becomes conscious of what naturalist literature itself reveals in its way, as we have lately seen, that 'far deeper and stranger reality than the pseudo-Linnaean one that [he] had sensed on the beach that early morning ... For it was less a profounder reality he seemed to see than universal chaos, looming behind the fragile structure of human order' (pp. 191–2). What is more, as Charles later reflects, this epistemological order is but one of 'so many orders beginning to melt and dissolve' (p. 259). More generally, in the fictional substance of the text, there are Flaubertian repetitions, reflections, substitutions (of women, for example, the Sarahs), emblematisation (Ernestina's brooch, for example), all betokening the typical naturalist levelling of experience. Indeed, for Charles, the novel represents a 'sentimental education' reminiscent of Frédéric Moreau's pursuit of his creator's 'phantoms of Trouville' in the 'Bible of Naturalism'. The chapter of his despondent travelling at the end of the novel (chapter 58) obviously recalls the archetypal wanderings of the wasted hero of *L'Education sentimentale*: 'Il voyagea ...'

But it is Fowles' heroine, Sarah, the 'French Loot'n'nts Hoer' as the dairyman calls her (p. 73), who seems to be a figure from a naturalist novel, potentially at least. Like one of our familiar victims of the catastrophic initial sexual act, she appears to be yet another fallen heroine, 'poor Tragedy' as she is nicknamed, 'living in a kind of long fall' (p. 82). Her confession to Charles, who has come to be interested in her 'case' – or so he persuades himself – that her father died in a lunatic asylum establishes another naturalist theme; and an epigraph from Darwin, according to which heredity is 'the chief part of the organization of every living creature' (chapter 3), confirms the point. There is even a certain 'bovarysm' in her character, for she 'had read far more fiction, and far more poetry, those two sanctuaries of the lonely, than most of her kind', judging people 'as much by the standards of Walter Scott and Jane Austen as by any empirically arrived at' (p. 48). As Charles observes her in the Undercliff, there is something disturbingly foreign, French, Parisian, in her face. He has read, 'very much in private', the celebrated novel: 'And as he looked down at the face beside him, it was suddenly, out of nowhere, that Emma Bovary's name sprang into his mind. Such allusions are comprehensions; and temptations' (p. 100).

However, *this* Charles has at his disposal scientific knowledge to explain her mystery. There is, of course, a doctor in the book, Dr Grogan: an ardent disciple of Darwin, naturally; a specialist in female hysteria, to be sure; and, even more ostensibly (and thus parodically) than in the usual naturalist work, a *voyeur*, for, equipped with a little brass Gregorian telescope in the window of his cabin, he overlooks the bay where, as he puts it, the 'nereids' come 'to take the waters' (p. 123). Like Moore's doctor, he pronounces on the heroine's fate with firm assurance: a hopeless case of 'obscure melancholia' as defined in the neat system of the learned German specialist in such matters, Doktor Hartmann. In a later discussion on the same specimen – Charles has again yielded to the temptation to discuss her clinically, naturalistically, 'to think of her locked in some small room' (p. 182), thus tamed, confined, categorised, dominated, possessed, safe – Dr Grogan passes him a French text, a marked copy of the *Observations médico-psychologiques* of Dr Karl Matthaei, where he reads the case history of an earlier French lieutenant's woman, an incidence of hysteria. Here again, as in *A Mummer's Wife*, a text inserted into the main narrative provides a *mise en abyme*, this time a *naturalist* document, which the novel itself will again undo, for it similarly establishes the same kind of generic predictability which the parodying effect of the text will come to frustrate.

Sarah, then, is presented as deranged by her sexuality, the hysterical madwoman, to be kept in the attic, a kind of 'folle sans logis' – 'Dark indeed. Very dark', as Dr Grogan observes (p. 127) – the dark figure, the dark continent, with her wildly inflaming hair and her fixed gaze, the body, the wound, the mystery, all that the Victorian age which Charles represents sought to suppress, the 'whole ungovernable torrent of things banned, romance, adventure, sin, madness, animality', all that 'coursed wildly through him' (p. 274) when finally he possesses her and is possessed by her – all that is only fantasised about in his philosophy. After one of his intoxicating evenings of discussion with his fellow Darwinian (none other than Dr Grogan), Charles, we learn, 'the naturally selected', is 'pure intellect', 'understanding all'. 'All except Sarah, that is', the narrator adds (p. 132). For Sarah and all that she represents escape his science. She escapes his literature too. Charles seeks the fallen woman in the streets and brothels of London, but this 'chair molle' is made of sterner stuff. She confounds his 'horizons of expectation', reverses the predictable pattern of the literary theme, escapes the degraded destiny of the naturalist heroine, becomes the New Woman, liberated from the thraldom of her literary role. The passive reader–victim that she was becomes herself the creator of fictions, the very opposite of the Emma Bovarys, the Kate Edes, the fallen angels of the literary type that Fowles' novel rejects. Sarah has stepped out of the naturalist novel prepared for her.

The famous alternative endings of *The French Lieutenant's Woman*, the bifurcations of the 'diegesis', open up the potentially naturalist text to a disruptive indeterminacy, for naturalist fiction is, in a sense, an extreme development of mimetic literature, thereby open to parody by virtue of its rigorous and absolute strategies of 'motivation', the manner in which the arbitrariness of the elements of the narrative are disguised by the logic of causal determination. Now Fowles – or rather his intrusive narrator who, in another famous scene, comes to 'life' in a railway compartment where he observes Charles – calls this process of 'motivation' more simply 'fixing the fight' (p. 317). In the naturalist novel, the fight is fixed, as it were, well before the first bell by those imperious laws of heredity, by those socio-economic determining forces, by those ingrained insufficiencies of life. As we saw in a previous chapter, the reader is subjected both to the strategies of verisimilitude and to the brutalities of the motivating system of naturalist thematics. Fowles, on the other hand, while using certain of the trappings of the naturalist system, restores the narrative to its essential arbitrariness and thematises the impossibility in a post-existentialist, post-*nouveau roman*, post-modernist age, of the naturalist novel being written. He thereby consigns naturalist literature to its own periodicity, even nipping it in the bud, in 1867.

These two novels illustrate, therefore, the processes by which the naturalist genre, which has been analysed in this book in its textual manifestations, largely through the medium of fiction, was imposed and deposed. They also illustrate many of the essential features of the genre which I have attempted to define. Clearly the innovations of naturalist fiction were thematic in the main. The attraction and odium that it caused were due to the combination that it entailed of the familiarising mimetic procedures of realist fiction and a fundamentally disturbing body of themes. It tended, therefore, to define and affirm its originality in relation to the acceptable conventions of the realist novel and the bourgeois novel. But it was also a type of literature situated at the end of the representational tradition such that parodying texts not only exposed the conventionality of its themes, characters and situations, but also undermined the very basis of its representationality. Yet, far from being the retrogressive, atavistic, repulsive mode of realism that it has often been taken to be, naturalist literature by its unflinching willingness to face certain truths, to treat certain themes, to strain certain constraining expectations, unquestioningly did much to liberate fiction from its fictions. It has taken the 'modernists' and 'post-modernists' to deconstruct the form, but the naturalists had already deconstructed the subject of the novel.

NOTES

Introduction

1 See Albert Thibaudet, 'Réflexions sur la littérature. Le Groupe de Médan', *La Nouvelle Revue française*, XV (1920), 923.

2 Throughout the book also, certain literary figures and texts will be introduced and discussed that may well be unfamiliar especially to the English-speaking reader – though about some of them, because of their crude methods or crude contents, I fear, the reader may wish to have remained in ignorance!

3 See Henryk Markiewicz, 'Le naturalisme dans les recherches littéraires et dans l'esthétique du XXe siècle', *Revue de Littérature comparée*, XLVII (1973), 271; Sigfrid Hoefert, 'Naturalism as an international phenomenon: the state of research', *Yearbook of Comparative and General Literature*, XXVII (1978), 84. This gap will soon be significantly filled by a collective work on naturalism currently being prepared under the auspices of the International Comparative Literature Association. See the two preliminary studies already published by the group in question: *Le Naturalisme dans les littératures de langues européennes*, ed. Yves Chevrel (Université de Nantes, 1983); *Le Naturalisme en question*, ed. Yves Chevrel (Presses de l'Université de Paris-Sorbonne, 1986). The eventual aim of the project is a comparative history of naturalism in literatures using European languages.

4 Lilian R. Furst and Peter N. Skrine, *Naturalism*, p. 5.

5 Cf. *ibid.*, p. 71: 'Naturalism succeeded best where it seemed to fail, i.e. where it departed from, or rather outstripped its own intentions.'

6 See Yves Chevrel, *Le Naturalisme*, p. 93: 'le premier mot de sa poétique pourrait bien être la "non-spécificité": indistinction, confusion ou désordre'.

7 *Ibid.*, p. 32.

8 *Naturalistic Triptych*, p. 14.

9 See Owen R. Morgan, 'Autopsie d'un journal républicain–naturaliste: *Le Rabelais* de Gustave Naquet', *Les Cahiers naturalistes*, 56 (1982), 221.

10 *Œuvres complètes de Gustave Flaubert*, vol. 16 (Paris, Club de l'Honnête Homme, 1975), pp. 160–1.

11 'La stratégie de la forme', *Poétique*, 27 (1976), 257.

12 *Validity in Interpretation*, p. 110.
13 *Introduction à l'architexte*, p. 73.
14 'It is time', Alastair Fowler writes in *Kinds of Literature*, p. 46, 'that genre theory acknowledged the historical mutability of the genres themselves, and dealt much more freely with temporal concepts.'
15 'Du texte au genre. Notes sur la problématique générique', *Poétique*, 53 (1983), 11.
16 *Beyond Genre*, p. 148.
17 *Introduction à l'architexte*, pp. 68−9.
18 *Genre*, p. 46. Cf. Philippe Lejeune, *Le Pacte autobiographique*, p. 322.
19 Naturalist theatre and (the almost non-existent) naturalist poetry, for example, have been largely excluded because of their relative insignificance in relation to the fiction and because they present certain specific formal and modal problems (e.g. the relationship between naturalist theatrical practices and those of the traditional and popular theatres) that are marginal to this study. Thematically, however, as a number of brief illustrations will show, I would claim that the approach and conclusions of this book are largely valid for these two forms.
20 *Literature as System*, p. 107.
21 *Introduction à la littérature fantastique*, p. 12; *Les Genres du discours*, p. 52.
22 Where significant passages are concerned, a number of references to standard English translations and, in some cases, my own translations appear at the end of the book for the benefit of readers unable to understand written French.

1 Histories

1 See Henri-Irénée Marrou, *De la connaissance historique*, pp. 35−6.
2 'Commentary', *New Literary History*, XVI (1985), 672.
3 See Paul Veyne, *Comment on écrit l'histoire*, pp. 23, 38.
4 All references to Zola's works included in the body of the text are to the following edition: *Emile Zola: Œuvres Complètes*, ed. Henri Mitterand (Paris, Cercle du Livre Précieux, 1966−9), 15 vols.
5 Cf. X, 1222; XI, 221−2, 281−5, 344; XII, 306−7.
6 *Le Naturalisme français*, p. 174.
7 12th revised edition, p. 1029. Cf. René Dumesnil's study, *Le Réalisme et le naturalisme*, p. 8. For a more balanced view, see the study by Alain Pagès, *Le Naturalisme* (Paris, PUF, 1989), in the series 'Que sais-je?'
8 Gustave Lanson, *Histoire de la littérature française*, pp. 1029, 1080.
9 'Critique d'un schème de périodisation: le naturalisme', in *Analyse de la périodisation littéraire*, ed. Ch. Bouazis, p. 41.
10 *Ibid.*, p. 46.
11 See Siegfried J. Schmidt, 'On writing histories of literature', *Poetics*, XIV (1985), 279−301.
12 *Sur Racine*, p. 138.

13 In Bouazis (ed.), *Analyse de la périodisation littéraire*, p.16.

14 'A propos d'une origine littéraire: *Les Soirées de Médan*', *Nineteenth-Century French Studies*, XII (1983–4), 207.

15 *Ibid.*, p.211.

16 See Jacques Patin, 'Du "bœuf nature" à "la table des Beylistes"', *Le Figaro*, 7 December 1930. See also *Emile Zola: Correspondance. II. 1868–1877*, eds. B. H. Bakker, Colette Becker *et al.* (Montreal, Presses de l'Université de Montréal/Paris, Editions du CNRS, 1980), pp.356–7. This edition, the first volume of which appeared in 1978 and which is still in the process of being issued, will be indicated hereafter by the abbreviation *Corr.* and the volume number.

17 *Corr. III*, pp.234–5.

18 *Le Naturalisme*, p.34.

19 Quoted in C. A. Burns, *Henry Céard et le naturalisme*, pp.95–6.

20 Léon Deffoux and Emile Zavie, *Le Groupe de Médan*, p.12.

21 See, for example, B. H. Bakker (ed.), *'Naturalisme pas mort'*. *Lettres inédites de Paul Alexis à Emile Zola 1871–1900*, p.107, on his series of satirical portraits of the naturalists published in *Les Cloches de Paris*.

22 *Corr. II*, p.79. Cf. pp.85, 114, and see p.80, note 8.

23 Quoted in Amédée Boyer, *La Littérature et les arts contemporains*, pp.93–4.

24 See Deffoux and Zavie, p.65.

25 'Henry Céard and his relations with Flaubert and Zola', *French Studies*, VI (1952), 311.

26 *'Naturalisme pas mort'*, pp.21–2.

27 'Léon Hennique and the disintegration of naturalism', *Nottingham French Studies*, I (1962), 29.

28 *Guy de Maupassant et l'art du roman*, p.20.

29 *Ibid.*, pp.253–4.

30 See Christophe Charle, *La Crise littéraire à l'époque du naturalisme*, p.66.

31 *Corr. III*, pp.138–9.

32 Cf. Flaubert's typical comment to Maupassant on Zola's 'Le Roman expérimental' (in a letter of 21 October 1879): 'Ne me parlez pas du réalisme, du naturalisme ou de l'expérimental! J'en suis gorgé. Quelles vides inepties!'

33 See *Corr. III*, p.16.

34 See '*Les Soirées de Médan*, comment ce livre a été fait', *Le Gaulois*, 17 April 1880; this frequently quoted account is reproduced in Colette Becker (ed.), *Les Soirées de Médan* (Paris, Le Livre à venir, 1981), pp.293–6.

35 See Becker (ed.), *ibid.*, p.16. The Huysmans story had already appeared in the Brussels paper *L'Artiste* from 19–21 October 1877, Zola's in *Vestnik Evropy* in July of the same year and Céard's, the most recently, in the *Slovo* of Saint Petersburg in September 1879. The other three stories, including Maupassant's 'Boule de suif', were written for the occasion.

36 It has been noted that there is only one reference to *Les Soirées de Médan* in the extant Zola correspondence of the time. See *Corr. III*, p. 439.

37 'Le mythe de Médan', *Les Cahiers naturalistes*, 55 (1981), 33.

38 *Ibid.*, p. 40.

39 For the intervening years, in addition to *L'Assommoir* and Zola's other novels, we should mention Goncourt's *La Fille Elisa* (1877), 'Un Cœur simple' in Flaubert's *Trois Contes* (1877), *Marthe* (1876) by Huysmans and perhaps Hennique's *La Dévouée*.

40 *Corr. V*, pp. 91, 247.

41 On the extensive spread of naturalist literature and of Zola's influence outside France, see, for a convenient summary, the introduction by Alain Pagès and Owen Morgan to *Corr. V*, p. 27.

42 The article, entitled in fact '*La Terre*. A Emile Zola', signed by Paul Bonnetain, J.-H. Rosny, Lucien Descaves, Paul Margueritte and Gustave Guiches (*Le Figaro*, 18 August 1887) has been reproduced by Henri Mitterand in *Les Rougon-Macquart IV* (Paris, Bibliothèque de la Pléiade, 1966), pp. 1525–9, where other works which also reproduce the text are listed (p. 1515). It appears in English in George J. Becker (ed.), *Documents of Modern Literary Realism*, pp. 345–9, and, more recently, in David Baguley (ed.), *Critical Essays on Emile Zola*, pp. 60–4.

43 See *Corr. V*, pp. 443–4, and A. A. Greaves, 'Paul Bonnetain: his attitudes to naturalism', *Nottingham French Studies*, V (1966), 80–1.

44 The article seems to have been planned by Bonnetain, Rosny and Descaves after a few drinks and some 'bouffées d'opium'. The contributions of Guiches and Margueritte are not clear. See Guy Robert, *'La Terre' d'Emile Zola. Etude historique et critique*, pp. 417–26.

45 *Ibid.*, p. 411.

46 Guy Robert, *'La Terre' d'Emile Zola*, p. 434.

47 Quoted in Maurice Le Blond, *La Publication de 'La Terre'*, p. 72.

48 *La Crise littéraire à l'époque du naturalisme*, p. 104.

49 See *ibid.*, p. 54.

50 *Ibid.*, p. 100.

51 '1871: la fausse coupure. Contribution à l'histoire du naturalisme', in *Recherches en Sciences des Textes*, p. 19.

52 J.-H. Bornecque and P. Cogny, *Réalisme et naturalisme*, p. 127.

53 *Naturalism*, p. 24.

54 'In France [naturalism] was at its height in the 1870s and early 1880s; in Germany and Italy it came a good decade later; in England it struggles from the 1890s into the opening years of this century, while in America, where its time-span is greatest, a vigorous Naturalism is in evidence between the two World Wars' (*ibid.*, p. 24).

55 *Ibid.*, pp. 37, 41.

56 *L'Influence du naturalisme français en Belgique de 1875 à 1900*, p. 297.

57 Quoted by Clarence R. Decker, in *The Victorian Conscience*, p. 10.

58 *Ibid.*, p. 11.

59 'The present position in Zola studies', in Charles B. Osburn (ed.), *The Present State of French Studies. A Collection of Research Reviews*, Metuchen, New York, Scarecrow Press, 1971, p. 604.

60 *Ibid.*, p. 604.

61 Ed. Margaret Drabble, Oxford University Press, 1985, p. 688.

62 *Vol. 6: From Dickens to Hardy*, ed. Boris Ford. Penguin Books, 1982: 'The naturalist phase inspired by Zola is represented by George Moore, but more adequately by Arnold Bennett's best work' (pp. 100–1).

63 *The English Novel. A Short Critical History*, p. 298.

64 Frierson, 'The English controversy over realism in fiction', *PMLA*, XLIII (1928), 549; McInnes, 'Naturalism and the English theatre', *Forum for Modern Language Studies*, I (1965), 197.

65 *Naturalism*, p. 32.

66 'The present state of the novel', *The Fortnightly Review*, XLII n.s. (1887), 412.

67 *From Gautier to Eliot. The Influence of France on English Literature 1851–1939*, p. 80. Contrast E. M. Forster's view: 'Can we, while discussing English fiction, quite ignore fiction written in other languages, particularly French and Russian? As far as influence goes, we could ignore it, for our writers have never been much influenced by the continentals' (*Aspects of the Novel*, p. 16).

68 *The Victorian Conscience*, p. 33.

69 *The English Novel in Transition*, p. 15.

70 'The present position in Zola studies', p. 605.

71 *The English Novel*, p. 298.

72 *Le Naturalisme*, chapter 2.

73 *Naturalism*, p. 32. Yet their bibliography includes Bennett's *Clayhanger* and plays by Galsworthy (*Strife*), Shaw (*Plays Unpleasant*) and D. H. Lawrence (*A Collier's Friday Night, The Daughter-in-Law, The Widowing of Mrs Holroyd*). For a survey of a number of other studies which bring in various other writers like Mark Rutherford, Edwin Pugh, William Pett Ridge, see the introduction and bibliography in *Naturalismus in England 1880–1920*, a collection of critical essays edited by Walter Greiner and Gerhard Stilz (Darmstadt, Wissenschaftliche Buchgesellschaft, 1983).

74 'George Moore, Zola, and the question of influence', *Canadian Review of Comparative Literature*, I (1974), 138–55.

75 See *Emile Zola, Novelist and Reformer*, pp. 242–99.

76 Reproduced in 'Pernicious literature', in *Documents of Modern Literary Realism*, ed. George J. Becker, pp. 353–4; also in *Naturalismus in England*, pp. 79–86.

77 See William E. Colburn, *Zola in England, 1883–1903*, p. 59.

78 For both letters see *Corr. V*, pp. 225–7.

79 The 'three-decker', so it seems, lasted until 1894 when publishers decided to discontinue the system. This meant the end of the 'circulating libraries', though the firm of Mudie's lasted until 1937 when the Select Library was

closed down. See Guinevere L. Griest, *Mudie's Circulating Library and the Victorian Novel* (Indiana University Press, 1970), p. 6.

80 See Colette Becker, 'L'audience d'Emile Zola', *Les Cahiers naturalistes*, 47 (1974), 40–69.

81 Quoted by Emily Crawford in 'Emile Zola', *The Contemporary Review*, LV (1889), 113.

82 *Ibid.*, p. 95.

83 Quoted in Frierson, 'The English controversy over realism in fiction 1885–1895', 539, and in George J. Becker (ed.), *Documents of Modern Literary Realism*, p. 355.

84 *From Gautier to Eliot*, p. 106.

85 'The moral teaching of Emile Zola', *The Contemporary Review*, LXIII (1893), 212.

86 That is *Nana* by Victor Plarr, *L'Assommoir* by Arthur Symons, *La Curée* by A. Teixeira de Mattos, *Germinal* by Havelock Ellis, *La Terre* by Ernest Dowson and *Pot-Bouille* by Percy Pinkerton. Vizetelly's fate was avoided, but the project was a commercial failure.

87 'The work of George Gissing', in George Gissing, *The House of Cobwebs*, p. viii.

88 From 'Mr. George Moore' (1901), in *The Author's Craft and Other Critical Writings of Arnold Bennett*, ed. Samuel Hynes, p. 144.

89 *Ibid.*, pp. 19, 93.

90 See Walter Allen, *Arnold Bennett*, pp. 15, 17.

91 *Arnold Bennett*, p. 3.

92 See Hynes (ed.), *The Author's Craft*, pp. 238–9. On Hardy's influence on Bennett, see Walter F. Wright, *Arnold Bennett. Romantic Realist*, p. 106.

93 See *The Literary Notebooks of Thomas Hardy*, vol. 1, ed. Lennart A. Björk (New York University Press, 1985), p. 385. See also William Newton, 'Hardy and the naturalists: their use of physiology', *Modern Philology*, XLIX (1951), p. 29; Hardy's article 'The science of fiction' (1891), reproduced in *Thomas Hardy's Personal Writings*, ed. Harold Orel (University of Kansas Press, 1966), pp. 134–8.

94 *Analyse de la périodisation littéraire*, ed. Ch. Bouazis, p. 18.

95 Cf. Françoise Gaillard, *ibid.*, p. 19: 'L'étude approfondie des différentes combinaisons instables et fluctuantes se situe dans une perspective à la fois synchronique et diachronique. Disons plutôt qu'étant dialectique elle fait éclater l'opposition synchronie vs diachronie, ce que les théoriciens formalistes russes ont, pour leur part, reconnu depuis longtemps, eux qui écrivent: "chaque système est présenté comme une évolution et, d'autre part, l'évolution a obligatoirement un caractère systématique".'

96 This analogy is not, by any means, original, of course, nor is it unproblematic. See Alastair Fowler, *Kinds of Literature*, pp. 41–2, where it is traced to, among other sources, a more famous analogy by Wittgenstein between games and language games. Fowler states that 'genres

appear to be much more like families than classes' (p. 41). For a criticism of the implicit conservatism of this analogy, see Mary Jacobus, 'The law of/and gender: genre theory and *The Prelude*', *Diacritics*, XIV (1984), 47–57.

2 Theories

1 *Kinds of Literature*, p. 24.
2 *L'Evolution naturaliste*, p. 94.
3 See F. W. J. Hemmings, 'The origin of the terms *naturalisme, naturaliste*', *French Studies*, VIII (1954), 109–21; Yves Chevrel, *Le Naturalisme*, chap. 1; Henri Mitterand, 'Le naturalisme théorique de Zola', *Lez Valenciennes*, 10 (1985), 183–6, reproduced in *Zola et le naturalisme*, chapitre 2, by the same author; Sylvie Thorel, 'Naturalisme, naturaliste', *Les Cahiers naturalistes*, 60 (1986), 76–88.
4 *American Literary Naturalism, a Divided Stream*, p. 23.
5 Cargill, 'A confusion of major critical terms', *The Ohio University Review*, IX (1967), 31; Rochat, 'The development and divergence of the two branches of naturalism', *The Durham University Journal*, XXXIX (1978), 155.
6 *Naturalism*, p. 2.
7 *Revue des deux Mondes*, XXXV (1879), 424–5.
8 *Corr. III*, pp. 294–5, in response to 'Emile Zola et le naturalisme', *La Jeune France*, 1 February 1879, 385.
9 'Some observations on naturalism, so called, in fiction', *The Antioch Review*, X (1950), 258.
10 Frank Lentricchia, 'Four types of nineteenth-century poetic', *The Journal of Aesthetics and Art Criticism*, XXVI (1968), 356.
11 See Thomas Munro, 'Meanings of "naturalism" in philosophy and aesthetics', *The Journal of Aesthetics and Art Criticism*, XIX (1960), 133–7, and Patrick Romanell, 'Prolegomena to any naturalistic aesthetics', *ibid.*, 139–43.
12 *The Monster in the Mirror. Studies in Nineteenth-Century Realism*, p. 2.
13 Arthur C. Danto, in *The Encyclopedia of Philosophy*, vol. 5 (London/New York, Collier-Macmillan, 1967), p. 449.
14 *Naturalism*, pp. 42–3.
15 Quoted by B. H. Bakker, in '*Naturalisme pas mort*', pp. 13–14. Cf. *ibid.*, pp. 475–6.
16 See *Henry Céard et le naturalisme*, pp. 14–15.
17 'Une lettre de M. Henry Céard', *L'Information*, 22 July 1918.
18 Furst and Skrine, *Naturalism*, p. 70.
19 *Le Naturalisme*, p. 12; *Naturalism*, p. 5.
20 *Documents of Modern Literary Realism*, p. 3.
21 *Ibid.*, p. vi.
22 For a catalogue of different types of realism, ranging in alphabetical

order from 'critical realism' to 'visionary realism', see the introduction to Damian Grant's little book, entitled (not surprisingly) *Realism* (London, Methuen, 1970).

23 'From Aristotelean mimesis to "bourgeois realism"', *Poetics*, XI (1982), 189–202.

24 *Ibid.*, pp. 190, 198–9.

25 *Naturalism*, p. 27.

26 *Emile Zola*, p. 17.

27 On the notion of the *vraisemblable*, see Jonathan Culler, *Structuralist Poetics*, pp. 138–9.

28 *Œuvres complètes de Guy de Maupassant. Pierre et Jean*, Paris, Conard, 1929, pp. XV.

29 *L'Esthétique de J.-K. Huysmans*, p. 63. The essay was first published in *L'Actualité* of Brussels, 11, 18, 25 March and 1 April 1877, and is reproduced in *Œuvres complètes de J.-K. Huysmans, II* (Paris, Crès, 1928), pp. 149–92.

30 'Pustules vertes ou chairs roses, peu nous importe; nous touchons aux unes et aux autres, parce que les unes et les autres existent, parce que le goujat mérite d'être étudié aussi bien que le plus parfait des hommes, parce que les filles perdues foisonnent dans nos villes et y ont droit de cité aussi bien que les filles honnêtes' (*ibid.*, p. 161).

31 *Ibid.*, pp. 162–3.

32 *Ibid.*, p. 166.

33 *Naturalism*, p. 33.

34 'Le naturalisme dans les recherches littéraires et dans l'esthétique du XXᵉ siècle', 261.

35 See Evert Sprinchorn, 'Strindberg and the greater naturalism', *Tulane Drama Review*, XIII (1968), p. 123.

36 'Le naturalisme dans les recherches littéraires et dans l'esthétique du XXᵉ siècle', p. 266.

37 *Naturalism*, p. 39. On Holz's theory, see also Yves Chevrel, *Le Naturalisme*, pp. 156–60.

38 'Le roman et l'expérience des limites', *Tel Quel*, 25 (1966), p. 26.

39 *Le Roman naturaliste*, p. 75.

40 4 March 1883. Yves Chevrel emphasises among the naturalists this 'incontestable malaise à se servir des termes usuels' (*Le Naturalisme*, p. 79).

41 There was, needless to say, little naturalist poetry written in France, though rather more than one at first might suppose. Christophe Charle, for instance, mentions J. Ajalbert as a naturalist poet (*La Crise littéraire à l'époque du naturalisme*, p. 100). Then there was Henry Céard who composed quite a lot of verse, though most of it remained unpublished (see C. A. Burns, *Henry Céard et le naturalisme*, chapter 8, 'Céard poète', pp. 197–219). A number of the naturalists contributed to *Le Nouveau Parnasse satyrique du dix-neuvième siècle* (Brussels, Sous le Manteau, 1881), in which there are three poems by Céard, two by Hennique,

two by Huysmans, one by Alexis and three by Maupassant. As one would expect, naturalist poetry tends to be irreverent, satirical and parodic, that is when it is not purely descriptive, as in the poem by Alexis 'La Bouchère' published by Auriant in 'Poésie et naturalisme', *Visages du monde*, 17 (15 July–15 August 1934), 156.

42 *Le Naturalisme français*, p. 157.
43 *Le Naturalisme*, p. 67.
44 *Ibid.*, p. 75.
45 There is, for instance, very little mention of the publication of *Le Roman expérimental* in Zola's correspondence and certainly no trace of any polemic. But the impact of Zola's ideas was largely overshadowed by the publication of *Nana* with its far more provocative themes.
46 'Décidément, il y a un sophisme capital dans votre étude sur le roman expérimental. Claude Bernard, quand il institue son expérience, sait parfaitement dans quelles conditions elle se produira et sous l'influence exacte de quelles lois déterminées. A chaque instant, il opère sur la modification du corps qu'il traite un contrôle scrupuleux, et toujours il arrive à un résultat mathématiquement indiscutable. En outre, il a en main le moyen précis de vérifier toutes ses expériences. En est-il identiquement de même pour le romancier? Certainement oui, pour ce qui est de la partie physiologique de son œuvre. Mais pour les modifications que l'hypertrophie ou l'atrophie d'un organe amènent nécessairement dans la psychologie d'un individu, où est son critérium? Les lois du cerveau n'étant que bien vaguement formulées, au lieu d'aboutir à une réalité scientifique, comme Claude Bernard, il aboutit simplement à une hypothèse, vraisemblable sans doute, mais qu'il ne peut appuyer sur aucun fait et qui laisse prise à toutes les discussions' (letter of 28 October 1879). See also C. A. Burns, *Henry Céard et le naturalisme*, pp. 14–15.
47 'Il est évident que M. Zola ne sait pas ce que c'est qu'*expérimenter*, car le romancier comme le poète, s'il expérimente, ne peut expérimenter que sur soi, nullement sur les autres. Expérimenter sur Coupeau, ce serait se procurer un Coupeau qu'on tiendrait en charte privée, qu'on enivrerait quotidiennement, à dosage déterminé, que d'ailleurs on empêcherait de rien faire qui risquât d'interrompre ou de détourner le cours de l'expérience, et qu'on ouvrirait sur la table de dissection aussitôt qu'il présenterait un cas d'alcoolisme nettement caractérisé. Il n'y a pas autrement ni ne peut y avoir d'expérimentation, il n'y a qu'observation, et dès là c'est assez pour que la théorie de M. Zola sur *le Roman expérimental* manque, et croule aussitôt par la base' ('Le Roman expérimental', p. 936).
48 See the article 'Une lettre de M. Henry Céard'.
49 *La Physiologie expérimentale et le 'Roman expérimental'. Claude Bernard et Monsieur Zola* (Paris, Hurtau, 1881), 23pp.
50 F. W. J. Hemmings, *Emile Zola*, pp. 151–2; Angus Wilson, *Emile Zola*.

An Introductory Study of His Novels, p. 39; Furst and Skrine, *Naturalism*, p. 30; Philip Walker, *Zola*, p. 139.

51 Introduction to the Garnier-Flammarion edition of *Le Roman expérimental* (Paris, 1971), p. 26. See also Alain Pagès, 'En partant de la théorie du roman expérimental', *Les Cahiers naturalistes*, 47 (1974), 70–87.

52 Cf. 'Etre maître du bien et du mal, régler la vie, régler la société, résoudre à la longue tous les problèmes du socialisme, apporter surtout des bases solides à la justice en résolvant par l'expérience les questions de criminalité, n'est-ce pas là être les ouvriers les plus utiles et les plus moraux du travail humain?' (X, 1188).

53 *Le Discours du roman*, p. 166. An earlier advocate of this view is René Wellek, who writes in *A History of Modern Criticism: 1750–1950. Vol. IV. The Later Nineteenth-Century* (Yale University Press, 1965), p. 14: 'We do an injustice to Zola in taking him literally. Quoting or paraphrasing Bernard was a rhetorical device – possibly an unfortunate device – to cloak his theories with the prestige of contemporary science.'

54 'Textes en intersection', *University of Ottawa Quarterly*, XLVIII (1978), p. 419.

55 *Mythologies de l'hérédité au XIXe siècle*, p. 92.

56 *Ibid.*, p. 29.

57 'Notes générales sur la nature de l'œuvre', reproduced in *Les Rougon-Macquart V*, ed. Henri Mitterand (Paris, Bibliothèque de la Pléiade, 1967), p. 1744.

58 'Plot and the analogy with science in later nineteenth-century novelists', in *Comparative Criticism. A Yearbook, 2*, ed. Elinor Shaffer, p. 134.

59 *Ibid.*, p. 143.

60 *Genre*, p. 45.

61 *Validity in Interpretation*, p. 76.

62 See Dubrow, *Genre*, pp. 83–4.

63 My emphasis.

64 Cf. *Thérèse Raquin* (tragedy), *Les Héritiers Rabourdin* (comedy), *Le Bouton de Rose* (farce), and the 'drames lyriques' of the later years.

65 'Du texte au genre', p. 9.

66 An earlier study by Zola of the same text was far more sensitive to the novel's literary qualities. On his evolving view of Flaubert's novel, see F. W. J. Hemmings, 'Zola and *L'Education sentimentale*', *The Romanic Review*, L (1959), 35–40.

67 *The Dialogic Imagination*, p. 5.

68 'Le "naturel" et le "conventionnel" dans la critique et la théorie', *Littérature*, 57 (1985), 19.

69 'Le naturalisme théorique de Zola', p. 192.

70 *Palimpsestes*, p. 11.

3 The founding texts

1 *Le Pacte autobiographique*, p. 327.
2 *Ibid.*, pp. 330, 329.
3 *Ibid.*, p. 334.
4 'Du texte au genre', pp. 13, 15.
5 See L. M. O'Toole and Ann Shukman (eds.), *Russian Poetics in Translation* (Oxford, Holdan Books, 1977), and Victor Erlich, *Russian Formalism. History – Doctrine*, 2nd edn (The Hague, Mouton, 1965).
6 'Literary history as a challenge to literary theory', in *Toward an Aesthetic of Reception*, pp. 27–8.
7 *Problems of Dostoevsky's Poetics*, p. 87.
8 'La stratégie de la forme', p. 264.
9 *Le Pacte autobiographique*, p. 318.
10 '1871: la fausse coupure. Contribution à l'histoire du naturalisme', p. 25.
11 Paris, Charpentier, 1911 (1864). References included in the text are to this edition.
12 Quoted in P. Martino, *Le Naturalisme français*, p. 21.
13 *Histoire du naturalisme français*, vol. 1, p. 344.
14 See chapter 7 'Dans le sillage de *Germinie Lacerteux*', in Pierre Sabatier, *'Germinie Lacerteux' des Goncourt*, and the final chapter of the same critic's study *L'Esthétique des Goncourt*.
15 Letter of 15 January 1865, quoted in *Lettres de Jules de Goncourt* (Paris, Charpentier, 1885), pp. 219–20.
16 *Correspondance. Cinquième série (1862–1868)* (Paris, Conard, 1929), p. 163.
17 See Robert Ricatte, *La Création romanesque chez les Goncourt: 1851–1870*, pp. 262, 250–1.
18 For other examples, see Chevrel, *Le Naturalisme*, pp. 155–6. The ultimate stage in this procedure was achieved by two American writers, James Brander Matthews and Henry Cuyler Bunner, who published in *Scribner's Monthly* (30 August 1879) a 'story' called 'The documents in the case', which is made up entirely of so-called documents (letters, tickets, newspaper clippings, etc.), leaving the reader to construct the plot. See Albert J. Salvan, 'Les correspondants américains de Zola', *Les Cahiers naturalistes*, 27 (1964), 103–4, and *Corr. III*, pp. 380–1. At the other extreme, Henry James mocked the naturalist mania for documentation (though still resorting to the procedure) in a letter to Thomas Sergeant Perry (2 December 1884): 'I have been all the morning at Millbank prison (horrible place) collecting notes for a fiction scene. You see I am quite the Naturalist. Look out for the same – a year hence.'
19 *Literary Theory*, p. 190.
20 Zola's 'ultra-nervous' character and appearance were noted by the Goncourts from the start of their association, his disposition 'où il mêle le mâle et le féminin' (*Journal*, 14 December 1868). With Jules de Goncourt an early 'martyr', Maupassant and Daudet (at least in this

respect one of the group) went to Charcot's lectures or received treatment from him. Nervous disabilities were, of course, a symptom of, and frequently a metaphor for, the ravages of syphilis.

21 Surprisingly, in his excellent study of this novel, even John C. Lapp, though briefly acknowledging the importance of the novelist's 'control experiment', writes: 'Zola commits himself, in *Thérèse Raquin*, to an essentially dramatic method. The author will choose to *present*, to *portray*, rather than to analyze' (*Zola before the 'Rougon-Macquart'*, p. 90).

22 There is no extant preparatory dossier for this novel. On its probable sources, in addition to Taine's ideas, see Henri Mitterand's introduction to the Garnier-Flammarion edition (1970). Taine himself gave general approval to the 'truth' of the novel, which he significantly compares to *Germinie Lacerteux*. See John C. Lapp (ed.), 'Taine et Zola: autour d'une correspondance', *Revue des Sciences humaines*, 87 (1957), 322–3.

23 *Validity in Interpretation*, p. 107.

24 In a BBC talk published in *The Listener*, 21 April 1966, and reprinted in D. Baguley (ed.), *Critical Essays on Emile Zola*, p. 93.

25 *Naturalism*, p. 43.

26 See Jean Rousset, *Leurs yeux se rencontrèrent. La scène de première vue dans le roman* (Paris, José Corti, 1981).

27 *Le Réveil*, 28 May 1882; quoted in Bakker (ed.), '*Naturalisme pas mort*', p. 472.

28 *Kinds of Literature*, p. 158.

29 See Victor Erlich, *Russian Formalism*, p. 260.

30 Notably a novel by Adolphe Belot and Ernest Daudet, *La Vénus de Gordes*; *L'Assassinat du Pont-Rouge* (1859) by Charles Barbara; *Atar-Gull* (1831) by Eugène Sue. See Henri Mitterand's introduction to the Garnier-Flammarion edition of Zola's novel, pp. 14–17.

31 See I, 584; also Yves Olivier-Martin, *Histoire du roman populaire en France de 1840 à 1980*, p. 161.

32 See *Anatomy of Criticism*, pp. 136, 42.

33 See, for one such interpretation, Michel Claverie's article '*Thérèse Raquin*, ou les Atrides dans la boutique du Pont-Neuf', *Les Cahiers naturalistes*, 36 (1968), 138–47.

34 The useful term 'hypotext', along with 'hypertext', derives from Gérard Genette's *Palimpsestes*, where may be found the following definition of 'hypertextualité': 'J'entends par là toute relation unissant un texte B (que j'appellerai *hypertexte*) à un texte antérieur A (que j'appellerai, bien sûr, *hypotexte*) sur lequel il se greffe d'une manière qui n'est pas celle du commentaire' (pp. 11–12).

35 'J.-K. Huysmans et le naturalisme', *L'Amateur d'autographes*, XL (1907), 164–6. Cf. his preface to the 1903 edition of *A Rebours*, in which he writes that the ideal of the representation of everyday life 's'était, en son genre, réalisé dans un chef d'œuvre qui a été beaucoup plus que *L'Assommoir* le parangon du naturalisme, *l'Education sentimentale* de Gustave

Flaubert; ce roman était, pour nous tous, des "Soirées de Médan", une véritable bible; mais il ne comportait que peu de moutures. Il'était parachevé, irrecommençable pour Flaubert même; nous en étions donc, tous, réduits, en ce temps-là, à louvoyer, à rôder par des voies plus ou moins explorées, tout autour' (in *Œuvres complètes de J.-K. Huysmans*, vol. VII (Paris, Crès, 1929), p. VIII).

36 *Lettres inédites à Emile Zola*, ed. C. A. Burns (Paris, Nizet, 1958), p. 116.
37 See Robert Baldick, *The Life of J.-K. Huysmans*, p. 28; also, on the influence of Flaubert's novel, Deffoux and Zavie, *Le Groupe de Médan*, pp. 122–6.
38 Cf. the following anecdote recounted by Deffoux and Zavie (*ibid.*, pp. 124–5): 'M. Henry Céard aime parfois, dans l'intimité, à imaginer un chapitre de *Madame Bovary* ou de *L'Education sentimentale* que Flaubert aurait pu écrire. Et, souriant à demi, à demi ému, M. Céard pastiche, en se jouant, l'épisode qu'il invente. – "Tout cela est facile, dit-il avec une modestie charmante, comme pour s'excuser, maintenant que Flaubert nous l'a montré ...".'
39 *Cosmopolis*, VII (1897), 59.
40 *Ibid.*, 58, 42.
41 (Paris, Conard, 1923), p. 35.
42 See Philip Walker, *Zola*, p. 81, who notes that Ulbach was 'an old friend' of Zola's with financial interests in the business of Zola's publisher, Lacroix. Ulbach's article is published in English in *Critical Essays on Emile Zola*, ed. D. Baguley, pp. 25–9.
43 Hans Robert Jauss, 'Literary history as a challenge to literary theory', *Toward an Aesthetic of Reception, p. 16.*

4 The tragic model

1 Gerrards Cross, Colin Smythe, 1981 (1886), p. 203.
2 *Characters in the Twilight*, p. 38.
3 London, Faber and Faber, 1961, p. 291.
4 *Le Naturalisme*, pp. 56–7, 75, 64.
5 *Ibid.*, pp. 73–4.
6 *Ibid.*, p. 76.
7 *Introduction à l'architexte*, p. 25.
8 *Anatomy of Criticism*, p. 208.
9 See the author's preface to the play and the article by Evert Sprinchorn, 'Strindberg and the greater naturalism', *Tulane Drama Review*, XIII (1968), 119–29.
10 Strindberg, *Five Plays*, trans. Harry G. Carlson (New York, Signet, 1984 [1981]), pp. 87, 54–5.
11 *Trente romans* (Paris, Charpentier, 1895), p. 172.
12 Brussels, Kistemaeckers, 1888 (1883) (Geneva, Slatkine Reprints, 1979), pp. 302–3.

13 *Five Plays*, p. 81.

14 *Zola et le naturalisme*, p. 31.

15 See Jean Borie, *Mythologies de l'hérédité au XIXe siècle*, p. 16.

16 'Le sang impur. Notes sur le concept de prostituée-née chez Lombroso', *Romantisme* 31 (1981), 174–6, 178.

17 Paris, Charpentier, 1891, p. 81.

18 *Ibid.*, p. 433.

19 Between Coupeau and Lantier, Gervaise 'mollissait' (II, 670); the heroine of *Le Calvaire d'Héloïse Pajadou* is 'de la cire molle' (p. 22); 'mollesse' and 'chute' are key terms in Zola's *Une Page d'amour*, as Brian Nelson has thoroughly shown (*Zola and the Bourgeoisie*, pp. 96–128); Germaine, in Camille Lemonnier's *Un Mâle*, feels 'un trouble vague, une sourde fermentation de son être ardent et jeune, avec des amollissements profonds' (p. 43); Arnold Bennett's *The Old Wives' Tale*, like its main source, Maupassant's *Une Vie*, deals amply with the theme of the prison of soft female flesh; and, to give a final example from an abundant supply, the mother of Paul Bonnetain's hero in *Charlot s'amuse* is 'prise d'une lascivité molle dont elle n'avait pas conscience', a state which is linked, as in *Madame Meuriot*, to religious devotion.

20 *Chair molle. Roman naturaliste*, with a preface by Paul Alexis (Brussels, Auguste Brancart, 1885).

21 *Ibid.*, p. 239.

22 *Ibid.*, pp. 169, 226.

23 See Hans-Jorg Neuschäfer's study, 'Naturalisme et feuilleton. Le "roman social" dans les journaux parisiens de 1884', in *Le Naturalisme en question*, ed. Yves Chevrel, pp. 123–9, and especially Yves Olivier-Martin, *Histoire du roman populaire en France de 1840 à 1980*, pp. 150–3.

24 On the second of these explanations, see Alain Corbin, 'L'hérédosyphilis ou l'impossible rédemption. Contribution à l'histoire de l'hérédité morbide', *Romantisme*, 31 (1981), 135; on the third, see Jean Borie, *Mythologies de l'hérédité au XIXe siècle*, p. 48: 'Le colonialisme féministe a donc pour conséquence une valorisation extraordinaire de la virginité, comme si de ce côté au moins, du côté du terroir, on voulait absolument s'assurer d'une page blanche.'

25 *Mythologies de l'hérédité au XIXe siècle*, p. 89.

26 Published in the collection *Autour de la caserne* (Paris, Victor Havard, 1885).

27 Brussels, Kistemaeckers, 1881, p. 145.

28 'Genèse et généalogie (Le cas du *Docteur Pascal*)', *Romantisme*, 31 (1981), 189.

29 Paris, Dentu, 1881.

30 *Ibid.*, pp. 208–9.

31 *Ibid.*, pp. 286, 287, 331, 332.

32 *Ibid.*, pp. 353, 355.

33 Paris, Charpentier, 1885, pp. 38–9.

34 *Ibid.*, pp. 78, 237, 269.

35 *Ibid.*, p. 345.

36 Brussels, Kistemaeckers, 1888, p. viii. The novel was reissued in 1979 by Slatkine Reprints of Geneva. References to this edition will be included in the text.

37 On these 'performances', see Stephen Heath, *The Sexual Fix* (New York, Schocken Books, 1984), pp. 35–6.

38 Cf. Lucie in *Chair molle*, who comes to see herself as 'la victime de quelque guigne mystérieuse' (p. 195), or Euchariste Moisan in the Quebec writer Radiguet's version of *La Terre*, *Trente arpents* (Paris, Flammarion, 1938): 'maintenant que la guigne semblait s'acharner sur lui, il s'attendait constamment au pire' (p. 226). In Verga's novel *I Malavoglia*, intended to be part of a series *I Vinti* ['The Doomed'], a sense of doom hangs over the whole Malavoglia family.

39 'Plot and the analogy with science', p. 137.

40 See Jacques Dubois, *'L'Assommoir' de Zola. Société, discours, idéologie*, pp. 28–40.

41 Quoted by T. R. Henn, in *The Harvest of Tragedy* (London, Methuen, 1956), p. 71.

42 See 'Tensions and ambiguities in Greek tragedy', in *Interpretation. Theory and Practice*, ed. Charles S. Singleton (Baltimore, 1969), p. 112.

43 Peter L. Hays, *The Limping Hero: Grotesques in Literature* (New York University Press, 1971). For more detailed studies of Gervaise's mythical and tragic fate, see Jacques Dubois, *'L'Assommoir' de Zola*, chapter 2, and D. Baguley, 'Rite et tragédie dans *L'Assommoir'*, *Les Cahiers naturalistes*, 52 (1978), 80–96.

44 *La Violence et le Sacré* (Paris, Grasset, 1972), p. 181.

45 *New York World*, 26 July 1896; quoted by Lars Åhnebrink, *The Beginnings of Naturalism in American Fiction*, p. 154.

46 See the New Wessex Edition of the novel: London, Macmillan, 1974, p. 163, and Arthur Mizener, '*Jude the Obscure* as a tragedy', in *Modern British Fiction*, ed. Mark Schorer (Oxford University Press, 1961), p. 48.

47 *George Moore. L'homme et l'œuvre (1852–1933)*, p. 239.

48 See Richard Allen Cave, *A Study of the Novels of George Moore*, p. 249.

5 Comic strains

1 *Les Genres du discours*, pp. 67–8.

2 Quoted in Bakker (ed.), *'Naturalisme pas mort'*, p. 205.

3 In his introduction to the Slatkine edition: Paris-Geneva, 1980, p. v, from which page references included in the text are taken.

4 *Le Roman naturaliste*, pp. 303, 305.

5 *Ibid.*, p. 304.

6 See *L'Evolution naturaliste*, p. 109; *Le Roman naturaliste*, p. 88; 'Plot-formation in modern novels', reprinted from the New Orleans

Times-Democrat, in Lafcadio Hearn, *Essays in European and Oriental Literature*, pp. 141–5.

7 *Guy de Maupassant et l'art du roman*, p. 32.

8 Brussels, Kistemaeckers, 1888, pp. 65, 68, 174, 214, 247.

9 *La Revue littéraire et artistique*, August–September 1881, p. 424. On this story, see C. A. Burns, *Henry Céard et le naturalisme*, pp. 61–7, and the same critic's edition of the text in *Visages du naturalisme* (1989), in the series *Naturalist Documents* (University of Western Ontario).

10 *La Fin de Lucie Pellegrin* (1880) [Paris–Geneva, Slatkine, 1979], p. 265.

11 See the informative articles by C. A. Burns in *Studi francesi*: 'En marge du Naturalisme: Gabriel Thyébaut (1854–1922)', III (1959), 231–42; 'Nouvelles perspectives sur le Naturalisme', IX (1965), 41–61; 'Documents naturalistes. Notes sur Gabriel Thyébaut et Henry Céard', XII (1968), 61–7; and several sections of his book *Henry Céard et le naturalisme*. See also Jean-Claude Le Blond-Zola, 'Gabriel Thyébaut, ami d'Emile Zola', *Les Cahiers naturalistes*, 49 (1975), 15–29; Deffoux and Zavie, *Le Groupe de Médan*, pp. 175–91.

12 'Je n'ai jamais connu d'homme plus subtil', wrote René Dumesnil; 'les admirations littéraires les plus profondes de Thyébaut étaient précisément si vivantes qu'il pouvait réciter, par exemple, tout *L'Education sentimentale* qu'il savait, littéralement, par cœur' (C. A. Burns, 'En marge du Naturalisme', p. 233).

13 In *Les Cahiers naturalistes*, 4 (1956), 165–8.

14 *Ibid.*, 165, and 'En marge du Naturalisme', 237.

15 *Le Groupe de Médan*, p. 184.

16 From *Promenades littéraires*; quoted in Deffoux and Zavie, *ibid.*, p. 179.

17 See *ibid.*, pp. 117–18.

18 See C. A. Burns, *Henry Céard et le naturalisme*, pp. 36–7.

19 In his much-quoted letter to Margaret Harkness; see David Caute, *The Illusion* (New York, Harper and Row, 1972), p. 98.

20 'The Zola Centenary', in *Studies in European Realism* (London, Hillway, 1950), pp. 90–1. The essay was first written in 1940 and first published in Hungarian in 1949.

21 Trans. by Hannah and Stanley Mitchell (Penguin Books, 1969 [1962 translation]), p. 237.

22 References included in the text are to the Garnier-Flammarion edition, 1972.

23 *Maupassant et l'art du roman*, p. 356. See the same author's *La Genèse d'"Une Vie", premier roman de Guy de Maupassant* (Paris, Les Belles Lettres, 1954), p. 43.

24 Rosalie gives birth in the parlour in chapter 7, then Jeanne is delivered of 'cette larve', 'cet avorton frippé, grimaçant' in the following chapter.

25 In *The Author's Craft*, ed. Samuel Hynes, p. 17.

26 *En ménage. A vau-l'eau* (Paris, Union Générale d'Editions, 1975 [série 10/18]), p. 81. For both works, subsequent references will appear in the text.

27 Nestor [Henry Fouquier], *Gil Blas*, 11 March 1882.

28 Robert Baldick, *The Life of J.-K. Huysmans*, p. 65.

29 *History of Western Philosophy* (London, George Allen and Unwin, 1961 [1946]), p. 727.

30 *The World as Will and Representation*, trans. E. F. J. Payne, vol. II (New York, Dover Publications, 1966), p. 513.

31 See *The Novels of Flaubert*, p. 133.

32 *Le Figaro*, 15 February 1886; quoted in René-Pierre Colin, *Schopenhauer en France: un mythe naturaliste*, p. 138.

33 *Influence de la philosophie de Schopenhauer en France (1860–1900)*, p. 16.

34 See Albert Thibaudet, *Gustave Flaubert* (Paris, Gallimard, 1935), p. 290. The 'Schopenhauerism' of the members of the Médan group has been well documented, particularly for Huysmans and Maupassant. See Baillot, *Influence de la philosophie de Schopenhauer en France*, pp. 228–34, and Colin, *Schopenhauer en France*, pp. 181–202, who has reservations about the previous study. See also Helen Trudgian, *L'Esthétique de J.-K. Huysmans*, pp. 195–200; Thomas G. West, 'Schopenhauer, Huysmans and French naturalism', *Journal of European Studies* (1977), 313–24; on Maupassant, see Vial, *Guy de Maupassant et l'art du roman*, pp. 115–20.

35 *Schopenhauer en France*, p. 205.

36 See *ibid.*, p. 181.

37 In an unpublished note quoted by Ronald Frazee, in *Henry Céard, idéaliste détrompé*, p. 19.

38 On these texts, see C. A. Burns, *Henry Céard et le naturalisme*, pp. 224–5.

39 'The esthetics of naturalism. Henry Céard's *Une Belle Journée*', *L'Esprit créateur*, IV (1964), 76.

40 *Le Groupe de Médan*, p. 110. They also note Edmond de Goncourt's significant reaction to the text: 'Défiez-vous de *L'Education sentimentale*.'

41 *Henry Céard et le naturalisme*, p. 102.

42 *Une Belle Journée* (Paris, Charpentier, 1881); references are to the Slatkine reprint of the novel (Geneva, 1980), with a preface by C. A. Burns.

43 See C. A. Burns, *Henry Céard et le naturalisme*, pp. 125–38.

44 Quoted in Frazee, *Henry Céard, idéaliste détrompé*, p. 103.

45 Quoted by C. A. Burns, *Henry Céard et le naturalisme*, p. 223.

46 *Emile Zola*, pp. 13–14.

47 *Marthe*, ed. Pierre Cogny (Paris, Le Cercle du Livre, 1955), p. 166.

6 In the ironic modes

1 *Kinds of Literature*, pp. 110, 188.

2 'Du texte au genre', p. 18.

3 'Ironie, satire, parodie. Une approche pragmatique de l'ironie', *Poétique*, 46 (1981), 141.

4 *Ibid.*, pp. 142–3.

5 On 'Verbal Irony' and 'Situational Irony', see D. C. Muecke, *Irony*, p. 28. In *The Anatomy of Satire*, pp. 13–14, Gilbert Highet similarly defines three main 'shapes' of satire: one, the 'monologue', in which the satirist speaks directly; two, the 'parody', which ridicules an existing work of literature (clearly a category somewhat out of place in a study of satire); three, 'satirical narratives', in which the satirist generally does not appear, as in *Candide*.

6 In an article published in *The Savoy*, I (January 1896), 67–80, and reproduced in *Affirmations* (London, Constable, 1898), pp. 131–57.

7 See 'Concord philosophy and Zola', *The Literary World* (Boston), XVII (7 August 1886), 264. Both this article and the one by Havelock Ellis mentioned above are reproduced in D. Baguley (ed.), *Critical Essays on Emile Zola*, pp. 41–4, 64–75.

8 See Wayne Booth, *A Rhetoric of Irony* (The University of Chicago Press, 1974).

9 Brussels, Kistemaeckers, 1884, p. 238. The text of this novel was reissued in 1980 by Slatkine Reprints, Geneva, with an introduction by Henri Mitterand.

10 See Eric Gans, 'Hyperbole et ironie', *Poétique*, 24 (1975), 493: 'L'ironie n'est donc pas le contraire de l'hyperbole mais une *réponse* à celle-ci, car elle constate comme elle, mais dans une perspective différente, la distance entre l'énoncé et l'état objectif des choses.'

11 See his article '*Les Soirées de Médan*, comment ce livre a été fait'.

12 *La Crise allemande de la pensée française*, pp. 52–3.

13 *The Fictions of Satire*, p. 3.

14 See Catherine Kerbrat-Orecchioni, 'L'ironie comme trope', *Poétique*, 41 (1980), 122.

15 References included in the text are to Colette Becker's edition of *Les Soirées de Médan* (Paris, Le Livre à venir, 1981).

16 *Anatomy of Criticism*, pp. 228–9.

17 See G. Hainsworth, 'Un thème des romanciers naturalistes: la Matrone d'Ephèse', *Comparative Literature*, III (1951), 141–2.

18 *Anatomy of Criticism*, p. 228.

19 *L'Ironie* (Paris, Flammarion, 1964), pp. 93, 96.

20 Alvin B. Kernan, *The Cankered Muse: Satire of the English Renaissance* (Yale University Press, 1959).

21 *L'Evolution naturaliste*, p. 178.

22 *Le Naturalisme*, p. 193.

23 *Madame Meuriot*, p. 427.

24 'Mais Mlle Célestine R ... était fort jolie ... Elle insista. Je finis par céder, car je suis un homme, après tout ...' (Paris, Fasquelle, 1959, p. 6).

25 *Ibid.*, p. 57.

26 *The Anatomy of Satire*, p. 206.

27 In *The Literary World* (Boston), 3 June 1882.

28 *Emile Zola*, p. 143.

29 Philippe Hamon writes in 'Zola, romancier de la transparence', *Europe*, 468–9 (1968), 386, of a 'complexe d'Asmodée', 'une tendance qui pousse le romancier à voir, à "expliquer", ... un art qui mettra tout en œuvre pour que le lecteur perçoive immédiatement les rouages les plus secrets d'un personnage comme les alcôves les plus cachées d'une maison'. H. Schütz Wilson, in an article on *L'Assommoir* in *The Gentleman's Magazine*, CCXLIII (1878), 738, invokes the figure of Asmodeus. Robida's famous cartoon, '*Pot-Bouille* ou tous détraqués mais tous vertueux' in *La Caricature*, 13 May 1882, showing a cross-section of the infamous house opened up to the public gaze graphically makes the same point.

30 In a letter to Céard, 24 August 1881 (*Corr. IV*, p. 217).

31 *Emile Zola*, p. 144. In chapter 18, the servant Adèle gives birth alone in her room: 'ça se détachait, tout un paquet finit par tomber, et elle s'en débarrassa en le jetent dans le pot. Cette fois, grâce à Dieu! c'était bien fini, elle ne souffrirait plus. Du sang tiède coulait seulement le long de ses jambes' (IV, 670–1).

32 *Zola and the Bourgeoisie*, pp. 141, 214.

33 11 February 1882; in *Corr. IV*, p. 276.

34 *Ibid.*, p. 295.

35 *The Anatomy of Satire*, p. 208.

36 *Le Roman naturaliste*, p. 308.

37 *The Anatomy of Satire*, p. 232.

38 In *The Novel in Motley* (Harvard University Press, 1936).

39 See *The Gates of Horn*, p. 47.

40 'Autour d'un livre', *Le Gaulois*, 4 October 1881; quoted in Vial, *Guy de Maupassant et l'art du roman*, p. 76.

41 See Auguste Dezalay, 'Les mystères de Zola', *Revue des Sciences humaines*, 160 (1975), 476–9, and, for a fuller study, D. Baguley, '*La Curée*: la Bête et la Belle', in *'La Curée' de Zola, ou 'la vie à outrance'* (Paris, SEDES, 1987), pp. 141–7.

42 *Pastoral and Romance* (Englewood Cliffs, New Jersey, Prentice Hall, 1969), p. 3.

43 See Kathryn Gravdal, 'Camouflaging rape: the rhetoric of sexual violence in the medieval pastourelle', *The Romanic Review* LXXVI (1985), 361–73.

44 Paris, Flammarion, 1938, p. 83.

45 See Jacques Viens, *'La Terre' de Zola et 'Trente arpents' de Ringuet. Etude comparée*, pp. 83–6.

46 See Alastair Fowler, *Kinds of Literature*, pp. 92–5.

47 In *Le Naturalisme*, pp. 94–8, he defines nine types referring to: (1) the monograph (*Germinie Lacerteux*); (2) the collectivity (*I Malavoglia*); (3) the type (*L'Evangéliste*); (4) the qualified name of a character (*Maggie, A Girl of the Streets*); (5) the qualification alone (*Mal Eclos*); (6) the series (*Les Hommes de Lettres*); (7) the place (*Mont-Oriol*); (8) the theme

(*L'Argent*); (9) the 'situation' or 'atmosphere' (*Germinal*, *La Bête humaine*).

48 See his letter to Kistemaeckers of 31 December 1881, reproduced in Robert Baldick, *The Life of J.-K. Huysmans*, p. 65.

7 The 'scandal' of naturalism

1 See Henri Mitterand's notes in the Pléiade edition of the text: *Les Rougon-Macquart*, vol. II (Paris, Fasquelle, 1961), pp. 1664, 1686, 1699.

2 Paris, Dentu, 1881.

3 *Ibid.*, pp. 492–3, 495.

4 *Emile Zola*, p. 150.

5 See 'Zola's plays in England 1870–1900', *French Studies*, XIII (1959), 28–38. The play premiered at the Princess's Theatre on 7 June 1879.

6 Reade's play is currently being edited (by D. Baguley) in the series *Naturalist Documents* published by the Mestengo Press (The French Department, University of Western Ontario).

7 *Literary Theory*, p. 74.

8 'Pour une pragmatique du discours fictionnel', *Poétique*, 39 (1979), 326–7.

9 *Ibid.*, p. 327.

10 *Ibid.*, p. 337.

11 *Le Naturalisme*, p. 201.

12 *L'Evolution naturaliste*, pp. 238–41.

13 *Le Naturalisme*, p. 211.

14 *Ibid.*, p. 199.

15 *The Parisian*, 26 February 1880, quoted here from *The House of Fiction* (London, Hart-Davis, 1957), p. 278.

16 *Corr. V.*, p. 94.

17 See *Corr. III*, p. 140.

18 For a series of examples in various countries, see Yves Chevrel, *Le Naturalisme*, pp. 184–5.

19 See *On Difficulty, and Other Essays*, pp. 108–9.

20 *Les Procès littéraires au XIXe siècle*, pp. 225–7.

21 See the *Journal*, 3 October 1876.

22 Fèvre, a minor, was exempt from prosecution. On Zola's letter, see *Corr. V*, pp. 113–15, 204–5. On the Desprez trial and its aftermath, see Guy Robert's edition of his letters to Zola (Paris, Les Belles Lettres, 1952); René-Pierre Colin, '1885: Zola et l'affaire Desprez', *Les Cahiers naturalistes*, 59 (1985), 144–50. See also Zola's letter of outrage at his death: 'Louis Desprez', *Le Figaro*, 9 December 1885, in XII, 641–2. The publisher of the book, Henry Kistemaeckers père, also wrote an account: 'Un procès littéraire: Louis Desprez (Souvenirs d'un éditeur)', *Mercure de France*, CLI, no. 560 (15 October 1921), 429–42.

23 *Autour d'un clocher*, p. 354.

24 See the preface by Céard (previously eliminated) and the introduction by Hubert Juin in the Slatkine reprint of the novel (Geneva, 1979), from which I have already quoted.

25 See J. Ann Duncan, *L'Epoque symboliste et le monde proustien à travers la correspondance de Paul Adam* (Paris, Nizet, 1982), pp. 17–22.

26 For details of the trial and the *cause célèbre*, see Henri Mitterand's edition of the novel: Geneva, Slatkine, 1980.

27 See René Fayt, 'Un éditeur des naturalistes: Henry Kistemaeckers', *Revue de l'Université de Bruxelles*, 4–5 (1984), 217–39.

28 *On Difficulty*, p. 128.

29 *Nouveau Discours du récit*, p. 32.

30 *La Feuille littéraire*, no. 149; quoted in Deffoux and Zavie, *Le Groupe de Médan*, p. 287. On naturalist 'bas-fondmanie', see Chevrel, *Le Naturalisme*, p. 98.

31 'A Note on Zola's method', in *Studies in Two Literatures* (London, Leonard Smithers, 1897), pp. 211–12.

32 'Uncovering *Nana*. The courtesan's new clothes', *L'Esprit créateur*, XXV (1985), pp. 47–9.

33 *Le Personnel du roman*, pp. 105–6.

34 *Nouveau Discours du récit*, p. 24.

35 *Corr. V*, p. 426.

36 See Colette Becker's edition of the preparatory dossier of this novel: *Emile Zola: la fabrique de 'Germinal'* (Paris, SEDES, 1986), p. 261.

37 *Ibid.*, p. 176.

38 *Corr. IV*, p. 297.

39 *Madame Meuriot*, p. 425.

40 See 'Haro sur la masturbation. Un spectre parmi d'autres hante le bourgeois au XIXe siècle: la masturbation', in *L'Amour et la sexualité*, ed. Georges Duby (Paris, Seuil, [1985?]) – a special number of the review *L'Histoire*.

41 See Heather Dubrow, *Genre*, p. 33.

42 *Mythologies de l'hérédité au XIXe siècle*, p. 102.

43 Léon Gandillot, *Entre Conjoints!*, p. 203.

44 Franc Schuerewegen, 'Réflexions sur le narrataire. Quidam et quilibet', *Poétique*, 70 (1987), 248.

45 *Adultery in the Novel*, p. 3.

46 *Le Pacte autobiographique*, p. 36.

47 'Un discours contraint', in R. Barthes *et al.*, *Littérature et réalité*, p. 129; article originally published in *Poétique*, 1973.

48 *Ibid.*, p. 132.

49 'Par où commencer?', *Poétique*, I (1970), p. 4.

50 *Réalité et mythe chez Zola*, p. 782. Cf. p. 783: 'Le roman dira ce que la littérature ne doit pas dire … le récit tend à montrer toujours davantage ce qu'il est scandaleux de montrer, les jambes écartées, la chair nue, les poils, le sperme.'

51 *La Crise littéraire à l'époque du naturalisme*, p. 98. See also René-Pierre Colin, *Zola. Renégats et alliés. La République naturaliste*, part I: 'Les conditions de la création'.
52 *Le Naturalisme français*, p. 184.
53 *Le Naturalisme*, p. 131.
54 For Zola's reservations on this 'naturalist novel', see *Corr. III*, p. 276. Charles Bigot took this novel as an example of the way in which Zola's disciples used and abused his methods and themes; see 'L'esthétique naturaliste', *Revue des deux Mondes*, XXXV (1879), 421.
55 'La stratégie de la forme', p. 260.
56 See below, in the conclusion of this book.
57 Paris, Albert Savine, 1890, pp. 34–5.
58 Published in *Génie et métier* (Paris, Armand Colin, 1894), pp. 291–328.

8 Naturalist description

1 See Sara Via, 'Description et anti-description chez Paul Alexis', in *La Description* (Textes réunis par Philippe Bonnefis et Pierre Reboul), p. 153.
2 *Anatomy of Criticism*, pp. 79–80.
3 *Génie et métier*, p. 296.
4 *Introduction à l'analyse du descriptif*, p. 28.
5 *Ibid.*, p. 100.
6 See Michèle Hirsch, '*Madame Bovary*, "l'éternel imparfait" et la description', in *La Description*, pp. 45–9.
7 *Le Roman naturaliste*, p. 134.
8 'Narrate or describe?', in *Writer and Critic*, ed. Arthur Kahn, pp. 113, 127, 133, 144, 147.
9 *Figures II*, p. 57.
10 'Description and event in narrative', *Orbis Litterarum*, XXXVII (1982), 202.
11 *Introduction à l'analyse du descriptif*, p. 5.
12 Hamon (*ibid.*, p. 83) gives a number of examples, like Edmond de Goncourt's preface to *Renée Mauperin* on the secondary importance of 'affabulation', or Zola's declaration (on *Nana*) that 'le drame est secondaire'.
13 *Le Naturalisme français*, p. 24.
14 *Writer and Critic*, pp. 132–4.
15 Genette, *Figures II*, pp. 58, 59.
16 *Introduction à l'analyse du descriptif*, p. 6.
17 *Littérature et réalité*, p. 89.
18 *Introduction à l'analyse du descriptif*, pp. 51–2.
19 *Emile Zola: carnets d'enquêtes*, p. 14.
20 *Ibid.*, p. 16.
21 *Introduction à l'analyse du descriptif*, p. 62.
22 *L'Innommable*, p. 20.

23 *The Order of Mimesis*, p. 6.
24 See J. Habermas, 'Technology and science as "ideology"' (1968), in *Toward a Rational Society* (Boston, Beacon Press, 1970), pp. 82, 85.
25 'Le réalisme et la peur du désir', in *Littérature et réalité*, pp. 59–60.
26 *Literary Reviews and Essays on American, English and French Literature*, ed. A. Mordell (New York, Twayne, 1957), pp. 158–9.
27 *Introduction à l'analyse du descriptif*, p. 49. Cf. p. 180.
28 *La Dévouée* (Paris, Charpentier, 1878), pp. 19, 24, 25.
29 *Le Besoin d'aimer* (Paris, Charpentier, 1885), pp. 295–6.
30 *La Relève du réel*, p. 16.
31 *Ibid.*, p. 16.
32 *L'Innommable*, p. 13.
33 *The Social History of Art, II* (London, 1952), p. 871.
34 *Guy de Maupassant et l'art du roman*, pp. 375–7.
35 *Journal*, August 1865, September 1866, 25 February 1866, 10 October 1865.
36 *Ibid.*, 21 June 1870.
37 In Zola's naturalism, Lukács complained, 'representation declines into genre' and 'the description of things no longer has anything to do with the lives of characters' (*Writer and Critic*, pp. 130, 132).
38 *Marthe*, in *Œuvres complètes de J.-K. Huysmans, II* (Paris, Crès, 1928), p. 113.
39 *Les Sœurs Vatard*, in *Œuvres complètes de J.-K. Huysmans, III* (Paris, Crès, 1928), p. 39.
40 Paris, PUF, 1957, p. 136.
41 *Le Groupe de Médan*, p. 16.
42 *McTeague. A Story of San Francisco* (New York, The New American Library, 1964), p. 259.
43 In the final chapter: 'La neige est venue, une neige qui n'est pas de la vraie neige, blanche et ferme et sèche, mais une neige qui est presque de la pluie, une neige qui sitôt touché terre n'est plus bientôt que flaques d'eau boueuse où se délaye une pâte grise' (p. 317).
44 *Introduction à l'analyse du descriptif*, p. 63.
45 Jean Ricardou, *Problèmes du nouveau roman* (Paris, Seuil, 1967), p. 109.
46 *Germinie Lacerteux*, p. 3.
47 Paris, Charpentier, 1879.
48 Lucien Descaves, *Le Calvaire d'Héloïse Pajadou* (Brussels, Kistemaeckers, 1883), p. 111.
49 Somerset Maugham, *Liza of Lambeth* [1897] (Penguin Books, 1967), pp. 115, 125.
50 *Principes d'une esthétique de la mort* (Paris, José Corti, 1967), p. 337.
51 See *Literary Theory*, p. 187.

9 The entropic vision

1 Viviane Alleton, Claude Bremond, Thomas Pavel, 'Vers une thématique', *Poétique*, 64 (1985), 395.

2 See Danièle Rachelle-Latin, 'La critique thématique', *Revue des Langues vivantes*, XLI (1975), 261–81.

3 See Michel Potet, 'Place de la thématologie', *Poétique*, 35 (1978), 374–84.

4 'Qu'est-ce qu'un thème?', *Poétique*, 64 (1985), 405.

5 For some useful definitions, see Gerald Prince, 'Thématiser', *Poétique*, 64 (1985), 425–433, as well as other articles in the same issue of *Poétique*, a special number entitled 'Du thème en littérature'.

6 See Shlomith Rimmon-Kenan (*ibid.*, 402), on the three stages of the operation: 'l'assemblage, la généralisation, l'étiquetage'.

7 *Ibid.*, p. 416 (in the article 'Concept et thème').

8 'Place de la thématologie', p. 384.

9 *Le Naturalisme*, p. 98.

10 *Ibid.*, pp. 99, 100.

11 'Thématique du naturalisme', in *Le Romantisme III: 1869–1896* (Paris, Arthaud, 1968), pp. 127–33.

12 In an even earlier study 'Discussions sur le naturalisme français', in *Studies in Philology*, XXXIX (1942), 696–726, Helmut A. Hatzfeld goes to the other extreme, defining the key naturalist themes as birth, marriage and death (p. 701), a thematic field which, though obviously coherent, lacks appropriate specificity.

13 'L'esthétique naturaliste', 420.

14 *Le Figaro*, 28 February 1881; see *Une Campagne* (XIV, 531–7).

15 See 'L'adultère', *Le Gaulois*, 23 January 1882.

16 From the Unpublished Notebook, 21: February 1886 – May 1887, p. 32; quoted in Sidney J. Krause, *Mark Twain as Critic* (The Johns Hopkins University Press, 1967), p. 282.

17 'La fascination de l'adultère', in *L'Amour et la sexualité*, ed. Georges Duby (Paris, Seuil, [1985?]), pp. 33, 35.

18 *Le Roman naturaliste*, pp. 287–8.

19 *Adultery in the Novel*, pp. 15, 17.

20 'Genèse et généalogie (Le cas du *Docteur Pascal*)', *Romantisme*, XI (1981), 188. See also Naomi Schor, *Zola's Crowds* (The Johns Hopkins University Press, 1978), chapter 1: 'The founding myth'.

21 Brian Nelson, *Zola and the Bourgeoisie*, pp. 96–7.

22 See *L'Opéra des 'Rougon-Macquart'* (Paris, Klincksieck, 1983).

23 *Ibid.*, p. 137.

24 In his article 'Un thème des romanciers naturalistes: La Matrone d'Ephèse', *Comparative Literature*, III (1951), 129–51, Hainsworth lists *L'Education sentimentale*, *Bel-Ami*, 'Les tombales' of Maupassant, 'La petite paroisse' by Daudet, 'Après la bataille' of Alexis, *L'Immortel* of Daudet, 'La sentinelle' by Hugues Le Roux, to which 'Nuit à trois', also by Alexis (in *L'Education amoureuse*), should be added.

25 *The Dialogic Imagination*, pp. 222–3.

26 *Mythologies de l'hérédité au XIXe siècle*, p. 147.

27 *Ibid.*, p. 143.

28 *Syphilis. Essai sur la littérature française du XIXe siècle*, p. 156.

29 *Ibid.*, p. 52.

30 *Edmond de Goncourt et Henry Céard: Correspondance inédite (1876–1896)*, ed. Colin Burns (Paris, Nizet, 1965), p. 31.

31 Arnold Bennett, *Clayhanger* [1910] (Penguin Books, 1954), p. 403.

32 Nelson, *Zola and the Bourgeoisie*, p. 86; Barthes, 'La mangeuse d'hommes', *Guilde du Livre*, XX (1955), 227.

33 Paris, Gallimard, 1980, p. 11.

34 Penguin edition, 1981, p. 73.

35 *McTeague*, pp. 27, 29.

36 Garden City, New York, Doubleday, Doran edition, 1928, pp. 24, 181, 213–14, 242–3.

37 *Histoire du naturalisme français, II*, pp. 106–7.

38 *Œuvres complètes de Guy de Maupassant. L'Inutile Beauté* (Paris, Conard, 1947), pp. 25–6.

39 '*En rade*, ou le roman des énergies bloquées', in *Le Naturalisme. Colloque de Cerisy*, pp. 268–70.

40 See, for example, Charles Child Walcutt, 'From scientific theory to aesthetic fact: the "naturalistic" novel', *Quarterly Review of Literature*, III (1946), 176–7.

41 See Yves Chevrel, *Le Naturalisme*, p. 35, and the anonymous review of Maupassant's *Bel-Ami*, the novel of an indomitable 'struggle-for-lifer' by an avowed disciple of Darwin and Herbert Spencer, 'Darwinisme littéraire', *Le Télégraphe*, 14 May 1885, a review that in all probability was written by Céard − it is listed by Frazee in his book on the same author − and criticises Maupassant for his intemperate and one-sided application of Darwinian ideas.

42 *Darwin, Marx, Wagner. Critique of a Heritage* (Garden City, New York, Doubleday, 1958 [1941]), p. 126.

43 *The Political Unconscious. Narrative as a Socially Symbolic Act* (Cornell University Press, 1981), p. 118.

44 *Le Naturalisme*, p. 107.

45 In *Le Naturalisme. Colloque de Cerisy*, pp. 114–6.

46 '*La Curée' de Zola, ou 'la vie à outrance'. Actes du colloque du 10 janvier 1987* (Paris, SEDES, 1987), p. 36.

47 *L'Innommable*, pp. 12–13.

48 *Une Belle Journée*, pp. 187, 201–4 [my emphasis].

49 *Ibid.*, pp. 230, 250.

50 The poem is published and introduced by Colin A. Burns in 'Documents naturalistes. Notes sur Gabriel Thyébaut et Henry Céard', 66–7.

51 'Plot and the analogy with science in later nineteenth-century novelists', pp. 131, 135–6.

52 *La Relève du réel*, p. 22.
53 *Feux et signaux de brume. Zola*, p. 78. Serres points out, quite naturally, that in Zola's works – and I would add, in those works in which he withdraws from or goes beyond the naturalist vision – there is the opposite movement: 'le flot de vie, le courant générique, la confiance aveugle en ce que nous nommons désormais les forces de néguentropie, le vivant, le discours, l'arbre et la science, le sperme et la lettre' (*ibid.*). For an interesting discussion of these issues, see Geoff Woollen, 'Zola's thermodynamic vitalism', *Romance Studies*, 6 (1985), 48–62.
54 See Gilbert Durand, *Les Structures anthropologiques de l'imaginaire* (Paris, Bordas, 1969).
55 *Etudes sur le temps humain* (Paris, Plon, 1949), pp. XLI–XLII.
56 *Charles Demailly* (Paris, Charpentier, 1880), pp. 389, 406. The novel was originally published in 1860 under the title *Les Hommes de Lettres*.

10 Conclusion

1 *The Order of Mimesis*, p. 45.
2 *Kinds of Literature*, p. 22.
3 *A Theory of Parody*, p. 94.
4 *Literary Theory*, p. 103.
5 '*Stigma indelebile*: *Gide's parodies of Zola* and the displacement of realism', *MLN*, [*Modern Language Notes*], CI September 1986, 858.
6 See *ibid.*, pp. 860–1.
7 From 'Mr. George Moore' (1901), in *The Author's Craft*, ed. Samuel Hynes, p. 148.
8 London, Walter Scott, 1893 edition, p. 6. Subsequent references to this edition will appear in parentheses in the text.
9 'George Moore's *A Mummer's Wife* and Zola', *Revue de Littérature comparée*, XXXI (1957), 85.
10 See *ibid.*, 86. As Chaikin notes, Moore was considering translating *Thérèse Raquin* at about the time he was writing this novel.
11 'Flaubert, Miss Braddon, and George Moore', *Comparative Literature*, XII (1960), 151–8.
12 *Interpretation and Genre*, p. 103.
13 *Ibid.*, pp. 104–5.
14 *The Fiction of John Fowles. Tradition, Art and the Loneliness of Selfhood* (University of Missouri Press, 1974), p. 65.
15 In 1867 the first volume of *Das Kapital* appeared, John Stuart Mill introduced a motion before parliament on women's rights and Hardy fell in love with Tryphena. See the New American Library edition of the novel, 1970, pp. 16, 95 and 215. Subsequent references to this edition will be included in the text.

TRANSLATIONS OF PASSAGES
IN FRENCH

In the following pages I either present translations (usually my own) for the longer and more important passages of French cited in the text or I provide references to certain standard translations of naturalist works.

p. 17 Céard: 'One day Zola wished to see the place where we used to meet: he accepted a dinner invitation and the dinner was so bad that, put to shame, we decided to offer him a better meal somewhere else where he would be able to eat decently. Then Maupassant suggested that Flaubert be brought along; when that had been decided, we thought of Goncourt; and we eliminated Daudet without any discussion. He was not considered to be a master. Then Charpentier was invited, with the ulterior motive in mind that this courtesy would induce him to publish future novels. We had a table at the Trapp restaurant near to St Lazare station and, due to Alexis's indiscretion, this quiet dinner was announced and commented upon in *La République des Lettres*. Even the Hugo clan took notice, taking offence somewhat, the regulars being worried by what they considered to be an affirmation of a new school hostile to Romanticism, whilst Daudet, humiliated by his exclusion, said in the presence of Mme Charpentier with tears in his eyes: "It's Zola's salon that did it."'

pp. 18–19 Goncourt: 'Flaubert attacks, – nonetheless with compliments paid to his genius, – attacks the naturalist prefaces, doctrines, professions of faith, indeed this whole slightly Mangin farce with which Zola helps his books to succeed. Zola replies somewhat like this: "You've had some money behind you to rely upon and to allow you to steer clear of many things. As for me, I've had to earn my living by my pen and I've had to resort to all kinds of shameful forms of writing, to journalism. I've retained, how shall I put it, a certain *banquisme* ... Yes, it's true that I don't care a damn any more than you do for the word *Naturalisme*; and yet I shall go on repeating it because things have to have a name so that the general public thinks they are new".'

p. 23 Preface to *Les Soirées de Médan*: 'Some of the stories that follow have been published in France, others abroad. They seemed to us to proceed from a single idea, to have the same philosophy: so we have collected them together.

We expect all the attacks, the bad faith and the ignorance of which to-day's critics have already given us such ample proof. Our only concern has been publicly to affirm our true friendships and, at the same time, our literary tendencies.'

p. 55 Zola, 'Le roman expérimental': 'I really only need to adapt, for the experimental method has been established with strength and marvellous clearness by Claude Bernard in his "Introduction à l'Etude de la Médecine Expérimentale." This work, by a savant whose authority is unquestioned, will serve me as a solid foundation. I shall here find the whole question treated, and I shall restrict myself to irrefutable arguments and to giving the quotations which may seem necessary to me. This will then be but a compiling of texts, as I intend on all points to entrench myself behind Claude Bernard. It will often be but necessary for me to replace the word "doctor" by the word "novelist" to make my meaning clear and to give it the rigidity of a scientific truth' (Trans. Belle M. Sherman, 1893).

p. 55 *Ibid.*: 'I am going to try to prove for my part that if the experimental method leads to the knowledge of physical life, it should also lead to the knowledge of the passionate and intellectual life. It is but a question of degree in the same path which runs from chemistry to physiology, then from physiology to anthropology and to sociology. The experimental novel is the goal' (Trans. Sherman).

pp. 56–7 *Ibid.*: 'Now, to return to the novel, we can easily see that the novelist is equally an observer and an experimentalist. The observer in him gives the facts as he has observed them, suggests the point of departure, displays the solid earth on which his characters are to tread and the phenomena to develop. Then the experimentalist appears and introduces an experiment, that is to say, sets his characters going in a certain story so as to show that the succession of facts will be such as the requirements of the determinism of the phenomena under examination call for. Here it is nearly always an experiment "*pour voir*" as Claude Bernard calls it. The novelist starts out in search of a truth' (Trans. Sherman).

p. 57 *Ibid.*: 'In fact, the whole operation consists in taking facts in nature, then in studying the mechanism of these facts, acting upon them, by the modification of circumstances and surroundings, without deviating from the laws of nature. Finally, you possess knowledge of the man, scientific knowledge of him, in both his individual and social relations' (Trans. Sherman).

pp. 74–5 Delfau: 'Now, it is curious that the experts have never thought to emphasise what the appearance together of these three works contributes by way of innovation to the history of the novel. Essentially, there are contained within them the thematics, the sensibility and the philosophy of what is yet to be called Naturalism; two themes, that will be constantly exploited: adultery and "the bad worker" with its many associated meanings: prostitution, alcoholism and revolution; a social milieu that is characteristic of the new school: the lower middle class, willingly provincial and still in contact with the working class – in short, in the ambiguous terminology of the time, the People; characters trying to rise up out of it: individuals detached from their familiar world, like Germinie Lacerteux, a prime example, since her job as a servant places her firmly in the camp of the exploited yet makes her part of the lower middle class that frequents Madame Jupillon's shop; finally, at a deeper level, at the level of the narrative: daily life lived in the shadow of failure, a failure that is often attributed to physiological disorders in conflict with social norms. That is what the three novels have in common.'

pp. 77–8 *Germinie Lacerteux*, preface: Trans. Leonard Tancock, Penguin Books, 1984, pp. 15–16.

p. 79 *Germinie Lacerteux*, 'Quand la flamme ...': Trans. Tancock, p. 136.

pp. 85–6 *Thérèse Raquin*, preface: Trans. Leonard Tancock, Penguin Books, 1962, pp. 22–3.

p. 86 *Thérèse Raquin*, 'La nature sèche et nerveuse ...': Trans. Tancock, p. 170.

p. 91 *Ibid.*, 'Une crise suprême les brisa ...': Trans. Tancock, p. 256.

p. 99 Genette: 'In fact, of course, there are here two distinct realities: one that is both modal and thematic, which the first few pages of the *Poetics* present and which is the noble or serious drama set in opposition to the noble narrative (the epic) and the low or gay forms of drama (comedy); this generic reality, which encompasses *The Persians* as well as *Oedipus the King*, is then traditionally called *tragedy*, and Aristotle clearly does not consider questioning the name. The other is purely thematic and belongs to a more anthropological than poetical order: it is the *tragic*, that is to say the sense of the irony of destiny or of the cruelty of the gods.'

p. 102 *Charlot s'amuse*, 'Charlot avait heureusement ...': 'Fortunately Charlot had some money, ordered a couple of beers and then the wretched creature told him her story. A banal, vulgar story, but one which was interesting like a novel to the poor fellow for whom Paris and its unfathomable mysteries were still unknown. Her name was Fanny Méjean and she was the daughter of honest folk. Her father was a stoker at the Lebaudy refinery in la Villette, her mother a mattress maker in the same district. She had been seduced when she was sixteen. In fact, she did not blame her first lover too much. She had more or less given herself to him. She loved the man. It was in her blood and the thrashings that her father had given her had not cured her of her passion. She had run away from her father's house and moved around a lot, falling into one liaison after another until she lapsed into the complete destitution that gradually landed her in the mire. Yet it was not entirely her fault. If her first lover had been honest, she would still have been with him, but he had taken a delight in depraving her and, when he had joined the vice-squad, he had registered her to live off her earnings without a second thought.

She told him all this calmly, in drawling tones, with crude words and cynical details as if she was not aware of the horror of what she was saying.'

p. 108 Gaillard: 'Zola's silence, like the scientists' too, on the original cause of the flaw/punishment, assimilates it to one of those mighty curses that strike down whole families in the legends of antiquity. In these stories there is always a guilty individual through whom evil declares itself and spreads, just as there is always in the natural history of heredity an accursed being through whom and because of whom that difference, with its concrete effects observed by the geneticists, invades the very core of the species which, theoretically, is undifferentiated and made up of a utopic fraternity of equals ...

Associated with the biblical idea of *Original Sin*, heredity emerges as an expiatory figure. Far from being absurdly iniquitous, it is the manifestation of a form of immanent justice. In point of fact, heredity is the new Goddess of Retribution, the positivist version of the Euminedes.'

p. 113 *Charlot s'amuse*, 'Elle était un exemple ...': 'She was an example of the morbid disorders transmitted by heredity, her father having died of *delirium tremens* and her mother, who was epileptic, having drowned herself in the poorhouse. Hers was a very curious case. When, after the crisis of menopause, she had decided to speak, her life story could be reconstructed. At eighteen she had been a nymphomaniac and had never been cured. As she got older, she became alcoholic and hysteria had replaced the nymphomania before leading in turn to a remarkable state of paraplegia after the menopause.'

p. 117 *L'Assommoir*, 'Une fois surtout ...': Trans. Leonard Tancock, Penguin Books, 1970, pp. 395–6.

pp. 123–4 Vial: 'Around 1880 there emerges thus a kind of Jansenism of Art; a dream haunts creative minds, the dream of an arid, ascetic perfection: the idea of a novel in which nothing would happen, in which nothing would take place, the dream of a blank work to which the name "novel" would even no longer apply, a work which would not fall into any of the traditional categories, which would subject itself to innumerable limiting constraints without refraining from deriving its material from reality and which, in length, volume and quality, would confine the substance that sustains it in the narrowest of fashions. It was as if writers were trying to outdo one another in concentrating on the most banal, the most annoying, the most sterile snippet of truth to extract from it a meaning that only a few initiates could understand. The novel – failing some other term that, even according to E. de Goncourt, has yet to be invented – aspires to be the complete opposite of the rhetorical, the epic, the tragic, the lyrical.'

p. 133 *A vau-l'eau*, 'M. Folantin descendit ...': 'Mr Folantin left this girl's place profoundly disgusted and, as he walked home, surveyed the desolate horizon of life; he perceived the uselessness of changes in direction, the sterility of impulses and efforts; one should just drift downstream; Schopenhauer is right, he said to himself, "man's life swings back and forth like a pendulum between anguish and boredom".'

pp. 137–8 *Une Belle Journée*, 'Pendant qu'elle coiffait …': 'As she was putting on her hair-net for the night and her blond hair settled neatly inside the large white meshes, philosophical thoughts arose obscurely in her mind. She understood that the miseries of the heart are not due to the constant anguish that invades it, but to the effort that it makes to escape its condition. The ideal to which it aspires as a deliverance revealed itself to be even more devastating than the vulgar compromises that it sought to elude, and then there were also the dangers, the fears, the broken habits, and also, and invariably, the more painful reversions when aspirations have not been fulfilled. She saw into the depths of stupidity which manifest themselves in the continual rebellions against this universal law of mediocrity which, like the unremitting force of gravitation and the unyielding power of gravity, bends the world to its will and submits it to its ordinances: she saw the necessity of remaining in one's little corner and of trying to make oneself as small as one can to reduce the risks of disturbing adventures and to prevent as much as possible stirring up the disconcerting consequences of the workings of fate.'

pp. 138–9 *Ibid.*, 'Ainsi de quelque côté …': 'And so, whichever way she turned, marriage or adultery opened up before her the same vistas of stupidity, and adultery, in addition, had the inconvenience of compromising one's reputation and bringing discredit upon oneself. Henceforth, her mind was made up. Like a despondent patient who gives up turning over in bed because any new position only brings him a new pain, she resigned herself to her fate. Banality for banality, she preferred the legal kind of platitudinous existence; tedium for tedium, she was more inclined to accept the one which did not prevent her from being respected and which would not sharpen the tongues of the neighbourhood gossips against her.'

p. 144 *Une Vie*, 'D'une inflexible sévérité …': 'Being inflexibly strict with himself, he was implacably intolerant with others. One thing especially provoked his anger and indignation, love. In his sermons he would speak animatedly about it in crude terms, in the customary ecclesiastical manner, casting before this audience of peasants thundering periods denouncing concupiscence; and he would tremble with rage, stamp his feet, his mind haunted by the visions that his outbursts would conjure up.'

p. 157 Maupassant, 'C'est toujours la jeune fille …': 'There is always a poor young girl marrying a rich young engineer with a rosy future; cousins who fall in love and marry, or a bankrupt young man who chooses a rich heiress, and it all takes place with surprises, unexpected inheritances to balance up situations, and dramatically touching adventures in the park of an old Breton castle. Without fail, there is the tower scene, the hunting scene, the duel scene and the grandmother scene … From this 'syrupy' literature for *ladies* there is just one step down to the treacly literature for middle class women;

and from this treacly stuff you just sink down to (if you will pardon the expression) the 'gut-rot' literature for washerwomen.'

p. 177 *Madame Meuriot*, 'Comme une chienne en folie, ...': 'Take up with the first man to come along, like a bitch in heat. Take the virginity of some innocent boy one mild evening in May; an hour later, galvanise an octogenarian into action! Then be beaten and raped by a ruffian, pay a pimp, extract gold from a millionaire, live for a day in a brothel! Even spend an hour alone with a condemned man on the morning of his execution! Having embarked upon this series of aberrations she did not stop, and went so far as to dream of couplings with men of every race, of every extraction; even with monkeys and other animals; with two men at once. And to try out her own sex? "Yes, know a woman ... Why not? ... Who knows? ..."'

pp. 184–5 Zola, 'Nous ne décrivons plus ...': 'We no longer describe for the sake of describing, out of a whim or for the pleasure of indulging in rhetoric. We consider that man cannot be separated from his environment, that his clothes, his home, his town, his province are all parts of his make-up; and so, we do not note down a single feature of his brain or of his heart without finding its causes or its repercussions in the environment. Hence what are called our endless descriptions.'

p. 185 Hamon, 'Le descriptif semble n'être ...': 'The descriptive seems to be no more than a kind of universal foil, a kind of general and convenient zero point serving to delimit more "marked" categories and theoretical areas more worthy of interest: sometimes, in fact, the descriptive is contrasted with the narrative mode, with the story; at other times it is contrasted with 'actions' or with the 'psychology' of characters, in contrast with objects or landscapes; at times it is a (subordinate) part of the narrative; at others (Valéry) it is contrasted with the poetic utterance; at others the descriptive is contrasted with the performative (Searle, Austin), the 'literal' (N. Frye), or the prescriptive and the normative; sometimes it is contrasted with the explicative.'

p. 192 *La Dévouée*, 'Maintenant, les regards ...': 'Now looks turned to the gates of the dreary city, to Passy, to Auteuil. In the background of the picture, the hills of Montmartre were sketched in almost pink tints in a late ray of light. In front of them, the dome of Les Invalides looked like a piece of a dying star, and the frieze of the triumphal arch, which could just be seen above the bluish swell of the roofs, was like a luxury skiff ready to sink.

Exactly opposite the plateau where Aristide was ambling about, ... the Seine appeared, glistening like a frozen lake, and behind the Seine, Paris, with its piles of houses and monuments drowned in the nascent darkness, studded with stars that hidden hands were lighting up; finally, hanging heavily over the colossus, whose hustle and bustle was dying down, a cloudless sky of a dense and faded whiteness.'

p. 196 *Charlot s'amuse*, 'Le soleil se couchait ...': 'The sun was setting. Above la Villette, the sky seemed to be bleeding and the canal, as it disappeared into the distance between the quays that were already almost indistinguishable in the shadow of the houses, was like a flow of molten gold in the midst of which barges and lighters quivered like black debris tossed about by the rolling waters. By contrast, to the right, the sky was fading away into gentle, vaporous lilac hues and, against this light backcloth, loomed tall factory chimney stacks, neat and erect, like pink grass snakes aimed at the clouds ...

And in this deluge of purple and indigo tones, in this orgy of pollen cascading down over Paris, it was as if, from the top of the bridge, a monstrous, invisible paint-brush, dipped in a dozen or more pots, were scattering everywhere a profusion of colours whose dazzling droplets riddled the city with magnificent blotches, agitating the surrounding space, like a schoolboy dauber making a streaming mess of his watercolour.'

p. 198 *Marthe*, 'La Seine charriait ...': 'That evening, the river Seine was heaving along its lead-coloured waters streaked here and there with reflections from the street lamps. To the right, in a coal-laden boat moored to an iron capstan the size of a brain, vague shadows of men and women moved about; to the left, the platform of the bridge stood out, bearing the statue of the King. The flimsy outline of a tattered tree, planted down below near the concert, could be seen against the slate-grey sky. Finally, further away, the Pont des Arts, with its crown of gas lamps, was vanishing into the mist and the shadow of its pillars was fading away into the river in a long black blot. A river boat slid under the arch of the bridge, sending out a warm gush of steam in Marthe's face, leaving in its wake a long trail of white foam which gradually disappeared into the sooty waters. A fine drizzle began to fall.'

p. 201 *Les Frères Zemganno*, 'De ce ciel défaillant ...': 'Imperceptibly, in the fading light from the sky, that greyish veil descended, bringing, in what remained of the day, uncertainty to the appearance of things, rendering them indeterminate and vague, drowning the shapes and contours of nature lapsing into sleep, disappearing into the twilight: those sad and gentle and indiscernible last agonies of the life of the light.'

'C'était un jour ...': 'It was a day at the end of October, during which it had rained from morning until night and at the end of which you could not really tell if it was still raining; one of those autumn days in Paris when her sky, her ground, her walls seem to dissolve, one of those days when, at night, the glimmerings of the gas lights on the pavements are like flames burning across the surface of rivers.'

p. 201 *Le Calvaire d'Héloïse Pajadou*, 'Héloïse perdit pied ...': 'Héloïse lost her footing and fell on her knees. Suddenly she felt a great chill and a light rain as gentle as a fog froze her to the marrow. All around was silence, the countryside beyond the Bièvre was sad and bare, blocked by a line of thin trees, with tufts on top that made them look like long feather-dusters growing out of the earth up to the vast ceiling of heavy, black clouds. The howling of a dog started up in the distance. It was a deep moaning, a long drawn-out sob like a suffering child's lament. Héloïse listened, her head bent low ... But she began to tremble and became vaguely aware that her feet were soaked in a puddle. A chill entered her body, ran over her skin, from her neck right down to her heels.'

p. 208 *La Bête humaine*, 'Puisqu'il ne les connaissait pas ...': Trans. Leonard Tancock, Penguin Books, 1977, p. 67.

p. 209 Gaillard, 'Les crimes ...': 'The crimes that are engraved in the now dulled mind of Tante Dide are but the consequence and the repetition of an earlier crime that is never really named or, at most, that is vaguely described as being the adultery of which she was once guilty, in the almost legendary era of the birth of the Rougon-Macquart family ... All the crimes that spatter the cursed family with blood are but the repetition of this primeval event that has remained imprinted in the collective memory.'

p. 221 Huyghe, 'Progressivement, ...': 'Science, which until then purposely confined itself to the measurable, the positive domain of the senses and to the logical, the rational domain of the mind, will progressively turn again to the disturbing and imponderable realities of life, those which in principle were reserved for the suggestive and intuitive arms of 'literary' thought. It will abandon its two major props: the dense, decomposable, divisible reality of "matter" and the fixed, code-like immutability of reason.'

p. 222 Serres, 'Il faut faire gloire à Zola ...': 'Zola, the engineer's son, must be given credit for having seen things clearly. Or for having written and produced his work as if he saw things clearly. There is no better picture than the Rougon-Macquart of destruction, waste, dispersion, loss, irreversible ebbing away towards death and disorder; decay, exhaustion, degeneration. The message is clear: it is all burning too fast. An epic of entropy ... Contrary to what the uninformed say, naturalism is exactly in tune with the science of its time and ahead of the philosophy.'

p. 223 *Charles Demailly*, 'Et il vécut ...': 'And he lived. He lives as if he had been destined to take on even to the most horrible limits the atonements and humiliations of human thought. He lives in order to be, in the hands of life, no more than the terrible example of the extreme forms of our wretchedness and of the nothingness of our pride ... Everything in human language, down to the names that we give to the necessities of life, everything has left his memory. No more past, no more memory, no more time, no more ideas! There is nothing left of him surviving death except a mass of flesh from which emerge little cries, grimaces, tears, laughter, inarticulate syllables, the chance manifestations of idiocy expressing themselves without any particular motive! There is nothing human left but this body, which only belongs to humanity through the process of digestion! this body tied to a chair, babbling away in monosyllables like a little baby, immobile except for the constant raising and lowering of his shoulders, uttering into the air at the sight of the sun this animal cry: *coc ... coc*, opening his mouth to the food that is brought and rubbing against the man who gives him his food with the gratitude and caresses of an animal.'

SELECT BIBLIOGRAPHY

Primary sources

Adam, Paul, *Chair molle. Roman naturaliste*, Brussels, Auguste Brancart, 1885.

Alexis, Paul, *La Fin de Lucie Pellegrin*, Paris, Charpentier, 1880 [Geneva, Slatkine, 1979, with an introduction by Jean de Palacio].

Le Besoin d'aimer, Paris, Charpentier, 1885.

L'Education amoureuse, Paris, Charpentier, 1890.

Madame Meuriot. Mœurs parisiennes, Paris, Charpentier, 1891.

Trente romans, Paris, Charpentier, 1895.

Bennett, Arnold, *The Old Wives' Tale* [1908], London, Dent, 1982.

Clayhanger [1910], Penguin Books, 1954.

Bonnetain, Paul, *Charlot s'amuse*, Brussels, Kistemaeckers, 1883 [Geneva, Slatkine, 1979, with a preface by Céard and an introduction by Hubert Juin].

Autour de la caserne, Paris, Victor Havard, 1885.

Céard, Henry, *Une Belle Journée*, Paris, Charpentier, 1881 [Geneva, Slatkine, 1980, with a preface by C. A. Burns].

'Mal Eclos', *Revue littéraire et artistique*, IV (August–September 1881), 354–65, 392–402, 417–28 [in *Visages du naturalisme*, ed. C. A. Burns, London, Ontario, Mestengo Press (French Dept., University of Western Ontario), 1989].

Claretie, Jules, *Les Amours d'un interne*, Paris, Dentu, 1881.

Crane, Stephen, *Maggie: A Girl of the Streets (A Story of New York)* [1893], ed. Thomas A. Gullason, New York, Norton, 1979.

Descaves, Lucien, *Le Calvaire d'Héloïse Pajadou*, Brussels, Kistemaeckers, 1883.

Une Vieille Rate, Brussels, Kistemaeckers, 1883.

La Caserne. Misères du sabre, Paris, Tresse and Stock, 1887.

Sous-Offs. Roman militaire, Paris, Stock, 1889 [Geneva, Slatkine, 1980, with an introduction by Henri Mitterand].

Dreiser, Theodore, *Sister Carrie* [1900], Penguin Books, 1981.

Fèvre-Desprez, Louis [Louis Desprez and Henry Fèvre], *Autour d'un clocher*, Brussels, Kistemaeckers, 1884 [Geneva, Slatkine, 1980, with an introduction by Henri Mitterand].

Flaubert, Gustave, *L'Education sentimentale* [1869], Paris, Conard, 1923.
 Œuvres complètes, tome XVI. Correspondance 1877–1880, Paris, Club de l'Honnête Homme, 1975.
Fowles, John, *The French Lieutenant's Woman* [1969], New York, The New American Library, 1970.
Gandillot, Léon, *Entre Conjoints!*, Brussels, Kistemaeckers, 1888.
Goncourt, Edmond de, *La Fille Elisa* [1877], Paris, Charpentier, 1911.
 Les Frères Zemganno, Paris, Charpentier, 1879.
Goncourt, Edmond de and Jules de Goncourt, *Charles Demailly*, Paris, Charpentier, 1880 [1860 under the title *Les Hommes de Lettres*].
 Germinie Lacerteux [1864], Paris, Charpentier, 1911.
 Journal. Mémoires de la vie littéraire, ed. Robert Ricatte, Paris, Fasquelle–Flammarion, 1956, 4 vols.
Hardy, Thomas, *Tess of the d'Urbervilles* [1891], London, Macmillan, 1974.
Hennique, Léon, *La Dévouée*, Paris, Charpentier, 1878.
 L'Accident de Monsieur Hébert [1883], Paris, Charpentier, 1884.
 Les Funérailles de Francine Cloarec, Brussels, Librairie nouvelle/Paris, Librairie universelle, 1887.
Huysmans, J.-K., *Marthe, histoire d'une fille* [1876], ed. Pierre Cogny, Paris, Le Cercle du Livre, 1955.
 Les Sœurs Vatard [1879], in *Œuvres complètes III*, Paris, Crès, 1928.
 En ménage. A vau-l'eau [1881, 1882], Paris, Union Générale d'Editions, 1975.
Lemonnier, Camille, *Un Mâle*, Brussels, Kistemaeckers, 1881.
 L'Hystérique, Paris, Charpentier, 1885.
Maugham, Somerset, *Liza of Lambeth* [1897], London, Penguin Books, 1967.
Maupassant, Guy de, *Une Vie* [1883], ed. Pierre Cogny, Paris, Garnier-Flammarion, 1974.
 'Le Roman', in *Pierre et Jean* [1888], *Œuvres complètes de Guy de Maupassant*, Paris, Conard, 1929, pp. V–XXVI.
Mirbeau, Octave, *Le Journal d'une femme de chambre* [1900], Paris, Fasquelle, 1959.
Moore, George, *A Mummer's Wife* [1885], London, Walter Scott, 1893.
 A Drama in Muslin [1886], Gerrards Cross, Colin Smythe, 1981.
 Esther Waters [1894], London, Dent, 1962.
Norris, Frank, *McTeague. A Story of San Francisco* [1899], New York, The New American Library, 1964.
 Vandover and the Brute [1914], Garden City, New York, Doubleday-Doran, 1928, with an introduction by H. L. Mencken.
Parigot, Hippolyte, 'Dialogue des morts. Naturalistes', in *Génie et métier*, Paris, Armand Colin, 1894, pp. 291–328.
Ringuet, *Trente arpents*, Paris, Flammarion, 1938.
Rosny, J.-H. [aîné], *Nell Horn de l'Armée du Salut. Roman de mœurs londoniennes*, Paris, Giraud, 1886.
 Le Termite. Roman de mœurs littéraires, Paris, Albert Savine, 1890.

Sirven, Alfred, and Henri Leverdier, *La Fille de Nana. Roman de mœurs parisiennes*, Paris, Dentu, 1881.

Strindberg, August, *Miss Julie* [1888], in *Five Plays*, trans. and ed. Harry G. Carlson, New York, Signet, 1984, pp. 50–102.

Thyébaut, Gabriel, 'Le vin en bouteilles', ed. C. A. Burns, in *Les Cahiers naturalistes*, 4 (1956), 165–8.

Vast-Ricouard [Raoul Vast and Georges Ricouard], *Vices parisiens, 2e série. Madame Bécart*, Paris, Derveaux, 1879.

Zola, Emile, *Œuvres complètes*, ed. Henri Mitterand, Paris, Cercle du Livre Précieux, 1966–9, 15 vols.

   Les Rougon-Macquart, ed. Henri Mitterand, Paris, Bibliothèque de la Pléiade, 1960–7, 5 vols.

   Emile Zola: Correspondance, ed. B. H. Bakker *et al.*, Les Presses de l'Université de Montréal/Paris, Editions du CNRS, 1978–.

   Emile Zola: carnets d'enquêtes. Une ethnographie inédite de la France, ed. Henri Mitterand, Paris, Plon, 1986.

Zola, Emile, Guy de Maupassant, J.-K. Huysmans, Henry Céard, Léon Hennique and Paul Alexis, *Les Soirées de Médan* [1880], ed. Colette Becker, Paris, Le Livre à venir, 1981.

Secondary sources

Åhnebrink, Lars, *The Beginnings of Naturalism in American Fiction*, Upsala, A.-B. Lundequistska Bokhandeln/Cambridge, Massachusetts, Harvard University Press, 1950.

Allen, Walter, *Arnold Bennett*, Denver, Alan Swallow, 1949.

   The English Novel. A Short Critical History, Penguin Books, 1978 [1954].

Alleton, Viviane, Claude Bremond and Thomas Pavel, 'Vers une thématique', *Poétique*, 64 (1985), 395–6.

Apter, Emily S., '*Stigma indelebile*: Gide's parodies of Zola and the displacement of realism', *MLN*, CI (1986), 857–70.

Baguley, David, 'Rite et tragédie dans *L'Assommoir*', *Les Cahiers naturalistes*, 52 (1978), 80–96.

   (ed.), *Critical Essays on Emile Zola*, Boston, G. K. Hall, 1986.

Baillot, A., *Influence de la philosophie de Schopenhauer en France (1860–1900)*, Paris, Vrin, 1927.

Bakhtin, Mikhail, *Problems of Dostoevsky's Poetics*, trans. R. W. Rotsel, n.p., Ardis, 1973 [1929].

Bakhtin, M., *The Dialogic Imagination. Four Essays*, ed. Michael Holquist, trans. Caryl Emerson and Michael Holquist, University of Texas Press, 1981.

Bakker, B. H. (ed.), '*Naturalisme pas mort*'. *Lettres inédites de Paul Alexis à Emile Zola 1871–1900*, University of Toronto Press, 1971.

Baldick, Robert, *The Life of J.-K. Huysmans*, Oxford, The Clarendon Press, 1955.

Barthes, Roland, *Sur Racine*, Paris, Seuil, 1963.

Barthes, R., L. Bersani, Ph. Hamon, M. Riffaterre and I. Watt, *Littérature et réalité*, Paris, Seuil, 1982.

Barzun, Jacques, *Darwin, Marx, Wagner. Critique of a Heritage*, Garden City, New York, Doubleday, 1958 [1941].

Becker, Colette, 'L'audience d'Emile Zola', *Les Cahiers naturalistes*, 47 (1974), 40–69.

Becker, George J. (ed.), *Documents of Modern Literary Realism*, Princeton University Press, 1963.

Beer, Gillian, 'Plot and the analogy with science in later nineteenth-century novelists', in Elinor Shaffer (ed.), *Comparative Criticism. A Yearbook, 2*, Cambridge University Press, 1980, pp. 131–49.

Beizer, Janet L., 'Uncovering *Nana*: the courtesan's new clothes', *L'Esprit créateur*, XXV (1985), 45–56.

Beuchat, Charles, *Histoire du naturalisme français*, 2 vols., Paris, Editions Corrêa, 1949.

Bigot, Charles, 'L'esthétique naturaliste', *Revue des deux Mondes*, XXV (1879), 415–32.

Block, Haskell M., *Naturalistic Triptych. The Fictive and the Real in Zola, Mann, and Dreiser*, New York, Random House, 1970.

Bonnefis, Philippe, *L'Innommable. Essai sur l'œuvre d'Emile Zola*, Paris, SEDES, 1984.

Bonnefis, Philippe, and Pierre Reboul (eds.), *La Description*, Presses Universitaires de Lille, 1981.

Bonnetain, Paul, J.-H. Rosny, Lucien Descaves, Paul Margueritte, Gustave Guiches, '*La Terre*. A Emile Zola', *Le Figaro*, 18 August 1887.

Borie, Jean, *Mythologies de l'hérédité au XIXe siècle*, Paris, Galilée, 1981.

Bornecque, J.-H., and P. Cogny, *Réalisme et naturalisme*, Paris, Hachette, 1958.

Bouazis, Ch. (ed.), *Analyse de la périodisation littéraire*, Paris, Editions universitaires, 1972 [articles by Jacques Dubois, pp. 11–22, and Françoise Gaillard, pp. 39–47].

Boyer, Amédée, *La Littérature et les arts contemporains*, Paris, Albert Méricant, 1910.

Bremond, Claude, 'Concept et thème', *Poétique*, 64 (1985), 415–23.

Brinker, Menachem, 'Le "naturel" et le "conventionnel" dans la critique et la théorie', *Littérature*, 57 (1985), 17–30.

Brombert, Victor, *The Novels of Flaubert. A Study of Themes and Techniques*, Princeton University Press, 1966.

Bruck, Jan, 'From Aristotelian mimesis to "bourgeois realism"', *Poetics*, XI (1982), 189–202.

Brunetière, Ferdinand, 'Le roman expérimental', *Revue des deux Mondes*, XXXVII (1880), 935–48.

  Le Roman naturaliste, Paris, Calmann-Lévy, 1897 [1883].

Burns, C. A., 'Henry Céard and his relations with Flaubert and Zola', *French Studies*, VI (1952), 308–24.

'En marge du Naturalisme: Gabriel Thyébaut (1854–1922)', *Studi francesi*, III (1959), 231–42.

'Nouvelles perspectives sur le Naturalisme', *Studi francesi*, IX (1965), 41–61.

'Documents naturalistes. Notes sur Gabriel Thyébaut et Henry Céard', *Studi francesi*, XII (1968), 61–7.

Henry Céard et le naturalisme, Birmingham, John Goodman, 1982.

Cargill, Oscar, 'A confusion of major critical terms', *The Ohio University Review*, IX (1967), 31–8.

Cave, Richard Allen, *A Study of the Novels of George Moore*, Gerrards Cross, Colin Smythe, 1978.

[Céard, Henry], 'Une lettre de M. Henry Céard: Zola et le prêt du livre de Claude Bernard. Pourquoi Henry Céard avait incité Zola à lire Claude Bernard', *L'Information*, 22 July 1918.

Chaikin, M., 'George Moore's *A Mummer's Wife* and Zola', *Revue de Littérature comparée*, XXXI (1957), 85–8.

Charle, Christophe, *La Crise littéraire à l'époque du naturalisme. Roman, théâtre, politique*, Paris, Presses de l'Ecole Normale Supérieure, 1979.

Chevrel, Yves, *Le Naturalisme*, Paris, PUF, 1982.

Chevrel, Yves (ed.), *Le Naturalisme dans les littératures de langues européennes*, Université de Nantes, 1983.

Le Naturalisme en question, Presses de l'Université de Paris-Sorbonne, 1986.

Claverie, Michel, '*Thérèse Raquin*, ou les Atrides dans la boutique du Pont-Neuf', *Les Cahiers naturalistes*, 36 (1968), 138–47.

Cogny, Pierre (ed.), *Le 'Huysmans Intime' de Henry Céard et Jean Caldain*, Paris, Nizet, 1957.

Colburn, William Elliot, *Zola in England, 1883–1903*, University of Illinois thesis, 1952.

Colin, René-Pierre, *Schopenhauer en France: un mythe naturaliste*, Presses Universitaires de Lyon, 1979.

'1885: Zola et l'affaire Desprez', *Les Cahiers naturalistes*, 59 (1985), 144–50.

Zola. Renégats et alliés. La République naturaliste, Presses Universitaires de Lyon, 1988.

Corbin, Alain, 'L'hérédosyphilis ou l'impossible rédemption. Contribution à l'histoire de l'hérédité morbide', *Romantisme*, 31 (1981), 131–49.

Crawford, Emily, 'Emile Zola', *The Contemporary Review*, LV (1889), 94–113.

Culler, Jonathan, *Structuralist Poetics. Structuralism, Linguistics and the Study of Literature*, London, Routledge and Kegan Paul, 1975.

Decker, Clarence R., *The Victorian Conscience*, New York, Twayne, 1952.

Deffoux, Léon, *Le Naturalisme*, Paris, Les Œuvres représentatives, 1929.

Deffoux, Léon, and Emile Zavie, *Le Groupe de Médan*. Nouvelle édition, Paris, Crès, 1924 [1920].

Delfau, Gérard, '1871: la fausse coupure: contribution à l'histoire du naturalisme', in *Recherches en Sciences des Textes*, Presses Universitaires de Grenoble, 1977, pp. 19–53.

Desprez, Louis, *L'Evolution naturaliste*, Paris, Tresse, 1884.

Dezalay, Auguste, 'Les mystères de Zola', *Revue des Sciences humaines*, 160 (1975), 475–87.

L'Opéra des 'Rougon-Macquart', Paris, Klincksieck, 1983.

Digeon, Claude, *La Crise allemande de la pensée française (1870–1914)*, Paris, PUF, 1959.

Dubois, Jacques, *'L'Assommoir' de Zola. Société, discours, idéologie*, Paris, Larousse, 1973.

Dubrow, Heather, *Genre*, The Critical Idiom Series, vol. 42, London, Methuen, 1982.

Eagleton, Terry, *Literary Theory. An Introduction*, University of Minnesota Press/Oxford, Blackwell, 1983.

Ellis, Havelock, 'Zola: the man and his work', *The Savoy*, I (1896), 67–80, and in *Affirmations*, London, Constable, 1898, pp. 131–57.

Erlich, Victor, *Russian Formalism. History – Doctrine*, 2nd ed., The Hague, Mouton, 1965.

Farrell, James T., 'Some observations on naturalism, so called, in fiction', *The Antioch Review*, X (1950), 247–64.

Fayt, René, 'Un éditeur des naturalistes: Henry Kistemaeckers', *Revue de l'Université de Bruxelles*, 4–5 (1984), 217–39.

Ferdas, Dr René, *La Physiologie expérimentale et le 'Roman expérimental'. Claude Bernard et Monsieur Zola*, Paris, Hurtau, 1881.

Ford, Boris (ed.), *New Pelican Guide to English Literature. Vol. 6: From Dickens to Hardy*, Penguin Books, 1982.

Forster, E. M., *Aspects of the Novel*, London, Edward Arnold, 1927.

Fowler, Alastair, *Kinds of Literature. An Introduction to the Theory of Genres and Modes*, Harvard University Press, 1982.

Frazee, Ronald, *Henry Céard, idéaliste détrompé*, University of Toronto Press, 1963.

Frierson, William C., 'The English controversy over realism in fiction', *PMLA*, XLIII (1928), 533–50.

The English Novel in Transition: 1885–1940, The University of Oklahoma Press, 1942/New York, Cooper Square Publishers, 1965.

Frye, Northrop, *Anatomy of Criticism*, Princeton University Press, 1957.

Furst, Lilian R., 'George Moore, Zola, and the question of influence', *Canadian Review of Comparative Literature*, I (1974), 138–55.

Furst, Lilian R., and Peter N. Skrine, *Naturalism*, The Critical Idiom Series, vol. 18, London, Methuen, 1971.

Gaillard, Françoise, '*En rade*, ou le roman des énergies bloquées', in *Le*

Naturalisme. Colloque de Cerisy, Paris, Union Générale d'Editions, 1978, pp. 263–77.

'Genèse et généalogie (Le cas du *Docteur Pascal*)', *Romantisme*, 31 (1981), 181–96.

Gans, Eric, 'Hyperbole et ironie', *Poétique*, 24 (1975), 488–94.

Genette, Gérard, *Figures II*, Paris, Seuil, 1969.

Introduction à l'architexte, Paris, Seuil, 1979.

Palimpsestes. La littérature au second degré, Paris, Seuil, 1982.

Nouveau discours du récit, Paris, Seuil, 1983.

Greaves, A. A., 'Paul Bonnetain: his attitudes to naturalism', *Nottingham French Studies*, V (1966), 80–8.

Guillén, Claudio, *Literature as System. Essays toward the Theory of Literary History*, Princeton University Press, 1971.

Hainsworth, G., 'Un thème des romanciers naturalistes: la Matrone d'Ephèse', *Comparative Literature*, III (1951), 129–51.

Hamon, Philippe, 'Zola, romancier de la transparence', *Europe*, 468–9 (1968), 385–91.

'Note sur un dispositif naturaliste', in *Le Naturalisme. Colloque de Cerisy*, Paris, Union Générale d'Editions, 1978, pp. 101–18.

Introduction à l'analyse du descriptif, Paris, Hachette, 1981.

Le Personnel du roman. Le système des personnages dans les 'Rougon-Macquart' d'Emile Zola, Geneva, Droz, 1983.

Hearn, Lafcadio, 'Plot-formation in modern novels', in *Essays in European and Oriental Literature*, ed. Albert Mordell, New York, Dodd, Mead and Co., 1923, pp. 141–5.

Hemmings, F. W. J., 'The origin of the terms *naturalisme, naturaliste*', *French Studies*, VIII (1954), 109–21.

Emile Zola, 2nd edition, Oxford, The Clarendon Press, 1966.

'The present position in Zola studies', in Charles B. Osborn (ed.), *The Present State of French Studies*, Metuchen, New York, Scarecrow Press, 1971, pp. 586–623, 951–4.

Hernadi, Paul, *Beyond Genre. New Directions in Literary Classification*, Cornell University Press, 1972.

Heywood, C., 'Flaubert, Miss Braddon, and George Moore', *Comparative Literature*, XII (1960), 151–8.

Highet, Gilbert, *The Anatomy of Satire*, Princeton University Press, 1962.

Hirsch, E. D. Jr, *Validity in Interpretation*, Yale University Press, 1967.

Hoefert, Sigfrid, 'Naturalism as an international phenomenon: the state of research', *Yearbook of Comparative and General Literature*, XXVII (1978), 84–93.

Hutcheon, Linda, 'Ironie, satire, parodie. Une approche pragmatique de l'ironie', *Poétique*, 46 (1981), 140–55.

A Theory of Parody, London, Methuen, 1985.

Huyghe, René, *La Relève du réel*, Paris, Flammarion, 1974.

Hynes, Samuel (ed.), *The Author's Craft and Other Critical Writings of Arnold Bennett*, University of Nebraska Press, 1968.

Jauss, Hans Robert, *Toward an Aesthetic of Reception*, trans. Timothy Bahti, University of Minnesota Press, 1982.

Jenny, Laurent, 'La stratégie de la forme', *Poétique*, 27 (1976), 257–81.

Kent, Thomas, *Interpretation and Genre. The Role of Generic Perception in the Study of Narrative Texts*, Bucknell University Press, 1986.

Kerbrat-Orecchioni, Catherine, 'L'ironie comme trope', *Poétique*, 41 (1980), 108–27.

Kistemaeckers père, Henry, 'Un procès littéraire: Louis Desprez (Souvenirs d'un éditeur)', *Mercure de France*, CLI (15 October 1921), 429–42.

Klaus, Peter, 'Description and event in narrative', *Orbis Litterarum*, XXXVII (1982), 201–16.

Lanson, Gustave, *Histoire de la littérature française*, 12th edn., Paris, Hachette, 1912 [1895].

Lapp, John C., *Zola before the 'Rougon-Macquart'*, University of Toronto Press, 1964.

(ed.), 'Taine et Zola: autour d'une correspondance', *Revue des Sciences humaines*, n.s. 87 (1957), 319–26.

Le Blond, Maurice, *La Publication de 'La Terre'*, Paris, Société d'Editions littéraires et techniques, 1937.

Le Blond-Zola, Jean-Claude, 'Gabriel Thyébaut, ami d'Emile Zola', *Les Cahiers naturalistes*, 49 (1975), 15–29.

Lee, Vernon, 'The moral teaching of Zola', *The Contemporary Review*, LXIII (1893), 196–212.

Lejeune, Philippe, *Le Pacte autobiographique*, Paris, Seuil, 1975.

Lentricchia, Frank, 'Four types of nineteenth-century poetic', *The Journal of Aesthetics and Art Criticism*, XXVI (1968), 351–66.

Levin, Harry, *The Gates of Horn. A Study of Five French Realists*, Oxford University Press, 1963.

Lukács, Georg, 'The Zola centenary' [1940], in *Studies in European Realism*, London, Hillway, 1950, pp. 85–96.

The Historical Novel, trans. Hannah and Stanley Mitchell, Penguin Books, 1969 [1962].

'Narrate or describe?', in *Writer and Critic*, trans. and ed. Arthur Kahn, London, Merlin Press, 1978, pp. 110–48.

McInnes, Edward, 'Naturalism and the English theatre', *Forum for Modern Language Studies*, I (1965), 197–206.

Markiewicz, Henryk, 'Le naturalisme dans les recherches littéraires et dans l'esthétique du XXᵉ siécle', *Revue de Littérature comparée*, XLVII (1973), 256–72.

Marrou, Henri-Irénée, *De la connaissance historique*, Paris, Seuil, 1954.

Martino, Pierre, *Le Naturalisme français (1870–1895)*. 8ᵉ édition revue et corrigée par Robert Ricatte, Paris, Armand Colin, 1969 [1923].

Maupassant, Guy de, '*Les Soirées de Médan*, comment ce livre a été fait',

Le Gaulois, 17 April 1880.

'Autour d'un livre', *Le Gaulois*, 4 October 1881.

Emile Zola, Paris, Quantin, 1883 [1882].

Mitterand, Henri, 'Textes en intersection: *Le Roman expérimental* et *Les Rougon-Macquart*', *Revue de l'Université d'Ottawa/University of Ottawa Quarterly*, XLVIII (1978), 415–28.

Le Discours du roman, Paris, PUF, 1980.

'Le naturalisme théorique de Zola', *Lez Valenciennes*, 10 (1985), 181–93.

Zola et le naturalisme, Que sais-je? Series, 2314, Paris, PUF, 1986.

(ed.), *Emile Zola: carnets d'enquêtes. Une ethnographie inédite de la France*, Paris, Plon, 1986.

Moore, George, *Literature at Nurse, or Circulating Morals*, London, Vizetelly, 1885.

'A Tragic Novel', *Cosmopolis*, VII (1897), 38–59.

Morgan, Owen R., 'Léon Hennique and the disintegration of naturalism', *Nottingham French Studies*, I (1962), 24–33.

'Autopsie d'un journal républicain–naturaliste: *Le Rabelais* de Gustave Naquet', *Les Cahiers naturalistes*, 56 (1982), 213–24.

Muecke, D. C., *Irony*, London, Methuen, 1970.

Munro, Thomas, 'Meanings of "naturalism" in philosophy and aesthetics', *The Journal of Aesthetics and Art Criticism*, XIX (1960), 133–7.

Nelson, Brian, *Zola and the Bourgeoisie*, London, Macmillan, 1983.

Newton, William, 'Hardy and the naturalists: their use of physiology', *Modern Philology*, XLIX (1951), 28–41.

Noël, Jean, *George Moore. L'homme et l'œuvre (1852–1933)*, Paris, Didier, 1966.

Nordau, Max, *Entartung*, Berlin, C. Duncker, 1892–3; English translation: *Degeneration*, New York, Appleton, 1895.

Olivier-Martin, Yves, *Histoire du roman populaire en France de 1840 à 1980*, Paris, Albin Michel, 1980.

Olrik, Hilde, 'Le sang impur. Notes sur le concept de prostituée-née chez Lombroso', *Romantisme*, 31 (1981), 166–78.

Pagès, Alain, 'En partant de la théorie du roman expérimental', *Les Cahiers naturalistes*, 47 (1974), 70–87.

'Le mythe de Médan', *Les Cahiers naturalistes*, 55 (1981), 31–40.

'A propos d'une origine littéraire: *Les Soirées de Médan*', *Nineteenth-Century French Studies*, XII (1983–4), 207–12.

Le Naturalisme, Que sais-je? Series, 604, Paris, PUF, 1989.

Patin, Jacques, 'Du "bœuf nature" à "la table des Beylistes"', *Le Figaro*, 7 December 1930.

Paulson, Ronald, *The Fictions of Satire*, The Johns Hopkins University Press, 1967.

Potet, Michel, 'Place de la thématologie', *Poétique*, 35 (1978), 374–84.

Prendergast, Christopher, *The Order of Mimesis. Balzac, Stendhal, Nerval, Flaubert*, Cambridge University Press, 1986.

Prince, Gerald, 'Thématiser', *Poétique*, 64 (1985), 425–33.

Pryme, Eileen, 'Zola's plays in England 1870–1900', *French Studies*, XIII (1959), 28–38.

Reed, Walter L., 'Commentary', *New Literary History*, XVI (1985), 671–9.

Ricatte, Robert, *La Création romanesque chez les Goncourt: 1851–1870*, Paris, Armand Colin, 1953.

Rimmon-Kenan, Shlomith, 'Qu'est-ce qu'un thème?', *Poétique*, 64 (1985), 387–406.

Ripoll, Roger, *Réalité et mythe chez Zola*, Université de Lille III/Paris, Champion, 1981.

Rivet, Gustave, 'Emile Zola et le naturalisme', *La Jeune France* I (1 February 1879), 379–85.

Robert, Guy, *'La Terre' d'Emile Zola. Etude historique et critique*, Paris, Les Belles Lettres, 1952.

Rochat, Joyce Hamilton, 'The development and divergence of the two branches of naturalism', *The Durham University Journal*, n.s. XXXIX (1978), 155–67.

Romanell, Patrick, 'Prolegomena to any naturalistic aesthetics', *The Journal of Aesthetics and Art Criticism*, XIX (1960), 139–43.

Sabatier, Pierre, *L'Esthétique des Goncourt*, Paris, Hachette, 1920.
  'Germinie Lacerteux' des Goncourt, Paris, Sfelt, 1948.

Sachs, Murray, 'The esthetics of naturalism. Henry Céard's *Une Belle Journée*', *L'Esprit créateur*, IV (1964), 76–83.

Saintsbury, George, 'The present state of the novel', *The Fortnightly Review*, XLII n.s. (1887), 410–17.

Salvan, Albert J., 'Les correspondants américains de Zola', *Les Cahiers naturalistes*, 27 (1964), 101–15.

Schaeffer, Jean-Marie, 'Du texte au genre. Notes sur la problématique générique', *Poétique*, 53 (1983), 3–18.

Schmidt, Siegfried J., 'On writing histories of literature. Some remarks from a constructivist point of view', *Poetics*, XIV (1985), 279–301.

Schuerewegen, Franc, 'Réflexions sur le narrataire. Quidam et quilibet', *Poétique*, 70 (1987), 247–54.

Seccombe, Thomas, 'The work of George Gissing', in George Gissing, *The House of Cobwebs*, London, Constable, 1906.

Serres, Michel, *Feux et signaux de brume. Zola*, Paris, Grasset, 1975.

Sollers, Philippe, 'Le roman et l'expérience des limites', *Tel Quel*, 25 (1966), 20–34.

Sprinchorn, Evert, 'Strindberg and the greater naturalism', *Tulane Drama Review*, XIII (1968), 119–29.

Starkie, Enid, *From Gautier to Eliot. The Influence of France on English Literature 1851–1939*, London, Hutchinson, 1960.

Steiner, George, *The Death of Tragedy*, London, Faber and Faber, 1961.
  On Difficulty, and Other Essays, Oxford University Press, 1978.

Tanner, Tony, *Adultery in the Novel. Contract and Transgression*, The Johns Hopkins University Press, 1979.

Thibaudet, Albert, 'Réflexions sur la littérature. Le Groupe de Médan, *La Nouvelle Revue française*, XV (1920), 923–33.

Thorel, Sylvie, 'Naturalisme, naturaliste', *Les Cahiers naturalistes*, 60 (1986), 76–88.

Todorov, Tzvetan, *Introduction à la littérature fantastique*, Paris, Seuil, 1970. *Les Genres du discours*, Paris, Seuil, 1978.

Trudgian, Helen, *L'Esthétique de J.-K. Huysmans*, Paris, Conard, 1934 [Geneva, Slatkine Reprints, 1970].

Vanwelkenhuyzen, Gustave, *L'Influence du naturalisme français en Belgique de 1875 à 1900*, Brussels, Palais des Académies/Liège, H. Vaillant-Carmanne, 1930.

Veyne, Paul, *Comment on écrit l'histoire*, Paris, Seuil, 1971.

Vial, André, *Guy de Maupassant et l'art du roman*, Paris, Nizet, 1954.

Viens, Jacques, *'La Terre' de Zola et 'Trente arpents' de Ringuet. Etude comparée*, Montreal, Editions Cosmos, 1970.

Vizetelly, Ernest A., *Emile Zola, Novelist and Reformer: An Account of His Life and Work*, London, Bodley Head/New York, J. Lane, 1904.

Wain, John, *Arnold Bennett*, Columbia University Press, 1967.

Walcutt, Charles Child, 'From scientific theory to aesthetic fact: the "naturalistic" novel', *Quarterly Review of Literature*, III (1946), 167–79.
American Literary Naturalism, a Divided Stream, University of Minnesota Press, 1965.

Wald Lasowski, Patrick, *Syphilis. Essai sur la littérature française du XIXe siècle*, Paris, Gallimard, 1982.

Walker, Philip, *Zola*, London, Routledge and Kegan Paul, 1985.

Warning, Rainer, 'Pour une pragmatique du discours fictionnel', *Poétique*, 39 (1979), 321–37.

West, Thomas G., 'Schopenhauer, Huysmans and French naturalism', *Journal of European Studies* (1977), 313–24.

Williams, D. A. (ed.), *The Monster in the Mirror. Studies in Nineteenth-Century Realism*, Oxford University Press, 1978.

Wilson, Angus, *Emile Zola. An Introductory Study of His Novels*, London, Mercury Books, 1965 [1952].

Winner, Anthony, *Characters in the Twilight. Hardy, Zola and Chekhov*, University Press of Virginia, 1981.

Wright, Walter F., *Arnold Bennett. Romantic Realist*, University of Nebraska Press, 1971.

Zévaès, A., *Les Procès littéraires au XIXe siècle*, Paris, Perrin, 1924.

'Concord philosophy and Zola', *The Literary World*, XVII (7 August 1886), 264.

'J.-K. Huysmans et le naturalisme', *L'Amateur d'autographes*, XL (1907), 164–6.

INDEX

281

Cambridge Studies in French

General editor: MALCOLM BOWIE

Also in the series

STIRLING HAIG
Flaubert and the Gift of Speech: Dialogue and Discourse in Four 'Modern' Novels

NATHANIEL WING
The Limits of Narrative: Essays on Baudelaire, Flaubert, Rimbaud and Mallarmé

MITCHELL GREENBERG
Corneille, Classicism, and the Ruses of Symmetry

HOWARD DAVIES
Sartre and 'Les Temps Modernes'

ROBERT GREER COHN
Mallarmé's Prose Poems: A Critical Study

CELIA BRITTON
Claude Simon: Writing the Visible

DAVID SCOTT
Pictorialist Poetics: Poetry and the Visual Arts in Nineteenth-Century France

ANN JEFFERSON
Reading Realism in Stendhal

DALIA JUDOVITZ
Subjectivity and Representation in Descartres: The Origins of Modernity

RICHARD D.E. BURTON
Baudelaire in 1859: A Study in the Sources of Poetic Creativity

MICHAEL MORIARTY
Taste and Ideology in Seventeenth-Century France

JOHN FORRESTER
The Seductions of Psychoanalysis: On Freud, Lacan and Derrida

JEROME SCHWARTZ
Irony and Ideology in Rabelais: Structures of Subversion